HORSE RACING
THE RECORDS

HORSE RACING

THE RECORDS

John Randall and Tony Morris

GUINNESS BOOKS

Acknowledgements

Arthur Ackermann & Son Ltd: 65
BBC Hulton Picture Library: 9, 21, 23, 25, 27, 28, 33, 44, 46, 59, 104, 140, 157
P. Bertrand et Fils: 76, 126
Bob Coglianese: 106
Gerry Cranham: 66, 99, 100, 101, 102, 109, 135, 136, 154
European Racehorse: 48, 91
Tony Leonard: 55
Werner Menzendorf: 123
Press Association: 85, 94, 97, 155
W.W. Rouch & Co: 36
Alec Russell: 117
Mike Sirico: 128
Sport & General: 12, 13, 29, 43, 61, 70, 72, 79, 80, 87, 142, 148
Sporting Pictures: 30
Reproduced by kind permission of the Stewards of the Jockey club: 65

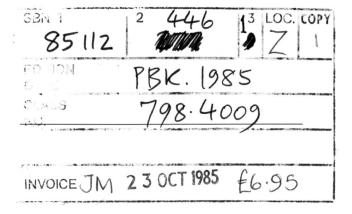
Editor: Beatrice Frei
Design and layout: Ian Wileman

Published in Great Britain by Guinness Superlatives Ltd,
2 Cecil Court, London Road, Enfield, Middlesex

Typeset in Times and Helvetica
Typeset by Input Typesetting Ltd., London, SW19.
Printed and bound in Great Britain by
Hazell Watson & Viney Ltd, Member of the BPCC Group,
Aylesbury, Buckinghamshire.

'Guinness' is a registered trade mark of
Guinness Superlatives Ltd

British Library Cataloguing in Publication Data

Randall John
    Guinness horse racing : the records.
    1. Horse-racing—Records
I. Title
798.4'009   SF325
ISBN 0-85112-446-1 Pbk

Contents

Introduction

If you have ever tried to trace your family tree, you will know how difficult it can be. Usually only the most aristocratic of the human race find it possible to progress beyond a few generations, and even when records enable us to identify our antecedents, we generally remain ignorant about how they lived their lives.

By contrast, the pedigree of the humblest Thoroughbred racehorse in any part of the world can be readily traced to its roots, in many cases for more than 30 generations, and we have access to the performance and breeding records of all its ancestors. No other animal species is better documented than the Thoroughbred horse; no other organised sport has a longer recorded history than horse racing.

The wealth of material available to the researcher is prodigious, and the following pages are the product of countless hours spent examining, checking and re-checking official and unofficial records, wherever possible from contemporary archives. Much of the data set out here has never been published before in this form, and in many instances our researches have enabled us to correct erroneous versions of events traditionally accepted as fact. It is our hope that *Horse Racing—The Records* will entertain, educate and settle many arguments about the history of the Sport of Kings.

Our cut-off date for entries was April 15th. Records brought to our notice subsequently are incorporated in the postscript on p 158.

John Randall & Tony Morris
1985

Abbreviations

colour
b   bay
bl black
br brown
ch chesnut
gr grey
ro roan

sex
c   colt
f   filly
g   gelding
h   horse
m   mare

J: jockey
T: trainer
B: breeder
a   age unknown
yr years
Fav favourite
Jt-Fav joint-favourite (of 2)
Co-Fav co-favourite (of 3)
Fr francs
l lengths

gns guineas
     (1 guinea = £1.05)
st, lb stones, pounds

I

HISTORICAL MILESTONES

Bloomsbury wins the 1839 Derby, the only renewal of the premier Classic to be run in a snowstorm.

1540 Racing is recorded for the first time on the Roodee at Chester, the oldest surviving course in England.

1580s Queen Elizabeth attends the races on Salisbury Plain.

1595 A racecourse appears on a map of Doncaster Town Moor.

1605 James I is the first monarch to visit Newmarket.

1619 The earliest known rules of racing are drawn up at Kiplingcotes, Yorkshire.

1640s Racing at Epsom is recorded for the first time.

1665 North America's first formal racecourse is laid out on Long Island, New York.

1660s Charles II's patronage makes Newmarket the main centre of racing in England.

1689 The Byerley Turk, earliest of the 3 male-line ancestors of the Thoroughbred, is imported into England.

c1704 The Darley Arabian, male-line ancestor of over 90 per cent of modern Thoroughbreds, is imported into England.

1709 York holds the first fully-reported race meeting.

1711 The first meeting at Ascot takes place at Queen Anne's instigation.

1713 First use of the term 'thro-bred' to describe horses.

1727 Death of Tregonwell Frampton, the Father of the Turf and controller of the royal horses at Newmarket during 4 reigns.
John Cheny of Arundel publishes the first annual racing calendar.

1730 The Godolphin Arabian, last of the 3 male-line ancestors of the Thoroughbred, is imported into England.

1731 Racing at York is transferred to the Knavesmire.
Bedale, Yorkshire stages the first race for 3-year-olds.

1740 In order to check the growth of the sport, Parliament outlaws nearly all races worth less than £50.

c1750 The Jockey Club is founded at the Star and Garter in Pall Mall, London.

1751 John Pond's first *Sporting Kalendar* contains regulations destined to evolve into the modern Rules of Racing.

1752 The earliest recorded steeplechase takes place when Mr Edmund Blake and Mr O'Callaghan ride a match of 4½ miles from the Church of Buttevant to St Leger Church, Co Cork.

1758 The Jockey Club passes its first resolution, requiring all riders at Newmarket to weigh in after a race.

1762 Racing colours are first registered at Newmarket.

1764 Birth of Eclipse, the greatest racehorse of the 18th century.

1766 Richard Tattersall starts to organise bloodstock sales at Hyde Park Corner, London.

1769 Newmarket sees the first appearance on a racecourse of a 2-year-old.

1770 The Orders of the Jockey Club, applicable only at Newmarket, are published for the first time.

1773 James Weatherby, Keeper of the Match-Book at Newmarket, publishes the first volume of his *Racing Calendar*.

1774 Birth of Highflyer, the greatest sire of the 18th century.

1776 Inaugural running at Doncaster of the sweepstakes which became the St Leger in 1778.
The first organised meeting in France is held near Paris.

1779 The Oaks Stakes at Epsom is run for the first time.

1780 Inaugural running of the Derby Stakes at Epsom.

c1790 The first bookmaker appears on a racecourse.

1790 Formation of the Turf Club, the governing body of racing in Ireland.

1791 James Weatherby publishes the first volume of the *General Stud Book*.
The Oatlands Stakes at Ascot is the first important handicap in England.
The Prince of Wales withdraws from Newmarket after a Jockey Club enquiry into the inconsistent running of his horse Escape.

1792 The earliest recorded steeplechases in England take place in Leicestershire.

1802 Goodwood holds its first recognised meeting.

1807 Inaugural running of the Gold Cup at Ascot.

1809 Inaugural running of the 2000 Guineas at Newmarket.

1810 The first recorded meeting in Australia is held in Sydney.

1811 Bedford stages the first steeplechase over an artificial course.

1814 Inaugural running of the 1000 Guineas at Newmarket.

1816 A trailer is used to convey a horse to the races for the first time.

1821 Death of Sir Charles Bunbury, permanent steward of the Jockey Club and the first dictator of the Turf.
The Jockey Club issues its first warning-off notice.
The first artificial dirt track comes into use at the Union Course on Long Island, New York.

1822 The first organised meeting in Germany is held at Doberan, Mecklenburg.

1827 Pest stages the first organised meeting in Hungary.

1828 Retirement of Robert Robson of Newmarket, credited with being the first trainer to refrain from 'sweating' his horses, i.e. wrapping them in heavy sheets and subjecting them to long gallops.

1829 Liverpool's new course at Aintree holds its first meeting.

1830 Thomas Coleman, the father of steeplechasing, organises the first St Albans steeplechase.

1831 Cheltenham races are held at Prestbury Park for the first time; they find a permanent home there in 1902.
The Jockey Club refuses to resolve any more disputes arising at meetings where its Rules are not in force.

1833 Randwick, Sydney holds its first meeting.
Formation of the Société d'Encouragement pour l'amélioration des races de chevaux en France; Lord Henry Seymour is its first president.

1834 Horses at Newmarket take their ages from 1 January instead of 1 May; horses elsewhere in Great Britain follow suit in 1858.
Chantilly holds its first meeting.

1836 Inaugural running of the Prix du Jockey-Club at Chantilly.

1837 Florence and Naples stage the first organised meetings in Italy.

1838 The first recorded meeting in Victoria is held in Melbourne.

1839 Inaugural running at Liverpool of the race which became the Grand National Steeple Chase in 1847.

1840 Flemington, Melbourne holds its first meeting.

1842 The first formal meeting in New Zealand is held in Auckland.
Formation of the Australian Jockey Club, the governing body of racing in New South Wales.
The Jockey Club refuses to settle any more disputes over betting.

1843 Inaugural running of the Prix de Diane at Chantilly.

1844 'Running Rein' wins the Derby but is exposed as a 4-year-old.

1848 Death of Lord George Bentinck, administrator, reformer and the second dictator of the Turf.

1850 Birth of Lexington, the greatest sire ever to stand in America.

1851 California's first formal racecourse opens near San Francisco.
Fairyhouse holds its first meeting.
The Flying Dutchman beats Voltigeur in a match at York.

1853 West Australian becomes the first Triple Crown winner.

1855 Admiral Henry Rous, author of the weight-for-age scale, is appointed handicapper to the Jockey Club.
Inaugural running of the Victoria Derby at Flemington.

1857 Ellerslie (Auckland) and Longchamp hold their first meetings.

1858 Baden-Baden holds its first meeting.

1860 Yearlings may no longer race in Great Britain.
The Queen's Plate, Canada's premier classic, is run for the first time.

1861 The first organised meeting in Japan is held in Yokohama.
The AJC Derby at Randwick and the Melbourne Cup at Flemington are both run for the first time.

1863 Inaugural running of the Grand Prix de Paris at Longchamp.
Formation of the Société des Steeple-Chases de France.

1864 Formation of the Victoria Racing Club, the governing body of racing in Victoria.
Saratoga and Deauville hold their first meetings.

1865 Parisian Pierre Oller devises the first system of pari-mutuel betting.
Gladiateur, the 'Avenger of Waterloo', becomes the first foreign-bred Derby winner.

1866 Formation of the Grand National Steeple Chase Committee, renamed the National Hunt Committee in 1889.

1867 The Belmont Stakes in New York is run for the first time.

Admiral Henry Rous, leading light of the Jockey Club and virtual ruler of the English Turf for more than 20 years until his death in 1877.

Hoppegarten, Berlin holds its first meeting.

Formation of the Union-Klub, the governing body of racing in Germany until World War II.

1869 The Norddeutsches Derby in Hamburg, forerunner of the Deutsches Derby, is staged for the first time.

The Marquess of Drogheda founds the Irish National Hunt Steeplechase Committee.

1870 The Jockey Club restricts the length of the Flat season and no longer recognises meetings which are not subject to its Rules.

1873 Inaugural running of the Preakness Stakes at Pimlico, Maryland.

Auteuil holds its first meeting.

1874 Birth of Kincsem, Hungary's champion racemare.

1875 Sandown Park, the first enclosed course in Great Britain, holds its inaugural meeting.

The Kentucky Derby at Churchill Downs and the Great Northern Derby (renamed the New Zealand Derby in 1973) at Ellerslie are both run for the first time.

1877 The Rules of Racing provide for a draw for starting positions.

1878 At Palo Alto, California, English-born photographer Eadweard Muybridge reveals in detail the gait of a galloping horse.

Kempton Park holds its first meeting.

1879 Jockeys in Great Britain are required to be licensed.

1881 Formation of the Jockey Club Italiano.

Birth of St Simon, the greatest sire of the 19th century.

Woodbine, Toronto holds its first meeting; the new track there opens in 1956.

1882 Racing at Newcastle is transferred to Gosforth Park.

Minimum requirements are laid down for the number and size of fences or hurdles in a race.

1883 Birth of Ormonde, the greatest racehorse of the 19th century.

1884 The Derby Reale, forerunner of the Derby Italiano, and the Gran Premio Nacional (Argentine Derby) are both staged for the first time.

1886 Inaugural running of the Eclipse Stakes, the first £10,000 race in England, at Sandown Park on 23 July.

Champion jockey Fred Archer shoots himself in a fit of depression on 8 November.

1887 First meeting of the body which became the New Zealand Racing Conference in 1897.

The Gran Premio Internacional in Buenos Aires, forerunner of the Gran Premio Carlos Pellegrini, is staged for the first time.

1888 Leopardstown holds its first meeting.

1890 Sheepshead Bay, New York pioneers the use of the camera to decide the finish of races.

Lingfield Park holds its first meeting.

1891 A pari-mutuel betting monopoly is established in France.

1894 Formation of the Jockey Club of New York, parent body of the American Turf.

Aqueduct, New York holds its first meeting; the new track there opens in 1959.

1895 American Willie Simms is the first to use the modern jockeys' seat in England.

The Derby is the first race to be recorded on film.

1897 The starting gate is introduced on British courses at Newmarket.

1898 Federico Tesio founds the Razza Dormello on the shores of Lake Maggiore.

1899 Haydock Park holds its first meeting.

1902 Sceptre wins all the Classics except the Derby.

Phoenix Park holds its first meeting.

1903 Doping is banned by the Jockey Club in response to the practices of some American trainers.

1905 The Jockey Club requires trainers to be licensed.

Belmont Park and Newbury hold their first meetings.

1909 Anti-betting legislation causes racing in California to be abandoned.

1910 The National Hunt Committee makes number-cloths compulsory, requires trainers to be licensed and bans doping.

Anti-betting legislation suspends racing in New York until 1913.

1911 The National Hunt meeting settles permanently at Cheltenham.

1913 The Jockey Club no longer allows races to be shorter than 5 furlongs or horses older than 2 to run unnamed.

The favourite is disqualified after the 'Suffragette Derby.'

The 'Jersey Act' bars many American-breds from the *General Stud Book*; the success of horses thus excluded causes its repeal in 1949.

1916 The National Stud is founded at Tully, Co Kildare; it is moved to England in 1943.

1917 Birth of Man o' War, America's champion racehorse.

c1920 American William Murray designs the first starting stalls.

1920 The Jockey Club no longer allows owners to use assumed names or amateur riders to compete against professionals.

Inaugural running of the Prix de l'Arc de Triomphe at Longchamp.

1922 Number-cloths are carried for the first time on the Flat in Great Britain.

1924 Inaugural running of the Cheltenham Gold Cup.

Skull caps are made compulsory under National Hunt Rules.

Federico Tesio, the outstanding owner-breeder-trainer of the 20th century, won the Derby Italiano 20 times. Donatello, Nearco and Ribot were among the champions with whom he was associated.

1925 Hialeah Park, Florida holds its first meeting.

1926 Chancellor of the Exchequer Winston Churchill introduces betting tax in his Budget but its failure forces him to abandon it in 1929.

The sporting papers agree on a combined return of starting prices.

Birth of Phar Lap, Australasia's champion racehorse.

1927 Inaugural running of the Champion Hurdle at Cheltenham.

The Grand National and the Derby are the first races in England to be broadcast on radio.

The Jockey Club requires all horses to be run on their merits; hitherto one horse could be stopped in favour of another in the same ownership.

Arlington Park, Chicago holds its first meeting.

1928 Formation of the Racecourse Betting Control Board, reconstituted as the Horserace Totalisator Board in 1961.

1929 A new type of starting gate is introduced on British courses at Lincoln.

Abolition of the 'void nominations' rule whereby the death of an owner rendered void all entries for his horses.

Totalisator betting is tried out at Newmarket and Carlisle on 2 July.

1930 Most American tracks adopt starting stalls.

1931 Dead-heats in Great Britain may no longer be run off.

1932 The Derby is the first race to be televised.

Inaugural running of the Japanese Derby.

1933 Racing with pari-mutuel betting is legalised in California.

1934 Santa Anita, California holds its first meeting.

1935 Hyperion starts his stud career in Newmarket.

1936 Most American tracks adopt the photo-finish camera.

1938 Hollywood Park, California holds its first meeting.

Nearco is imported from Italy to stand at stud in Newmarket.

1942 National Hunt racing in Great Britain is suspended for 2 seasons in order not to hamper the war effort.

1945 California pioneers the air transport of racehorses.

1946 No horse in Great Britain may run unnamed.

Nearly all French races are opened to foreign-bred horses.

1947 The photo-finish camera is introduced on British courses at Epsom on 22 April.

The first evening meeting in Great Britain is held at Hamilton Park on 18 July.

1949 The first East European international meeting is staged in Prague.

1950 Nasrullah is exported from Ireland to stand at stud in Kentucky.

1951 Citation becomes the first equine dollar millionaire.

Inaugural running of the King George VI and Queen Elizabeth Stakes at Ascot.

1952 Birth of Ribot, Italy's champion racehorse.

Electrical timing and loudspeaker commentaries are introduced on British courses at Newmarket and Goodwood respectively.

1954 The pari-mutuel tiercé bet is introduced, greatly increasing the flow of revenue into French racing.

Formation of the Japan Racing Association.

1957 Birth of champion steeplechaser Arkle.

1960 The patrol camera is introduced on British courses at Newmarket on 30 June.

1961 The Jockey Club introduces overnight declarations.

Betting shops become legal on 1 May.

The start of the Chesterfield Stakes on Newmarket's July Course in 1965, the first race ever started from stalls in Great Britain. The winner, Track Spare (Lester Piggott), is on the extreme right.

The Horserace Betting Levy Board, the controlling body of British racing finances, comes into being on 1 September.

1962 Birth of Sea-Bird, France's champion racehorse.

Inaugural running of the Irish Sweeps Derby at The Curragh.

1963 France is the first major racing nation in Europe to adopt starting stalls.

1965 Starting stalls are introduced on British courses at Newmarket on 8 July; they are first used in the Classics in 1967.

1966 The Jockey Club is forced to grant trainers' licences to women.

Chancellor of the Exchequer James Callaghan reintroduces betting tax in his Budget; it comes into effect on 24 October.

1968 The Jockey Club and the National Hunt Committee amalgamate on 12 December.

1971 Introduction of Pattern Race classifications in Europe.

Inaugural year of the Eclipse Awards in America.

1972 The Jockey Club permits races for women riders.

Australian racing goes metric on 1 August.

1973 Introduction of Graded Stakes classifications in North America.

The Jockey Club adopts computer-assisted centralised handicapping.

Secretariat becomes the first American Triple Crown winner for 25 years.

New Zealand racing goes metric on 1 August.

1975 Introduction of graded handicaps on the Flat in Great Britain.

1978 Sha Tin, Hong Kong's £100 million racecourse, holds its first meeting.

1981 The Arlington Million in Chicago and the Japan Cup in Tokyo are both run for the first time.

1984 All the English Classics are sponsored.

Inaugural year of the European Breeders' Fund, whereby half the maiden 2-year-old races in Great Britain, Ireland and France are open only to the progeny of nominated stallions.

Inaugural year of the Breeders' Cup programme in North America, culminating in Breeders' Cup Day at Hollywood Park on 10 November with $10 million in prize money.

II
RACE RESULTS
AND RECORDS

Dahlia achieves a unique second victory in the King George VI and Queen Elizabeth Stakes in 1974. This French-trained filly was later based in her native America and became the world's leading female earner.

The English Classic Races

For much of their history, the English Classic races have been regarded as the supreme tests of the Thoroughbred, victory in any one of the five events conferring a degree of prestige unmatched in any other branch of the sport anywhere.

But that distinction is something which evolved over a period of years; it was not the product of a grand design. Nobody conceived the idea of a Classic series until all five races were well established and a neat, logical pattern already seemed to exist.

Until the last quarter of the 18th century, races for 3-year-olds were few and far between. Most events were contested by older horses over long distances, often in heats, with the prize going to the first horse to win two heats. The St Leger, instituted in 1776, albeit still without a name, was the first single-heat race for 3-year-olds to attain popularity. Within a few years this North-country event open to both sexes was joined in the fixture list by two South-country races which swiftly assumed significance, the Oaks for fillies only, and the Derby, open to colts and fillies.

By the end of the 18th century these occasions were already regarded as 'the three great races' on the Turf, and they continued to be regarded as something apart from and above all else, even after the 2000 Guineas (both sexes) and 1000 Guineas (fillies only) had become established features of the Newmarket calendar in the spring.

It was not until the 1850s that the Guineas races began to be recognised as something more significant than 'stepping-stones' to the Derby and the Oaks in terms of prestige and prize money. But by the mid-1860s it had become generally accepted that the five races, all confined to 3-year-olds, and characterised by a graduation in distance through the season, constituted a 'set'.

The term 'Classics' was coined to describe the series, and at around the same time the expressions 'Triple Crown', denoting the three Classics open to colts, and 'Fillies' Triple Crown', indicating the 1000 Guineas, Oaks and St Leger, also came into use.

Once the Classic pattern had been recognised, it swiftly caught the imagination, and the concept was adopted in many overseas countries.

Although official records have been kept throughout the period in which the Classics have been run, most of the early reports lacked detail, so that it is now impossible to compile fully comprehensive data of all the races. The following pages comprise the most complete records we have been able to produce after many years' research into contemporary archives.

2000 Guineas

Title

2000 Guineas Stakes 1809–1939
New 2000 Guineas Stakes 1940–44
2000 Guineas Stakes 1945–83
General Accident 2000 Guineas from 1984

Venue

Rowley Mile Course, Newmarket, Suffolk 1809–1939
Summer Course, Newmarket, Cambridgeshire 1940–45
Rowley Mile Course, Newmarket, Suffolk from 1946

Distance

1 mile 1 yard 1809–51
1 mile 17 yards 1852–88
1 mile 11 yards 1889–1901
1 mile from 1902

Weights

Colts/geldings 8 st 3 lb, fillies 8 st 0 lb 1809
Colts/geldings 8 st 5 lb, fillies 8 st 2 lb 1810–13
Colts/geldings 8 st 7 lb, fillies 8 st 4 lb 1814–59
Colts/geldings 8 st 7 lb, fillies 8 st 2 lb 1860–61
Colts/geldings 8 st 10 lb, fillies 8 st 5 lb 1862–81
Colts/geldings 9 st 0 lb, fillies 8 st 9 lb 1882–1903
Colts 9 st 0 lb, fillies 8 st 9 lb from 1904

1809 Christopher Wilson's ch c **Wizard** J: Bill Clift 4/5 Fav £1,522 2. Robin 3. Fair Star 8 ran
1810 2nd Earl Grosvenor's b c **Hephestion** J: Frank Buckle 5/1 £1,885 2. The Dandy 3. Oporto 9 ran
1811 Robert Andrew's bl c **Trophonius** J: Sam Barnard 5/2 Fav £1,680 2. Barrosa 3. Magus 11 ran
1812 3rd Earl of Darlington's br c **Cwrw** J: Sam Chifney, jr 7/1 £1,522 2. Cato 3. Octavius 7 ran
1813 Sir Charles Bunbury's bl c **Smolensko** J: H. Miller 7/4 Fav £2,047 2. Music 3. Phosphor 12 ran
1814 Charles Wyndham's b c **Olive** J: Bill Arnull 5/1 £2,257 2. Perchance 3. b c by Sorceror 14 ran
1815 1st Baron Rous's ch c **Tigris** J: Bill Arnull 7/4 Fav £1,575 2. Castanet 3. Original 10 ran
1816 Lord George Cavendish's b c **Nectar** J: Bill Arnull 5/2 Fav £1,942 2. Milton 3. Bobadil 12 ran

1817 Scott Stonehewer's b c **Manfred** J: Will Wheatley 4/1 £1,575 2. Sylvanus 3. Havoc 8 ran
1818 3rd Baron Foley's b c **Interpreter** J: Bill Clift 7/4 and 5/4 Fav £1,102 2. Secundus 3. Picaroon 9 ran
1819 Sir John Shelley's b c **Antar** J: Edward Edwards 4/1 £1,207 2. Truth 3. Euphrates 6 ran
1820 4th Duke of Grafton's b c **Pindarrie** J: Frank Buckle Evens Fav £1,260 2. Oracle 3. Hoopoe 5 ran
1821 4th Duke of Grafton's b c **Reginald** J: Frank Buckle 11/10 Fav £1,050 2. Newmarket 3. Incantator 4 ran
1822 4th Duke of Grafton's b f **Pastille** J: Frank Buckle 4/6 Fav £735 2. Midsummer 3. b c by Marmion 3 ran
1823 Joe Rogers's ch c **Nicolo** J: Will Wheatley 5/1 £1,417 2. Talisman 3. Cinder 7 ran
1824 James Haffenden's b c **Schahriar** J: Will Wheatley 10/1 £850 2. Tiara 3. Conviction 7 ran
1825 2nd Marquis of Exeter's ch c **Enamel** J: Jem Robinson 7/4 Fav £700 2. Château Margaux 3. Bolero 6 ran

1826 4th Duke of Grafton's b c **Dervise** J: John Barham Day 7/2 £850 2. Hobgoblin 3. Black Swan 7 ran

1827 4th Duke of Grafton's br c **Turcoman** J: Frank Buckle 5/1 £950 2. Chrysalis 3. Grampus 5 ran

1828 5th Duke of Rutland's br c **Cadland** J: Jem Robinson 5/2 £1,500 2. Lepanto 3. Enthusiast 5 ran

1829 2nd Marquis of Exeter's ch c **Patron** J: Frank Boyce 1/8 Fav £600 2. Kean 2 ran

1830 2nd Marquis of Exeter's ch c **Augustus** J: Patrick Conolly 4/7 Fav £750 2. Burlington 2 ran

1831 5th Earl of Jersey's ch c **Riddlesworth** J: Jem Robinson 1/5 Fav £1,500 2. Sarpedon 3. Bohemian 6 ran

1832 Jonathan Peel's b c **Archibald** J: Arthur Pavis 7/4 and 2/1 Fav £1,450 2. Posthumus 3. Spencer 7 ran

1833 3rd Earl of Orford's gr c **Clearwell** J: Jem Robinson 5/4 Fav £1,700 2. Sir Robert 3. Boscobel 6 ran

1834 5th Earl of Jersey's ch c **Glencoe** J: Jem Robinson 6/1 £1,650 2. Flatterer 3. Bentley 7 ran

1835 5th Earl of Jersey's br c **Ibrahim** J: Jem Robinson 1/7 Fav £1,400

2. Paulus 3. Stockport 4 ran

1836 5th Earl of Jersey's b c **Bay Middleton** J: Jem Robinson 4/6 Fav £1,600 2. Elis 3. Jack in the Green 6 ran

1837 5th Earl of Jersey's b c **Achmet** J: Edward Edwards 4/6 Fav £1,500 2. Mustee 3. Troilus 9 ran

1838 Lord George Bentinck's gr c **Grey Momus** J: John Barham Day 4/1 £1,650 2. Saintfoin 3. Bamboo 6 ran

1839 1st Earl of Lichfield's bl c **The Corsair** J: Bill Wakefield 10/1 £1,050 2. Caesar 3. Aether 3 ran

1840 Lord George Bentinck's b f **Crucifix** J: John Barham Day 8/11 Fav £1,450 2. Confederate 3. Angelo 6 ran

1841 4th Earl of Albemarle's ch c **Ralph** J: John Barham Day 5/2 Fav £1,300 2. Joachim 3. Mustapha 8 ran

1842 John Bowes's ch c **Meteor** J: Bill Scott 6/4 Fav £1,500 2. Wiseacre 3. Misdeal 8 ran

1843 John Bowes's b c **Cotherstone** J: Bill Scott 1/3 Fav £1,350 2. Cornopean 3. Mallard 3 ran

1844 John Barham Day's b c **The Ugly Buck** J: John Day, jr 2/7 Fav £1,500 2. The Devil to Pay 3. Joe Lovell 7 ran

1845 2nd Earl of Stradbroke's b c **Idas**

J: Nat Flatman 5/6 Fav £1,050 2. Worthless 3. Winchelsea 5 ran

1846 Bill Scott's b c **Sir Tatton Sykes** J: Bill Scott 5/1 £1,700 2. Tom Tulloch 3. St Demetri 6 ran

1847 Sir Robert Pigot's b c **Conyngham** J: Jem Robinson 4/1 £1,800 2. Planet 3. Ziska 10 ran

1848 B. Green's b c **Flatcatcher** J: Jem Robinson 4/1 £1,700 2. Glendower 3. Blaze 5 ran

1849 Anthony Nichol's bl c **Nunnykirk** J: Frank Butler 5/6 Fav £2,050 2. Honeycomb 3. Vatican 8 ran

1850 Harry Hill's ch c **Pitsford** J: Alfred Day 5/2 £1,400 2. The Bee Hunter 3. Hardinge 5 ran

1851 Viscount Enfield's br c **Hernandez** J: Nat Flatman 5/1 £1,850 2. The Mountain Deer 3. Glenhawk 10 ran

1852 2nd Marquis of Exeter's ch c **Stockwell** J: John Norman 10/1 £1,900 2. Homebrewed 3. Filius 9 ran

1853 John Bowes's b c **West Australian** J: Frank Butler 4/6 Fav £1,940 2. Sittingbourne 3. Barbatus 7 ran

1854 John Gully's br c **The Hermit** J: Alfred Day 12/1 £2,700 2. Middlesex 3. Champagne 9 ran

1855 James Merry's b c **Lord of the**

Unbeaten Bay Middleton, the 2000 Guineas hero of 1836, was the greatest of the early winners of that Classic.

Isles J: Tom Aldcroft 5/2 £2,600 2. St Hubert 3. Kingstown 9 ran

1856 14th Earl of Derby's b c **Fazzoletto** J: Nat Flatman 5/1 £2,100 2. Yellow Jack 3. Pitapat 10 ran

1857 2nd Earl of Eglinton's br c **Vedette** J: John Osborne 5/2 Fav £2,600 2. Anton 3. Loyola 12 ran

1858 Sir Joseph Hawley's ch c **Fitzroland** J: John Wells 100/6 £2,750 2. The Happy Land 3. Clydesdale 14 ran

1859 William Day's b c **Promised Land** J: Alfred Day Evens Fav £2,850 2. Cynricus 3. Crafton 9 ran

1860 Anthony Nichol's b c **The Wizard** J: Tom Ashmall 20/1 £3,700 2. The Rap 3. Traducer 15 ran

1861 7th Earl of Stamford's ch c **Diophantus** J: Arthur Edwards 25/1 £3,300 2. Kettledrum 3. Klarikoff 16 ran

1862 Stanhope Hawke's b c **The Marquis** J: Tom Ashmall 5/1 Co-Fav £4,150 2. Caterer 3 = Knowsley and Nottingham 17 ran

1863 Richard Naylor's b c **Macaroni** J: Tom Chaloner 10/1 £4,500 2. Saccarometer 3. King of the Vale 9 ran

1864 5th Earl of Glasgow's b c **General Peel** J: Tom Aldcroft 7/2 £4,400 2. Paris 3. Historian 13 ran

1865 Comte Frédéric de Lagrange's b c **Gladiateur** J: Harry Grimshaw 7/1 £5,100 2. Archimedes 3. Liddington 18 ran

1866 Richard Sutton's b c **Lord Lyon** J: R. Thomas 4/7 Fav £4,850 2. Monarch of the Glen 3. Knight of the Crescent 15 ran

1867 8th Duke of Beaufort's br c **Vauban** J: George Fordham 5/2 Fav £5,350 2. Knight of the Garter 3. Marksman 18 ran

1868 William Stirling Crawfurd's b c **Moslem** J: Tom Chaloner 100/7 £2,775 *dead-heated with* William Graham's ch f **Formosa** J: George Fordham 3/1 £2,775 3. St Ronan 14 ran

1869 John Johnstone's b c **Pretender** J: John Osborne 3/1 Fav £4,400 2. Belladrum 3. Perrydown 19 ran

1870 James Merry's b c **Macgregor** J: John Daley 100/30 £4,400 2. Normanby 3. Kingcraft 10 ran

1871 John Johnstone's br c **Bothwell** J: John Osborne 11/2 £4,350 2. Sterling 3. King of the Forest 13 ran

1872 Joe Dawson's ch c **Prince Charlie** J: John Osborne 2/1 Fav £4,350 2. Cremorne 3. Queen's Messenger 14 ran

1873 William Stirling Crawfurd's ch c **Gang Forward** J: Tom Chaloner 8/1 £3,650 2. Kaiser 3. Suleiman 10 ran

1874 6th Viscount Falmouth's ch c **Atlantic** J: Fred Archer 10/1 £4,200 2. Reverberation 3. Ecossais 12 ran

1875 Clare Vyner's b c **Camballo** J: John Osborne 7/2 Fav £4,550 2. Picnic 3. Breechloader 13 ran

1876 Viscount Dupplin's b c **Petrarch** J: Harry Luke 20/1 £4,100 2. Julius Caesar 3. Kaleidoscope 14 ran

1877 Comte Frédéric de Lagrange's b c **Chamant** J: Jem Goater 2/1 Jt-Fav £5,200 2. Brown Prince 3. Silvio 11 ran

1878 4th Earl of Lonsdale's ch f **Pilgrimage** J: Tom Cannon 2/1 Fav £4,650 2. Insulaire 3. Sefton 10 ran

1879 6th Viscount Falmouth's ch c **Charibert** J: Fred Archer 25/1 £6,250 2. Cadogan 3. Rayon d'Or 15 ran

1880 8th Duke of Beaufort's bl c **Petronel** J: George Fordham 20/1 £4,850 2. Muncaster 3. The Abbot 17 ran

1881 1st Duke of Westminster's br c **Peregrine** J: Fred Webb 15/2 £6,150 2. Iroquois 3. Don Fulano 14 ran

1882 1st Duke of Westminster's ch f **Shotover** J: Tom Cannon 10/1 £5,000 2. Quicklime 3. Marden 18 ran

1883 6th Viscount Falmouth's br c **Galliard** J: Fred Archer 9/2 £4,550 2. Goldfield 3. The Prince 15 ran

1884 John Foy's br c **Scot Free** J: Billy Platt 3/1 Fav £4,150 2. St Medard 3. Harvester 10 ran

1885 William Brodrick Cloete's b c **Paradox** J: Fred Archer 1/3 Fav £4,300 2. Crafton 3. The Child of the Mist 7 ran

1886 1st Duke of Westminster's b c **Ormonde** J: George Barrett 7/2 £4,000 2. Minting 3. Mephisto 6 ran

1887 Douglas Baird's ch c **Enterprise** J: Tom Cannon 2/1 Fav £3,550 2. Phil 3. Eglamore 8 ran

1888 6th Duke of Portland's b c **Ayrshire** J: John Osborne 8/1 £3,550 2. Johnny Morgan 3. Orbit 6 ran

1889 Douglas Baird's ch c **Enthusiast** J: Tom Cannon 25/1 £4,000 2. Donovan 3. Pioneer 9 ran

1890 Archie Merry's b c **Surefoot** J: John Liddiard 5/4 Fav £4,100 2. Le Nord 3. Blue Green 9 ran

1891 1st Baron Alington's br c **Common** J: George Barrett 9/1 £4,250 2. Orvieto 3. Peter Flower 9 ran

1892 Charles Day Rose's ch c **Bona Vista** J: Jack Robinson 10/1 £4,400 2. St Angelo 3. Curio 14 ran

1893 Harry McCalmont's b c **Isinglass** J: Tommy Loates 4/5 Fav £4,250 2. Ravensbury 3. Raeburn 10 ran

1894 5th Earl of Rosebery's b c **Ladas** J: Jack Watts 5/6 Fav £3,500 2. Matchbox 3. Athlone 8 ran

1895 Sir John Blundell Maple's b c **Kirkconnel** J: Jack Watts 10/1 £4,000 2. Laveno 3. Sir Visto 8 ran

1896 Leopold de Rothschild's br c **St Frusquin** J: Tommy Loates 12/100 Fav £4,250 2. Love Wisely 3. Labrador 7 ran

1897 John Gubbins's b c **Galtee More** J: Charlie Wood 5/4 Fav £3,700 2. Velasquez 3. Minstrel 8 ran

1898 Wallace Johnstone's b c **Disraeli** J: Sam Loates 100/8 £4,900

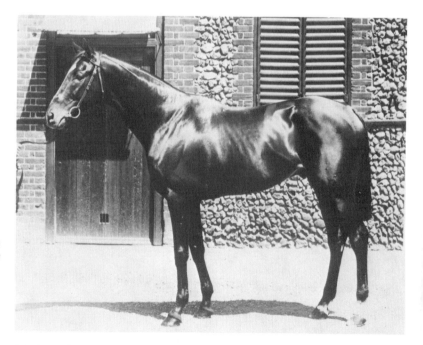

Isinglass, whose defeat of Ravensbury in the 2000 Guineas of 1893 was repeated in both the other two Triple Crown races.

2. Wantage 3. Ninus 14 ran

1899 1st Duke of Westminster's b c **Flying Fox** J: Morny Cannon 5/6 Fav £4,250 2. Caiman 3. Trident 8 ran

1900 HRH Prince of Wales's b c **Diamond Jubilee** J: Herbert Jones 11/4 £4,700 2. Bonarosa 3. Sidus 10 ran

1901 Sir Ernest Cassel's br c **Handicapper** J: William Halsey 33/1 £5,300 T: Fred Day, Newmarket B: Donald Fraser Sire: Matchmaker 2. Doricles 3. Osboch 2l, neck 1:43.0 17 ran

1902 Bob Sievier's b f **Sceptre** J: Bert Randall 4/1 £5,050 T: Owner, Shrewton, Wiltshire B: 1st Duke of Westminster Sire: Persimmon 2. Pistol 3. Ard Patrick 2l, 3l 1:39.0 14 ran

1903 Sir James Miller's br c **Rock Sand** J: Skeets Martin 6/4 Fav £4,500 T: George Blackwell, Newmarket B: Owner Sire: Sainfoin 2. Flotsam 3. Rabelais 1½l, 3l 1:42.0 11 ran

1904 Leopold de Rothschild's b c **St Amant** J: Kempton Cannon 11/4 Fav £5,300 T: Alfred Hayhoe, Newmarket B: Owner Sire: St Frusquin 2. John o' Gaunt 3. Henry the First 4l, 2l 1:38.8 14 ran

1905 West de Wend-Fenton's b or br c **Vedas** J: Herbert Jones 11/2 £4,650 T: Jack Robinson, Foxhill, Wiltshire B: Lady Meux Sire: Florizel 2. Signorino 3. Llangibby 2l, head 1:41.2 13 ran

1906 Arthur James's br c **Gorgos** J: Herbert Jones 20/1 £3,700 T: Richard Marsh, Newmarket B: Owner Sire: Ladas 2. Sancy 3. Ramrod head, neck 1:43.8 12 ran

1907 Henry Greer's br or bl c **Slieve Gallion** J: Billy Higgs 4/11 Fav £5,300 T: Sam Darling, Beckhampton, Wiltshire B: Owner Sire: Gallinule 2. Bezonian 3. Linacre 3l, ¾l 1:41.8 10 ran

1908 August Belmont, jr's b c **Norman** J: Otto Madden 25/1 £5,600 T: John Watson, Newmarket B: Owner Sire: Octagon 2. White Eagle 3l, ¾l 1:44.6 17 ran

1909 H M King Edward VII's br c **Minoru** J: Herbert Jones 4/1 £5,000 T: Richard Marsh, Newmarket B: William Hall Walker Sire: Cyllene 2. Phaleron 3. Louviers 2l, 1½l 1:37.8 11 ran

1910 5th Earl of Rosebery's ch c **Neil Gow** J: Danny Maher 2/1 Fav £6,200 T: Percy Peck, Exning, Suffolk B: Owner Sire: Marco 2. Lemberg 3. Whisk Broom short head, 2l 1:40.4 13 ran

1911 Jack Joel's br c **Sunstar** J: George Stern 5/1 £5,600 T: Charles Morton, Wantage, Berkshire B: Owner Sire: Sundridge 2. Stedfast 3. Lycaon 2l, ½l 1:37.6 14 ran

1912 Herman Duryea's ch c **Sweeper** J: Danny Maher 6/1 £6,105 T: Atty Persse, Stockbridge, Hampshire B: Owner Sire: Broomstick 2. Jaeger 3. Hall Cross 1l, ½l 1:38.4 14 ran

1913 Walter Raphael's b c **Louvois** J: Johnny Reiff 25/1 £6,800 T: Dawson Waugh, Newmarket B: Owner Sire: Isinglass 2. Craganour 3. Meeting House head, 2l 1:38.8 15 ran

1914 Sir John Thursby's b c **Kennymore** J: George Stern 2/1 Fav £7,100 T: Alec Taylor, Manton, Wiltshire B: Owner Sire: John o' Gaunt 2. Corcyra 3. Black Jester short head, 2l 1:38.0 18 ran

1915 Solly Joel's b c **Pommern** J: Steve Donoghue 2/1 Fav £7,100 T: Charley Peck, Newmarket B: Owner Sire: Polymelus 2. Tournament 3. The Vizier 3l, head 1:43.4 16 ran

1916 7th Viscount Falmouth's ch c **Clarissimus** J: Jimmy Clark 100/7 £5,400 T: Willie Waugh, Kingsclere, Berkshire B: Owner Sire: Radium 2. Kwang-Su 3. Nassovian ¾l, ½l 1:39.6 17 ran

1917 Alfred Cox's b c **Gay Crusader** J: Steve Donoghue 9/4 Fav £3,950 T: Alec Taylor, Manton, Wiltshire B: Owner Sire: Bayardo 2. Magpie 3. Athdara head, 3l 1:40.8 14 ran

1918 Lady James Douglas's b c **Gainsborough** J: Joe Childs 4/1 £5,100 T: Alec Taylor, Manton, Wiltshire B: Owner Sire: Bayardo 2. Somme Kiss 3. Blink 1½l, 6l 1:44.6 13 ran

1919 Sir Alec Black's br c **The Panther** J: Dick Cooper 10/1 £4,950 T: George Manser, Newmarket B: National Stud Sire: Tracery 2. Buchan 3. Dominion neck, ¾l 1:44.4 12 ran

1920 Dermot McCalmont's gr c **Tetratema** J: Brownie Carslake 2/1 Fav £5,750 T: Atty Persse, Stockbridge, Hampshire B: Owner Sire: The Tetrarch 2. Allenby 3. Paragon ½l, 3l 1:43.2 17 ran

1921 2nd Viscount Astor's b c **Craig an Eran** J: Jack Brennan 100/6 £8,300 T: Alec Taylor, Manton, Wiltshire B: Owner Sire: Sunstar 2. Lemonora 3. Humorist ¾l, ¾l 1:41.6 26 ran

1922 1st Baron Queenborough's b c **St Louis** J: George Archibald 6/1 £10,645 T: Peter Gilpin, Newmarket B: James Maher Sire: Louvois 2. Pondoland 3. Captain Cuttle 3l, 4l 1:43.6 22 ran

1923 5th Earl of Rosebery's b c **Ellangowan** J: Charlie Elliott 7/1 £9,765 T: Jack Jarvis, Newmarket B: Owner Sire: Lemberg 2. Knockando. D'Orsay head, ½l 1:37.8 18 ran

1924 HH Aga Khan III's ch c **Diophon** J: George Hulme 11/2 £10,315 T: Dick Dawson, Whatcombe,

Berkshire B: 1st Viscount D'Abernon Sire: Grand Parade 2. Bright Knight 3. Green Fire head, neck 1:39.0 20 ran

1925 Henry Morriss's b c **Manna** J: Steve Donoghue 100/8 £10,240 T: Fred Darling, Beckhampton, Wiltshire B: James Maher Sire: Phalaris 2. St Becan 3. Oojah 2l, 4l 1:39.4 13 ran

1926 17th Earl of Derby's br c **Colorado** J: Tommy Weston 100/8 £9,630 T: George Lambton, Newmarket B: Owner Sire: Phalaris 2. Coronach 3. Apple Sammy 5l, 3l 1:43.6 19 ran

1927 Charles Sofer Whitburn's b c **Adam's Apple** J: Jack Leach 20/1 £10,915 T: Harry Cottrill, Lambourn, Berkshire B: Owner Sire: Pommern 2. Call Boy 3. Sickle short head, ½l 1:38.2 23 ran

1928 Sir Laurence Philipps's b c **Flamingo** J: Charlie Elliott 5/1 £10,945 T: Jack Jarvis, Newmarket B: Sir John Robinson Sire: Flamboyant 2. Royal Minstrel 3. O'Curry head, 1½l 1:38.8 17 ran

1929 Dermot McCalmont's gr c **Mr Jinks** J: Harry Beasley 5/2 Fav £10,440 T: Atty Persse, Stockbridge, Hampshire B: Owner Sire: Tetratema 2. Cragadour 3. Gay Day head, 1½l 1:39.8 22 ran

1930 Sir Hugo Hirst's b c **Diolite** J: Freddie Fox 10/1 £9,947 T: Fred Templeman, Lambourn, Berkshire B: Charles Birkin Sire: Diophon 2. Paradine 3. Silver Flare 2l, 1l 1:42.4 28 ran

1931 Arthur Dewar's b c **Cameronian** J: Joe Childs 100/8 £11,472 T: Fred Darling, Beckhampton, Wiltshire B: 1st Baron Dewar Sire: Pharos 2. Goyescas 3. Orpen 2l, 3l 1:39.4 24 ran

1932 Washington Singer's b c **Orwell** J: Bobby Jones Evens Fav £8,459 T: Joe Lawson, Manton, Wiltshire B: 1st Viscount Furness Sire: Gainsborough 2. Dastur 3. Hesperus 2l, 1½l 1:42.4 11 ran

1933 Princesse de Faucigny-Lucinge's ch c **Rodosto** J: Roger Brethès 9/1 £9,037 T: Harry Count, Chantilly, France B: Henri Corbière Sire: Epinard 2. King Salmon 3. Gino 1l, ¾l 1:40.4 27 ran

1934 1st Baron Glanely's b c **Colombo** J: Rae Johnstone 2/7 Fav £8,272 T: Tommy Hogg, Newmarket B: Sir Alec Black Sire: Manna 2. Easton 3. Badruddin 1l, 1½l 1:40.0 12 ran

1935 HH Aga Khan III's b c **Bahram** J: Freddie Fox 7/2 £9,339 T: Frank Butters, Newmarket B: Owner Sire: Blandford 2. Theft 3. Sea Bequest 1½l, 2l 1:41.4 16 ran

1936 2nd Viscount Astor's br c **Pay Up** J: Bobby Dick 11/2 £9,449 T: Joe Lawson, Manton, Wiltshire B: Cliveden Stud Sire: Fairway

2. Mahmoud 3. Thankerton short head, 3l 1:39.6 19 ran

1937 Evremond de Saint-Alary's b c **Le Ksar** J: Charles Semblat 20/1 £9,318 T: Frank Carter, Chantilly, France B: Léon Volterra Sire: Ksar 2. Goya 3. Mid-day Sun 4l, ½l 1:44.6 18 ran

1938 Henry Morriss's b c **Pasch** J: Gordon Richards 5/2 Fav £9,241 T: Fred Darling, Beckhampton, Wiltshire B: Banstead Manor Stud Sire: Blandford 2. Scottish Union 3. Mirza 2l, 1½l 1:38.8 18 ran

1939 6th Earl of Rosebery's ch c **Blue Peter** J: Eph Smith 5/1 Jt-Fav £9,556 T: Jack Jarvis, Newmarket B: Owner Sire: Fairway 2. Admiral's Walk 3. Fairstone ½l, ¾l 1:39.4 25 ran

1940 Marcel Boussac's b c **Djebel** J: Charlie Elliott 9/4 Fav £5,340 T: Albert Swann, Chantilly, France B: Owner Sire: Tourbillon 2. Stardust 3. Tant Mieux 2l, head 1:43.0 21 ran

1941 2nd Duke of Westminster's b c **Lambert Simnel** J: Charlie Elliott 10/1 £1,930 T: Fred Templeman, Lambourn, Berkshire B: Owner Sire: Fair Trial 2. Morogoro 3. Sun Castle 2l, 1½l 1:43.2 19 ran

1942 HM King George VI's b c **Big Game** J: Gordon Richards 8/11 Fav £2,083 T: Fred Darling, Beckhampton, Wiltshire B: National Stud Sire: Bahram 2. Watling Street 3. Gold Nib 4l, 2l 1:41.0 14 ran

1943 Alfred Saunders's b c **Kingsway** J: Sam Wragg 18/1 £2,049 T: Joe Lawson, Manton, Wiltshire B: 1st Viscount Furness Sire: Fairway 2. Pink Flower 3. Way In short head, head 1:37.4 19 ran

1944 17th Earl of Derby's br f **Garden Path** J: Harry Wragg 5/1 £3,857 T: Walter Earl, Newmarket B: Owner Sire: Fairway 2. Growing Confidence 3. Tehran head, 1½l 1:39.8 26 ran

1945 2nd Viscount Astor's ch c **Court Martial** J: Cliff Richards 13/2 £8,684 T: Joe Lawson, Manton, Wiltshire B: Cliveden Stud Sire: Fair Trial 2. Dante 3. Royal Charger neck, 2l 1:40.6 20 ran

1946 Sir William Cooke's b c **Happy Knight** J: Tommy Weston 28/1 £8,642 T: Henri Jelliss, Newmarket B: Owner Sire: Colombo 2. Khaled 3. Radiotherapy 4l, head 1:38.0 13 ran

1947 Arthur Dewar's br c **Tudor Minstrel** J: Gordon Richards 11/8 Fav £10,040 T: Fred Darling, Beckhampton, Wiltshire B: Owner Sire: Owen Tudor 2. Saravan 3. Sayajirao 8l, short head 1:37.8 15 ran

1948 HH Maharaja of Baroda's b c **My Babu** J: Charlie Smirke 2/1 Fav £14,099 T: Sam Armstrong, Newmarket B: Peter Beatty Sire: Djebel 2. The Cobbler 3. Pride of India head, 4l 1:35.8 18 ran

1949 Mrs Marion Glenister's b c

Nimbus J: Charlie Elliott 10/1 £13,606 T: George Colling, Newmarket B: William Hill Sire: Nearco 2. Abernant 3. Barnes Park short head, 4l 1:38.0 13 ran

1950 HH Aga Khan III's gr c **Palestine** J: Charlie Smirke 4/1 £12,982 T: Marcus Marsh, Newmarket B: Owner and Prince Aly Khan Sire: Fair Trial 2. Prince Simon 3. Masked Light short head, 5l 1:36.8 19 ran

1951 Ley On's br c **Ki Ming** J: Scobie Breasley 100/8 £14,631 T: Michael Beary, Wantage, Berkshire B: John Sullivan Sire: Ballyogan 2. Stokes 3. Malka's Boy 1½l, short head 1:42.0 27 ran

1952 Eugène Constant's ch c **Thunderhead** J: Roger Poincelet 100/7 £14,516 T: Etienne Pollet, Chantilly, France B. Jean Desbons Sire: Merry Boy 2. King's Bench 3. Argur 5l, ½l 1:42.48 26 ran

1953 William Humble's b c **Nearula** J: Edgar Britt 2/1 Fav £13,921 T: Charles Elsey, Malton, Yorkshire B: Roderic More O'Ferrall and Charles Sweeny Sire: Nasrullah 2. Bebe Grande 3. Oleandrin 4l, 3l 1:38.26 16 ran

1954 Sir Percy Loraine's b c **Darius** J: Manny Mercer 8/1 £13,211 T: Harry Wragg, Newmarket B: Owner Sire: Dante 2. Ferriol 3. Poona 1l, 5l 1:39.45 19 ran

1955 David Robinson's b c **Our Babu** J: Doug Smith 13/2 £13,666 T: Geoffrey Brooke, Newmarket B: Sir Oliver Lambart Sire: My Babu 2. Tamerlane 3. Klairon neck, short head 1:38.83 23 ran

1956 Anthony Samuel's b c **Gilles de Retz** J: Frank Barlow 50/1 £11,622 T: Mrs Helen Johnson Houghton, Blewbury, Berkshire B: Eveton Stud Sire: Royal Charger 2. Chantelsey 3. Buisson Ardent 1l, 1½l 1:38.76 19 ran

1957 Sir Victor Sassoon's ch c **Crepello** J: Lester Piggott 7/2 £13,598 T: Noel Murless, Newmarket B: Eve Stud Ltd Sire: Donatello 2. Quorum 3. Pipe of Peace ½l, head 1:38.24 14 ran

1958 HM Queen Elizabeth II's ch c **Pall Mall** J: Doug Smith 20/1 £13,917 T: Cecil Boyd-Rochfort, Newmarket B: Owner Sire: Palestine 2. Major Portion 3. Nagami ½l, 3l 1:39.43 14 ran

1959 Prince Aly Khan's b c **Taboun** J: George Moore 5/2 Fav £15,341 T: Alec Head, Chantilly, France B: Owner and HH Aga Khan III Sire: Tabriz 2. Masham 3. Carnoustie 3l, neck 1:42.42 13 ran

1960 Reginald Webster's ch c **Martial** J: Ron Hutchinson 18/1 £16,854 T: Paddy Prendergast, The Curragh, Co Kildare, Ireland B: Tim Rogers Sire: Hill Gail 2. Venture 3. Auroy head, 4l 1:38.33 17 ran

1961 Thomas Yuill's b c **Rockavon** J: Norman Stirk 66/1 £22,801 T: George Boyd, Dunbar, East Lothian, Scotland B: Biddlesden Park Stud Sire: Rockefella 2. Prince Tudor 3. Time Greine 2l, short head 1:39.46 22 ran

1962 Gerald Glover's ch c **Privy Councillor** J: Bill Rickaby 100/6 £32,839 T: Tom Waugh, Newmarket B: Owner Sire: Counsel 2. Romulus 3. Prince Poppa 3l, 2l 1:38.74 19 ran

1963 Miss Monica Sheriffe's b c **Only for Life** J: Jimmy Lindley 33/1 £31,369 T: Jeremy Tree, Beckhampton, Wiltshire B: Hanstead Stud Sire: Chanteur 2. Ionian 3. Corpora short head, 3l 1:45.00 21 ran.

1964 Mrs Howell Jackson's b c **Baldric** J: Bill Pyers 20/1 £40,302 T: Ernie Fellows, Chantilly, France B: Bull Run Stud Sire: Round Table 2. Fabergé 3. Balustrade 2l, 1l 1:38.44 27 ran

1965 Wilfred Harvey's ch c **Niksar** J: Duncan Keith 100/8 £30,230 T: Walter Nightingall, Epsom, Surrey B: Marquis de Nicolay Sire: Le Haar 2. Silly Season 3. Présent 1l, 1l 1:43.31 22 ran

1966 Peter Butler's br c **Kashmir** J: Jimmy Lindley 7/1 £30,595 T: Mick Bartholomew, Chantilly, France B: Mrs Jane Levins Moore Sire: Tudor Melody 2. Great Nephew 3. Celtic Song short head, 2½l 1:40.68 25 ran

1967 Jim Joel's b c **Royal Palace** J: George Moore 100/30 Jt-Fav £31,000 T: Noel Murless, Newmarket B: Owner Sire: Ballymoss 2. Taj Dewan 3. Missile short head, 1½l 1:39.37 18 ran

1968 Raymond Guest's b c **Sir Ivor** J: Lester Piggott 11/8 Fav £22,586 T: Vincent O'Brien, Cashel, Co Tipperary, Ireland B: Mrs Alice Headley Bell Sire: Sir Gaylord 2. Petingo 3. Jimmy Reppin 1½l, 2½l 1:39.26 10 ran

1969 Jim Brown's b c **Right Tack** J: Geoff Lewis 15/2 £24,757 T: John Sutcliffe, Epsom, Surrey B: Paul Larkin Sire: Hard Tack 2. Tower Walk 3. Welsh Pageant 2½l, head 1:41.65 13 ran

1970 Charles Engelhard's b c **Nijinsky** J: Lester Piggott 4/7 Fav £28,295 T: Vincent O'Brien, Cashel, Co Tipperary, Ireland B: Eddie Taylor Sire: Northern Dancer 2. Yellow God 3. Roi Soleil 2½l, 2½l 1:41.54 14 ran

1971 Mrs Jean Hislop's b c **Brigadier Gerard** J: Joe Mercer 11/2 £27,283 T: Dick Hern, West Ilsley, Berkshire B: John Hislop Sire: Queen's Hussar 2. Mill Reef 3. My Swallow 3l, ¾l 1:39.20 6 ran

1972 Sir Jules Thorn's b c **High Top** J: Willie Carson 85/40 Fav £27,538

T: Bernard van Cutsem, Newmarket
B: Bob McCreery Sire: Derring-Do
2. Roberto 3. Sun Prince ½l, 6l
1:40.82 12 ran

1973 Mrs Brenda Davis's br c **Mon Fils**
J: Frankie Durr 50/1 £29,970
T: Richard Hannon, East Everleigh,
Wiltshire B: Jack Davis Sire:
Sheshoon 2. Noble Decree 3. Sharp
Edge head, 3l 1:42.97 18 ran

1974 Mme Maria-Felix Berger's b c
Nonoalco J: Yves Saint-Martin 19/2
£45,327 T: François Boutin,
Lamorlaye, France B: Forrest E. Mars
Sire: Nearctic 2. Giacometti
3. Apalachee 1½l, 1l 1:39.58 12 ran

1975 Carlo D'Alessio's ch c **Bolkonski**
J: Gianfranco Dettori 33/1 £36,868
T: Henry Cecil, Newmarket
B: Woodpark Ltd Sire: Balidar
2. Grundy 3. Dominion ½l, 3l 1:39.49
24 ran

1976 Carlo D'Alessio's b c **Wollow**
J: Gianfranco Dettori Evens Fav
£49,581 T: Henry Cecil, Newmarket
B: Tally Ho Stud Sire: Wolver Hollow
2. Vitigès 3 Thieving Demon 1½l, 2l
1:38.09 17 ran

1977 Niels Schibbye's ch c **Nebbiolo**
J: Gabriel Curran 20/1 £45,232
T: Kevin Prendergast, The Curragh,
Co Kildare, Ireland B: Owner Sire:
Yellow God 2. Tachypous 3. The
Minstrel 1l, 1l 1:38.54 18 ran

1978 John Hayter's b c **Roland
Gardens** J: Frankie Durr 28/1
£51,940 T: Duncan Sasse, Upper
Lambourn, Berkshire B: Mrs Peggy
Ryan Sire: Derring-Do 2. Remainder
Man 3. Weth Nan 1½l, head 1:47.33
19 ran

1979 Tony Shead's ch c **Tap on Wood**
J: Steve Cauthen 20/1 £55,840
T: Barry Hills, Lambourn, Berkshire
B: Irish National Stud Sire: Sallust
2. Kris 3. Young Generation
1½l, short head 1:43.60 20 ran

1980 Khalid Bin Abdullah's b c **Known
Fact** J: Willie Carson 14/1 £56,620
T: Jeremy Tree, Beckhampton,
Wiltshire B: William O. Reed Sire: In
Reality 2. Posse 3. Night Alert ¾l, 3l
1:40.46 14 ran (Nureyev finished
first, disqualified)

1981 Mrs Andry Muinos's br c **To-
Agori-Mou** J: Greville Starkey
5/2 Fav £64,136 T: Guy Harwood,
Pulborough, Sussex B: Rathduff
Stud Sire: Tudor Music 2. Mattaboy
3. Bel Bolide neck, 1½l 1:41.43
19 ran

1982 Gerry Oldham's b c **Zino**
J: Freddy Head 8/1 £80,080
T: François Boutin, Lamorlaye,
France B: Citadel Stud
Establishment Sire: Welsh Pageant
2. Wind and Wuthering 3. Tender
King head, 2l 1:37.13 26 ran

1983 Robert Sangster's b c **Lomond**
J: Pat Eddery 9/1 £73,462 T: Vincent
O'Brien, Cashel, Co Tipperary,

American-bred El Gran Senor records the best performance seen on a British racecourse during 1984 when trouncing Chief Singer in the 2000 Guineas.

Ireland B: Warner Jones, Will Farish
and William Kilroy Sire: Northern
Dancer 2. Tolomeo 3. Muscatite
2l, ¾l 1:43.87 16 ran

1984 Robert Sangster's b c **El Gran
Senor** J: Pat Eddery 15/8 Fav
£87,408 T: Vincent O'Brien, Cashel,
Co Tipperary, Ireland B: Eddie Taylor
Sire: Northern Dancer 2. Chief Singer
3. Lear Fan 2½l, 4l 1:37.41 9 ran

RECORDS FOR WINNING HORSES

Greatest margins

8 lengths — Tudor Minstrel (1947)
5 lengths — Macgregor (1870), Scot-
Free (1884), Colorado (1926),
Thunderhead (1952)

Smallest margins

dead-heat — Moslem and Formosa
(1868)
short head — Gang Forward (1873), Neil
Gow (1910), Kennymore (1914),
Adam's Apple (1927), Pay Up (1936),
Kingsway (1943), Nimbus (1949),
Palestine (1950), Only for Life (1963),
Kashmir (1966), Royal Palace
(1967).

Fillies

Pastille (1822), Crucifix (1840),
Formosa (1868, dead-heat),
Pilgrimage (1878), Shotover (1882),
Sceptre (1902), Garden Path (1944).

Twin

Nicolo (1823).

Grey

Clearwell (1833), Grey Momus (1838),
Tetratema (1920), Mr Jinks (1929),
Palestine (1950).

Black

Trophonius (1811), Smolensko (1813),
The Corsair (1839), Nunnykirk
(1849), Petronel (1880). Slieve
Gallion (1907) was described as
brown or black.

Longest odds

66/1 — Rockavon (1961)
50/1 — Gilles de Retz (1956), Mon Fils
(1973)
33/1 — Handicapper (1901), Only for
Life (1963), Bolkonski (1975)
28/1 — Happy Knight (1946), Roland
Gardens (1978)

25/1—Diophantus (1861), Charibert (1879), Enthusiast (1889), Norman (1908), Louvois (1913)

Shortest odds

12/100—St Frusquin (1896)
1/8—Patron (1829)
1/7—Ibrahim (1835)
1/5—Riddlesworth (1831)
2/7—The Ugly Buck (1844), Colombo (1934)
1/3—Cotherstone (1843), Paradox (1885)

Winner carrying overweight

Macgregor (1870) carried 1 lb overweight at 8 st 11 lb.

Winner on disqualification

Known Fact (1980) was awarded the race after finishing a neck behind Nureyev, who was disqualified and placed last for bumping Posse.

Dubious winner

Louvois (1913) was declared the winner, although the Judge was almost alone in believing that Craganour had not finished first.

Trained in Scotland

Rockavon (1961).

Trained in Ireland

Martial (1960), Sir Ivor (1968), Nijinsky (1970), Nebbiolo (1977), Lomond (1983), El Gran Senor (1984).

Trained in France

Rodosto (1933), Le Ksar (1937), Djebel (1940), Thunderhead (1952), Taboun (1959), Baldric (1964), Kashmir (1966), Nonoalco (1974), Zino (1982).

Bred in France

Gladiateur (1865), Prince Charlie (1872), Chamant (1877), Sweeper (1912), Rodosto (1933), Le Ksar (1937), Djebel (1940), My Babu (1948), Thunderhead (1952), Taboun (1959), Niksar (1965).

Bred in USA

Norman (1908), Baldric (1964), Sir Ivor (1968), Nonoalco (1974), Known Fact (1980), Lomond (1983), El Gran Senor (1984).

Bred in Canada

Nijinsky (1970).

Siblings

Bay Middleton (1836) and Achmet (1837) were brothers.
Pindarrie (1820) and Pastille (1822) were half-brother and half-sister.

Unnamed at time of victory

Bay Middleton (1836).

Raced under two names

My Babu (1948) had been champion two-year-old under the name Lérins.

Winners in two countries

Rodosto (1933) and Djebel (1940) also won the equivalent French classic, the Poule d'Essai des Poulains.
Right Tack (1969) also won the Irish 2000 Guineas.

Oldest and youngest sires

Doctor Syntax was 26 years old when he got Ralph (1841). Grand Parade sired Diophon (1924) at the age of four.

Oldest and youngest dams

Lisette was 24 years old when she produced Clearwell (1833). Monstrosity produced The Ugly Buck (1844) at the age of three.

RECORDS FOR PLACED HORSES

Fillies

Music (1813), Bebe Grande (1953).

Grey

Paulus (1835), Angelo (1840), Royal Minstrel (1928), Gino (1933), Badruddin (1934), Mahmoud (1936), Morogoro (1941), Abernant (1949), Quorum (1957), Sharp Edge (1973), Weth Nan (1978).

Black

Black Swan (1826), Loyola (1857), Clydesdale (1858), Insulaire (1878), Magpie (1917), Paradine (1930).

Longest odds

100/1—Don Fulano (1881), Sidus (1900), Jaeger (1912), Barnes Park (1949)
66/1—Perry Down (1869), Normanby (1870), Athlone (1894), Prince Tudor (1961), Great Nephew (1966), Thieving Demon (1976)
60/1—Sun Prince (1972)
50/1—Historian (1864), Iroquois (1881), Minstrel (1897), Bonarosa (1900), Pistol (1902), Lycaon (1911), Meeting House (1913), D'Orsay (1923), Badruddin (1934), Tehran (1944), Mattaboy (1981).

Trained in Ireland

Time Greine (1961), Prince Poppa (1962), Ionian (1963), Celtic Song (1966), Missile (1967), Roberto (1972), Apalachee (1974), The Minstrel (1977), Night Alert (1980).

Trained in France

Easton (1934), Argur (1952), Ferriol (1954), Klairon (1955), Buisson Ardent (1956), Venture (1960), Corpora (1963), Présent (1965), Taj

Dewan (1967), Roi Soleil (1970), Vitigès (1976).

Bred in France

Insulaire (1878), Rayon d'Or (1879), Le Nord (1890), Goyescas (1931), Hesperus (1932), Easton (1934), Badruddin (1934), Mahmoud (1936), Goya (1937), Mirza (1938), Tant Mieux (1940), Argur (1952), Ferriol (1954), Klairon (1955), Buisson Ardent (1956), Présent (1965), Taj Dewan (1967), Vitigès (1976).

Bred in USA

Brown Prince (1877), Iroquois (1881), Don Fulano (1881), Caiman (1899), Whisk Broom (1910), Meeting House (1913), Prince Simon (1950), Corpora (1963), Silly Season (1965), Mill Reef (1971), Roberto (1972), Noble Decree (1973), Apalachee (1974), Weth Nan (1978), Posse (1980), Night Alert (1980), Bel Bolide (1981), Wind and Wuthering (1982), Lear Fan (1984).

Bred in Canada

The Minstrel (1977).

Ridden by amateur

John o' Gaunt (1904) and Sir Archibald (1908) both finished second under amateur rider George Thursby.

MISCELLANEOUS RECORDS

Fastest times

1:35.8—My Babu (1948)
1:36.8—Palestine (1950)
1:37.13—Zino (1982)

Largest entry

1,001—1974

Smallest entry

10—1825

Largest fields

28—1930
27—1933, 1951, 1964
26—1921, 1944, 1952, 1982

Smallest fields

2—1829, 1830
3—1822, 1839, 1843
4—1821, 1835

Richest first prizes

£87,408—1984
£80,080—1982
£73,462—1983

Smallest first prizes

£600—1829
£700—1825
£735—1822

Hottest losing favourite

1/7—Caesar was 2nd in 1839.

Most consecutive winning favourites
6 — 1840 to 1845

Most consecutive losing favourites
8 — 1921 to 1928

Race postponed
1921, because of national coal strike.

Earliest date
14 April — 1812

Latest date
25 May — 1943

Latest peacetime date
10 May — 1859

Run on
Tuesday: 1809–71, 1942–43
Wednesday: 1872–1920, 1922–41, 1944–70, 1976–77
Friday: 1921
Saturday: 1971–75, from 1978

Foreign-bred horses placed 1, 2, 3
In 1980 the first four to finish — Nureyev, Known Fact, Posse and Night Alert – were all bred in the USA. Nureyev was subsequently disqualified and relegated to last.

Most successful owners
5 wins — 4th Duke of Grafton: 1820, 1821, 1822, 1826, 1827
5th Earl of Jersey: 1831, 1834, 1835, 1836, 1837
4 wins — 2nd Marquis of Exeter: 1825, 1829, 1830, 1852
1st Duke of Westminster: 1881, 1882, 1886, 1899.
3 wins — John Bowes: 1842, 1843, 1853
6th Viscount Falmouth: 1874, 1879, 1883
5th Earl of Rosebery: 1894, 1910, 1923
2nd Viscount Astor: 1921, 1936, 1945
HH Aga Khan III: 1924, 1935, 1950
2 wins — Lord George Bentinck: 1838, 1840
Anthony Nichol: 1849, 1860
James Merry: 1855, 1870
John Johnstone: 1869, 1871
William Stirling Crawfurd: 1868, 1873
Comte Frédéric de Lagrange: 1865, 1877
8th Duke of Beaufort: 1867, 1880
Douglas Baird: 1887, 1889
Leopold de Rothschild: 1896, 1904
HM King Edward VII: 1900, 1909
Dermot McCalmont: 1920, 1929
Henry Morriss: 1925, 1938
17th Earl of Derby: 1926, 1944
Arthur Dewar: 1931, 1947
Carlo D'Alessio: 1975, 1976
Robert Sangster: 1983, 1984

Owned winner and 2nd
6th Duke of Portland: 1888
HH Aga Khan III: 1935

Most successful breeders
5 wins — 4th Duke of Grafton: 1820, 1821, 1822, 1826, 1827
5th Earl of Jersey: 1831, 1834, 1835, 1836, 1837.
4 wins — 2nd Marquis of Exeter: 1825, 1829, 1830, 1868
5th Earl of Rosebery: 1892, 1894, 1910, 1923
3 wins — 6th Viscount Falmouth: 1874, 1879, 1883
Yardley Stud: 1885, 1887, 1889
1st Duke of Westminster: 1886, 1899, 1902
2nd Viscount Astor/Cliveden Stud: 1921, 1936, 1945
HH Aga Khan III: 1935, 1950, 1959 (2 in partnership).
2 wins — John Bowes: 1843, 1853
Jonathan Peel: 1832, 1854;
HM Queen Victoria: 1858, 1861
James Cookson: 1868, 1878
8th Duke of Beaufort: 1867, 1880
Leopold de Rothschild: 1896, 1904
James Maher: 1922, 1925
Dermot McCalmont: 1920, 1929
1st Viscount Furness: 1932, 1943
17th Earl of Derby: 1926, 1944
Eddie Taylor: 1970, 1984

Bred winner and 2nd
6th Duke of Portland: 1888
HH Aga Khan III: 1935

Jem Robinson, whose record of nine winning 2000 Guineas rides has gone unchallenged for more than a century.

Most successful trainers
7 wins — John Scott: 1842, 1843, 1849, 1853, 1856, 1860, 1862
6 wins — Robert Robson: 1810, 1820, 1821, 1822, 1826, 1827
James Edwards: 1819, 1831, 1834, 1835, 1836, 1837
5 wins — Dixon Boyce: 1811, 1814, 1815, 1816, 1828
Mat Dawson: 1874, 1875, 1879, 1883, 1894
John Porter: 1882, 1885, 1886, 1891, 1899
Fred Darling: 1925, 1931, 1938, 1942, 1947
4 wins — John Day, jr: 1847, 1850, 1854, 1867
Alec Taylor: 1914, 1917, 1918, 1921
Joe Lawson: 1932, 1936, 1943, 1945
Vincent O'Brien: 1968, 1970, 1983, 1984
3 wins — Charles Marson: 1825, 1829, 1830
John Barham Day: 1838, 1840, 1844
Tom Dawson: 1864, 1869, 1871
Richard Marsh: 1900, 1906, 1909
Atty Persse: 1912, 1920, 1929
Jack Jarvis: 1923, 1928, 1939
2 wins — William Day: 1855, 1859
Joe Dawson: 1861, 1872
Alec Taylor, sr: 1868, 1873
Tom Jennings: 1865, 1877
Joe Cannon: 1878, 1880
Jimmy Ryan: 1887, 1889
John Dawson: 1876, 1898
Alfred Hayhoe: 1896, 1904
Sam Darling: 1897, 1907
Fred Templeman: 1930, 1941
Noel Murless: 1957, 1967
Henry Cecil: 1975, 1976
Jeremy Tree: 1963, 1980
François Boutin: 1974, 1982

Trained winner and 2nd
George Dawson: 1888
George Blackwell: 1903
Alec Taylor: 1917, 1921
Frank Butters: 1935
Jack Jarvis: 1939

Most successful jockeys
9 wins — Jem Robinson: 1825, 1828, 1831, 1833, 1834, 1835, 1836, 1847, 1848
6 wins — John Osborne: 1857, 1869, 1871, 1872, 1875, 1888.
5 wins — Frank Buckle: 1810, 1820, 1821, 1822, 1827
Charlie Elliott: 1923, 1928, 1940, 1941, 1949
4 wins — John Barham Day: 1826, 1838, 1840, 1841
Fred Archer: 1874, 1879, 1883, 1885
Tom Cannon: 1878, 1882, 1887, 1889
Herbert Jones: 1900, 1905, 1906, 1909
3 wins — Bill Arnull: 1814, 1815, 1816
Will Wheatley: 1817, 1823, 1824
Bill Scott: 1842, 1843, 1846
Nat Flatman: 1845, 1851, 1856

Continued on page 24

POCAHONTAS

Whereas the best stallions generally come from the ranks of the best racehorses, the best broodmares are often those who failed to distinguish themselves on the racecourse. Far from that being illogical, it is a natural consequence of a system whereby colts are generally required to earn their right to stand as stallions by dint of racing prowess, while fillies are virtually destined from birth to become broodmares, whether or not they succeed as runners.

A comprehensive search of the 39 volumes of the *General Stud Book* will reveal no greater broodmare than Pocahontas, but reference to the *Racing Calendar* shows that Pocahontas was anything but an outstanding racemare. It is true that she finished a close fifth in the Oaks, but it is equally true that she failed to win a race of any description, though she raced until she was five and descended into the humblest company.

Pocahontas was bred in 1837 by King William IV and was sent to auction when only a few months old. At the fall of the hammer she passed from the ownership of royalty into the possession of a rather unsavoury bookmaker, John Greatorex. Her price was just 62 gns, a disappointing sum for a filly whose sire, Glencoe, had won a 2000 Guineas and an Ascot Gold Cup, and whose dam, Marpessa, had a victory to her credit over the Oaks winner of her generation.

But as far as racing merit was concerned, the price for Pocahontas was not unreasonable; she won precisely nothing in prize-money. In view of her failure to win, Greatorex must have congratulated himself on getting as much as £500 for her when he passed her on to breeder William Theobald, whose prominent Stockwell Stud was situated in what is now London SW9.

In addition to being an unsuccessful runner, Pocahontas was a 'roarer', suffering from an affliction in the wind which was known to be hereditary, and which she could

be expected to pass on to at least some of her produce. Sure enough, she did transmit the defect to a number of her foals, but it is as the dam of a dozen individual winners of 72 races that she was to become a legend in her own lifetime.

She accumulated that record after her first four foals had managed only one win between them. Her fifth was a colt by The Baron called Stockwell, who won the 2000 Guineas, the St Leger, 12 races in all and rapidly acquired the soubriquet 'Emperor of Stallions'. Stockwell headed the sires' list 7 times, set records—still unmatched—for the number of races won by his progeny in a season (132) and the most individual Classic winners (12). He dominated the scene just as St Simon and Northern Dancer did in later times.

The sixth foal of Pocahontas was Rataplan, a full brother to Stockwell who was campaigned rigorously by a tough trainer and won 42 of his 71 starts. Just below top Classic standard, he ran fourth in the Derby and third in the St Leger, but he proved formidable over long distances and as a 5-year-old he accumulated 20 wins. Rataplan was not so effective as Stockwell at stud, but he did get a Derby winner in Kettledrum and one of his daughters bred the influential sire Hampton.

Pocahontas next produced King Tom, who won only 3 races, but was runner-up in the Derby and the best son of the famous Irish horse Harkaway. King Tom also made his name as a sire, heading the table in 1870 (when his son Kingcraft won the Derby) and again in 1871 (when his daughter Hannah was a triple Classic heroine).

Those were the best of Pocahontas's sons, but in due course they were joined in the stallion ranks by two others, the relatively minor winners Knight of Kars and Knight of St Patrick, who each carved a niche in Turf history, the former as sire of dual Grand National winner The Colonel, and the latter

Stockwell, the greatest of Pocahontas's sons, won the 2000 Guineas and St Leger of 1852. His outstanding stud career earned him the accolade "Emperor of Stallions".

as sire of a 2000 Guineas dead-heater in Moslem.

The extent of Pocahontas's influence in her own lifetime is exemplified by the fact that in 1866 (when she was 29 years old), those 5 stallion sons were responsible for 109 individual winners of 285 races on the British Turf.

But Pocahontas's claim as the greatest broodmare in history does not rest solely on the records of her sons. Her non-winning daughter Indiana became the dam of Humming Bird, who founded an important branch of the family in France. Another daughter, Ayacanora, won 3 good races, ran third in the 1000 Guineas, and produced the talented, unbeaten Chattanooga, himself sire of Wellingtonia, in turn sire of the outstanding French mare Plaisanterie.

At the age of 25 Pocahontas produced her last, but by no means least, foal, in the shape of Araucaria, who won only a single race, but became the dam of 3 Classic winners in 4 years—Camélia (1000 Guineas, dead-heat Oaks), Chamant (2000 Guineas) and Rayon d'Or (St Leger). Rayon d'Or was to become a champion sire in North America.

From 1852 Pocahontas was owned by the 2nd Marquis of Exeter, whose death in 1867 resulted in the auction of all his bloodstock. For Pocahontas, 30 years old and very dipped in the back, that meant the indignity of another appearance in the sale ring, but luckily nobody bid against the 3rd Marquis, who got her back for 10 gns and allowed her to end her days peacefully in the Burghley paddocks. Pocahontas died at 33, one of the oldest Thoroughbred mares on record, but her influence persisted, reaching a remarkable peak in the pedigree of Clover, winner of the 1889 Prix du Jockey-Club, the French Derby. All 4 of Clover's grandparents were descendants of Pocahontas. It is doubtful whether any other individual, male or female, has figured in each quarter of a prominent winner's pedigree so soon after his or her death.

Alfred Day: 1850, 1854, 1859
Tom Chaloner: 1863, 1868, 1873
George Fordham: 1867, 1868, 1880
Steve Donoghue: 1915, 1917, 1925
Gordon Richards: 1938, 1942, 1947
Lester Piggott: 1957, 1968, 1970
2 wins—Bill Clift: 1809, 1818
Edward Edwards: 1819, 1837
Frank Butler: 1849, 1853
Tom Ashmall: 1860, 1862
Tom Aldoroft: 1855, 1864
George Barrett: 1886, 1891
Jack Watts: 1894, 1895
Tommy Loates: 1893, 1896
Danny Maher: 1910, 1912
George Stern: 1911, 1914
Joe Childs: 1918, 1931
Freddie Fox: 1930, 1935
Tommy Weston: 1926, 1946
Charlie Smirke: 1948, 1950
Doug Smith: 1955, 1958
Jimmy Lindley: 1963, 1966
George Moore: 1959, 1967
Gianfranco Dettori: 1975, 1976
Frankie Durr: 1973, 1978
Willie Carson: 1972, 1980
Pat Eddery: 1983, 1984

Successful owner-breeder-trainer
John Barham Day—The Ugly Buck
(1844).

Successful owner-rider
Bill Scott—Sir Tatton Sykes (1846).

Sucessful trainer-rider
John Barham Day—Grey Momus
(1838), Crucifix (1840).

Successful owner-trainers
Joe Rogers—Nicolo (1823).
John Barham Day—The Ugly Buck
(1844).
William Day—Promised Land (1859).
Joe Dawson—Prince Charlie (1872).
Bob Sievier—Sceptre (1902).

Successful woman trainer
Helen Johnson Houghton trained Gilles
de Retz (1956), but was not officially

recognised. The licence was held by
Charles Jerdein.

*Successful as both jockey and
trainer*
John Barham Day rode Dervise (1826),
Grey Momus (1838), Crucifix (1840)
and Ralph (1841), trained Grey
Momus (1838), Crucifix (1840) and
The Ugly Buck (1844).
John Day, jr rode The Ugly Buck (1844),
trained Conyngham (1847), Pitsford
(1850), The Hermit (1854) and
Vauban (1867).
Tom Chaloner rode Macaroni (1863),
Moslem (1868) and Gang Forward
(1873), trained Scot-Free (1884).
Jack Robinson rode Bona Vista (1892),
trained Vedas (1905).
Harry Wragg rode Garden Path (1944),
trained Darius (1954).

*Successful as both breeder and
trainer*
John Scott bred Pitsford (1850), trained
Meteor (1842), Cotherstone (1843),
Nunnykirk (1849), West Australian
(1853), Fazzoletto (1856), The
Wizard (1860) and The Marquis
(1862).

Most successful sires
5 wins—Sultan: Augustus (1830),
Glencoe (1834), Ibrahim (1835),
Bay Middleton (1836), Achmet
(1837)
4 wins—Touchstone: Cotherstone
(1843), Flatcatcher (1848),
Nunnykirk (1849), Lord of the Isles
(1855)
Stockwell: The Marquis (1862), Lord
Lyon (1866), Bothwell (1871),
Gang Forward (1873)
Fairway: Pay Up (1936), Blue Peter
(1939), Kingsway (1943), Garden
Path (1944).
3 wins—Sorceror: Wizard (1809),
Trophonius (1811), Smolensko
(1813)

Orlando: Fazzoletto (1856),
Fitzroland (1858), Diophantus
(1861)
Sterling: Paradox (1885), Enterprise
(1887), Enthusiast (1889)
Fair Trial: Lambert Simnel (1941),
Court Martial (1945), Palestine
(1950)
Northern Dancer: Nijinsky (1970),
Lomond (1983), El Gran Senor
(1984).
2 wins—Haphazard: Antar (1819),
Reginald (1821)
Phantom: Pindarrie (1820), Enamel
(1825)
Selim: Nicolo (1823), Turcoman
(1827)
Melbourne: Sir Tatton Sykes (1846),
West Australian (1853)
Thormanby: Atlantic (1874), Charibert
(1879)
Bend Or: Ormonde (1886), Bona
Vista (1892)
Isonomy: Common (1891), Isinglass
(1893)
Hampton: Ayrshire (1888), Ladas
(1894)
Galopin: Galliard (1883), Disraeli
(1898)
St Simon: St Frusquin (1896),
Diamond Jubilee (1900)
Bayardo: Gay Crusader (1917),
Gainsborough (1918)
Phalaris: Manna (1925), Colorado
(1926)
Blandford: Bahram (1935), Pasch
(1938)
Derring-Do: High Top (1972), Roland
Gardens (1978)

Sired winner and 2nd
Emilius (1831)
West Australian (1860)
Stockwell (1862, 1866)
Sweetmeat (1863)
Isonomy (1893)
In 1862 Stockwell was responsible for
winner (The Marquis) and 2nd
(Caterer), plus Knowsley, one of the
dead-heaters for 3rd place.

1000 Guineas

Title
1000 Guineas Stakes 1814–1939
New 1000 Guineas Stakes 1940–44
1000 Guineas Stakes 1945–83
General Accident 1000 Guineas Stakes
from 1984

Venue
Rowley Mile Course, Newmarket,
Suffolk 1814–1939
Summer Course, Newmarket,
Cambridgeshire 1940–45
Rowley Mile Course, Newmarket,
Suffolk from 1946

Distance
7 furlongs 178 yards 1814–51
7 furlongs 201 yards 1852–56
7 furlongs 210 yards 1857–88
1 mile 11 yards 1889–1901
1 mile from 1902

Weight
8 st 4 lb 1814–39
8 st 7 lb 1840–61
8 st 10 lb 1862–81
8 st 12 lb 1882–97
9 st 0 lb from 1898

1814 Christopher Wilson's b f **Charlotte**
J: Bill Clift 11/5 Fav £682 2. Vestal
3. Medora 5 ran
1815 3rd Baron Foley's unnamed br f by
Selim J: Bill Clift 3/1 £735 2. Minuet
3. Discord 4 ran
1816 5th Duke of Rutland's b f **Rhoda**
J: Sam Barnard 3/1 and 5/2 £892
2. Duenna 3. Guendolen 6 ran
1817 George Watson's b f **Neva** J: Bill
Arnull 7/4 Fav £1,522 2. Clearwell
Lass 3. Trictrac 10 ran
1818 John Udney's br f **Corinne**
J: Frank Buckle 7/1 £1,050 2. Loo

3. Tredrille 8 ran
1819 4th Duke of Grafton's br f **Catgut** no jockey recorded 20/1 £1,260 2. Espagnolle 3. Nina 7 ran
1820 4th Duke of Grafton's ch f **Rowena** J: Frank Buckle 7/4 Fav £1,312 2. Caroline 3. Rebecca 6 ran
1821 4th Duke of Grafton's b f **Zeal** J: Frank Buckle 4/6 Fav £682 2. Amy 3. Breeze 6 ran
1822 4th Duke of Grafton's ch f **Whizgig** J: Frank Buckle 2/5 Fav £620 2. Rosalind 3. Varnish 4 ran
1823 4th Duke of Grafton's br f **Zinc** J: Frank Buckle 4/6 Fav £577 2. Spermaceti 3. Apparition 5 ran
1824 5th Earl of Jersey's b f **Cobweb** J: Jem Robinson 5/2 £650 2. Rebecca 3. Milto 4 ran
1825 4th Duke of Grafton's ch f **Tontine** no jockey recorded £350 walked over
1826 4th Duke of Grafton's ch f **Problem** J: John Barham Day 5/1 £800 2. Tears 3. Butterfly 5 ran
1827 4th Duke of Grafton's br f **Arab** J: Frank Buckle 8/1 £950 2. Monody 3. Young Barrosa 7 ran
1828 Arthur Molony's b f **Zoe** J: Jem Robinson 6/5 Fav £1,200 2. Trampoline 3. Scribe 7 ran
1829 Lord George Cavendish's b f **Young Mouse** J: Bill Arnull no odds recorded £1,050 2. Green Mantle 3. Pauline 4 ran
1830 5th Earl of Jersey's ch f **Charlotte West** J: Jem Robinson 5/1 £1,250 2. Zillah 3. Brambilla 7 ran
1831 Sir Mark Wood's b f **Galantine** J: Patrick Conolly 10/1 £1,550 2. Lioness 3. Oxygen 8 ran
1832 2nd Marquis of Exeter's br f **Galata** J: Bill Arnull 1/2 Fav £1,250 2. Olga 3. Salute 4 ran
1833 T. H. Cookes's ch f **Tarentella** J: E. Wright 2/1 Fav £1,800 2. Falernia 3. Vespa 10 ran
1834 4th Baron Berners's ch f **May-day** J: John Barham Day 6/1 £1,750 2. Velocity 3. Amadou 7 ran
1835 Charles Greville's ch f **Preserve** J: Nat Flatman 1/3 Fav £1,000 2. Observatory 3. ch f by Emilius 3 ran
1836 Thomas Houldsworth's ch f **Destiny** J: John Barham Day 6/4 Fav £1,400 2. Toga 3. Zenana 7 ran
1837 Lord George Bentinck's b f **Chapeau d'Espagne** J: John Barham Day 2/5 Fav £900 2. Velure 3. Comate 5 ran
1838 4th Earl of Albemarle's b f **Barcarolle** J: Edward Edwards 4/1 £1,300 2. Mecca 3. Romania 6 ran
1839 Richard Watt's b f **Cara** J: George Edwards 7/4 £1,300 2. Caenis 3. Alexandrina 5 ran
1840 Lord George Bentinck's b f **Crucifix** J: John Barham Day 1/10 Fav £1,500 2. Rosa Bianca 3. Spangle 4 ran
1841 Stanlake Batson's ch f **Potentia**

J: Jem Robinson 6/4 Jt-Fav £1,100 2. Florence 3. Queen of Beauty 5 ran
1842 Lord George Bentinck's ch f **Firebrand** J: Sam Rogers no odds recorded £1,300 2. Celia 3. Eliza 7 ran
1843 Thomas Thornhill's b f **Extempore** J: Sam Chifney, jr 7/1 £1,350 2. Spiteful 3. Fräulein 9 ran
1844 George Osbaldeston's ch f **Sorella** J: Jem Robinson 10/1 £1,650 2. Merope 3. Emerald 9 ran
1845 5th Duke of Richmond's b f **Picnic** J: William Abdale 5/2 £1,350 2. Pug 3. Heather Bell 8 ran
1846 John Gully's br f **Mendicant** J: Sam Day Evens Fav £1,550 2. Mowerina 3. Prussic Acid 7 ran
1847 George Payne's b f **Clementina** J: Nat Flatman 5/2 £1,650 2. Slander 3. Brown Bess 5 ran
1848 Baron Stanley's br f **Canezou** J: Frank Butler 5/1 £1,950 2. Vexation 3. Prairie Bird 9 ran
1849 Frank Clarke's b f **The Flea** J: Alfred Day no odds recorded £2,050 2. Clarissa 3. St Rosalia 10 ran
1850 3rd Earl of Orford's ch f **Lady Orford** J: Frank Butler 5/6 Fav £1,350 2. Tiff 3. Cora 5 ran
1851 Sir Joseph Hawley's br f **Aphrodite** J: Job Marson 5/6 Fav £1,750 2. Anspach 3. Iris 6 ran
1852 J. Sargent's b f **Kate** J: Alfred Day 4/1 £1,350 2. Lady in Waiting 3. b f by Launcelot 6 ran
1853 Baron Meyer de Rothchild's b f **Mentmore Lass** J: Jack Charlton 12/1 £2,350 2. Comfit 3. Sylphine 11 ran
1854 Henry Padwick's ch f **Virago** J: John Wells 1/3 Fav £2,150 2. Meteora 3. Honey-suckle 3 ran

1855 7th Duke of Bedford's ch f **Habena** J: Sam Rogers Evens Fav £2,400 2. Capucine 3. Clotilde 11 ran
1856 John King's ch f **Manganese** J: John Osborne 2/1 £1,950 2. Mincepie 3. Queen's Head 5 ran
1857 John Scott's b f **Impérieuse** J: Nat Flatman 100/8 £1,950 2. Tasmania 3. Ayacanora 8 ran
1858 G. W. K. Gratwicke's ch f **Governess** J: Tom Ashmall 6/1 £2,050 2. Hepatica 3. Perfection 9 ran
1859 William Stirling Crawfurd's b f **Mayonaise** J: George Fordham 9/2 £1,950 2. Ariadne 3. Prelude 4 ran
1860 14th Earl of Derby's b f **Sagitta** J: Tom Aldcroft 5/2 Fav £2,850 2. Aurora 3. b f by Longbow 13 ran
1861 G. Hilton's b f **Nemesis** J: George Fordham 10/1 £2,300 2. Fairwater 3. Brown Duchess 9 ran
1862 6th Viscount Falmouth's b f **Hurricane** J: Tom Ashmall 11/2 £2,800 2. Bertha 3. Sappho 11 ran
1863 7th Earl of Stamford's ch f **Lady Augusta** J: Arthur Edwards 3/1 Fav £3,600 2. Flying Fish 3. Cadeau .10 ran
1864 Baron Meyer de Rothschild's b f **Tomato** J: John Wells 10/1 £3,650 2. Breeze 3. Tooi-Tooi 15 ran
1865 8th Duke of Beaufort's br f **Siberia** J: George Fordham 3/1 £3,550 2. The White Duck 3. La Fortune 11 ran
1866 4th Marquis of Hastings's b f **Repulse** J: Tom Cannon 1/2 Fav £3,250 2. Baïonnette 3. Mirella 9 ran
1867 Mark Pearson's br f **Achievement** J: Harry Custance 1/8 Fav £4,150 2. Soeur de Charité 3. Mayflower 7 ran

Virago, probably the greatest filly of the 19th century, won Epsom's City and Suburban and Great Metropolitan Handicaps on the same afternoon a month before her 1000 Guineas triumph in 1854.

1868 William Graham's ch f **Formosa**
J: George Fordham 10/11 Fav
£3,750 2. Athena 3. Lady Coventry
8 ran

1869 8th Duke of Beaufort's ch f
Scottish Queen J: George Fordham
100/8 £3,750 2. Morna 3. Brigantine
9 ran

1870 Joe Dawson's b f **Hester**
J: Jemmy Grimshaw 6/4 Fav £3,650
2. Frivolity 3. Mahonia 10 ran

1871 Baron Meyer de Rothschild's b f
Hannah J: Charlie Maidment 2/1 Fav
£3,400 2. Steppe 3. Noblesse 7 ran

1872 Joachim Lefèvre's b f **Reine**
J: Henry Parry 20/1 £3,150
2. Derelict 3. Highland Fling 11 ran

1873 6th Viscount Falmouth's b f
Cecilia J: Jack Morris 100/3 £2,900
2. Angela 3. Windermere 14 ran

1874 John King's ch f **Apology** J: John
Osborne 5/2 Fav £3,050 2. La
Coureuse 3. Blanchefleur 9 ran

1875 6th Viscount Falmouth's b f
Spinaway J: Fred Archer 10/1
£2,350 2. Per Se 3. Chaplet 6 ran

1876 Comte Frédéric de Lagrange's ch f
Camélia J: Tom Glover 4/1 £3,100
2. Allumette 3. La Seine 13 ran

1877 Marquis of Hartington's b f
Belphoebe J: Harry Jeffery 100/6
£4,750 2. Lady Ronald 3. Lady
Golightly 19 ran

1878 4th Earl of Lonsdale's ch f
Pilgrimage J: Tom Cannon 4/5 Fav
£4,500 2. Jannette 3. Clementine
9 ran

1879 6th Viscount Falmouth's b f **Wheel
of Fortune** J: Fred Archer 40/75 Fav
£4,200 2. Abbaye 3. Reconciliation
8 ran

1880 T. E. Walker's b f **Elizabeth**
J: Charlie Wood 9/2 £3,950
2. Versigny 3. Evasion 10 ran

1881 William Stirling Crawfurd's ch f
Thebais J: George Fordham 5/6 Fav
£4,750 2. Thora 3. Bal Gal 13 ran

1882 William Stirling Crawfurd's ch f **St
Marguerite** J: Charlie Wood 10/1
£2,900 2. Shotover 3. Nellie 6 ran

1883 Joachim Lefèvre's br f **Hauteur**
J: George Fordham 9/4 Fav £2,900
2. Malibran 3. Lovely 9 ran

1884 George Baird's b f **Busybody**
J: Tom Cannon 85/40 Fav £3,000
2. Queen Adelaide 3. Whitelock
6 ran

1885 1st Duke of Westminster's ch f
Farewell J: George Barrett 20/1
£3,600 2. Jane 3. Satchel 16 ran

1886 12th Duke of Hamilton's b f **Miss
Jummy** J: Jack Watts 3/1 £2,950
2. Argo Navis 3. Jewel Song 10 ran

1887 8th Duke of Beaufort's ch f **Rêve
d'Or** J: Charlie Wood Evens Fav
£3,300 2. Porcelain 3. Freedom
12 ran

1888 Douglas Baird's b f **Briarroot**
J: Billy Warne 100/9 £3,500
2. Seabreeze 3. Belle Mahone 14 ran

1889 Robert Vyner's b f **Minthe**

J: Jimmy Woodburn 4/1 £2,700
2. Wrinkle 3. Polka 14 ran

1890 6th Duke of Portland's b f
Semolina J: Jack Watts 1/2 Fav
£3,400 2. Memoir 3. Fatuité 10 ran

1891 Noel Fenwick's b f **Mimi** J: Fred
Rickaby 7/1 £4,050 2. Melody
3. Siphonia 12 ran

1892 Baron Maurice de Hirsch's br f **La
Flèche** J: George Barrett 1/2 Fav
£3,650 2. The Smew 3. Adoration
7 ran

1893 Sir John Blundell Maple's ch f
Siffleuse J: Tommy Loates 33/1
£3,750 2. Dame President
3. Tressure 11 ran

1894 6th Duke of Portland's b f
Amiable J: Walter Bradford 100/8
£3,550 2. Lady Minting 3. Mecca
13 ran

1895 Alfred Cox's b f **Galeottia** J: Fred
Pratt 100/8 £4,550 2. La Sagesse
3. Gas 15 ran

1896 HRH Prince of Wales's br f **Thaïs**
J: Jack Watts 5/1 £5,100 2. Santa
Maura 3. Jolly Boat 19 ran

1897 5th Earl of Rosebery's b f
Chélandry J: Jack Watts 9/4 £4,250
2. Galatia 3. Goletta 9 ran

1898 Sir John Blundell Maple's b or br f
Nun Nicer J: Sam Loates
11/2 Jt-Fav £4,800 2. Airs and Graces
3. Alt Mark 15 ran

1899 Lord William Beresford's b f
Sibola J: Tod Sloan 13/8 Fav £3,800
2. Fascination 3. Musa 14 ran

1900 Leonard Brassey's b f **Winifreda**
J: Sam Loates 11/2 £4,150
2. Inquisitive 3. Vain Duchess 10 ran

1901 Sir James Miller's b f **Aïda**
J: Danny Maher 13/8 Fav £4,450
T: George Blackwell, Newmarket
B: Blankney Stud Sire: Galopin
2. Fleur d'Eté 3. Santa Brigida
neck, 2l 1:44.6 15 ran

1902 Bob Sievier's b f **Sceptre** J: Bert
Randall 1/2 Fav £5,450 T: Owner,
Shrewton, Wiltshire B: 1st Duke of
Westminster Sire: Persimmon 2. St
Windeline 3. Black Fancy 1½l, 4l
1:40.2 15 ran

1903 7th Viscount Falmouth's b f
Quintessence J: Bert Randall 4/1
£3,800 T: Jim Chandler, Lambourn,
Berkshire B: Owner Sire: St
Frusquin 2. Sun-Rose 3. Skyscraper
1½l, 2l 1:48.0 12 ran

1904 Eustace Loder's ch f **Pretty Polly**
J: Willie Lane 1/4 Fav £3,800
T: Peter Gilpin, Newmarket B: Owner
Sire: Gallinule 2. Leucadia
3. Flamma 3l, 4l 1:40.0 7 ran

1905 William Hall Walker's b f **Cherry
Lass** J: George McCall 5/4 Fav
£3,650 T: Jack Robinson, Foxhill,
Wiltshire B: Owner Sire: Isinglass
2. Koorhaan 3. Jongleuse 1l, 3l 1:43.4
19 ran

1906 Sir Daniel Cooper's b or br f **Flair**
J: Bernard Dillon 10/11 Fav £4,000
T: Peter Gilpin, Newmarket B: Owner

Sire: St Frusquin 2. Lischana 3. Paid
Up 3l, ¾l 1:40.6 12 ran

1907 William Hall Walker's b f **Witch
Elm** J: Barrington Lynham 4/1 Fav
£4,450 T: Jack Robinson, Foxhill,
Wiltshire B: Owner Sire: Orme
2. Frugality 3. Sixty 3l, 1½l 1:42.6
17 ran

1908 Richard Croker's br f **Rhodora**
J: Lucien Lyne 100/8 £5,550
T: James Allen, Sandyford, Co
Dublin, Ireland B: Owner Sire: St
Frusquin 2. Bracelet 3. Ardentrive
2l, neck 1:43.8 19 ran

1909 Ludwig Neumann's b f **Electra**
J: Bernard Dillon 9/1 £4,100 T: Peter
Gilpin, Newmarket B: Owner Sire:
Eager 2. Princesse de Galles
3. Perola 1l, 4l 1:40.4 10 ran

1910 Waldorf Astor's b f **Winkipop**
J: Barrington Lynham 5/2 Fav £4,650
T: Willie Waugh, Kingsclere,
Berkshire B: Owner Sire: William the
Third 2. Maid of Corinth 3. Rosedrop
1½l, head 1:41.0 13 ran

1911 Jimmy de Rothschild's b f **Atmah**
J: Freddie Fox 7/1 £4,600 T: Fred
Pratt, Newmarket B: Owner Sire:
Galeazzo 2. Radiancy
3. Knockfeerna short head, 2l 1:38.4
16 ran

1912 Walter Raphael's gr f **Tagalie**
J: Les Hewitt 20/1 £4,750 T: Dawson
Waugh, Newmarket B: Owner Sire:
Cyllene 2. Alope 3. Belleisle 1½l, ¾l
1:39.6 13 ran

1913 Jack Joel's ch f **Jest** J: Fred
Rickaby, jr 9/1 £6,400 T: Charles
Morton, Wantage, Berkshire
B: Owner Sire: Sundridge 2. Taslett
3. Prue head, ½l 1:40.8 22 ran

1914 Jack Joel's br f **Princess Dorrie**
J: Bill Huxley 100/9 £4,950
T: Charles Morton, Wantage,
Berkshire B: Owner Sire: Your
Majesty 2. Glorvina 3. Torchlight
¾l, neck 1:42.0 13 ran

1915 5th Earl of Rosebery's b f
Vaucluse J: Fred Rickaby, jr 5/2 Fav
£6,200 T: Frank Hartigan, Weyhill,
Hampshire B: Owner Sire: Dark
Ronald 2. Silver Tag 3. Bright
¾l, 1½l 1:40.8 15 ran

1916 17th Earl of Derby's b f **Canyon**
J: Fred Rickaby, jr 9/2 £4,300
T: George Lambton, Newmarket
B: Owner Sire: Chaucer 2. Fifinella
3. Salamandra ¾l, 3l 1:40.0 10 ran

1917 1st Viscount D'Abernon's ch f
Diadem J: Fred Rickaby, jr 6/4 Fav
£4,150 T: George Lambton,
Newmarket B: Owner Sire: Orby
2. Sunny Jane 3. Nonpareil ½l, 4l
1:43.0 14 ran

1918 17th Earl of Derby's b f **Ferry**
J: Brownie Carslake 50/1 £4,100
T: George Lambton, Newmarket
B: Owner Sire: Swynford 2. My Dear
3. Herself 2l, 3l 1:46.4 8 ran

1919 Sir Edward Hulton's b or br f
Roseway J: Albert Whalley 2/1 Fav

La Flèche, who took the Fillies' Triple Crown in 1892 and was prevented only by incompetent jockeyship from winning the Derby as well.

£4,300 T: Frank Hartigan, Weyhill, Hampshire B: Owner Sire: Stornoway 2. Britannia 3. Glaciale 6*l*, 1½*l* 1:47.6 15 ran
1920 Sir Robert Jardine's b f **Cinna** J: Billy Griggs 4/1 £5,500 T: Tom Waugh, Newmarket B: Owner Sire: Polymelus 2. Cicerole 3. Valescure 3*l*, 1*l* 1:40.4 21 ran
1921 Walter Raphael's b or br f **Bettina** J: George Bellhouse 33/1 £8,200 T: Percy Linton, Newmarket B: Owner Sire: Swynford 2. Petrea 3. Pompadour 1½*l*, ¾*l* 1:44.6 24 ran
1922 Barney Parr's ch f **Silver Urn** J: Brownie Carslake 10/1 £8,365 T: Atty Persse, Stockbridge, Hampshire B: Owner Sire: Juggernaut 2. Soubriquet 3. Golden Corn 2*l*, ¾*l* 1:40.0 20 ran
1923 17th Earl of Derby's b f **Tranquil** J: Ted Gardner 5/2 Fav £8,100 T: George Lambton, Newmarket B: Owner Sire: Swynford 2. Cos 3. Shrove 1½*l*, 1*l* 1:39.0 16 ran
1924 5th Earl of Rosebery's ch f **Plack** J: Charlie Elliott 8/1 £8,080 T: Jack Jarvis, Newmarket B: Owner Sire: Hurry On 2. Mumtaz Mahal 3. Straitlace 1½*l*, ½*l* 1:39.6 16 ran

1925 2nd Viscount Astor's br f **Saucy Sue** J: Frank Bullock 1/4 Fav £7,640 T: Alec Taylor, Manton, Wiltshire B: Owner Sire: Swynford 2. Miss Gadabout 3. Firouze Mahal 6*l*, 2*l* 1:42.4 11 ran
1926 Anthony de Rothschild's b f **Pillion** J: Dick Perryman 25/1 £8,365 T: John Watson, Newmarket B: Owner Sire: Chaucer 2. Trilogy 3. Short Story 1*l*, ½*l* 1:42.0 29 ran
1927 Giles Loder's b f **Cresta Run** J: Arthur Balding 10/1 £9,660 T: Peter Gilpin, Newmarket B: Owner Sire: Hurry On 2= Book Law and Endowment 2*l*, dead-heat 1:38.0 28 ran
1928 HM King George V's b f **Scuttle** J: Joe Childs 15/8 Fav £8,470 T: Willie Jarvis, Newmarket B: Owner Sire: Captain Cuttle 2. Jurisdiction 3. Toboggan 1*l*, 6*l* 1:44.2 14 ran
1929 Simon Guthmann's gr f **Taj Mah** J: Wally Sibbritt 33/1 £7,570 T: Juan Torterolo, Chantilly, France B: HH Aga Khan III Sire: Lemberg 2. Sister Anne 3. Ellanvale ¾*l*, short head 1:40.4 19 ran
1930 17th Earl of Derby's b or br f **Fair Isle** J: Tommy Weston 7/4 Fav

£8,366 T: Frank Butters, Newmarket B: Owner Sire: Phalaris 2. Torchère 3. Sister Clover short head, neck 1:42.0 19 ran
1931 4th Earl of Ellesmere's b f **Four Course** J: Charlie Elliott 100/9 £8,854 T: Fred Darling, Beckhampton, Wiltshire B: John Arkwright Sire: Tetratema 2. Lady Marjorie 3. Lindos Ojos head, 1*l* 1:39.8 20 ran
1932 Evremond de Saint-Alary's b f **Kandy** J: Charlie Elliott 33/1 £8,034 T: Frank Carter, Chantilly, France B: Owner Sire: Alcantara 2. Thorndean 3. Safe Return 1*l*, 1*l* 1:44.0 19 ran
1933 William Woodward's b or br f **Brown Betty** J: Joe Childs 8/1 £6,865 T: Cecil Boyd-Rochfort, Newmarket B: Sir Alec Black Sire: Friar Marcus 2. Fur Tor 3. Myrobella ½*l*, ¾*l* 1:39.4 22 ran
1934 Sir George Bullough's b f **Campanula** J: Harry Wragg 2/5 Fav £6,500 T: Jack Jarvis, Newmarket B: Owner Sire: Blandford 2. Light Brocade 3. Spend a Penny 1*l*, 6*l* 1:39.0 10 ran
1935 Pierre Wertheimer's b f **Mesa** J: Rae Johnstone 8/1 £7,397 T: Albert Swann, Chantilly, France B: Pierre Corbière Sire: Kircubbin

2. Hyndford Bridge 3. Caretta 3*l*, 1½*l*
1:43.0 22 ran

1936 17th Earl of Derby's br f **Tide-way**
J: Dick Perryman 100/30 £7,533
T: Colledge Leader, Newmarket
B: Owner Sire: Fairway 2. Feola
3. Ferrybridge 1½*l*, neck 1:42.0
22 ran

1937 Sir Victor Sassoon's b f
Exhibitionnist J: Steve Donoghue
10/1 £7,422 T: Joe Lawson, Manton,
Wiltshire B: Owner Sire: Solario
2. Spray 3. Gainsborough Lass
½*l*, head 1:43.8 20 ran

1938 Sir Hugo Cunliffe-Owen's br f
Rockfel J: Sam Wragg 8/1 £8,051
T: Ossie Bell, Lambourn, Berkshire
B: Weir Bank Stud Sire: Felstead
2. Laughing Water 3. Solar Flower
1½*l*, 3*l* 1:38.0 20 ran

1939 Robert Sterling Clark's br f
Galatea J: Bobby Jones 6/1 £7,592
T: Joe Lawson, Manton, Wiltshire
B: Owner Sire: Dark Legend
2. Aurora 3. Olein 3*l*, ½*l* 1:38.6
18 ran

1940 Esmond Harmsworth's b f **Godiva**
J: Doug Marks 10/1 £3,087 T: Willie
Jarvis, Newmarket B: Owner Sire:
Hyperion 2. Golden Penny 3. Allure
5*l*, 4*l* 1:40.8 11 ran

1941 1st Baron Glanely's b f **Dancing
Time** J: Dick Perryman 100/8
£1,184 T: Joe Lawson, Manton,
Wiltshire B: Owner Sire: Colombo
2. Beausite 3. Keystone 1*l*, 2*l* 1:41.4
13 ran

1942 HM King George VI's b f **Sun
Chariot** J: Gordon Richards Evens
Fav £1,736 T: Fred Darling,
Beckhampton, Wiltshire B: National
Stud Sire: Hyperion 2. Perfect Peace
3. Light of Day 4*l*, 2*l* 1:39.6 18 ran

1943 17th Earl of Derby's b f
Herringbone J: Harry Wragg 15/2
£1,273 T: Walter Earl, Newmarket
B: Owner Sire: King Salmon
2. Ribbon 3. Bongrace neck, 1½*l*
1:41.8 12 ran

1944 Jim Joel's b f **Picture Play**
J: Charlie Elliott 15/2 £1,777 T: John
Watts, Foxhill, Wiltshire B: Owner
Sire: Donatello 2. Grande Corniche
3. Superior 4*l*, 2*l* 1:40.6 11 ran

1945 17th Earl of Derby's ch f **Sun
Stream** J: Harry Wragg 5/2 Fav
£7,507 T: Walter Earl, Newmarket
B: Owner Sire: Hyperion 2. Blue
Smoke 3. Mrs Feather 3*l*, 2*l* 1:45.4
14 ran

1946 HM King George VI's b f
Hypericum J: Doug Smith 100/6
£7,146 T: Cecil Boyd-Rochfort,
Newmarket B: Owner Sire: Hyperion
2. Neolight 3. Iona 1½*l*, ¾*l* 1:41.4
13 ran

1947 Mme Pierre Corbière's br f
Imprudence J: Rae Johnstone
4/1 Fav £8,106 T: Joseph Lieux,
Maisons-Laffitte, France B: Pierre
Corbière Sire: Canot 2. Rose o' Lynn

Sun Chariot, the best horse to race in England during World War II and winner of the Fillies' Triple Crown in 1942. She is pictured here with Fred Darling, the outstanding Classic trainer of his time.

3. Wild Child neck, head 1:46.0
20 ran

1948 Sir Percy Loraine's br f **Queenpot**
J: Gordon Richards 6/1 £12,433
T: Noel Murless, Beckhampton,
Wiltshire B: Owner Sire: Big Game
2. Ariostar 3. Duplicity head, 1½*l*
1:41.8 22 ran

1949 Norman Donaldson's b f
Musidora J: Edgar Britt 100/8
£12,612 T: Charles Elsey, Malton,
Yorkshire B: Frank Tuthill Sire:
Nasrullah 2. Unknown Quantity
3. Solar Myth 1½*l*, 2*l* 1:40.0 18 ran

1950 Jean Ternynck's gr f **Camarée**
J: Rae Johnstone 10/1 £10,895
T: Alexandre Lieux, Maisons-Laffitte,
France B: Owner Sire: Maurepas
2= Catchit and Tambara 3*l*, dead-
heat 1:37.0 17 ran

1951 Henry Tufton's b f **Belle of All**
J: Gordon Richards 4/1 Fav £11,885
T: Norman Bertie, Newmarket
B: Viscount Adare Sire: Nasrullah

2. Subtle Difference 3. Bob Run
neck, 2*l* 1:44.8 18 ran

1952 Sir Malcolm McAlpine's ch f
Zabara J: Ken Gethin 7/1 £13,368
T: Vic Smyth, Epsom, Surrey B: Lady
Wyfold Sire: Persian Gulf 2. La
Mirambule 3. Refreshed ½*l*, 5*l*
1:40.92 20 ran

1953 David Wills's ch f **Happy Laughter**
J: Manny Mercer 10/1 £13,071
T: Jack Jarvis, Newmarket
B: Ballykisteen Stud Sire: Royal
Charger 2. Tessa Gillian 3. Bebe
Grande 2*l*, 5*l* 1:45.05 14 ran

1954 Arthur Dewar's ch f **Festoon**
J: Scobie Breasley 9/2 £11,111
T: Noel Cannon, Middle Woodford,
Wiltshire B: Owner Sire: Fair Trial
2. Big Berry 3. Welsh Fairy 2*l*, 1*l*
1:38.90 12 ran

1955 Lady Zia Wernher's b f **Meld**
J: Harry Carr 11/4 Fav £10,631
T: Cecil Boyd-Rochfort, Newmarket
B: Someries Stud Sire: Alycidon

2. Aberlady 3. Feria 2*l*, 1½*l* 1:42.16 12 ran

1956 Sir Victor Sassoon's b f **Honeylight** J: Edgar Britt 100/6 £12,752 T: Charles Elsey, Malton, Yorkshire B: Eve Stud Ltd Sire: Honeyway 2. Midget 3. Arietta 2*l*, 3*l* 1:38.01 19 ran

1957 HH Aga Khan III's b f **Rose Royale** J: Charlie Smirke 6/1 £13,602 T: Alec Head, Chantilly, France B: Owner and Prince Aly Khan Sire: Prince Bio 2. Sensualita 3. Angelet 1*l*, 2*l* 1:39.15 20 ran

1958 François Dupré's br f **Bella Paola** J: Serge Boullenger 8/11 Fav £12,773 T: François Mathet, Chantilly, France B: Owner Sire: Ticino 2. Amante 3. Alpine Bloom 1½*l*, 5*l* 1:38.75 11 ran

1959 Prince Aly Khan's gr f **Petite Etoile** J: Doug Smith 8/1 £13,254 T: Noel Murless, Newmarket B: Owner and H H Aga Khan III Sire: Petition 2. Rosalba 3. Paraguana 1*l*, 4*l* 1:40.36 14 ran

1960 Mrs Howell Jackson's ch f **Never Too Late** J: Roger Poincelet 8/11 Fav £14,023 T: Etienne Pollet, Chantilly, France B: Bull Run Stud Sire: Never Say Die 2. Lady in Trouble 3. Running Blue 2*l*, ½*l* 1:39.89 14 ran

1961 Mrs Magnus Castello's ch f **Sweet Solera** J: Bill Rickaby 4/1 Jt-Fav £16,233 T: Reg Day, Newmarket B: Mrs Dorothy Walker Sire: Solonaway 2. Ambergris 3. Indian Melody 1½*l*, 6*l* 1:38.14 14 ran

1962 Roderic More O'Ferrall's gr f **Abermaid** J: Bill Williamson 100/6 £21,597 T: Harry Wragg, Newmarket B: Owner and Sir Percy Loraine Sire: Abernant 2. Display 3. West Side Story ½*l*, ¾*l* 1:39.36 14 ran

1963 Mrs Gertrude Widener's gr f **Hula Dancer** J: Roger Poincelet 1/2 Fav £22,829 T: Etienne Pollet, Chantilly, France B: Owner Sire: Native Dancer 2. Spree 3. Royal Cypher 1*l*, 1*l* 1:42.34 12 ran

1964 Beatrice, Lady Granard's b f **Pourparler** J: Garnie Bougoure 11/2 £29,102 T: Paddy Prendergast, The Curragh, Co Kildare, Ireland B: Peter FitzGerald Sire: Hugh Lupus 2. Gwen 3= Petite Gina and Royal Danseuse 1*l*, 1½*l* 1:38.82 18 ran

1965 Lionel Holliday's b f **Night Off** J: Bill Williamson 9/2 Fav £22,570 T: Walter Wharton, Newmarket B: Owner Sire: Narrator 2. Yami 3. Mabel neck, 3*l* 1:45.43 16 ran

1966 Mrs Alice Mills's ch f **Glad Rags** J: Paul Cook 100/6 £25,214 T: Vincent O'Brien, Cashel, Co

Tipperary, Ireland B: Tim Rogers Sire: High Hat 2. Berkeley Springs 3. Miliza neck, 2*l* 1:40.30 21 ran

1967 Bob Boucher's b f **Fleet** J: George Moore 11/2 £24,848 T: Noel Murless, Newmarket B: Peter FitzGerald Sire: Immortality 2. St Pauli Girl 3. Lacquer ½*l*, head 1:44.76 16 ran

1968 Mrs Gwen Murless's ch f **Caergwrle** J: Sandy Barclay 4/1 £19,682 T: Noel Murless, Newmarket B: Owner Sire: Crepello 2. Photo Flash 3. Sovereign 1*l*, short head 1:40.38 14 ran

1969 Ralph Moller's b f **Full Dress** J: Ron Hutchinson 7/1 £21,048 T: Harry Wragg, Newmarket B: White Lodge Stud Sire: Shantung 2. Hecuba 3. Motionless 1½*l*, 1*l* 1:44.53 13 ran

1970 Jean, Lady Ashcombe's gr f **Humble Duty** J: Lester Piggott 3/1 Jt-Fav £21,015 T: Peter Walwyn, Lambourn, Berkshire B: Frank Tuthill Sire: Sovereign Path 2. Gleam 3. Black Satin 7*l*, 2*l* 1:42.13 12 ran

1971 Roger Hue-Williams's ch f **Altesse Royale** J: Yves Saint-Martin 25/1 £22,703 T: Noel Murless, Newmarket B: Mrs Vera Hue-Williams Sire: Saint Crespin 2. Super Honey 3. Catherine Wheel 1½*l*, ¾*l* 1:40.90 10 ran

1972 Mrs Susan Stanley's ch f **Waterloo** J: Edward Hide 8/1 £23,085 T: Bill Watts, Richmond, Yorkshire B: New England Stud Sire:

The grey Petite Etoile wins the 1000 Guineas as part of a brilliant unbeaten campaign in 1959. Doug Smith had the mount as Lester Piggott chose to ride her stablemate Collyria, seen here on the far right.

The Queen's filly, the blinkered Highclere, beats subsequent Oaks winner Polygamy by a short head in the 1000 Guineas of 1974. This was the first royal victory in the race for 28 years.

Bold Lad 2. Marisela 3. Rose Dubarry 2l, neck 1:39.49 18 ran

1973 George Pope, jr's ch f **Mysterious** J: Geoff Lewis 11/1 £25,239 T: Noel Murless, Newmarket B: Owner Sire: Crepello 2. Jacinth 3. Shellshock 3l, 2l 1:42.12 14 ran

1974 HM Queen Elizabeth II's b f **Highclere** J: Joe Mercer 12/1 £35,494 T: Dick Hern, West Ilsley, Berkshire B: Owner Sire: Queen's Hussar 2. Polygamy 3. Mrs Tiggywinkle short head, 4l 1:40.32 15 ran

1975 Mrs Anne-Hart O'Kelly's gr f **Nocturnal Spree** J: Johnny Roe 14/1 £27,303 T: Stuart Murless, The Curragh, Co Kildare, Ireland B: Jerry Dillon Sire: Supreme Sovereign 2. Girl Friend 3. Joking Apart short head, 1l

1:41.65 16 ran

1976 Daniel Wildenstein's ch f **Flying Water** J: Yves Saint-Martin 2/1 Fav £39,447 T: Angel Penna, Chantilly, France B: Dayton Ltd Sire: Habitat 2. Konafa 3. Kesar Queen 1l, neck 1:37.83 25 ran

1977 Mrs Edith Kettlewell's b f **Mrs McArdy** J: Edward Hide 16/1 £37,238 T: Mick Easterby, Sheriff Hutton, Yorkshire B: 4th Baron Grimthorpe Sire: Tribal Chief 2. Freeze the Secret 3. Sanedtki 2l, 1l 1:40.07 18 ran

1978 Dick Bonnycastle's b f **Enstone Spark** J: Ernie Johnson 35/1 £41,130 T: Barry Hills, Lambourn, Berkshire B: William Hill Studs Sire: Sparkler 2. Fair Salinia 3. Seraphima 1l, 2½l 1:41.56 16 ran

1979 Helena Springfield Ltd's b f **One in a Million** J: Joe Mercer Evens Fav £44,760 T: Henry Cecil, Newmarket B: Mount Coote Waverton Stud Sire: Rarity 2. Abbeydale 3. Yanuka 1½l, head 1:43.06 17 ran

1980 Ogden Mills Phipps's b f **Quick as Lightning** J: Brian Rouse 12/1 £49,376 T: John Dunlop, Arundel, Sussex B: Owner Sire: Buckpasser 2. Our Home 3. Mrs Penny neck, ½l 1:41.89 23 ran

1981 Jim Joel's b f **Fairy Footsteps** J: Lester Piggott 6/4 Fav £52,180 T: Henry Cecil, Newmarket B: Owner Sire: Mill Reef 2. Tolmi 3. Go Leasing neck, neck 1:40.43 14 ran

1982 Sir Philip Oppenheimer's b f **On the House** J: John Reid 33/1 £75,630 T: Harry Wragg, Newmarket B: Owner Sire: Be My Guest 2. Time Charter 3. Dione 2½l, 2l 1:40.45 15 ran

1983 Maktoum al Maktoum's br f **Ma Biche** J: Freddy Head 5/2 Fav

£71,472 T: Mme Criquette Head, Chantilly, France B: Mme Galina Tkatch de Briones Sire: Key to the Kingdom 2. Favoridge 3. Habibti 1¾l, ½l 1:41.71 18 ran (Royal Heroine finished second, disqualified)

1984 Marcos Lemos's ch f **Pebbles** J: Philip Robinson 8/1 £87,009 T: Clive Brittain, Newmarket B: Warren Hill Stud and Mimika Financiera Sire: Sharpen Up 2. Meis El-Reem 3. Desirable 3l, neck 1:38.18 15 ran

RECORDS FOR WINNING HORSES

Greatest margins
20 lengths — Mayonaise (1859)
7 lengths — Humble Duty (1970)
6 lengths — Roseway (1919), Saucy Sue (1925)
5 lengths — Godiva (1940)

Smallest margins
short head — Atmah (1911), Fair Isle (1930), Highclere (1974), Nocturnal Spree (1975)
head — Arab (1827), Extempore (1843), The Flea (1849), Lady Orford (1850), Kate (1852), Governess (1858), Repulse (1866), Camélia (1876), Hauteur (1883), Siffleuse (1893), Thaïs (1896), Jest (1913), Four Course (1931), Queenpot (1948)

Grey
Tagalie (1912), Taj Mah (1929), Camarée (1950), Petite Etoile (1959), Abermaid (1962), Hula Dancer (1963), Humble Duty (1970), Nocturnal Spree (1975)

Longest odds
50/1 — Ferry (1918)
35/1 — Enstone Spark (1978)
100/3 — Cecilia (1873)
33/1 — Siffleuse (1893), Bettina (1921), Taj Mah (1929), Kandy (1932), On the House (1982)
25/1 — Pillion (1926), Altesse Royale (1971)

Shortest odds
1/10 — Crucifix (1840)
1/8 — Achievement (1867)
1/4 — Pretty Polly (1904), Saucy Sue (1925)
1/3 — Preserve (1835), Virago (1854)

No odds recorded
Young Mouse (1829), Firebrand (1842), The Flea (1849)

Trained in Ireland
Rhodora (1908), Pourparler (1964), Glad Rags (1966), Nocturnal Spree (1975)

Trained in France
Camélia (1876), Taj Mah (1929), Kandy (1932), Mesa (1935), Imprudence (1947), Camarée (1950), Rose Royale (1957), Bella Paola (1958), Never Too Late (1960), Hula Dancer (1963), Flying Water (1976), Ma Biche (1983)

Bred in France
Reine (1872), Camélia (1876), Kandy (1932), Mesa (1935), Galatea (1939), Imprudence (1947), Camarée (1950), Rose Royale (1957), Bella Paola (1958), Full Dress (1969), Flying Water (1976), On the House (1982).

Bred in USA
Sibola (1899), Never Too Late (1960), Hula Dancer (1963), Quick as Lightning (1980), Ma Biche (1983).

Siblings
May-day (1834) and Firebrand (1842), and Thebais (1881) and St Marguerite (1882) were sisters. Zeal (1821) and Zinc (1823), Cobweb (1824) and Charlotte West (1830), Spinaway (1875) and Wheel of Fortune (1879), and Pourparler (1964) and Fleet (1967) were half-sisters.

Winners who produced winners
Zeal (1821) produced Arab (1827)
Cobweb (1824) produced Clementina (1847)
Pic-nic (1845) produced Mayonaise (1859)
Mentmore Lass (1853) produced Hannah (1871)
Siberia (1865) produced Cecilia (1873)
Spinaway (1875) produced Busybody (1884)

Unnamed at time of victory
Filly by Selim (1815), Young Mouse (1829), Galantine (1831), Galata (1832), Lady Orford (1850).

Raced under two names
Siffleuse (1893) had raced unsuccessfully as a two-year-old under the name La Belle Siffleuse.

Winner in two countries
Imprudence (1947) also won the equivalent French classic, the Poule d'Essai des Pouliches.

Oldest and youngest sires
Asparagus (Rhoda, 1816), Orville (Zoe, 1828) and Galopin (Aïda, 1901) got winners when 25 years old. Blair Athol (Scottish Queen, 1869), Goldfinch (Chélandry, 1897), Stornoway (Roseway, 1919), Bold Lad (Waterloo, 1972) and Be My Guest (On the House, 1982) sired winners at the age of four.

Oldest and youngest dams
Cobweb was 23 years old when she produced Clementina (1847). Groat produced Plack (1924) and Singe produced One in a Million (1979) at the age of four.

RECORDS FOR PLACED HORSES

Grey or roan
Zenana (1836), The White Duck (1865), Mumtaz Mahal (1924), Firouze Mahal (1925), Lindos Ojos (1931), Myrobella (1933), Spray (1937), Keystone (1941), Cincture (1943), Aberlady (1955), Midget (1956), Dione (1982), Desirable (1984).

Black
Olga (1832), Lovely (1883). Dame Pretender (1893) and Ellanvale (1929) were described as black or brown.

Longest odds
100/1 — Flamma (1904)
66/1 — St Pauli Girl (1967), Shellshock (1973), Konafa (1976).
50/1 — Allumette (1876), Wrinkle (1889), Polka (1889), Catchit (1950), Bob Run (1951), Petite Gina (1964).

Trained in Ireland
Angelet (1957), Display (1962), Royal Danseuse (1964).

Trained in France
Versigny (1880), Rose o' Lynn (1947), La Mirambule (1952), Midget (1956), Sensualita (1957), Amante (1958), Paraguana (1959), Royal Cypher (1963), Yami (1965), Miliza (1966), Hecuba (1969), Gleam (1970), Marisela (1972), Girl Friend (1975), Kesar Queen (1976), Sanedtki (1977)

Bred in France
La Fortune (1865), Baionnette (1866), Allumette (1876), La Seine (1876), Clementine (1878), Versigny (1880), Malibran (1883), Fatuité (1890), La Mirambule (1952), Midget (1956), Yami (1965), Miliza (1966), Gleam (1970).

Bred in USA
Sensualita (1957), Berkeley Springs (1966), Kesar Queen (1976), Freeze the Secret (1977), Mrs Penny (1980), Favoridge (1983).

Bred in Canada
Konafa (1976).

Placed horse disqualified
Royal Heroine finished 2nd, beaten 1½ lengths by Ma Biche, in 1983, but was subsequently disqualified and relegated to last place after returning a positive test.

MISCELLANEOUS RECORDS

Fastest times
1:37.0 — Camarée (1950)
1:37.83 — Flying Water (1976)
1:38.0 — Cresta Run (1927), Rockfel (1938).

Largest entry
836 — 1974

Smallest entry
8 — 1823, 1825

Largest fields
29 — 1926
28 — 1927
25 — 1976

Smallest fields
walk-over — 1825
3 — 1835, 1854
4 — 1815, 1822, 1824, 1829, 1832, 1840, 1859

Richest first prizes
£87,009 — 1984
£75,630 — 1982
£71,472 — 1983

Smallest first prizes
£350 — 1825
£577 — 1823
£620 — 1822

Hottest losing favourite
1/4 — Shotover was 2nd in 1882

Most consecutive winning favourites
4 — 1904 to 1907

Most consecutive losing favourites
7 — 1935 to 1941

Earliest date
18 April — 1839

Latest date
26 May — 1943

Latest peacetime date
12 May — 1859

Run on
Tuesday: 1944–45
Wednesday: 1942–43
Thursday: 1814–71, 1941, from 1961
Friday: 1872–1940, 1946–60

Run before 2000 Guineas
1944–45, 1971–75, from 1978

Foreign-trained horses placed 1, 2, 3
In 1957 winner and 2nd (Rose Royale and Sensualita) were trained in France and 3rd (Angelet) in Ireland.

Foreign-bred horses placed 1, 2, 3
In 1876 winner, 2nd and 3rd (Camélia, Allumette and La Seine) were all French-bred.
In 1976 winner Flying Water was French-bred, 2nd Konafa Canadian-bred and 3rd Kesar Queen US-bred.

Most successful owners
8 wins — 4th Duke of Grafton: 1819, 1820, 1821, 1822, 1823, 1825, 1826, 1827
7 wins — 17th Earl of Derby: 1916, 1918, 1923, 1930, 1936, 1943, 1945
4 wins — 6th Viscount Falmouth: 1862, 1873, 1875, 1879
3 wins — Lord George Bentinck: 1837, 1840, 1842
   Baron Meyer de Rothschild: 1853, 1864, 1871
   William Stirling Crawfurd: 1859, 1881, 1882
   8th Duke of Beaufort: 1865, 1869, 1887
   5th Earl of Rosebery: 1897, 1915, 1924
2 wins — 5th Earl of Jersey: 1824, 1830
   14th Earl of Derby: 1848, 1860
   John King: 1856, 1874
   Joachim Lefèvre: 1872, 1883
   6th Duke of Portland: 1890, 1894
   Sir John Blundell Maple: 1893, 1898
   William Hall Walker: 1905, 1907
   Jack Joel: 1913, 1914
   Walter Raphael: 1912, 1921
   2nd Viscount Astor: 1910, 1925
   HM King George VI: 1942, 1946
   Sir Victor Sassoon: 1937, 1956
   Jim Joel: 1944, 1981

Owned winner and 2nd
4th Duke of Grafton: 1827
Lord George Bentinck: 1840
7th Earl of Stamford: 1863
Baron Meyer de Rothschild: 1864
6th Duke of Portland: 1890
Sir John Blundell Maple: 1893
2nd Viscount Astor: 1925

Most successful breeders
8 wins — 4th Duke of Grafton: 1819, 1820, 1821, 1822, 1823, 1825, 1826, 1827
7 wins — 17th Earl of Derby: 1916, 1918, 1923, 1930, 1936, 1943, 1945.
4 wins — 6th Viscount Falmouth: 1873, 1875, 1879, 1884
3 wins — Thomas Thornhill: 1835, 1838, 1843
   5th Earl of Jersey: 1824, 1830, 1847
   Baron Meyer de Rothschild: 1853, 1864, 1871
   William Stirling Crawfurd: 1859, 1881, 1882
   HM Queen Victoria: 1857, 1888, 1892
   5th Earl of Rosebery: 1897, 1915, 1924
2 wins — Lord George Bentinck: 1842, 1849
   John King: 1856, 1874
   James Cookson: 1868, 1878

8th Duke of Beaufort: 1865, 1887
6th Duke of Portland: 1890, 1894
1st Duke of Westminster: 1885, 1902
Sir Daniel Cooper: 1900, 1906
William Hall Walker: 1905, 1907
Jack Joel: 1913, 1914
Walter Raphael: 1912, 1921
2nd Viscount Astor: 1910, 1925
Sir Victor Sassoon/Eve Stud: 1937, 1956
HH Aga Khan III and Prince Aly Khan: 1957, 1959
Peter FitzGerald: 1964, 1967
Frank Tuthill: 1949, 1970
Jim Joel: 1944, 1981

Bred winner and 2nd
4th Duke of Grafton: 1827
Baron Meyer de Rothschild: 1864
2nd Viscount Astor: 1925

Most successful trainers
9 wins — Robert Robson: 1818, 1819, 1820, 1821, 1822, 1823, 1825, 1826, 1827
6 wins — Mat Dawson: 1873, 1875, 1879, 1884, 1889, 1891
   Noel Murless: 1948, 1959, 1967, 1968, 1971, 1973
4 wins — John Barham Day: 1837, 1840, 1846, 1854
   John Scott: 1848, 1857, 1860, 1862
   John Day, jr: 1849, 1865, 1866, 1869
   George Lambton: 1916, 1917, 1918, 1923
   Peter Gilpin: 1904, 1906, 1909, 1927.
3 wins — Dixon Boyce: 1816, 1817, 1829
   Joe Dawson: 1863, 1870, 1880
   Alec Taylor, sr: 1851, 1881, 1887
   Joe Lawson: 1937, 1939, 1941
   Jack Jarvis: 1924, 1934, 1953
   Cecil Boyd-Rochfort: 1933, 1946, 1955
   Harry Wragg: 1962, 1969, 1982
2 wins — James Edwards: 1824, 1830
   Charles Marson: 1832, 1839
   Bobby Pettit: 1828, 1843
   John Kent, jr: 1842, 1845
   William Butler, jr: 1844, 1855
   Joe Hayhoe: 1864, 1871
   John Porter: 1885, 1892
   George Dawson: 1890, 1894
   Jimmy Ryan: 1888, 1895
   Richard Marsh: 1886, 1896
   Tom Jennings, jr: 1883, 1900
   Jack Robinson: 1905, 1907
   Willie Waugh: 1898, 1910
   Charles Morton: 1913, 1914
   Frank Hartigan: 1915, 1919
   Willie Jarvis: 1928, 1940
   Fred Darling: 1931, 1942
   Walter Earl: 1943, 1945
   Charles Elsey: 1949, 1956
   Etienne Pollet: 1960, 1963
   Henry Cecil: 1979, 1981

Trained winner, 2nd and 3rd
Robert Robson: 1818

Trained winner and 2nd
Robert Robson: 1826, 1827
John Barham Day: 1840
John Kent, jr: 1845
Joe Dawson: 1863, 1870
Joe Hayhoe: 1864
George Dawson: 1890
Mat Dawson: 1891
Joe Day: 1893
Alec Taylor: 1925
Jack Jarvis: 1953
Alec Head: 1957

Most successful jockeys
7 wins — George Fordham: 1859, 1861,
    1865, 1868, 1869, 1881, 1883
6 wins — Frank Buckle: 1818, 1820,
    1821, 1822, 1823, 1827
5 wins — Jem Robinson: 1824, 1828,
    1830, 1841, 1844
    John Barham Day: 1826, 1834, 1836,
    1837, 1840
4 wins — Jack Watts: 1886, 1890, 1896,
    1897
    Fred Rickaby, jr: 1913, 1915, 1916,
    1917
    Charlie Elliott: 1924, 1931, 1932,
    1944
3 wins — Bill Arnull: 1817, 1829, 1832
    Nat Flatman: 1835, 1847, 1857
    Tom Cannon: 1866, 1878, 1884
    Charlie Wood: 1880, 1882, 1887
    Dick Perryman: 1926, 1936, 1941
    Harry Wragg: 1934, 1943, 1945
    Rae Johnstone: 1935, 1947, 1950
    Gordon Richards: 1942, 1948, 1951
2 wins — Bill Clift: 1814, 1815
    Frank Butler: 1848, 1850
    Alfred Day: 1849, 1852
    Sam Rogers: 1842, 1855
    Tom Ashmall: 1858, 1862
    John Wells: 1854, 1864
    John Osborne: 1856, 1874
    Fred Archer: 1875, 1879
    George Barrett: 1885, 1892
    Sam Loates: 1898, 1900
    Bert Randall: 1902, 1903
    Bernard Dillon: 1906, 1909
    Barrington Lynham: 1907, 1910
    Brownie Carslake: 1918, 1922
    Joe Childs: 1928, 1933
    Edgar Britt: 1949, 1956
    Doug Smith: 1946, 1959
    Roger Poincelet: 1960, 1963
    Bill Williamson: 1962, 1965
    Yves Saint-Martin: 1971, 1976
    Edward Hide: 1972, 1977
    Joe Mercer: 1974, 1979
    Lester Piggott: 1970, 1981

Successful trainer-rider
John Barham Day — Chapeau
    d'Espagne (1837), Crucifix (1840)

Successful owner-trainers
John Scott — Impérieuse (1857)
Joe Dawson — Hester (1870)
Bob Sievier — Sceptre (1902)

George Fordham, whose record seven successful mounts in the 1000 Guineas included a 20–length win on Mayonaise in 1859. This remains the greatest margin of victory in any English Classic.

Successful woman trainer
Mme Criquette Head — Ma Biche (1983)

Successful as both jockey and trainer
John Barham Day rode Destiny (1836),
    Chapeau d'Espagne (1837) and
    Crucifix (1840), trained Chapeau
    d'Espagne (1837), Crucifix (1840)
    and Mendicant (1846).
Fred Pratt rode Galeottia (1895), trained
    Atmah (1911).
Harry Wragg rode Campanula (1934),
    Herringbone (1943) and Sun Stream,
    (1945), trained Abermaid (1962), Full
    Dress (1969) and On the House
    (1982).

Most successful sires
4 wins — St Simon: Semolina (1890), La
    Flèche (1892), Amiable (1894),
    Winifreda (1900).
    Swynford: Ferry (1918), Bettina
    (1921), Tranquil (1923), Saucy
    Sue (1925).
    Hyperion: Godiva (1940), Sun Chariot
    (1942), Sun Stream (1945),
    Hypericum (1946)
3 wins — Emilius: Preserve (1835),
    Barcarolle (1838), Extempore
    (1843)
    Stockwell: Lady Augusta (1863),
    Repulse (1866), Achievement
    (1867)
    St Frusquin: Quintessence (1903),
    Flair (1906), Rhodora (1908).
2 wins — Woful: Zinc (1823), Arab
    (1827)
    Orville: Charlotte (1814), Zoe (1828)
    Tramp: Charlotte West (1830),
    Tarantella (1833)
    Sultan: Galata (1832), Destiny (1836)

Lamplighter: May-day (1834),
    Firebrand (1842)
Melbourne: Canezou (1848),
    Mentmore Lass (1853)
Irish Birdcatcher: Habena (1855),
    Manganese (1856).
King Tom: Tomato (1864), Hannah
    (1871)
Blair Athol: Scottish Queen (1869),
    Cecilia (1873)
Macaroni: Spinaway (1875), Camélia
    (1876)
Adventurer: Apology (1874), Wheel of
    Fortune (1879)
Hermit: Thebais (1881), St Marguerite
    (1882)
Petrarch: Busybody (1884), Miss
    Jummy (1886)
Galopin: Galeottia (1895), Aïda
    (1901)
Chaucer: Canyon (1916), Pillion
    (1926)
Hurry On: Plack (1924), Cresta Run
    (1927)
Nasrullah: Musidora (1949), Belle of
    All (1951)
Crepello: Caergwrle (1968),
    Mysterious (1973).

Sired winner, 2nd and 3rd
Rubens (1822)
Sultan (1836)
Hermit (1882)

Sired winner and 2nd
Waxy (1818)
Woful (1827)
Touchstone (1846)
Slane (1850)
King Tom (1864)
St Simon (1890, 1892)
Hyperion (1940)

Derby

Title

Derby Stakes 1780–1914
New Derby Stakes 1915–18
Derby Stakes 1919–39
New Derby Stakes 1940–44
Derby Stakes 1945–83
Ever Ready Derby Stakes from 1984.

Venue

Epsom Downs, Surrey 1780–1914
Summer Course, Newmarket,
    Cambridgeshire 1915–18
Epsom Downs, Surrey 1919–39
Summer Course, Newmarket,
Cambridgeshire 1940–45
Epsom Downs, Surrey from 1946.

Distance

1 mile 1780–83
1 mile 4 furlongs 1874–1871
1 mile 4 furlongs 29 yards 1872–1914
1 mile 4 furlongs 1915–18
1 mile 4 furlongs 29 yards 1919–20
1 mile 4 furlongs 1921–33
1 mile 4 furlongs 5 yards 1934–37
1 mile 4 furlongs from 1938.

Weights

Colts/geldings 8 st 0 lb fillies 7 st 11 lb
    1780–83
Colts/geldings 8 st 3 lb, fillies 8 st 0 lb
    1784–1800
Colts/geldings 8 st 3 lb, fillies 7 st 12 lb
    1801–02
Colts/geldings 8 st 5 lb, fillies 8 st 0 lb
    1803–06
Colts/geldings 8 st 7 lb, fillies 8 st 2 lb
    1807–61
Colts/geldings 8 st 10 lb, fillies 8 st 5 lb
    1862–83
Colts/geldings 9 st 0 lb, fillies 8 st 9 lb
    1884–1905
Colts 9 st 0 lb, fillies 8 st 9 lb from 1906.

1780 Sir Charles Bunbury's ch c
    Diomed J: Sam Arnull 6/4 Fav
    £1,128 2. Boudrow 3. Spitfire 9 ran
1781 Dennis O'Kelly's b c **Young
    Eclipse** J: Charles Hindley 10/1
    £1,260 2. Crop 3. Prince of Orange
    15 ran
1782 3rd Earl of Egremont's b c
    Assassin J: Sam Arnull 5/1 £1,102
    2. Sweet Robin 3. Fortunio 13 ran
1783 John Parker's br c **Saltram**
    J: Charles Hindley 5/2 Jt-Fav £892
    2. Dungannon 3. Parlington 6 ran
1784 Dennis O'Kelly's b c **Serjeant**
    J: John Arnull 3/1 Fav £918 2. Carlo
    Khan 3. Dancer 11 ran
1785 1st Earl of Clermont's br c
    Aimwell J: Charles Hindley 7/1 £866
    2. Grantham 3. Verjuice 10 ran
1786 Tommy Panton's b c **Noble** J: J.
    White 30/1 £997 2. Meteor 3. Claret
    15 ran
1787 12th Earl of Derby's br c **Sir Peter
    Teazle** J: Sam Arnull 2/1 £892
    2. Gunpowder 3. Bustler 7 ran
1788 HRH Prince of Wales's ch c **Sir
    Thomas** J: William South 5/6 Fav
    £918 2. Aurelius 3. Feenow 11 ran
1789 5th Duke of Bedford's b c
    Skyscraper J: Sam Chifney 4/7 Fav
    £918 2. Sir George 3. Skylark 11 ran
1790 1st Earl Grosvenor's b c
    Rhadamanthus J: John Arnull
    5/4 Fav £1,050 2. Asparagus 3. Lee
    Boo 10 ran
1791 5th Duke of Bedford's b c **Eager**
    J: Matt Stephenson 5/2 £1,030
    2. Vermin 3. Proteus 9 ran
1792 1st Earl Grosvenor's b c **John
    Bull** J: Frank Buckle 4/6 Fav £971
    2. Speculator 3. Bustard 7 ran
1793 Sir Ferdinando Poole's b c **Waxy**
    J: Bill Clift 12/1 £1,496 2. Gohanna
    3. Triptolemus 13 ran
1794 1st Earl Grosvenor's b c **Daedalus**
    J: Frank Buckle 6/1 £1,233
    2. Ragged Jack 3. Leon 4 ran
1795 Sir Frank Standish's b c **Spread
    Eagle** J: Anthony Wheatley 3/1 and
    5/2 £1,362 2. Caustic 3. Pelter 11 ran
1796 Sir Frank Standish's b c **Didelot**
    J; John Arnull no odds recorded
    £1,312 2. Stickler 3. Leviathan 11 ran
1797 5th Duke of Bedford's unnamed
    br c by Fidget J: John Singleton, jr
    10/1 £997 2. Esculus 3. Plaistow
    7 ran
1798 Joseph Cookson's br c **Sir Harry**
    J: Sam Arnull 6/4 and 7/4 Fav £1,066
    2. Telegraph 3. Young Spear 10 ran
1799 Sir Frank Standish's br c
    Archduke J: John Arnull 12/1 £997
    2. Gislebert 3. Eagle 11 ran
1800 Christopher Wilson's b c
    Champion J: Bill Clift 7/4 Fav £1,050
    2. Tag 3. Mystery 13 ran
1801 Sir Charles Bunbury's b f **Eleanor**
    J: John Saunders 5/4 Fav £945
    2. br c by Fidget 3. Remnant 11 ran
1802 3rd Duke of Grafton's b c **Tyrant**
    J: Frank Buckle 7/1 £866 2. Young
    Eclipse 3. Orlando 9 ran
1803 Sir Hedworth Williamson's b c
    Ditto J: Bill Clift 7/2 £918 2. Sir Oliver
    3. br c by Sir Peter Teazle 6 ran
1804 3rd Earl of Egremont's b c
    Hannibal J: Bill Arnull 5/2 and 3/1
    £918 2. Pavilion 3. Hippocampus
    8 ran
1805 3rd Earl of Egremont's b c
    Cardinal Beaufort J: Dennis
    Fitzpatrick 20/1 £1,260
    2. Plantagenet 3. Goth 15 ran
1806 3rd Baron Foley's br c **Paris**
    J: John Shepherd 5/1 £1,181
    2. Trafalgar 3. Hector 12 ran
1807 3rd Earl of Egremont's ch c
    Election J: John Arnull 3/1 Fav
    £1,181 2. Giles Scroggins
    3. Coriolanus 13 ran
1808 Sir Hedworth Williamson's ch c
    Pan J: Frank Collinson 25/1 £1,102
    2. Vandyke 3. Chester 10 ran
1809 3rd Duke of Grafton's b c **Pope**
    J: Tom Goodisson 20/1 £1,286
    2. Wizard 3. Salvator 10 ran
1810 3rd Duke of Grafton's b c
    Whalebone J: Bill Clift 2/1 Fav
    £1,312 2. The Dandy 3. Eccleston
    11 ran
1811 Sir John Shelley's b c **Phantom**
    J: Frank Buckle 5/1 £1,522 2. Magic
    3. Rival 16 ran
1812 Robert Ladbroke's br c **Octavius**
    J: Bill Arnull 7/1 £1,443 2. Sweep
    3. Comus 14 ran
1813 Sir Charles Bunbury's bl c
    Smolensko J: Tom Goodisson
    Evens Fav £1,496 2. Caterpillar
    3. Illusion 5 ran
1814 2nd Baron Stawell's b c **Blücher**
    J: Bill Arnull 5/2 Fav £1,548
    2. Perchance 3. Bourbon 14 ran
1815 4th Duke of Grafton's b c **Whisker**
    J: Tom Goodisson 8/1 £1,522
    2. Raphael 3. Busto 13 ran
1816 HRH Duke of York's b c **Prince
    Leopold** J: Will Wheatley 20/1
    £1,470 2. Nectar 3. Pandour 11 ran
1817 John Payne's ch c **Azor** J: Jem
    Robinson 50/1 £1,653 2. Young
    Wizard 3. Sylvanus 13 ran
1818 Thomas Thornhill's ch c **Sam**
    J: Sam Chifney, jr 7/2 £1,732
    2. Raby 3. Prince Paul 16 ran
1819 4th Duke of Portland's br c
    Tiresias J: Bill Clift 2/1 and 5/2 Fav
    £1,680 2. Sultan 3. Euphrates 16 ran
1820 Thomas Thornhill's ch c **Sailor**
    J: Sam Chifney, jr 4/1 and 7/2 £1,601
    2. Abjer 3. Tiger 15 ran
1821 John Hunter's gr c **Gustavus**
    J: Sam Day 2/1 Fav £1,601
    2. Reginald 3. Sir Huldibrand 13 ran
1822 HRH Duke of York's b c **Moses**
    J: Tom Goodisson 6/1 £1,548
    2. Figaro 3. Hampden 12 ran
1823 John Udney's b f **Emilius**
    J: Frank Buckle 5/4 and 11/8 Fav
    £1,706 2. Tancred 3. Talisman 11 ran
1824 Sir John Shelley's ch c **Cedric**
    J: Jem Robinson 9/2 £1,811
    2. Osmond 3. Sir Gray 17 ran
1825 5th Earl of Jersey's ch c
    Middleton J: Jem Robinson 7/4 Fav
    £1,750 2. Rufus 3. Hogarth 18 ran
1826 3rd Earl of Egremont's b c **Lap-
    dog** J: George Dockeray 50/1
    £1,750 2. Shakspeare 3. Dervise
    19 ran
1827 5th Earl of Jersey's b c **Mameluke**
    J: Jem Robinson 9/1 £2,650
    2. Glenartney 3. Edmund 23 ran
1828 5th Duke of Rutland's br c
    Cadland J: Jem Robinson 4/1
    £2,450 2. The Colonel 3. Zinganee
    15 ran
1829 G. W. K. Gratwicke's b c
    Frederick J: John Forth 40/1 £2,500
    2. The Exquisite 3. Oatlands 17 ran
1830 Bill Chifney's b c **Priam** J: Sam
    Day 4/1 Fav £2,650 2. Little Red
    Rover 3. Mahmoud 23 ran
1831 Viscount Lowther's b c **Spaniel**
    J: Will Wheatley 50/1 £3,000

2. Riddlesworth 3. Incubus 23 ran

1832 Robert Ridsdale's ch c **St Giles** J: Bill Scott 3/1 Fav £2,825 2. Perion 3. Trustee 22 ran

1833 Isaac Sadler's ch c **Dangerous** J: Jem Chapple 30/1 £3,475 2. Connoisseur 3. Revenge 25 ran

1834 Stanlake Batson's ch c **Plenipotentiary** J: Patrick Conolly 9/4 Fav £3,375 2. Shilelagh 3. Glencoe 22 ran

1835 John Bowes's ch c **Mündig** J: Bill Scott 6/1 £3,300 2. Ascot 3. Pelops 14 ran

1836 5th Earl of Jersey's b c **Bay Middleton** J: Jem Robinson 7/4 Fav £3,475 2. Gladiator 3. Venison 21 ran

1837 4th Baron Berners's b c **Phosphorus** J: George Edwards 40/1 £3,450 2. Caravan 3. Mahometan 17 ran

1838 Sir Gilbert Heathcote's br c **Amato** J: Jem Chapple 30/1 £3,675 2. Ion 3. Grey Momus 23 ran

1839 William Ridsdale's b c **Bloomsbury** J: Sim Templeman 25/1 £3,850 2. Deception 3. Euclid 21 ran

1840 David Robertson's b c **Little Wonder** J: William Macdonald 50/1 £3,775 2. Launcelot 3. Discord 17 ran

1841 Abraham Rawlinson's b c **Coronation** J: Patrick Conolly 5/2 Fav £4,325 2. Van Amburgh 3. Mustapha Muley 29 ran

1842 George Anson's b c **Atilla** J: Bill Scott 5/1 £4,850 2. Robert de Gorham 3. Belcoeur 24 ran

1843 John Bowes's b c **Cotherstone** J: Bill Scott 13/8 Fav £4,200 2. Gorhambury 3. Sirikol 23 ran

1844 Jonathan Peel's b c **Orlando** J: Nat Flatman 20/1 £4,300 2. Ionian 3. Bay Momus 29 ran ('Running Rein' finished first, disqualified)

1845 G. W. K. Gratwicke's b c **The Merry Monarch** J: Foster Bell 15/1 £3,950 2. Annandale 3. Old England 31 ran

1846 John Gully's ch c **Pyrrhus the First** J: Sam Day 8/1 £5,250 2. Sir Tatton Sykes 3. Brocardo 27 ran

1847 T. H. Pedley's ch c **Cossack** J: Sim Templeman 5/1 £5,250 2. War Eagle 3. Van Tromp 32 ran

1848 3rd Viscount Clifden's b c **Surplice** J: Sim Templeman Evens Fav £5,550 2. Springy Jack 3. Shylock 17 ran

1849 13th Earl of Eglinton's br c **The Flying Dutchman** J: Charlie Marlow 2/1 Jt-Fav £6,325 2. Hotspur 3. Tadmor 26 ran

1850 2nd Earl of Zetland's br c **Voltigeur** J: Job Marson 16/1 £5,425 2. Pitsford 3. Clincher 24 ran

1851 Sir Joseph Hawley's ch c **Teddington** J: Job Marson 3/1 Fav £5,325 2. Marlborough Buck 3. Neasham 33 ran

1852 John Bowes's ch c **Daniel**

Blair Athol proved himself the best of a vintage crop of colts in England in a brief career which began with victory in the 1864 Derby.

O'Rourke J: Frank Butler 25/1 £4,900 2. Barbarian 3. Chief Baron Nicholson 27 ran

1853 John Bowes's b c **West Australian** J: Frank Butler 6/4 Fav £5,250 2. Sittingbourne 3. Cineas 28 ran

1854 John Gully's b c **Andover** J: Alfred Day 7/2 £5,800 2. King Tom 3. The Hermit 27 ran

1855 Francis Popham's br c **Wild Dayrell** J: Robert Sherwood Evens Fav £4,775 2. Kingstown 3. Lord of the Isles 12 ran

1856 Octavius Vernon Harcourt's br c **Ellington** J: Tom Aldcroft 20/1 £5,575 2. Yellow Jack 3. Cannobie 24 ran

1857 Wiliam I'Anson's b f **Blink Bonny** J: Jack Charlton 20/1 £5,500 2. Black Tommy 3. Adamas 30 ran

1858 Sir Joseph Hawley's br c **Beadsman** J: John Wells 10/1 £5,275 2. Toxophilite 3. The Hadji 23 ran

1859 Sir Joseph Hawley's br c **Musjid** J: John Wells 9/4 Fav £6,600 2. Marionette 3. Trumpeter 30 ran

1860 James Merry's ch c **Thormanby** J: Harry Custance 4/1 £6,050 2. The Wizard 3. Horror 30 ran

1861 Charles Towneley's ch c **Kettledrum** J: Ralph Bullock 16/1 £6,050 2. Dundee 3. Diophantus 18 ran

1862 Charles Snewing's b c **Caractacus** J: John Parsons 40/1 £6,375 2. The Marquis 3. Buckstone 34 ran

1863 Richard Naylor's b c **Macaroni** J: Tom Chaloner 10/1 £6,850 2. Lord Clifden 3. Rapid Rhone 31 ran

1864 William I'Anson's ch c **Blair Athol** J: Jim Snowden 14/1 £6,450 2. General Peel 3. Scottish Chief 30 ran

1865 Comte Frédéric de Lagrange's b c **Gladiateur** J: Harry Grimshaw 5/2 Fav £6,825 2. Christmas Carol 3. Eltham 29 ran

1866 Richard Sutton's b c **Lord Lyon** J: Harry Custance 5/6 Fav £7,350 2. Savernake 3. Rustic 26 ran

1867 Henry Chaplin's ch c **Hermit** J: John Daley 1000/15 £7,000 2. Marksman 3. Vauban 30 ran

1868 Sir Joseph Hawley's b c **Blue Gown** J: John Wells 7/2 £6,800 2. King Alfred 3. Speculum 18 ran

1869 John Johnstone's b c **Pretender** J: John Osborne 11/8 Fav £6,225 2. Pero Gomez 3. The Drummer 22 ran

1870 6th Viscount Falmouth's b c **Kingcraft** J: Tom French 20/1 £6,125 2. Palmerston 3. Muster 15 ran

1871 Baron Meyer de Rothschild's ch c **Favonius** J: Tom French 9/1 £5,125 2= Albert Victor and King of the Forest 17 ran

1872 Henry Savile's b c **Cremorne** J: Charlie Maidment 3/1 £4,850 2. Pell Mell 3. Queen's Messenger 23 ran

1873 James Merry's ch c **Doncaster** J: Fred Webb 45/1 £4,825 2= Gang Forward and Kaiser 12 ran

1874 W. S. Cartwright's ch c **George Frederick** J: Harry Custance 9/1 £5,350 2. Couronne de Fer 3. Atlantic 20 ran

1875 Prince Gustavus Batthyany's b or br c **Galopin** J: Jack Morris 2/1 Fav £4,950 2. Claremont 3. Remorse 18 ran

1876 Alexander Baltazzi's b c **Kisber** J: Charlie Maidment 4/1 £5,575 2. Forerunner 3. Julius Caesar 15 ran

1877 6th Viscount Falmouth's b c **Silvio** J: Fred Archer 100/9 £6,050 2. Glen Arthur 3. Rob Roy 17 ran

1878 William Stirling Crawfurd's b c **Sefton** J: Harry Constable 100/12 £5,825 2. Insulaire 3. Childeric 22 ran

1879 Baron Lionel Nathan de Rothschild's br c **Sir Bevys** J: George Fordham 20/1 £7,025 2. Palmbearer 3. Visconti 23 ran

1880 1st Duke of Westminster's ch c **Bend Or** J: Fred Archer 2/1 Fav £6,375 2. Robert the Devil 3. Mask 19 ran

1881 Pierre Lorillard's br c **Iroquois** J: Fred Archer 11/2 £5,925 2. Peregrine 3. Town Moor 15 ran

1882 1st Duke of Westminster's ch f **Shotover** J: Tom Cannon 11/2 £4,775 2. Quicklime 3. Sachem 14 ran

1883 Sir Frederick Johnstone's ch c **St Blaise** J: Charlie Wood 5/1 £5,150 2. Highland Chief 3. Galliard 11 ran

1884 Jack Hammond's b c **St Gatien** J: Charlie Wood 100/8 £2,375 *dead-heated with* Sir John Willoughby's br c **Harvester** J: Sam Loates 100/7 £2,375 3. Queen Adelaide 15 ran

1885 20th Baron Hastings's b c **Melton** J: Fred Archer 75/40 Fav £4,525 2. Paradox 3. Royal Hampton 12 ran

1886 1st Duke of Westminster's b c **Ormonde** J: Fred Archer 4/9 Fav £4,700 2. The Bard 3. St Mirin 9 ran

1887 George Baird's b c **Merry Hampton** J: Jack Watts 100/9 £4,525 2. The Baron 3. Martley 11 ran

1888 6th Duke of Portland's b c **Ayrshire** J: Fred Barrett 5/6 Fav £3,680 2. Crowberry 3. Van Diemen's Land 9 ran

1889 6th Duke of Portland's b c **Donovan** J: Tommy Loates 8/11 Fav £4,050 2. Miguel 3. El Dorado 13 ran

1890 Sir James Miller's ch c **Sainfoin** J: Jack Watts 100/15 £5,940 2. Le Nord 3. Orwell 8 ran

1891 Sir Frederick Johnstone's br c **Common** J: George Barrett 10/11 Fav £5,510 2. Gouverneur 3. Martenhurst 11 ran

1892 3rd Earl of Bradford's ch c **Sir Hugo** J: Fred Allsopp 40/1 £6,960 2. La Flèche 3. Bucentaure 13 ran

1893 Harry McCalmont's b c **Isinglass** J: Tommy Loates 4/9 Fav £5,515 2. Ravensbury 3. Raeburn 11 ran

1894 5th Earl of Rosebery's b c **Ladas** J: Jack Watts 2/9 Fav £5,450 2. Matchbox 3. Reminder 7 ran

1895 5th Earl of Rosebery's b c **Sir Visto** J: Sam Loates 9/1 £5,450 2. Curzon 3. Kirkconnel 15 ran

1896 HRH Prince of Wales's b c **Persimmon** J: Jack Watts 5/1 £5,450 2. St Frusquin 3. Earwig 11 ran

1897 John Gubbins's b c **Galtee More** J: Charlie Wood 1/4 Fav £5,450 2. Velasquez 3. History 11 ran

1898 James Larnach's ch c **Jeddah** J: Otto Madden 100/1 £5,450 2. Batt 3. Dunlop 18 ran

1899 1st Duke of Westminster's b c **Flying Fox** J: Morny Cannon 2/5 Fav £5,450 2. Damocles 3. Innocence 12 ran

1900 HRH Prince of Wales's b c **Diamond Jubilee** J: Herbert Jones

Persimmon, pictured here with Jack Watts in the saddle, is the last horse to win both the Derby and the Ascot Gold Cup, a double he achieved in 1896–7. At his head is trainer Richard Marsh and on the left is his owner, the future King Edward VII.

6/4 Fav £5,450 2. Simon Dale
3. Disguise 14 ran

1901 William Collins Whitney's b c
Volodyovski J: Lester Reiff 5/2 Fav
£5,670 T: John Huggins, Newmarket
B: Lady Meux Sire: Florizel
2. William the Third 3. Veronese
¾l, 4l 2:40.8 25 ran

1902 John Gubbins's br c **Ard Patrick**
J: Skeets Martin 100/14 £5,450
T: Sam Darling, Beckhampton,
Wiltshire B: Owner Sire: St Florian
2. Rising Glass 3. Friar Tuck 3l, 3l
2:42.2 18 ran

1903 Sir James Miller's br c **Rock Sand**
J: Danny Maher 4/6 Fav £6,450
T: George Blackwell, Newmarket
B: Owner Sire: Sainfoin 2. Vinicius
3. Flotsam 2l, 2l 2:42.8 7 ran

1904 Leopold de Rothschild's b c
St Amant J: Kempton Cannon 5/1
£6,450 T: Alfred Hayhoe, Newmarket
B: Owner Sire: St Frusquin 2. John
o' Gaunt 3. St Denis 3l, 6l 2:45.4 8 ran

1905 5th Earl of Rosebery's ch c **Cicero**
J: Danny Maher 4/11 Fav £6,450
T: Percy Peck, Exning, Suffolk
B: Owner Sire: Cyllene 2. Jardy
3. Signorino ¾l, head 2:39.6 9 ran

1906 Eustace Loder's b c **Spearmint**
J: Danny Maher 6/1 £6,450 T: Peter
Gilpin, Newmarket B: Sir Tatton
Sykes Sire: Carbine 2. Picton
3. Troutbeck 1½l, 2l 2:36.8 22 ran

1907 Richard Croker's ch c **Orby**
J: Johnny Reiff 100/9 £6,450 T: Fred
MacCabe, Sandyford, Co Dublin,
Ireland B: Owner Sire: Orme 2. Wool
Winder 3. Slieve Gallion 2l, ½l 2:44.0
9 ran

1908 Odoardo Ginistrelli's b or br f
Signorinetta J: Billy Bullock 100/1
£6,450 T: Owner, Newmarket
B: Owner Sire: Chaleureux 2. Primer
3. Llangwm 2l, neck 2:39.8 18 ran

1909 HM King Edward VII's br c **Minoru**
J: Herbert Jones 7/2 £6,450 T: Dick
Marsh, Newmarket B: William Hall
Walker Sire: Cyllene 2. Louviers
3. William the Fourth short head, ½l
2:42.4 15 ran

1910 Alfred Cox's b c **Lemberg**
J: Bernard Dillon 7/4 Fav £6,450
T: Alec Taylor, Manton, Wiltshire
B: Owner Sire: Cyllene
2. Greenback 3. Charles O'Malley
neck, 2l 2:35.2 15 ran

1911 Jack Joel's br c **Sunstar**
J: George Stern 13/8 Fav £6,450
T: Charles Morton, Wantage,
Berkshire B: Owner Sire: Sundridge
2. Stedfast 3. Royal Tender 2l, 4l
2:36.8 26 ran

1912 Walter Raphael's gr f **Tagalie**
J: Johnny Reiff 100/8 £6,450
T: Dawson Waugh, Newmarket
B: Owner Sire: Cyllene 2. Jaeger
3. Tracery 4l, 2l 2:38.8 20 ran

1913 Alan Cunliffe's b c **Aboyeur**
J: Edwin Piper 100/1 £6,450 T: Tom
Lewis, Middle Woodford, Wiltshire

B: Tom Laidlaw Sire: Desmond
2. Louvois 3. Great Sport neck, 1l
2:37.6 15 ran (Craganour finished
first, disqualified)

1914 Herman Duryea's b c **Durbar**
J: Matt MacGee 20/1 £6,450 T: Tom
Murphy, Lamorlaye, France B: Owner
Sire: Rabelais 2. Hapsburg 3. Peter
the Hermit 3l, 1½l 2:28.4 30 ran

1915 Solly Joel's b c **Pommern** J: Steve
Donoghue 11/10 Fav £2,400
T: Charley Peck, Newmarket
B: Owner Sire: Polymelus 2. Let Fly
3. Rossendale 2l, 3l 2:32.8 17 ran

1916 Sir Edward Hulton's ch f **Fifinella**
J: Joe Childs 11/2 £2,900 T: Dick
Dawson, Newmarket B: Owner Sire:
Polymelus 2. Kwang-Su
3. Nassovian neck, head 2:36.6
10 ran

1917 Alfred Cox's b c **Gay Crusader**
J: Steve Donoghue 7/4 Fav £2,050
T: Alec Taylor, Manton, Wiltshire
B: Owner Sire: Bayardo 2. Dansellon
3. Dark Legend 4l, head 2:40.6
12 ran

1918 Lady James Douglas's b c
Gainsborough J: Joe Childs
8/13 Fav £4,000 T: Alec Taylor,
Manton, Wiltshire B: Owner Sire:
Bayardo 2. Blink 3. Treclare 1½l, 2l
2:33.2 13 ran

1919 1st Baron Glanely's bl c **Grand
Parade** J: Fred Templeman 33/1
£6,450 T: Frank Barling, Newmarket
B: Richard Croker Sire: Orby
2. Buchan 3. Paper Money ½l, 2l
2:35.8 13 ran

1920 Giles Loder's b c **Spion Kop**
J: Frank O'Neill 100/6 £6,450
T: Peter Gilpin, Newmarket B: Owner
Sire: Spearmint 2. Archaic
3. Orpheus 2l, 1½l 2:34.8 19 ran

1921 Jack Joel's ch c **Humorist**
J: Steve Donoghue 6/1 £6,450
T: Charles Morton, Wantage,
Berkshire B: Owner Sire: Polymelus
2. Craig an Eran 3. Lemonora
neck, 3l 2:35.8 23 ran

1922 1st Baron Woolavington's ch c
Captain Cuttle J: Steve Donoghue
10/1 £10,625 T: Fred Darling,
Beckhampton, Wiltshire B: Owner
Sire: Hurry On 2. Tamar
3. Craigangower 4l, 3l 2:34.6 30 ran

1923 Ben Irish's br c **Papyrus** J: Steve
Donoghue 100/15 £11,325 T: Basil
Jarvis, Newmarket B: Sir John
Robinson Sire: Tracery 2. Pharos
3. Parth 1l, 1½l 2:38.0 19 ran

1924 17th Earl of Derby's b c
Sansovino J: Tommy Weston
9/2 Fav £11,755 T: George Lambton,
Newmarket B: Owner Sire:
Swynford 2. St Germans
3. Hurstwood 6l, neck 2:46.6 27 ran

1925 Henry Morriss's b c **Manna**
J: Steve Donoghue 9/1 £11,095
T: Fred Darling, Beckhampton,
Wiltshire B: James Maher Sire:
Phalaris 2. Zionist 3. The Sirdar 8l, 2l

2:40.6 27 ran

1926 1st Baron Woolavington's ch c
Coronach J: Joe Childs 11/2
£10,950 T: Fred Darling,
Beckhampton, Wiltshire B: Owner
Sire: Hurry On 2. Lancegaye
3. Colorado 5l, short head 2:47.8
19 ran

1927 Frank Curzon's ch c **Call Boy**
J: Charlie Elliott 4/1 Fav £12,615
T: John Watts, Newmarket B: Owner
Sire: Hurry On 2. Hot Night 3. Shian
Mor 2l, 8l 2:34.4 23 ran

1928 Sir Hugo Cunliffe-Owen's b c
Felstead J: Harry Wragg 33/1
£11,605 T: Ossie Bell, Lambourn,
Berkshire B: Owner Sire: Spion Kop
2. Flamingo 3. Black Watch 1½l, 6l
2:34.4 19 ran

1929 William Barnett's b c **Trigo** J: Joe
Marshall 33/1 £11,965 T: Dick
Dawson, Whatcombe, Berkshire
B: Owner Sire: Blandford 2. Walter
Gay 3. Brienz 1½l, 2l 2:36.4 26 ran

1930 HH Aga Khan III's b c **Blenheim**
J: Harry Wragg 18/1 £10,036 T: Dick
Dawson, Whatcombe, Berkshire
B: 6th Earl of Carnarvon Sire:
Blandford 2. Iliad 3. Diolite 1l, 2l
2:38.2 17 ran

1931 Arthur Dewar's b c **Cameronian**
J: Freddie Fox 7/2 Fav £12,161
T: Fred Darling, Beckhampton,
Wiltshire B: 1st Baron Dewar Sire:
Pharos 2. Orpen 3. Sandwich ¾l, ¾l
2:36.6 25 ran

1932 Tom Walls's br c **April the Fifth**
J: Fred Lane 100/6 £9,730 T: Owner,
Epsom, Surrey B: Graeme Whitelaw
Sire: Craig an Eran 2. Dastur
3. Miracle ¾l, short head 2:43.0
21 ran

1933 17th Earl of Derby's ch c **Hyperion**
J: Tommy Weston 6/1 Fav £9,836
T: George Lambton, Newmarket
B: Owner Sire: Gainsborough 2. King
Salmon 3. Statesman 4l, 1l 2:34.0
24 ran

1934 HH Maharaja of Rajpipla's b c
Windsor Lad J: Charlie Smirke
15/2 £9,352 T: Marcus Marsh,
Lambourn, Berkshire B: Dan Sullivan
Sire: Blandford 2. Easton 3. Colombo
1l, neck 2:34.0 19 ran

1935 HH Aga Khan III's b c **Bahram**
J: Freddie Fox 5/4 Fav £9,216
T: Frank Butters, Newmarket
B: Owner Sire: Blandford 2. Robin
Goodfellow 3. Field Trial 2l, ½l 2:36.0
16 ran

1936 HH Aga Khan III's gr c **Mahmoud**
J: Charlie Smirke 100/8 £9,934
T: Frank Butters, Newmarket
B: Owner Sire: Blenheim 2. Taj
Akbar 3. Thankerton 3l, ¾l 2:33.8
22 ran

1937 Mrs Lettice Miller's b c **Mid-day
Sun** J: Michael Beary 100/7 £9,441
T: Fred Butters, Kingsclere,
Berkshire B: William Sears Sire:
Solario 2. Sandsprite 3. Le Grand Duc

1½l, 1½l 2:37.2 21 ran
1938 Peter Beatty's br c **Bois Roussel**
J: Charlie Elliott 20/1 £9,228 T: Fred
Darling, Beckhampton, Wiltshire
B: Léon Volterra Sire: Vatout
2. Scottish Union 3. Pasch 4l, 2l
2:38.5 22 ran
1939 6th Earl of Rosebery's ch c **Blue
Peter** J: Eph Smith 7/2 Fav £10,625
T: Jack Jarvis, Newmarket B: Owner
Sire: Fairway 2. Fox Cub
3. Heliopolis 4l, 3l 2:36.5 27 ran
1940 Fred Darling's b c **Pont l'Evêque**
J: Sam Wragg 10/1 £5,892
T: Owner, Beckhampton, Wiltshire
B: Henry Morriss Sire: Barneveldt
2. Turkhan 3. Lighthouse 3l, short
head 2:30.8 16 ran
1941 Mrs Catherine Macdonald-
Buchanan's br c **Owen Tudor** J: Billy
Nevett 25/1 £4,473 T: Fred Darling,
Beckhampton, Wiltshire B: Owner
Sire: Hyperion 2. Morogoro 3. Firoze
Din 1½l, 2l 2:29.6 20 ran
1942 17th Earl of Derby's b c **Watling
Street** J: Harry Wragg 6/1 £3,844
T: Walter Earl, Newmarket B: Owner
Sire: Fairway 2. Hyperides 3. Ujiji
neck, 2l 2:29.6 13 ran
1943 Miss Dorothy Paget's br c
Straight Deal J: Tommy Carey
100/6 £4,388 T: Walter Nightingall,
Epsom, Surrey B: Owner Sire:
Solario 2. Umiddad 3. Nasrullah
head, ½l 2:30.4 23 ran
1944 6th Earl of Rosebery's b c **Ocean
Swell** J: Billy Nevett 28/1 £5,901
T: Jack Jarvis, Newmarket B: Owner
Sire: Blue Peter 2. Tehran 3. Happy
Landing neck, short head 2:31.0
20 ran
1945 Sir Eric Ohlson's br c **Dante**
J: Billy Nevett 100/30 Fav £8,339
T: Matt Peacock, Middleham,
Yorkshire B: Owner Sire: Nearco
2. Midas 3. Court Martial 2l, head
2:26.6 27 ran
1946 John Ferguson's gr c **Airborne**
J: Tommy Lowrey 50/1 £8,415
T: Dick Perryman, Newmarket
B: Harold Boyd-Rochfort Sire:
Precipitation 2. Gulf Stream
3. Radiotherapy 1l, 2l 2:45.0 17 ran
1947 Baron Geoffroy de Waldner's b c
Pearl Diver J: George Bridgland
40/1 £9,601 T: Percy Carter,
Chantilly, France B: Edward Esmond
Sire: Vatellor 2. Migoli 3. Sayajirao
4l, ¾l 2:38.4 15 ran
1948 HH Aga Khan III's b c **My Love**
J: Rae Johnstone 100/9 £13,059
T: Dick Carver, Chantilly, France
B: Léon Volterra Sire: Vatellor
2. Royal Drake 3. Noor 1½l, 4l 2:40.0
32 ran
1949 Mrs Marion Glenister's b c
Nimbus J: Charlie Elliott 7/1 £14,245
T: George Colling, Newmarket
B: William Hill Sire: Nearco 2. Amour
Drake 3. Swallow Tail head, head
2:42.0 32 ran

1950 Marcel Boussac's ch c **Galcador**
J: Rae Johnstone 100/9 £17,010
T: Charles Semblat, Chantilly, France
B: Owner Sire: Djebel 2. Prince
Simon 3. Double Eclipse head, 4l
2:36.8 25 ran
1951 Joe McGrath's br c **Arctic Prince**
J: Charlie Spares 28/1 £19,386
T: Willie Stephenson, Royston,
Hertfordshire B: Owner Sire: Prince
Chevalier 2. Sybil's Nephew 3. Signal
Box 6l, head 2:39.4 33 ran
1952 HH Aga Khan III's br c **Tulyar**
J: Charlie Smirke 11/2 Fav £20,487
T: Marcus Marsh, Newmarket
B: Owner and Prince Aly Khan Sire:
Tehran 2. Gay Time 3. Faubourg
¾l, 1l 2:36.4 33 ran
1953 Sir Victor Sassoon's b c **Pinza**
J: Sir Gordon Richards 5/1 Jt-Fav
£19,118 T: Norman Bertie,
Newmarket B: Fred Darling Sire:
Chanteur 2. Aureole 3. Pink Horse
4l, 1½l 2:35.6 27 ran
1954 Robert Sterling Clark's ch c **Never
Say Die** J: Lester Piggott 33/1
£16,959 T: Joe Lawson, Newmarket
B: Owner Sire: Nasrullah 2. Arabian
Night 3. Darius 2l, neck 2:35.8 22 ran
1955 Mme Suzy Volterra's br c **Phil
Drake** J: Freddie Palmer 100/8
£18,702 T; François Mathet,
Chantilly, France B: Owner Sire:
Admiral Drake 2. Panaslipper
3. Acropolis 1½l, 1½l 2:39.8 23 ran
1956 Pierre Wertheimer's b c **Lavandin**
J: Rae Johnstone 7/1 Fav £17,282
T: Alec Head, Chantilly, France
B: Owner Sire: Verso 2. Montaval
3. Roistar neck, 2l 2:36.4 27 ran
1957 Sir Victor Sassoon's ch c **Crepello**
J: Lester Piggott 6/4 Fav £18,659
T: Noel Murless, Newmarket B: Eve
Stud Ltd Sire: Donatello 2. Ballymoss
3. Pipe of Peace 1½l, 1l 2:35.4
22 ran
1958 Sir Victor Sassoon's b c **Hard
Ridden** J: Charlie Smirke 18/1
£20,036 T: Mick Rogers, The
Curragh, Co Kildare, Ireland B: Sir
Oliver Lambart Sire: Hard Sauce
2. Paddy's Point 3. Nagami 5l, 1½l
2:41.2 20 ran
1959 Sir Humphrey de Trafford's b c
Parthia J: Harry Carr 10/1 £36,078
T: Cecil Boyd-Rochfort, Newmarket
B: Owner Sire: Persian Gulf
2. Fidalgo 3. Shantung 1½l, 1½l
2:36.0 20 ran
1960 Sir Victor Sassoon's b c **St Paddy**
J: Lester Piggott 7/1 £33,052 T: Noel
Murless, Newmarket B: Eve Stud Ltd
Sire: Aureole
2. Alcaeus 3. Kythnos 3l, ½l 2:35.8
17 ran
1961 Mme Etti Plesch's ch c **Psidium**
J: Roger Poincelet 66/1 £34,548
T: Harry Wragg, Newmarket
B: Owner Sire: Pardal 2. Dicta Drake
3. Pardao 2l, neck 2:36.4 28 ran
1962 Raymond Guest's ch c **Larkspur**

J: Neville Sellwood 22/1 £34,786
T: Vincent O'Brien, Cashel, Co
Tipperary, Ireland B: Messrs Philip
A. Love Ltd Sire: Never Say Die
2. Arcor 3. Le Cantilien 2l, ½l 2:37.6
26 ran
1963 François Dupré's b c **Relko**
J: Yves Saint-Martin 5/1 Fav £35,338
T: François Mathet, Chantilly, France
B: Owner Sire: Tanerko 2. Merchant
Venturer 3. Ragusa 6l, 3l 2:39.4
26 ran
1964 John Ismay's b c **Santa Claus**
J: Scobie Breasley 15/8 Fav £72,067
T: Mick Rogers, The Curragh, Co
Kildare, Ireland B: Frank Smorfitt
Sire: Chamossaire 2. Indiana
3. Dilettante 1l, 2l 2:41.98 17 ran
1965 Jean Ternynck's ch c **Sea-Bird**
J: Pat Glennon 7/4 Fav £65,301
T: Etienne Pollet, Chantilly, France
B: Owner Sire: Dan Cupid
2. Meadow Court 3. I Say 2l, 1½l
2:38.41 22 ran
1966 Lady Zia Wernher's b c
Charlottown J: Scobie Breasley 5/1
£74,489 T: Gordon Smyth, Lewes,
Sussex B: Someries Stud Sire:
Charlottesville 2. Prétendre 3. Black
Prince neck, 5l 2:37.63 25 ran
1967 Jim Joel's b c **Royal Palace**
J: George Moore 7/4 Fav £61,918
T: Noel Murless, Newmarket
B: Owner Sire: Ballymoss 2. Ribocco
3. Dart Board 2½l, 2l 2:38.36 22 ran
1968 Raymond Guest's b c **Sir Ivor**
J: Lester Piggott 4/5 Fav £58,525
T: Vincent O'Brien, Cashel, Co
Tipperary, Ireland B: Mrs Alice
Headley Bell Sire: Sir Gaylord
2. Connaught 3. Mount Athos
1½l, 2½l 2:38.73 13 ran
1969 Arthur Budgett's b c **Blakeney**
J: Ernie Johnson 15/2 £63,108
T: Owner, Whatcombe, Berkshire
B: Park Farm Stud Sire: Hethersett
2. Shoemaker 3. Prince Regent
1l, 1l 2:40.30 26 ran
1970 Charles Engelhard's b c **Nijinsky**
J: Lester Piggott 11/8 Fav £62,311
T: Vincent O'Brien, Cashel, Co
Tipperary, Ireland B: Eddie Taylor
Sire: Northern Dancer 2. Gyr
3. Stintino 2½l, 3l 2:34.68 11 ran
1971 Paul Mellon's b c **Mill Reef**
J: Geoff Lewis 100/30 Fav £61,625
T: Ian Balding, Kingsclere, Berkshire
B: Owner Sire: Never Bend 2. Linden
Tree 3. Irish Ball 2l, 2½l 2:37.14
21 ran
1972 John Galbreath's b c **Roberto**
J: Lester Piggott 3/1 Fav £63,735
T: Vincent O'Brien, Cashel, Co
Tipperary, Ireland B: Owner Sire:
Hail to Reason 2. Rheingold
3. Pentland Firth short head, 3l
2:36.09 22 ran
1973 Arthur Budgett's ch c **Morston**
J: Edward Hide 25/1 £66,348
T: Owner, Whatcombe, Berkshire
B: Park Farm Stud Sire: Ragusa

Troy wins the 200th Derby by the widest margin officially recorded in the race for more than half a century.

2. Cavo Doro 3. Freefoot ½l, 2½l
2:35.92 25 ran

1974 Mrs Sharon Phillips's ch c **Snow Knight** J: Brian Taylor 50/1 £89,229 T: Peter Nelson, Lambourn, Berkshire B: Claude Lilley Sire: Firestreak 2. Imperial Prince 3. Giacometti 2l, 1l 2:35.04 18 ran

1975 Carlo Vittadini's ch c **Grundy** J: Pat Eddery 5/1 £106,465 T: Peter Walwyn, Lambourn, Berkshire B: Overbury Stud Sire: Great Nephew 2. Nobiliary 3. Hunza Dancer 3l, 4l 2:35.35 18 ran

1976 Nelson Bunker Hunt's b c **Empery** J: Lester Piggott 10/1 £111,825 T: Maurice Zilber, Chantilly, France B: Owner Sire: Vaguely Noble 2. Relkino 3. Oats 3l, head 2:35.69 23 ran

1977 Robert Sangster's ch c **The Minstrel** J: Lester Piggott 5/1 £107,530 T: Vincent O'Brien, Cashel, Co Tipperary, Ireland B: Eddie Taylor Sire: Northern Dancer 2. Hot Grove 3. Blushing Groom neck, 5l 2:36.44 22 ran

1978 2nd Earl of Halifax's b c **Shirley Heights** J: Greville Starkey 8/1 £98,410 T: John Dunlop, Arundel, Sussex B: Owner and Baron Irwin Sire: Mill Reef 2. Hawaiian Sound 3. Remainder Man head, 1½l 2:35.30 25 ran

1979 Sir Michael Sobell's b c **Troy** J: Willie Carson 6/1 £153,980 T: Dick Hern, West Ilsley, Berkshire

B: Ballymacoll Stud Farm Sire: Petingo 2. Dickens Hill 3. Northern Baby 7l, 3l 2:36.59 23 ran

1980 Mme Etti Plesch's b c **Henbit** J: Willie Carson 7/1 £166,820 T: Dick Hern, West Ilsley, Berkshire B: Mrs Jack G. Jones Sire: Hawaii 2. Master Willie 3. Rankin ¾l, 1½l 2:34.77 24 ran

1981 HH Aga Khan IV's b c **Shergar** J: Walter Swinburn 10/11 Fav £149,900 T: Michael Stoute, Newmarket B: Owner Sire: Great Nephew 2. Glint of Gold 3. Scintillating Air 10l, 2l 2:44.21 18 ran

1982 Robert Sangster's b c **Golden Fleece** J: Pat Eddery 3/1 Fav £146,720 T: Vincent O'Brien, Cashel, Co Tipperary, Ireland B: Paul and Helen Hexter Sire: Nijinsky 2. Touching Wood 3. Silver Hawk 3l, 1l 2:34.27 18 ran

1983 Eric Moller's b c **Teenoso** J: Lester Piggott 9/2 Fav £165,080 T: Geoffrey Wragg, Newmarket B: Owner Sire: Youth 2. Carlingford Castle 3. Shearwalk 3l, 3l 2:49.07 21 ran

1984 Luigi Miglietti's b c **Secreto** J: Christy Roche 14/1 £227,680 T: David O'Brien, Cashel, Co Tipperary, Ireland B: Eddie Taylor Sire: Northern Dancer 2. El Gran Senor 3. Mighty Flutter short head, 3l 2:39.12 17 ran

RECORDS FOR WINNING HORSES

Greatest margins

10 lengths — Shergar (1981)
8 lengths — Manna (1925)
7 lengths — Troy (1979)
6 lengths — Sansovino (1924), Arctic Prince (1951), Relko (1963)
5 lengths — Kisber (1876), Coronach (1926), Hard Ridden (1958).

Smallest margins

dead-heat — Cadland and The Colonel (1828), St Gatien and Harvester (1884).
short head — Paris (1806), Whisker (1815), Minoru (1909), Roberto (1972), Secreto (1984).
head — Phantom (1811), Blücher (1814), Tiresias (1819), Moses (1822), Frederick (1829), Mündig (1835), Phosphorus (1837), Macaroni (1863), Lord Lyon (1866), Pretender (1869), Cremorne (1872), Bend Or (1880), Melton (1885), Straight Deal (1943), Nimbus (1949), Galcador (1950), Shirley Heights (1978).

Fillies

Eleanor (1801), Blink Bonny (1857), Shotover (1882), Signorinetta (1908), Tagalie (1912), Fifinella (1916).

Grey

Gustavus (1821), Tagalie (1912), Mahmoud (1936), Airborne (1946).

Black

Smolensko (1813), Grand Parade (1919).

Longest odds

100/1 — Jeddah (1898), Signorinetta
(1908), Aboyeur (1913)
1000/15 — Hermit (1867)
66/1 — Psidium (1961).
50/1 — Azor (1817), Lap-dog (1826),
Spaniel (1831), Little Wonder (1840),
Airborne (1946), Snow Knight (1974)
45/1 — Doncaster (1873)
40/1 — Frederick (1829), Phosphorus
(1837), Caractacus (1862), Sir Hugo
(1892), Pearl Diver (1947)
33/1 — Grand Parade (1919), Felstead
(1928), Trigo (1929), Never Say Die
(1954)
30/1 — Noble (1786), Dangerous
(1833), Amato (1838).

Shortest odds

2/9 — Ladas (1894)
1/4 — Galtee More (1897)
4/11 — Cicero (1905)
2/5 — Flying Fox (1899)
4/9 — Ormonde (1886), Isinglass (1893)
4/7 — Skyscraper (1789)
8/13 — Gainsborough (1918)
4/6 — John Bull (1792), Rock Sand
(1903)
8/11 — Donovan (1889)
4/5 — Sir Ivor (1968)
5/6 — Sir Thomas (1788), Lord Lyon
(1866), Ayrshire (1888)
10/11 — Common (1891), Shergar
(1981).

No odds recorded

Didelot (1796).

Dead-heat run off

In 1828 Cadland beat The Colonel by
half a length in a run-off after the pair
had dead-heated for first place. On
the occasion of the only other dead-
heat, in 1884, the owners of St Gatien
and Harvester divided the stakes.

Winners on disqualification

The outcome of the 1844 Derby was
determined in a court of law almost six
weeks after the race, when it was
established that the colt who finished
first was not the so-called Running
Rein, but a four-year-old named
Maccabeus. The race was duly
awarded to Orlando, who had finished
three-quarters of a length behind the
'winner'.

In 1913 Craganour finished first, beating
Aboyeur by a head. After an
objection to the winner by the
Stewards, on the grounds that he
had jostled the second horse,
Craganour was disqualified for
having caused serious interference to
three other runners and for having
'bumped and bored Aboyeur so as to
prevent his winning'.

Trained in Ireland

Orby (1907), Hard Ridden (1958),
Larkspur (1962), Santa Claus

(1964), Sir Ivor (1968), Nijinsky
(1970), Roberto (1972), The Minstrel
(1977), Golden Fleece (1982),
Secreto (1984).

Trained in France

Durbar (1914), Pearl Diver (1947), My
Love (1948), Galcador (1950), Phil
Drake (1955), Lavandin (1956),
Relko (1963), Sea-Bird (1965),
Empery (1976).

Bred in France

Gladiateur (1865), Durbar (1914),
Mahmoud (1936), Bois Roussel
(1938), Pearl Diver (1947), My Love
(1948), Galcador (1950), Phil Drake
(1955), Lavandin (1956), Relko
(1963), Sea-Bird (1965), Morston
(1973).

Bred in Hungary

Kisber (1876).

Bred in USA

Iroquois (1881), Never Say Die (1954),
Sir Ivor (1968), Mill Reef (1971),
Roberto (1973), Empery (1976),
Henbit (1980), Golden Fleece
(1982), Teenoso (1983), Secreto
(1984).

Bred in Canada

Nijinsky (1970), The Minstrel (1977).

Siblings

Rhadamanthus (1790) and Daedalus
(1794), Archduke (1799) and Paris
(1806), Whalebone (1810) and
Whisker (1815), Lap-dog (1826) and
Spaniel (1831), and Persimmon
(1896) and Diamond Jubilee (1900)
were brothers.
Spread Eagle (1795) and Didelot
(1796), Ditto (1803) and Pan (1808),
St Giles (1832) and Bloomsbury
(1839), Mündig (1835) and
Cotherstone (1843), Galtee More
(1897) and Ard Patrick (1902), and
Blakeney (1969) and Morston (1973)
were half-brothers.

Unnamed at time of victory

Eager (1791), Colt by Fidget (1797),
Middleton (1825), Lap-dog (1826).

Never beaten

Sailor (1820), Middleton (1825), Bay
Middleton (1836), Amato (1838),
Ormonde (1886), Bahram (1935),
Morston (1973), Golden Fleece
(1982).

Winners in two countries

Orby (1907), Santa Claus (1964),
Nijinsky (1970), Grundy (1975), The
Minstrel (1977), Shirley Heights
(1978), Troy (1979) and Shergar
(1981) all also won the Irish Derby.

Oldest and youngest sires

Muley was 26 years old when he got
Little Wonder (1840). Blue Peter
sired Ocean Swell (1944) and Prince
Chevalier sired Arctic Prince (1951)
at the age of four.

Oldest and youngest dams

Horatia was 25 years old when she
produced Paris (1806). Betty's Secret
produced Secreto (1984) at the age
of four.

RECORDS FOR PLACED HORSES

Fillies

Remnant (1801), Deception (1839),
Queen Adelaide (1884), La Flèche
(1892), Nobiliary (1975).

Gelding

Curzon (1895).

Grey or roan

Crop (1781), Carlo Khan (1784),
Grantham (1785), Hector (1806), Raby
(1818), The Exquisite (1829), Grey
Momus (1838), Rapid Rhone (1863),
Morogoro (1941), Migoli (1947),
Shearwalk (1983).

Black

Shylock (1848), Chief Baron Nicholson
(1852), Black Tommy (1857), Insulaire
(1878), Miguel (1889), Rossendale
(1915), Robin Goodfellow (1935),
Black Prince (1966). Slieve Gallion
(1907) was described as brown or
black.

Longest odds

200/1 — Black Tommy (1857)
100/1 — Speculator (1792), Incubus
(1831), Connoisseur (1833), Pelops
(1835), Robert de Gorham (1842),
Belcoeur (1842), Barbarian (1852),
Eltham (1865), Palmbearer (1879),
Orwell (1890), Bucentaure (1892),
Dunlop (1898), Peter the Hermit
(1914), Sandsprite (1937), Firoze Din
(1941), Panaslipper (1955), Paddy's
Point (1958), Dilettante (1964).
66/1 — Gorhambury (1843), Visconti
(1879), Tracery (1912), Northern
Baby (1979), Mighty Flutter (1984).
50/1 — Young Wizard (1817), Sir
Huldibrand (1821), Sirikol (1843),
Annandale (1845), Hotspur (1849),
Rapid Rhone (1863), King Alfred
(1868), Pell Mell (1872), Glen Arthur
(1877), Martenhurst (1891),
Innocence (1899), St Denis (1904),
Signorino (1905), Orpheus (1920),
The Sirdar (1925), Brienz (1929),
Robin Goodfellow (1935), Sybil's
Nephew (1951), Pentland Firth
(1972), Hunza Dancer (1975),
Scintillating Air (1981).

Trained in Ireland

Signal Box (1951), Panaslipper (1955), Roistar (1956), Ballymoss (1957), Paddy's Point (1958), Alcaeus (1960), Kythnos (1960), Ragusa (1963), Dilettante (1964), Meadow Court (1965), Cavo Doro (1973), Dickens Hill (1979), Carlingford Castle (1983), El Gran Senor (1984).

Trained in France

Gouverneur (1891), Bucentaure (1892), Vinicius (1903), Jardy (1905), The Sirdar (1925), Royal Drake (1948), Amour Drake (1949), Faubourg (1952), Pink Horse (1953), Montaval (1956), Shantung (1959), Dicta Drake (1961), Arcor (1962), Le Cantilien (1962), Prince Regent (1969), Gyr (1970), Stintino (1970), Irish Ball (1971), Nobiliary (1975), Blushing Groom (1977), Northern Baby (1979).

Bred in France

Insulaire (1878), Le Nord (1890), Gouverneur (1891), Bucentaure (1892), Vinicius (1903), Jardy (1905), The Sirdar (1925), Easton (1934), Le Grand Duc (1937), Fox Cub (1939), Lighthouse (1940), Royal Drake (1948), Amour Drake (1949), Faubourg (1952), Pink Horse (1953), Montaval (1956), Shantung (1959), Dicta Drake (1961), Arcor (1962), Le Cantilien (1962), Dilettante (1964), Prince Regent (1969), Gyr (1970), Linden Tree (1971), Irish Ball (1971), Blushing Groom (1977), Rankin (1980).

Bred in USA

Sachem (1882), Disguise (1900), Prince Simon (1950), Black Prince (1966), Ribocco (1967), Nobiliary (1975), Hunza Dancer (1975), Hawaiian Sound (1978), Touching Wood (1982), Silver Hawk (1982), El Gran Senor (1984).

Bred in Canada

Northern Baby (1979).

Ridden by amateur

John o' Gaunt (1904) and Picton (1906) both finished second under amateur rider George Thursby.

Placed but unplaced

Day Comet finished 3rd behind disqualified Craganour and promoted Aboyeur in 1913, but was overlooked by the Judge and assigned no official place. The mistake was never corrected.

MISCELLANEOUS RECORDS

Fastest times

2:33.8 — Mahmoud (1936)
2:34.0 — Hyperion (1933), Windsor Lad (1934)
2:34.27 — Golden Fleece (1982)
2:34.68 — Nijinsky (1970)
2:34.77 — Henbit (1980)
In substitute races at Newmarket:
2:26.6 — Dante (1945)
2:29.6 — Owen Tudor (1941), Watling Street (1942).

Largest entry

920 — 1974

Smallest entry

29 — 1785, 1786 (17 for substitute race 1917)

Largest fields

34 — 1862
33 — 1851, 1951, 1952
32 — 1847, 1948, 1949

Smallest fields

4 — 1794
6 — 1783, 1803
7 — 1792, 1797, 1894, 1903

Richest first prizes

£227,680 — 1984
£166,820 — 1980
£153,980 — 1979

Smallest first prizes

£866 — 1785, 1802
£892 — 1783, 1787
£918 — 1784, 1788, 1789, 1803, 1804

Hottest losing favourites

40/95 — Surefoot was 4th in 1890
4/9 — Macgregor was 4th in 1870
4/7 — Tudor Minstrel was 4th in 1947.

Other odds-on losing favourites

Gohanna (1793), Leon (1794), Wizard (1809), Riddlesworth (1831), The Baron (1887), St Frusquin (1896), Slieve Gallion (1907), Big Game (1942), El Gran Senor (1984).

Most consecutive winning favourites

3 — 1778 to 1790, 1899 to 1901, 1963 to 1965, 1970 to 1972, 1981 to 1983.

Most consecutive losing favourites

8 — 1973 to 1980.

Race venue switched

The 1940 New Derby was to have been run at Newbury on 12 June, but the course became unavailable, so the race was switched to Newmarket.

Earliest date

4 May — 1780

Latest date

31 July — 1917

Latest peacetime date

9 June — 1791

Run on

Tuesday: 1915–18
Wednesday: 1786, 1838–1914, 1919–41, 1946, 1951–52, from 1954
Thursday: 1780–85, 1787–1837
Saturday: 1942–45, 1947–50, 1953

First sponsorship

The 17th Earl of Derby provided all the added money (£1,000) for the 1915 New Derby.

Foreign-trained horses placed 1, 2, 3

In 1956 winner and 2nd (Lavandin and Montaval) were trained in France and 3rd (Roistar) in Ireland.
In 1962 winner Larkspur was trained in Ireland and 2nd and 3rd (Arcor and Le Cantilien) in France.
In 1970 winner Nijinsky was trained in Ireland and 2nd and 3rd (Gyr and Stintino) in France.

Foreign-bred horses placed 1, 2, 3

In 1971 winner Mill Reef was US-bred, and 2nd and 3rd (Linden Tree and Irish Ball) were French-bred.

Foreign-bred horses first 5 to finish

In 1982 winner, 2nd, 3rd and 5th (Golden Fleece, Touching Wood, Silver Hawk and Norwick) were US-bred, and 4th (Persepolis) was French-bred.

Most successful owners

5 wins — 3rd Earl of Egremont: 1782, 1804, 1805, 1807, 1826
HH Aga Khan III: 1930, 1935, 1936, 1948, 1952.
4 wins — John Bowes: 1835, 1843, 1852, 1853
Sir Joseph Hawley: 1851, 1858, 1859, 1868
1st Duke of Westminster: 1880, 1882, 1886, 1899
Sir Victor Sassoon: 1953, 1957, 1958, 1960
3 wins — 1st Earl Grosvenor: 1790, 1792, 1794
5th Duke of Bedford: 1789, 1791, 1797
Sir Frank Standish: 1795, 1796, 1799
3rd Duke of Grafton: 1802, 1809, 1810
Sir Charles Bunbury: 1780, 1801, 1813
5th Earl of Jersey: 1825, 1827, 1836
5th Earl of Rosebery: 1894, 1895, 1905
HM King Edward VII: 1896, 1900, 1909
17th Earl of Derby: 1924, 1933, 1942

2 wins—Dennis O'Kelly: 1781, 1784
Sir Hedworth Williamson: 1803, 1808
Thomas Thornhill: 1818, 1820
HRH Frederick, Duke of York: 1816, 1822
Sir John Shelley: 1811, 1824
G. W. K. Gratwicke: 1829, 1845
John Gully: 1846, 1854
William I'Anson: 1857, 1864
James Merry: 1860, 1873
6th Viscount Falmouth: 1870, 1877
6th Duke of Portland: 1888, 1889
Sir Frederick Johnstone: 1883, 1891
John Gubbins: 1897, 1902
Sir James Miller: 1890, 1903
Alfred Cox: 1910, 1917
Jack Joel: 1911, 1921
1st Baron Woolavington: 1922, 1926
6th Earl of Rosebery: 1939, 1944
Raymond Guest: 1962, 1968
Arthur Budgett: 1969, 1973
Mme Etti Plesch: 1961, 1980
Robert Sangster: 1977, 1982

Owned winner and 2nd

5th Duke of Bedford: 1789
1st Earl Grosvenor: 1790
5th Earl of Jersey: 1827
Jonathan Peel: 1844
HH Aga Khan III: 1936

Most successful breeders

6 wins—3rd Earl of Egremont: 1789, 1804, 1805, 1807, 1826, 1831
4 wins—Sir Frank Standish: 1795, 1796, 1799, 1806
John Bowes: 1835, 1843, 1852, 1853
3 wins—1st Earl Grosvenor: 1790, 1792, 1794
3rd Duke of Grafton: 1802, 1809, 1810
Sir John Shelley: 1811, 1824, 1830
6th Viscount Falmouth: 1870, 1877, 1884
1st Duke of Westminster: 1880, 1886, 1899
5th Earl of Rosebery: 1894, 1895, 1905
17th Earl of Derby: 1924, 1933, 1942
HH Aga Khan III: 1935, 1936, 1952 (one in partnership)
Eddie Taylor: 1970, 1977, 1984
2 wins—5th Duke of Bedford: 1791, 1797
12th Earl of Derby: 1787, 1798
Sir Charles Bunbury: 1801, 1813
Thomas Thornhill: 1818, 1820
HRH Frederick, Duke of York: 1816, 1822
5th Earl of Jersey: 1825, 1836
G. W. K. Gratwicke: 1829, 1845
R. C. Elwes: 1827, 1847
William I'Anson: 1857, 1864
William Blenkiron: 1862, 1867
Sir Joseph Hawley: 1858, 1868
6th Duke of Portland: 1888, 1889
1st Baron Alington: 1883, 1891
HM King Edward VII: 1896, 1900
John Gubbins: 1897, 1902

Sir Tatton Sykes: 1873, 1906
Alfred Cox: 1910, 1917
Richard Croker: 1907, 1919
Jack Joel: 1911, 1921
1st Baron Woolavington: 1922, 1926
6th Earl of Rosebery: 1939, 1944
Léon Volterra: 1938, 1948
Eve Stud: 1957, 1960
Park Farm Stud: 1969, 1973

Bred winner and 2nd

12th Earl of Derby: 1798
Jonathan Peel: 1844
James Cookson: 1861
William Blenkiron: 1867
HH Aga Khan III: 1936
Léon Volterra: 1948
Eddie Taylor: 1984

Most successful trainers

7 wins—Robert Robson: 1793, 1802, 1809, 1810, 1815, 1817, 1823
John Porter: 1868, 1882, 1883, 1886, 1890, 1891, 1899
Fred Darling: 1922, 1925, 1926, 1931, 1938, 1940, 1941
6 wins—Frank Neale: 1782, 1783, 1786, 1788, 1798, 1804
Mat Dawson: 1860, 1870, 1877, 1885, 1894, 1895
Vincent O'Brien: 1962, 1968, 1970, 1972, 1977, 1982
5 wins—Richard Prince: 1795, 1796, 1799, 1806, 1819
Dixon Boyce: 1805, 1807, 1812, 1814, 1828
James Edwards: 1811, 1824, 1825, 1827, 1836
John Scott: 1835, 1842, 1843, 1852, 1853
4 wins—John Pratt: 1785, 1790, 1792, 1794
Richard Marsh: 1896, 1898, 1900, 1909
3 wins—Matt Stephenson: 1789, 1791, 1797
John Forth: 1829, 1840, 1845
Joe Hayhoe: 1871, 1876, 1879
Alec Taylor: 1910, 1917, 1918
Dick Dawson: 1916, 1929, 1930
Noel Murless: 1957, 1960, 1967
2 wins—John Lonsdale: 1803, 1808
Tom Perren: 1800, 1818
Crouch: 1813, 1821
William Butler: 1816, 1822
William Chifney: 1820, 1830
John Day, jr: 1847, 1854
George Manning: 1858, 1859
William I'Anson: 1857, 1864
Tom Dawson: 1856, 1869
Alec Taylor, sr: 1851, 1878
Robert Peck: 1873, 1880
George Dawson: 1888, 1889
James Jewitt: 1884, 1893
Sam Darling: 1897, 1902
Peter Gilpin: 1906, 1920
Charles Morton: 1911, 1921
George Lambton: 1924, 1933
Frank Butters: 1935, 1936

Jack Jarvis: 1939, 1944
Marcus Marsh: 1934, 1952
François Mathet: 1955, 1963
Mick Rogers: 1958, 1964
Arthur Budgett: 1969, 1973
Dick Hern: 1979, 1980

Trained winner and 2nd

John Pratt: 1785, 1790, 1792
Matt Stephenson: 1789
Tom Perren: 1818
James Edwards: 1827
John Forth: 1829
William Cooper: 1844
Alec Taylor: 1918
Frank Butters: 1936
Fred Darling: 1941
Dick Carver: 1948

Most successful jockeys

9 wins—Lester Piggott: 1954, 1957, 1960, 1968, 1970, 1972, 1976, 1977, 1983
6 wins—Jem Robinson: 1817, 1824, 1825, 1827, 1828, 1836
Steve Donoghue: 1915, 1917, 1921, 1922, 1923, 1925.
5 wins—John Arnull: 1784, 1790, 1796, 1799, 1807
Bill Clift: 1793, 1800, 1803, 1810, 1819
Frank Buckle: 1792, 1794, 1802, 1811, 1823
Fred Archer: 1877, 1880, 1881, 1885, 1886
4 wins—Sam Arnull: 1780, 1782, 1787, 1798
Tom Goodisson: 1809, 1813, 1815, 1822
Bill Scott: 1832, 1835, 1842, 1843
Jack Watts: 1887, 1890, 1894, 1896
Charlie Smirke: 1934, 1936, 1952, 1958
3 wins—Charles Hindley: 1781, 1783, 1785
Bill Arnull: 1804, 1812, 1814
Sam Day: 1821, 1830, 1846
Sim Templeman: 1839, 1847, 1848
John Wells: 1858, 1859, 1868
Harry Custance: 1860, 1866, 1874
Charlie Wood: 1883, 1884, 1897
Danny Maher: 1903, 1905, 1906
Joe Childs: 1916, 1918, 1926
Harry Wragg: 1928, 1930, 1942
Billy Nevett: 1941, 1944, 1945
Charlie Elliott: 1927, 1938, 1949
Rae Johnstone: 1948, 1950, 1956
2 wins—Sam Chifney, jr: 1818, 1820
Will Wheatley: 1816, 1831
Jem Chapple: 1833, 1838
Patrick Conolly: 1834, 1841
Job Marson: 1850, 1851
Frank Butler: 1852, 1853
Tom French: 1870, 1871
Charlie Maidment: 1872, 1876
Tommy Loates: 1889, 1894
Sam Loates: 1884, 1895
Herbert Jones: 1900, 1909
Johnny Reiff: 1907, 1912

Lester Piggott had achieved three of his record nine Derby victories when this photograph was taken in 1964.

Tommy Weston: 1924, 1933
Freddie Fox: 1931, 1935
Scobie Breasley: 1964, 1966
Willie Carson: 1979, 1980
Pat Eddery: 1975, 1982

Successful owner-breeder-trainers

Isaac Sadler — Dangerous (1833)
William I'Anson — Blink Bonny (1857), Blair Athol (1864)
Odoardo Ginistrelli — Signorinetta (1908)
Arthur Budgett — Blakeney (1969), Morston (1973)

Successful trainer-riders

Matt Stephenson — Eager (1791)
John Forth — Frederick (1829)

Successful owner-trainers

William Chifney — Priam (1830)
William Ridsdale — Bloomsbury (1839)
Fred Darling — Pont l'Evêque (1940)

Successful as both jockey and trainer

Matt Stephenson rode Eager (1791), trained Skyscraper (1789), Eager (1791) and unnamed Fidget colt (1797).
John Forth rode Frederick (1829), trained Frederick (1829), Little Wonder (1840) and The Merry Monarch (1845).
Robert Sherwood rode Wild Dayrell (1855), trained St Gatien (1884).
Harry Wragg rode Felstead (1928), Blenheim (1930) and Watling Street (1942), trained Psidium (1961).

Most successful sires

4 wins — Sir Peter Teazle: Sir Harry (1798), Archduke (1799), Ditto (1803), Paris (1806)
Waxy: Pope (1809), Whalebone (1810), Blücher (1814), Whisker (1815)
Cyllene: Cicero (1905), Minoru (1909), Lemberg (1910), Tagalie (1912)
Blandford: Trigo (1929), Blenheim (1930), Windsor Lad (1934), Bahram (1935)
3 wins — Eclipse: Young Eclipse (1781), Saltram (1783), Serjeant (1784)
Highflyer: Noble (1786), Sir Peter Teazle (1787), Skyscraper (1789)
Potooooooo: Waxy (1793), Champion (1800), Tyrant (1802)
Whalebone: Moses (1822), Lap-dog (1826), Spaniel (1831)
Touchstone: Cotherstone (1843), Orlando (1844), Surplice (1848)
Stockwell: Blair Athol (1864), Lord Lyon (1866), Doncaster (1873)
Hampton: Merry Hampton (1887), Ayrshire (1888), Ladas (1894)
Polymelus: Pommern (1915), Fifinella (1916), Humorist (1921)
Hurry On: Captain Cuttle (1922), Coronach (1926), Call Boy (1927)
Northern Dancer: Nijinsky (1970), The Minstrel (1977), Secreto (1984)
2 wins — Florizel: Diomed (1780), Eager (1791)
Justice: Rhadamanthus (1790), Daedalus (1794)

Gohanna: Cardinal Beaufort (1805), Election (1807)
Scud: Sam (1818), Sailor (1820)
Orville: Octavius (1812), Emilius (1823)
Phantom: Cedric (1824), Middleton (1825)
Tramp: St Giles (1832), Dangerous (1833)
Emilius: Priam (1830), Plenipotentiary (1834)
Bay Middleton: The Flying Dutchman (1849), Andover (1854)
Melbourne: West Australian (1853), Blink Bonny (1857)
Newminster: Musjid (1859), Hermit (1867)
Parmesan: Favonius (1871), Cremorne (1872)
Hermit: Shotover (1882), St Blaise (1883)
Isonomy: Common (1891), Isinglass (1893)
St Simon: Persimmon (1896), Diamond Jubilee (1900)
Orme: Flying Fox (1899), Orby (1907)
Bayardo: Gay Crusader (1917), Gainsborough (1918)
Fairway: Blue Peter (1939), Watling Street (1942)
Solario: Mid-day Sun (1937), Straight Deal (1943)
Vatellor: Pearl Diver (1947), My Love (1948)
Nearco: Dante (1945), Nimbus (1949)
Great Nephew: Grundy (1975), Shergar (1981)

Sired winner, 2nd and 3rd

Sir Peter Teazle (1803)
Stockwell (1866)

Sired winner and 2nd

Sweetbriar (1782)
Eclipse (1783)
Sir Peter Teazle (1798)
Isonomy (1893)
St Simon (1896, 1900)
Swynford (1924)
Northern Dancer (1984)
In 1873 Stockwell was responsible for winner Doncaster and Gang Forward, one of the dead-heaters for second place.

Oaks

Title

Oakes Stakes 1779–86
Oaks Stakes 1787–1914
New Oaks Stakes 1915–18
Oaks Stakes 1919–39
New Oaks Stakes 1940–44
Oaks Stakes 1945–83
Gold Seal Oaks Stakes from 1984

Venue

Epsom Downs, Surrey 1779–1914
Summer Course, Newmarket, Cambridgeshire 1915–18
Epsom Downs, Surrey 1919–39
Summer Course, Newmarket, Cambridgeshire 1940–45
Epsom Downs, Surrey from 1946

Distance

1 mile 4 furlongs 1779–1871
1 mile 4 furlongs 29 yards 1872–1914
1 mile 4 furlongs 1915–18
1 mile 4 furlongs 29 yards 1919–20
1 mile 4 furlongs 1921–33
1 mile 4 furlongs 5 yards 1934–37
1 mile 4 furlongs from 1938

Continued on page 46

FRED ARCHER

The most romantic and tragic figure of his time on the Turf, Frederick James Archer was arguably also the greatest jockey of any era. His was an age when the nobility and gentry dominated the racing scene, but the professionals, the horsemen who were their paid servants, were beginning to advance in status and receive the respect which their skills merited. Archer, by far the most gifted of his generation, became the sport's first folk hero.

Born at Cheltenham on 11 January 1857, Fred Archer was the son of a celebrated jump jockey whose career reached its zenith in a Grand National victory aboard Little Charley in 1858. There was never much doubt that Fred would also become a jockey, his father having no qualms about neglecting his formal education and concentrating on developing his talents on horseback. The boy soon learned to decipher the form book and to appreciate the meaning of weights and distances, while money was a subject which he seemed to know instinctively, but otherwise he had no use for reading and arithmetic. Writing he made no attempt to master, even the execution of his signature being almost beyond him, but there was always his friend Joseph Davis to attend to his correspondence.

Fred was only 11 years old when he was taken to Newmarket to be apprenticed to

Mathew Dawson, the foremost trainer of his age. At first he felt desperately lonely and homesick, but in time he overcame his fears in his devotion to his chosen profession and the development of an obsessive ambitious streak. Dawson was not slow to realise the boy's talent and determination to succeed, and he knew well how to exploit those traits.

Archer had his first mount in public at the age of 12 and his first winner at 13, on a 2-year-old filly called Athol Daisy at Malton. At 15, though still required to fulfil the usual stable lad's duties at home, he was given regular employment in races, and from 180 mounts he recorded 27 wins. During the following season, 1873, Dawson's stable jockey, Tom French, died, and the youngster was entrusted with many more opportunities; he used them well and his tally of 107 victories brought him second place in the jockeys' table, only three behind Harry Constable. Thereafter there was only one champion in Archer's lifetime.

From 1874, a season he began at 6 st 2 lb, until 1886, when he weighed out for his last mount, a pound overweight at 9 st, he reigned supreme, the idol of the public and acknowledged as the master by his fellow professionals. His style was not pretty—vigorous always, often active with whip and spur—but none could match the effect he produced. Out of the saddle he was a soft-spoken, unassuming character, but in competition he displayed a ruthless will to win which his rivals found intimidating and inspired his legions of followers to countless displays of admiration and affection.

For all his lack of education, Archer had a shrewd tactical brain and was rarely outwitted. His judgment of pace was exemplary, his nerve and his strength in a finish apparently superhuman. In common with many of the other leading practitioners of his profession, he owned the ideal temperament for the big occasion, but such was his brand of dedication that any race, whether it was the Derby or a selling plate in the provinces, would inspire him to peak performance. He was addicted to winners, of any description, and the public naturally loved him for it. At his death it was rightly said, 'Backers have lost the best friend they ever had.'

Archer's record of 13 consecutive championships has yet to be matched and his career ratio of 34.33 per cent winners to mounts (2,748 to 8,004) seems destined to stand for all time. He exceeded 200 winners on 8 occasions, twice (in 1881 and 1884) winning on more than 41 per cent of his rides. His tally of 21 Classic victories accrued from only 62 such mounts, the triumphs including five in the Derby and six in the St Leger.

Archer was inevitably associated with many of the great horses of his time, among them St Simon (as a 2-year-old only), Ormonde and the superb filly Wheel of Fortune. But the most striking illustrations of his courage, determination, dedication and incomparable brilliance in the saddle came in 1880 after he had been savaged on the gallops by a horse called Muley Edris. The injuries he received were severe, but he could not be persuaded to give up promising mounts in the Prix du Jockey-Club (French Derby) and the Derby. Riding with one arm held together by an iron splint, he won at Chantilly by a short head on Beauminet and at Epsom by a head on Bend Or. Only after the double had been achieved would he take the two-month break from racing which the injury required to heal.

While Archer's deeds in the saddle brought him fame and considerable fortune (his will was proved at £60,000), he enjoyed little luck in his personal life. A happy marriage to Mat Dawson's niece Nellie was destined to be brief and grief-stricken. Their first-born son died on the day of his birth, and Nellie herself died after delivering their only other child, a daughter. Archer was inconsolable, and though his incessant quest for winners continued, he became increasingly morose and liable to fits of depression, especially when the necessity to waste sapped his energy. He was already losing his battle against the scales and he could not have continued riding much longer, even if the final tragedy had not occurred in November 1886. Then, desperately weak from wasting, he took to his bed and typhoid fever was diagnosed. When the delirium passed and he seemed to be over the worst, a morbid depression overtook him and he shot himself. He died instantly, at the age of 29.

Weight
8 st 4 lb 1779–84
8 st 0 lb 1785–1806
8 st 3 lb 1807
8 st 4 lb 1808–40
8 st 7 lb 1841–61
8 st 10 lb 1862–91
9 st 0 lb from 1892

1779 12th Earl of Derby's b f **Bridget**
J: Dick Goodisson 5/2 Fav £840
2. Fame 3. Lavinia 12 ran
1780 Thomas Douglas's b f **Tetotum** no
jockey recorded 6/4 Jt-Fav £840
2. Thetis 3. b f by Goldfinder 11 ran
1781 1st Earl Grosvenor's b f **Faith** no
jockey recorded 4/1 £787 2. Dido
3. Camilla 6 ran
1782 1st Earl Grosvenor's b f **Ceres**
J: Sam Chifney 4/7 Fav £955
2. Countess 3. Catchfly 12 ran
1783 1st Earl Grosvenor's ch f **Maid of
the Oaks** J: Sam Chifney 4/1 Fav
£834 2. Hebae 3. Primrose 10 ran
1784 Philip Burlton's b f **Stella**
J: Charles Hindley 20/1 £829 2. Lady
Teazle 3. Elden 10 ran
1785 1st Earl of Clermont's br f **Trifle**
J: J. Bird 5/1 £787 2. br f by Trentham
3. Miss Kitty 8 ran
1786 Sir Frank Standish's ch f **Yellow
Filly** J: James Edwards 5/2 Fav £918
2. Letitia 3. Scota 13 ran
1787 Richard Vernon's b f **Annette**
J: Dennis Fitzpatrick 4/6 Fav £787
2. Augusta 3. b f by Alfred 8 ran
1788 3rd Earl of Egremont's b f
Nightshade J: Dennis Fitzpatrick
1/2 Fav £603 2. Busy 3. b f by Alfred
7 ran
1789 3rd Earl of Egremont's b f **Tag**
J: Sam Chifney 5/2 Jt-Fav £603
2. Olivia 3. Hope 7 ran
1790 5th Duke of Bedford's ch f
Hippolyta J: Sam Chifney 6/1 £735
2. Mistletoe 3. b f by Giant 12 ran
1791 5th Duke of Bedford's ch f **Portia**
J: John Singleton, jr 2/1 and 5/2
£1,181 2. Astraea 3. Kezia 9 ran
1792 1st Earl of Clermont's b f **Volante**
J: Charles Hindley 4/1 £1,200
2. Trumpetta 3. Boldface 11 ran
1793 5th Duke of Bedford's br f **Caelia**
J: John Singleton, jr 4/1 £1,181
2. Black Puss 3. Rachel 10 ran
1794 12th Earl of Derby's br f **Hermione**
J: Sam Arnull 5/2 £971 2. Eliza
3. Jessica 8 ran
1795 3rd Earl of Egremont's ch f **Platina**
J: Dennis Fitzpatrick 3/1 £1,233
2. Ariadne 3. b f by Justice 11 ran
1796 Sir Frank Standish's br f **Parisot**
J: John Arnull 7/2 £1,286
2. Miss Whip 3. Outcast 13 ran
1797 1st Earl Grosvenor's b f **Niké**
J: Frank Buckle 15/8 Fav £797
2. Mother Shipton 3. Rose 5 ran
1798 John Durand's b f **Bellissima**
J: Frank Buckle 6/4 Fav £840

2. Duchess of Limbs 3. Lady Bull
7 ran
1799 1st Earl Grosvenor's ch f **Bellina**
J: Frank Buckle 5/2 £682 2. Lady
Jane 3. St Ann 4 ran
1800 3rd Earl of Egremont's ch f
Ephemera J: Dennis Fitzpatrick
9/4 Fav £787 2. Wowski 3. Miss
Totteridge 8 ran
1801 Sir Charles Bunbury's b f **Eleanor**
J: John Saunders 4/7 and 1/2 Fav
£577 2. Tulip 3. Crazy Poetess 6 ran
1802 John Wastell's gr f **Scotia**
J: Frank Buckle 5/4 and 6/4 Fav
£551 2. Julia 3. Tooee 6 ran
1803 Sir Thomas Gascoigne's b f
Theophania J: Frank Buckle 5/2
£656 2. Fanny 3. Parasol 7 ran
1804 3rd Duke of Grafton's br f **Pelisse**
J: Bill Clift 4/5 Fav £656 2. Slipper
3. Maud 8 ran
1805 2nd Earl Grosvenor's b f **Meteora**
J: Frank Buckle 7/2 and 3/1 £761
2. Dodona 3. b f by Sir Peter Teazle
8 ran
1806 Berkeley Craven's br f **Bronze**
J: William Edwards 10/1 £866
2. Jerboa 3. Rosabella 12 ran
1807 Thomas Grosvenor's b f **Briseïs**
J: Sam Chifney, jr 15/1 £1,007
2. Margaret 3. Pantina 13 ran
1808 3rd Duke of Grafton's ch f **Morel**
J: Bill Clift 3/1 Fav £918
2. Goosander 3. Miranda 10 ran
1809 John Leveson Gower's b f **Maid
of Orleans** J: Ben Moss 100/6 £997
2. Zaïda 3. Spindle 11 ran
1810 Sir William Gerard's b f **Oriana**
J: Bill Peirse 4/1 £1,097 2. Pirouette
3. Donna Clara 11 ran
1811 5th Duke of Rutland's b f **Sorcery**
J: Sam Chifney, jr 3/1 Fav £1,207
2. b f by Young Eagle 3. Arquebusade
12 ran
1812 W.N.W. Hewett's b f **Manuella**
J: Bill Peirse 20/1 £1,207
2. Elizabeth 3. b f by Gohanna 12 ran
1813 4th Duke of Grafton's b f **Music**
J: Tom Goodisson 5/2 Fav £1,233
2. Vulpecula 3. Wilful 9 ran
1814 5th Duke of Rutland's ch f **Medora**
J: Sam Barnard 10/1 £1,233
2. Vestal 3. Wire 9 ran
1815 4th Duke of Grafton's b f **Minuet**
J: Tom Goodisson 3/1 Jt-Fav £1,417
2. Mouse 3. Nadejda 12 ran
1816 John Leveson Gower's b f
Landscape J: Sam Chifney, jr
2/1 Fav £1,391 2. Duenna 3. Johanna
11 ran
1817 George Watson's b f **Neva**
J: Frank Buckle Evens Fav £1,365
2. Amabel 3. b f by Election 11 ran
1818 John Udney's br f **Corinne**
J: Frank Buckle 5/2 £1,338 2. Fay
3. Fanny 10 ran
1819 Thomas Thornhill's b f **Shoveler**
J: Sam Chifney, jr 2/1 £1,881
2. Espagnolle 3. Schedam 10 ran
1820 3rd Earl of Egremont's b f
Caroline J: Harry Edwards 8/1

*Lord George Bentinck, the dominant
figure of his time on the English Turf,
owned Crucifix, the brilliant triple Classic
heroine of 1840. He was instrumental in
exposing the fraud over 'Running Rein' in
the 1844 Derby.*

£1,217 2. Rowena 3. Bombasine
13 ran
1821 2nd Marquis of Exeter's b f
Augusta J: Jem Robinson 20/11 Fav
£1,155 2. Ibla 3. My Lady 7 ran
1822 4th Duke of Grafton's b f **Pastille**
J: Harry Edwards 7/2 £1,207 2. ch f by
Rubens 3. Madelina 10 ran
1823 4th Duke of Grafton's br f **Zinc**
J: Frank Buckle Evens and 5/6 Fav
£1,233 2. Dandizette 3. b f by Pioneer
10 ran
1824 5th Earl of Jersey's b f **Cobweb**
J: Jem Robinson 8/11 Fav £1,260
2. Fille de Joie 3. Rebecca 13 ran
1825 Thomas Grosvenor's ch f **Wings**
J: Sam Chifney, jr 13/1 £1,350
2. Pastime 3. Tontine 10 ran
1826 John Forth's b f **Lilias** J: Tommy
Lye 15/1 £1,450 2. Problem
3. Mignonette 15 ran
1827 5th Duke of Richmond's b f
Gulnare J: Frank Boyce 14/1 £2,300
2. Translation 3. Brocard 19 ran
1828 4th Duke of Grafton's br f
Turquoise J: John Barham Day
25/1 £2,150 2. Ruby 3. Rosetta
14 ran
1829 2nd Marquis of Exeter's b f **Green
Mantle** J: George Dockeray 5/2
£2,125 2. Varna 3. Clotilde 14 ran
1830 Scott Stonehewer's b f **Variation**
J: George Edwards 28/1 £2,225
2. Mouche 3. Jenny Vertpré 18 ran
1831 4th Duke of Grafton's b f **Oxygen**
J: John Barham Day 12/1 £2,425
2. Marmora 3. Guitar 21 ran
1832 2nd Marquis of Exeter's br f
Galata J: Patrick Conolly 9/4 £2,300
2. Lady Fly 3. Eleanor 19 ran

1833 Sir Mark Wood's br f **Vespa**
J: Jem Chapple 50/1 £2,625
2. Octave 3. Revelry 19 ran

1834 Thomas Cosby's br f **Pussy**
J: John Barham Day 20/1 £2,500
2. Louisa 3. Lady Le Gros 15 ran

1835 Edward Lloyd Mostyn's br f **Queen of Trumps** J: Tommy Lye 8/1 £2,450
2. Preserve 3. Bodice 10 ran

1836 John Scott's b f **Cyprian** J: Bill Scott 9/4 Fav £2,500 2. Destiny
3. Marmalade 12 ran

1837 Thomas Orde-Powlett's b f **Miss Letty** J: John Holmes 7/1 £2,375
2. Chapeau d'Espagne 3. Velure
13 ran

1838 6th Earl of Chesterfield's br f **Industry** J: Bill Scott 9/2 £2,575
2. Callisto 3. Mecca 16 ran

1839 Fulwar Craven's b f **Deception**
J: John Barham Day 8/13 Fav £2,450
2. Carolina 3. Louisa 13 ran

1840 Lord George Bentinck's b f **Crucifix** J: John Barham Day
1/3 Fav £2,700 2. Welfare 3. Teleta
15 ran

1841 1st Marquis of Westminster's b f **Ghuznee** J: Bill Scott 7/4 Fav £3,250
2. Miss Stilton 3. Disclosure 22 ran

1842 George Dawson's ch f **Our Nell**
J: Tommy Lye 8/1 £3,025 2. Meal
3. Firebrand 16 ran

1843 George Ford's ch f **Poison**
J: Frank Butler 30/1 £2,600
2. Extempore 3. Mania 23 ran

1844 George Anson's ch f **The Princess** J: Frank Butler 5/1 £3,300
2. Merope 3. Barricade 25 ran

1845 5th Duke of Richmond's br f **Refraction** J: Henry Bell 25/1 £3,475
2. Hope 3. Miss Sarah 21 ran

1846 John Gully's br f **Mendicant**
J: Sam Day 9/4 Fav £3,750
2. Laundry Maid 3. Conspiracy 24 ran

1847 Sir Joseph Hawley's b f **Miami**
J: Sim Templeman 9/1 £4,125
2. Clementina 3. Ellerdale 23 ran

1848 Harry Hill's br f **Cymba** J: Sim Templeman 7/1 £4,250 2. Attraction
3. Queen of the May 26 ran

1849 6th Earl of Chesterfield's br f **Lady Evelyn** J: Frank Butler 3/1 Jt-Fav
£4,425 2. Lady Superior 3. Woodlark
15 ran

1850 George Hobson's b f **Rhedycina**
J: Frank Butler 6/1 £3,285
2. Kathleen 3. Countess 15 ran

1851 Baron Stanley's ch f **Irish** J: Frank Butler 4/1 £3,370 2. Miserrima
3. Hesse Homburg 15 ran

1852 John Scott's b f **Songstress**
J: Frank Butler 2/1 Fav £3,145
2. Bird on the Wing 3. Gossamer
14 ran

1853 John Don Wauchope's br f **Catherine Hayes** J: Charlie Marlow
2/1 Fav £3,670 2. Dove 3. Miss Sarah
17 ran

1854 William Cookson's b f **Mincemeat**
J: Jack Charlton 10/1 £3,995
2. Meteora 3. Bribery 15 ran

1855 William Rudston Read's b f **Marchioness** J: Sim Templeman
12/1 £4,045 2. Blooming Heather
3. Capucine 11 ran

1856 Harry Hill's ch f **Mincepie** J: Alfred Day 5/2 Fav £3,345 2. Melissa
3. Victoria 10 ran

1857 Wiliam I'Anson's b f **Blink Bonny**
J: Jack Charlton 4/5 Fav £3,295
2. Sneeze 3. Moestissima 13 ran

1858 G. W. K. Gratwicke's ch f **Governess** J; Tom Ashmall 4/1
£3,845 2. Gildermire 3. Tunstall Maid
13 ran

1859 1st Baron Londesborough's br f **Summerside** J: George Fordham
4/1 £4,295 2. Scent 3. Wild Rose
15 ran

1860 Richard Eastwood's ch f **Butterfly**
J: Jim Snowden 10/1 £3,995
2. Avalanche 3. Contadina 13 ran

1861 Joseph Saxon's br f **Brown Duchess** J: Luke Snowden 100/7
£4,420 2. Lady Ripon 3. Fairwater
17 ran

1862 Richard Naylor's ch f **Feu de Joie**
J: Tom Chaloner 20/1 £4,045
2. Imperatrice 3. Hurricane 19 ran

1863 6th Viscount Falmouth's b f **Queen Bertha** J: Tom Aldcroft 40/1 £4,845
2. Marigold 3. Vivid 20 ran

1864 Comte Frédéric de Lagrange's ch f **Fille de l'Air** J: Arthur Edwards
6/4 Fav £5,025 2. Breeze 3. Tomato
19 ran

1865 William Graham's ch f **Regalia**
J: John Norman 20/1 £5,225 2. Wild Agnes 3. Zephyr 18 ran

1866 Benjamin Ellam's b f **Tormentor**
J: Jimmy Mann 5/1 £4,650 2. Mirella
3. Ischia 17 ran

1867 Baron Meyer de Rothschild's b f **Hippia** J: John Daley 11/1 £5,200
2= Achievement and Romping Girl
8 ran

1868 William Graham's ch f **Formosa**
J: George Fordham 8/11 Fav £5,450
2. Lady Coventry 3. Athena 9 ran

1869 Sir Frederick Johnstone's b f **Brigantine** J: Tom Cannon 7/2
£4,550 2. Morna 3. Martinique 15 ran

1870 William Graham's ch f **Gamos**
J: George Fordham 100/8 £4,350
2. Sunshine 3. Paté 7 ran

1871 Baron Meyer de Rothschild's b f **Hannah** J: Charlie Maidment 6/5 Fav
£4,100 2. Noblesse 3. Hopbine 9 ran

1872 Joachim Lefèvre's b f **Reine**
J: George Fordham 3/1 £4,175
2. Louise Victoria 3. Guadaloupe
17 ran

1873 James Merry's ch f **Marie Stuart**
J: Tom Cannon 2/1 Fav £3,425
2. Wild Myrtle 3. Angela 18 ran

1874 John King's ch f **Apology** J: John Osborne 5/2 £4,375 2. Miss Toto
3. Lady Patricia 11 ran

1875 6th Viscount Falmouth's b f **Spinaway** J: Fred Archer 5/4 Fav
£2,925 2. Ladylove 3. Empress 7 ran

1876 Auguste Lupin's b f **Enguerrande**
J: Hudson 4/1 £2,150 *dead-heated with* Comte Frédéric de Lagrange's
ch f **Camélia** J: Tom Glover 5/4 Fav
£2,150 3. Merry Duchess 14 ran

1877 John Fiennes's br f **Placida**
J: Harry Jeffery 2/1 Fav £4,150
2. Belphoebe 3. Muscatel 9 ran

1878 6th Viscount Falmouth's b f **Jannette** J: Fred Archer 65/40
£5,000 2. Pilgrimage 3. Clementine
8 ran

1879 6th Viscount Falmouth's b f **Wheel of Fortune** J: Fred Archer 1/3 Fav
£4,425 2. Coromandel 3. Adventure
8 ran

1880 Charles Perkins's ch f **Jenny Howlet** J: Jim Snowden 33/1 £4,500
2. Bonnie Marden 3. War Horn 13 ran

1881 William Stirling Crawfurd's ch f **Thebais** J: George Fordham 4/6 Fav
£4,050 2. Lucy Glitters 3. Myra 12 ran

1882 7th Earl of Stamford's br f **Geheimniss** J: Tom Cannon 4/6 Fav
£3,375 2. St Marguerite 3. Nellie
5 ran

1883 5th Earl of Rosebery's b f **Bonny Jean** J: Jack Watts 5/1 £3,475
2. Malibran 3. Ettarre 14 ran

1884 George Baird's b f **Busybody**
J: Tom Cannon 100/105 Fav £3,425
2. Superba 3. Queen Adelaide 9 ran

1885 5th Earl Cadogan's b f **Lonely**
J: Fred Archer 85/40 Fav £3,350
2. St Helena 3. Cipollina 10 ran

1886 12th Duke of Hamilton's b f **Miss Jummy** J: Jack Watts Evens Fav
£3,250 2. Argo Navis 3. Braw Lass
12 ran

1887 8th Duke of Beaufort's ch f **Rêve d'Or** J: Charlie Wood 8/11 Fav
£3,275 2. St Helen 3. Freedom 9 ran

1888 5th Baron Calthorpe's ch f **Seabreeze** J: Jack Robinson 7/4
£2,950 2. Rada 3. Belle Mahone
6 ran

1889 Lord Randolph Churchill's bl f **L'Abbesse de Jouarre** J: Jimmy Woodburn 20/1 £2,600 2. Minthe
3. Seclusion 12 ran

1890 6th Duke of Portland's br f **Memoir** J: Jack Watts 100/30
£4,400 2. Signorina 3. Ponza 7 ran

1891 Noel Fenwick's b f **Mimi** J: Fred Rickaby 4/7 Fav £4,405
2. Corstorphine 3. Lady Primrose
6 ran

1892 Baron Maurice de Hirsch's br f **La Flèche** J: George Barrett 8/11 Fav
£5,270 2. The Smew 3. Lady Hermit
7 ran

1893 6th Duke of Portland's b f **Mrs Butterwick** J: Jack Watts 100/7
£5,130 2. Tressure 3. Cypria 17 ran

1894 6th Duke of Portland's b f **Amiable** J: Walter Bradford 7/1
£4,825 2. Sweet Duchess 3. Sarana
11 ran

1895 Sir James Miller's b f **La Sagesse**
J: Sam Loates 5/1 £4,150
2. Galeottia 3. Penkridge 15 ran

1896 16th Earl of Derby's ch f

Canterbury Pilgrim J: Fred Rickaby 100/8 £4,150 2. Thaïs 3. Proposition 11 ran

1897 2nd Baron Hindlip's ch f **Limasol** J: Walter Bradford 100/8 £4,195 2. Chélandry 3. Fortalice 8 ran

1898 W. T. Jones's br f **Airs and Graces** J: Walter Bradford 100/8 £4,375 2. Nun Nicer 3. Cauliflower 13 ran

1899 Douglas Baird's b f **Musa** J: Otto Madden 20/1 £4,150 2. Sibola 3. Corposant 12 ran

1900 6th Duke of Portland's b f **La Roche** J: Morny Cannon 5/1 £4,550 2. Merry Gal 3. Lady Schomberg 14 ran

1901 Foxhall Keene's b or br f **Cap and Bells** J: Milton Henry 9/4 Fav £5,305 T: Sam Darling, Beckhampton, Wiltshire B: Owner and James R. Keene Sire: Domino 2. Sabrinetta 3. Minnie Dee 6*l*, 2*l* 2:44.4 21 ran

1902 Bob Sievier's b f **Sceptre** J: Bert Randall 5/2 Fav £4,150 T: Owner, Shrewton, Wiltshire B: 1st Duke of Westminster Sire: Persimmon 2. Glass Jug 3. Elba 3*l*, 1½*l* 2:46.6 14 ran

1903 Jack Joel's b f **Our Lassie** J: Morny Cannon 6/1 £4,950 T: Charles Morton, Wantage, Berkshire B: Owner Sire: Ayrshire 2. Hammerkop 3. Skyscraper 3*l*, head 2:44.6 10 ran

1904 Eustace Loder's ch f **Pretty Polly** J: Willie Lane 8/100 Fav £4,950 T: Peter Gilpin, Newmarket B: Owner Sire: Gallinule 2. Bitters 3. Fiancée 3*l*, bad 2:46.2 4 ran

1905 William Hall Walker's b f **Cherry Lass** J: Herbert Jones 4/5 Fav £4,950 T: Jack Robinson, Foxhill, Wiltshire B: Owner Sire: Isinglass 2. Queen of the Earth 3. Amitié 3*l*, 6*l* 2:38.0 12 ran

1906 16th Earl of Derby's b f **Keystone** J: Danny Maher 5/2 Fav £4,950 T: George Lambton, Newmarket B: Owner Sire: Persimmon 2. Gold Riach 3. Snow Glory 3*l*, 1½*l* 2:38.6 12 ran

1907 Jack Joel's b f **Glass Doll** J: Bert Randall 25/1 £4,950 T: Charles Morton, Wantage, Berkshire B: Owner Sire: Isinglass 2. Laomedia 3. Lady Hasty ½*l*, ¾*l* 2:42.0 14 ran

1908 Odoardo Ginistrelli's b or br f **Signorinetta** J: Billy Bullock 3/1 £4,950 T: Owner, Newmarket B: Owner Sire: Chaleureux 2. Courtesy 3. Santeve ¾*l*, 2*l* 2:42.4 13 ran

1909 William Cooper's ch f **Perola** J: Frank Wootton 5/1 £4,950 T: Saunders Davies, Michel Grove, Sussex B: Sir Daniel Cooper Sire: Persimmon 2. Princesse de Galles 3. Verne 2*l*, 2*l* 2:39.8 14 ran

1910 Sir William Bass's ch f **Rosedrop** J: Charlie Trigg 7/1 £4,950 T: Alec

Taylor, Manton, Wiltshire B: J. A. Doyle Sire: St Frusquin 2. Evolution 3. Pernelle 4*l*, neck 2:38.2 11 ran

1911 William Brodrick Cloete's b or br f **Cherimoya** J: Fred Winter 25/1 £4,950 T: Charlie Marsh, Newmarket B: Owner Sire: Cherry Tree 2. Tootles 3. Hair Trigger 3*l*, 5*l* 2:41.6 21 ran

1912 Jean Prat's b f **Mirska** J: Joe Childs 33/1 £4,950 T: Tom Jennings, jr, Newmarket B: Douglas Baird Sire: St Frusquin 2. Equitable 3. Bill and Coo 3*l*, ¾*l* 2:43.0 14 ran

1913 Jack Joel's ch f **Jest** J: Fred Rickaby, jr 8/1 £4,950 T: Charles Morton, Wantage, Berkshire B: Owner Sire: Sundridge 2. Dépêche 3. Arda 2*l*, ½*l* 2:37.6 12 ran

1914 Jack Joel's br f **Princess Dorrie** J: Bill Huxley 11/4 Fav £4,950 T: Charles Morton, Wantage, Berkshire B: Owner Sire: Your Majesty 2. Wassilissa 3. Torchlight 2*l*, 4*l* 2.38.2 21 ran

1915 Ludwig Neumann's b f **Snow Marten** J: Walter Griggs 20/1 £1,400 T: Peter Gilpin, Newmarket B: Owner Sire: Martagon 2. Bright 3. Silver Tag 4*l*, head 2:36.2 11 ran

1916 Sir Edward Hulton's ch f **Fifinella** J: Joe Childs 8/13 Fav £1,100 T: Dick Dawson, Newmarket B: Owner Sire: Polymelus 2. Salamandra 3. Market Girl 5*l*, ½*l* 2:35.0 7 ran

1917 Waldorf Astor's ch f **Sunny Jane** J: Otto Madden 4/1 £875 T: Alec Taylor, Manton, Wiltshire B: Owner Sire: Sunstar 2. Diadem 3. Moravia ½*l*, 4*l* 2:43.4 11 ran

1918 Alfred Cox's b f **My Dear** J: Steve Donoghue 3/1 Fav £3,400 T: Alec Taylor, Manton, Wiltshire B: Owner Sire: Beppo 2= Ferry and Silver Bullet 4*l*, dead-heat 2:34.8 15 ran

(Stony Ford finished first, disqualified)

1919 Lady James Douglas's b f **Bayuda** J: Joe Childs 100/7 £4,950 T: Alec Taylor, Manton, Wiltshire B: Owner Sire: Bayardo 2. Roseway 3. Mapledurham 1½*l*, 1½*l* 2:37.2 10 ran

1920 Alan Cunliffe's bl f **Charlebelle** J: Albert Whalley 7/2 £4,950 T: Sandy Braime, Burbage, Wiltshire B: Owner Sire: Charles O'Malley 2. Cinna 3. Roselet neck, 4*l* 2:38.2 17 ran

1921 Joseph Watson's b or br f **Love in Idleness** J: Joe Childs 5/1 Fav £4,950 T: Alec Taylor, Manton, Wiltshire B: Sir Gilbert Greenall Sire: Bachelor's Double 2. Lady Sleipner 3. Long Suit 3*l*, neck 2:38.4 22 ran

1922 2nd Viscount Astor's b f **Pogrom** J: Ted Gardner 5/4 Fav £6,620 T: Alec Taylor, Manton, Wiltshire B: Owner Sire: Lemberg 2. Soubriquet 3. Mysia ¾*l*, 3*l* 2:36.2 11 ran

1923 Vicomte de Fontarce's b f **Brownhylda** J: Vic Smyth 10/1 £8,105 T: Dick Dawson, Whatcombe, Berkshire B: F. W. Dunn Sire: Stedfast 2. Shrove 3. Teresina neck, head 2:37.0 12 ran

1924 Sir Edward Hulton's br f **Straitlace** J: Frank O'Neill 100/30 £8,645 T: Dawson Waugh, Newmarket B: Lady Sykes Sire: Son-in-Law 2. Plack 3. Mink 1½*l*, head 2:47.0 12 ran

1925 2nd Viscount Astor's br f **Saucy Sue** J: Frank Bullock 30/100 Fav £7,625 T: Alec Taylor, Manton, Wiltshire B: Owner Sire: Swynford 2. Miss Gadabout 3. Riding Light 8*l*, 8*l* 2:38.2 12 ran

Pretty Polly was by far the best racehorse of her time in England, and her odds of 8/100 in the 1904 Oaks are the shortest ever returned in any Classic. She later became an influential broodmare.

1926 2nd Viscount Astor's b f **Short Story** J: Bobby Jones 5/1 Fav £8,485 T: Alec Taylor, Manton, Wiltshire B: Owner Sire: Buchan 2. Resplendent 3. Gay Bird 4l, 2l 2:43.6 16 ran

1927 3rd Earl of Durham's b f **Beam** J: Tommy Weston 4/1 £9,410 T: Frank Butters, Newmarket B: Owner Sire: Galloper Light 2. Book Law 3. Grande Vitesse head, 6l, 2:34.6 16 ran

1928 17th Earl of Derby's b f **Toboggan** J: Tommy Weston 100/15 £8,745 T: Frank Butters, Newmarket B: Owner Sire: Hurry On 2. Scuttle 3. Flégère 4l, 6l 2:37.4 13 ran

1929 2nd Viscount Astor's b f **Pennycomequick** J: Henri Jelliss 11/10 Fav £8,015 T: Joe Lawson, Manton, Wiltshire B: Owner Sire: Hurry On 2. Golden Silence 3. Sister Anne 5l, 2l 2:35.8 13 ran

1930 1st Baron Glanely's br f **Rose of England** J: Gordon Richards 7/1 £8,153 T: Tommy Hogg, Newmarket B: Lady James Douglas Sire: Teddy 2. Wedding Favour 3. Micmac 3l, 2l 2:39.0 15 ran

1931 Charles Birkin's b f **Brulette** J: Charlie Elliott 7/2 Jt-Fav £9,067 T: Frank Carter, Chantilly, France B: Owner Sire: Brûleur 2. Four Course 3. Links Tor 1l, ¾l 2:39.2 15 ran

1932 HH Aga Khan III's br f **Udaipur** J: Michael Beary 10/1 £7,205 T: Frank Butters, Newmarket B: Owner Sire: Blandford 2. Will O' the Wisp 3. Giudecca 2l, 2l 2:43.2 12 ran

1933 Ernest Thornton-Smith's b f **Châtelaine** J: Sam Wragg 25/1 £6,725 T: Fred Templeman, Lambourn, Berkshire B: Lady Sykes Sire: Phalaris 2. Solfatara 3. Fur Tor 1½l, 2l 2:36.8 14 ran

1934 5th Earl of Durham's br f **Light Brocade** J: Brownie Carslake 7/4 Fav £6,436 T: Frank Butters, Newmarket B: Owner Sire: Galloper Light 2. Zelina 3. Instantaneous 1½l, ½l 2:35.2 8 ran

1935 Baron Stanley's br f **Quashed** J: Henri Jelliss 33/1 £7,159 T: Colledge Leader, Newmarket B: Lady Barbara Smith Sire: Obliterate 2. Ankaret 3. Mesa short head, 2l 2:41.4 17 ran

1936 Sir Abe Bailey's b f **Lovely Rosa** J: Tommy Weston 33/1 £7,669 T: Harry Cottrill, Lambourn, Berkshire B: E. J. Hope Sire: Tolgus 2. Barrowby Gem 3. Feola ¾l, 2l 2:36.0 17 ran

1937 Sir Victor Sassoon's b f **Exhibitionnist** J: Steve Donoghue 3/1 Fav £7,133 T: Joe Lawson, Manton, Wiltshire B: Owner Sire: Solario 2. Sweet Content 3. Sculpture 3l, head 2:36.8 13 ran

1938 Sir Hugo Cunliffe-Owen's br f **Rockfel** J: Harry Wragg 3/1 Fav £7,320 T: Ossie Bell, Lambourn, Berkshire B: Weir Bank Stud Sire: Felstead 2. Radiant 3. Solar Flower 4l, 1½l 2:37.0 14 ran

1939 Robert Sterling Clark's br f **Galatea** J: Bobby Jones 10/11 Fav £8,043 T: Joe Lawson, Manton, Wiltshire B: Owner Sire: Dark Legend 2. White Fox 3. Superbe head, 3l 2:40.6 21 ran

1940 Esmond Harmsworth's b f **Godiva** J: Doug Marks 7/4 Fav £2,457 T: Willie Jarvis, Newmarket B: Owner Sire: Hyperion 2. Silverlace 3. Valeraine 3l, 4l 2:29.4 14 ran

1941 Arthur Dewar's b f **Commotion** J: Harry Wragg 8/1 £1,939 T: Fred Darling, Beckhampton, Wiltshire B: Owner Sire: Mieuxcé 2. Turkana 3. Dancing Time 2l, ¾l 2:35.6 12 ran

1942 HM King George VI's b f **Sun Chariot** J: Gordon Richards 1/4 Fav £1,879 T: Fred Darling, Beckhampton, Wiltshire B: National Stud Sire: Hyperion 2. Afterthought 3. Feberion 1l, 1½l 2:33.4 12 ran

1943 Jimmy Rank's ch f **Why Hurry** J: Charlie Elliott 7/1 £1,956 T: Noel Cannon, Middle Woodford, Wiltshire B: Owner Sire: Precipitation 2. Ribbon 3. Tropical Sun neck, 1l 2:32.6 13 ran

1944 William Woodward's ch f **Hycilla** J: George Bridgland 8/1 £3,483 T: Cecil Boyd-Rochfort, Newmarket B: Owner Sire: Hyperion 2. Monsoon 3. Kannabis 1½l, 1½l 2:31.2 16 ran

1945 17th Earl of Derby's ch f **Sun Stream** J: Harry Wragg 6/4 Fav £6,357 T: Walter Earl, Newmarket B: Owner Sire: Hyperion 2. Naishapur 3. Solar Princess short head, ¾l 2:30.0 16 ran

1946 Sir Alfred Butt's b f **Steady Aim** J: Harry Wragg 7/1 £6,540 T: Frank Butters, Newmarket B: Owner Sire: Felstead 2. Iona 3. Nelia 3l, 3l 2:41.0 10 ran

1947 Mme Pierre Corbière's br f **Imprudence** J: Rae Johnstone 7/4 Fav £7,165 T: Joseph Lieux, Maisons-Laffitte, France B: Pierre Corbière Sire: Canot 2. Netherton Maid 3. Mermaid 5l, 2l 2:40.0 11 ran

1948 HH Aga Khan III's b f **Masaka** J: Billy Nevett 7/1 £10,679 T: Frank Butters, Newmarket B: Owner Sire: Nearco 2. Angelola 3. Folie 6l, 3l 2:40.6 25 ran

1949 Norman Donaldson's b f **Musidora** J: Edgar Britt 4/1 Fav £10,670 T: Charles Elsey, Malton, Yorkshire B: Frank Tuthill Sire: Nasrullah 2. Coronation 3. Vice Versa neck, 2l 2:40.0 17 ran

1950 Marcel Boussac's ch f **Asmena** J: Rae Johnstone 5/1 £13,508 T: Charles Semblat, Chantilly, France B: Owner Sire: Goya 2. Plume

3. Stella Polaris 1l, 1½l 2:42.4 19 ran

1951 Lionel Holliday's b f **Neasham Belle** J: Stan Clayton 33/1 £15,285 T: Geoffrey Brooke, Newmarket B: Owner Sire: Nearco 2. Chinese Cracker 3. Belle of All 4l, 2l 2:41.2 16 ran

1952 Alexander Keith's b f **Frieze** J: Edgar Britt 100/7 £16,500 T: Charles Elsey, Malton, Yorkshire B: Owner Sire: Phideas 2. Zabara 3. Moon Star 3l, 1½l 2:35.8 19 ran

1953 3rd Viscount Astor's b f **Ambiguity** J: Joe Mercer 18/1 £15,336 T: Jack Colling, West Ilsley, Berkshire B: 2nd Viscount Astor and Sons Sire: Big Game 2. Kerkeb 3. Noémi 1l, 1l 2:36.8 21 ran

1954 Mme Robert Forget's gr f **Sun Cap** J: Rae Johnstone 100/8 £14,027 T: Dick Carver, Chantilly, France B: Robert Forget Sire: Sunny Boy 2. Altana 3. Philante 6l, 1l 2:39.2 21 ran

1955 Lady Zia Wernher's b f **Meld** J: Harry Carr 7/4 Fav £14,078 T: Cecil Boyd-Rochfort, Newmarket B: Someries Stud Sire: Alycidon 2. Ark Royal 3. Reel In 6l, 3l 2:47.6 13 ran

1956 Mme Suzy Volterra's b f **Sicarelle** J: Freddie Palmer 3/1 Fav £15,013 T: François Mathet, Chantilly, France B: Owner Sire: Sicambre 2. Janiari 3. Yasmin 3l, 6l 2:42.0 14 ran

1957 HM Queen Elizabeth II's br f **Carrozza** J: Lester Piggott 100/8 £16,101 T: Noel Murless, Newmarket B: National Stud Sire: Dante 2. Silken Glider 3. Rose Royale short head, 3l 2:37.4 11 ran

1958 François Dupré's br f **Bella Paola** J: Max Garcia 6/4 Fav £15,557 T: François Mathet, Chantilly, France B: Owner Sire: Ticino 2. Mother Goose 3. Cutter 3l, 3l 2:40.8 17 ran

1959 Prince Aly Khan's gr f **Petite Etoile** J: Lester Piggott 11/2 £21,155 T: Noel Murless, Newmarket B: Owner and HH Aga Khan III Sire: Petition 2. Cantelo 3. Rose of Medina 3l, 5l 2:35.8 11 ran

1960 Mrs Howell Jackson's ch f **Never Too Late** J: Roger Poincelet 6/5 Fav £17,836 T: Etienne Pollet, Chantilly, France B: Bull Run Stud Sire: Never Say Die 2. Paimpont 3. Imberline head, 2l 2:39.2 10 ran

1961 Mrs Magnus Castello's ch f **Sweet Solera** J: Bill Rickaby 11/4 Fav £18,103 T: Reg Day, Newmarket B: Mrs Dorothy Walker Sire: Solonaway 2. Ambergris 3. Anne la Douce 1½l, neck 2:39.4 12 ran

1962 George Goulandris's br f **Monade** J: Yves Saint-Martin 7/1 £18,435 T: Joseph Lieux, Maisons-Laffitte, France B: Achille Fould Sire: Klairon 2. West Side Story 3. Tender Annie short head, 1½l 2:38.2 18 ran

1963 Mrs Evelyn Olin's ch f **Noblesse**
J: Garnie Bougoure 4/11 Fav
£18,129 T: Paddy Prendergast, The
Curragh, Co Kildare, Ireland B: Mrs
Doreen Margetts Sire: Mossborough
2. Spree 3. Pouponne 10*l*, neck
2:39.6 9 ran

1964 Sir Foster Robinson's ch f
Homeward Bound J: Greville
Starkey 100/7 £32,311 T: John
Oxley, Newmarket B: Owner Sire:
Alycidon 2. Windmill Girl 3. La Bamba
2*l*, neck 2:49.36 18 ran

1965 Jimmy Cox Brady's b f **Long Look**
J: Jack Purtell 100/7 £30,747
T: Vincent O'Brien, Cashel, Co
Tipperary, Ireland B: Owner Sire:
Ribot 2. Mabel 3. Ruby's Princess
1½*l*, ¾*l* 2:39.56 18 ran

1966 Charles Clore's br f **Valoris**
J: Lester Piggott 11/10 Fav £35,711
T: Vincent O'Brien, Cashel, Co
Tipperary, Ireland B: Robert Forget
Sire: Tiziano 2. Berkeley Springs
3. Varinia 2½*l*, 3*l* 2:39.35 13 ran

1967 Gräfin Margit Batthyany's br f **Pia**
J: Edward Hide 100/7 £28,137 T: Bill
Elsey, Malton, Yorkshire B: Owner
Sire: Darius 2. St Pauli Girl
3. Ludham ¾*l*, 2*l* 2:38.34 12 ran

1968 Henry Berlin's b f **La Lagune**
J: Gérard Thiboeuf 11/8 Fav £28,773
T: François Boutin, Chantilly, France
B: Marquis du Vivier Sire: Val de Loir
2. Glad One 3. Pandora Bay 5*l*, short
head 2:41.66 14 ran

1969 6th Earl of Rosebery's gr f
Sleeping Partner J: John Gorton
100/6 £30,422 T: Doug Smith,
Newmarket B: Owner Sire: Parthia
2. Frontier Goddess 3. Myastrid
¾*l*, 4*l* 2:39.94 15 ran

1970 Mrs Gladys Joel's b f **Lupe**
J: Sandy Barclay 100/30 Fav
£31,319 T: Noel Murless, Newmarket
B: Snailwell Stud Sire: Primera
2. State Pension 3. Arctic Wave
4*l*, ½*l* 2:41.46 16 ran

1971 Roger Hue-Williams's ch f **Altesse
Royale** J: Geoff Lewis 6/4 Fav
£30,214 T: Noel Murless, Newmarket
B: Mrs Vera Hue-Williams Sire: Saint
Crespin 2. Maina 3. La Manille
3*l*, 1½*l* no official time 11 ran

1972 Charles St George's b f **Ginevra**
J: Tony Murray 8/1 £29,879 T: Ryan
Price, Findon, Sussex B: 21st Earl of
Suffolk Sire: Shantung 2. Regal
Exception 3. Arkadina 1½*l*, neck
2:39.35 17 ran

1973 George Pope, jr's ch f **Mysterious**
J: Geoff Lewis 13/8 Fav £35,417
T: Noel Murless, Newmarket
B: Owner Sire: Crepello 2. Where You
Lead 3. Aureoletta 4*l*, 4*l* 2:36.31
10 ran

1974 Louis Freedman's b f **Polygamy**
J: Pat Eddery 3/1 Fav £40,639
T: Peter Walwyn, Lambourn,
Berkshire B: Cliveden Stud Sire:
Reform 2. Furioso 3. Matuta 1*l*, ½*l*
2:39.39 15 ran (Dibidale finished
third, disqualified)

1975 James Morrison's b f **Juliette
Marny** J: Lester Piggott 12/1
£44,958 T: Jeremy Tree,
Beckhampton, Wiltshire B: Fonthill
Stud Sire: Blakeney 2. Val's Girl
3. Moonlight Night 4*l*, ¾*l* 2:39.10
12 ran

1976 Daniel Wildenstein's b f
Pawneese J: Yves Saint-Martin
6/5 Fav £50,117 T: Angel Penna,
Chantilly, France B: Dayton Ltd Sire:
Carvin 2. Roses For the Star
3. African Dancer 5*l*, 4*l* 2:35.25 14 ran

1977 HM Queen Elizabeth II's b f
Dunfermline J: Willie Carson 6/1
£48,515 T: Dick Hern, West Ilsley,
Berkshire B: Owner Sire: Royal

Sun Princess gallops home a record dozen lengths clear in the 1983 Oaks. She was the first maiden to win an English Classic since Asmena took the same race in 1950.

Palace 2. Freeze the Secret
3. Vaguely Deb ¾l, 3l 2:36.53 13 ran
1978 Sven Hanson's b f **Fair Salinia**
J: Greville Starkey 8/1 £45,960
T: Michael Stoute, Newmarket
B: Oldtown Stud Sire: Petingo
2. Dancing Maid 3. Suni short head,
1½l 2:36.82 15 ran
1979 James Morrison's b f **Scintillate**
J: Pat Eddery 20/1 £47,310
T: Jeremy Tree, Beckhampton,
Wiltshire B: Fonthill Stud Sire:
Sparkler 2. Bonnie Isle 3. Britannia's
Rule 3l, 1l 2:43.74 14 ran
1980 Dick Hollingsworth's ch f **Bireme**
J: Willie Carson 9/2 £69,280 T: Dick
Hern, West Ilsley, Berkshire
B: Owner Sire: Grundy 2. Vielle 3. The
Dancer 2l, short head 2:34.33 11 ran
1981 Mrs Diana Firestone's ch f **Blue
Wind** J: Lester Piggott 3/1 Jt-Fav
£74,568 T: Dermot Weld, The
Curragh, Co Kildare, Ireland B: Miss
Betty Laidlaw Sire: Lord Gayle
2. Madam Gay 3. Leap Lively
7l, 10l 2:40.93 12 ran
1982 Robert Barnett's b f **Time Charter**
J: Billy Newnes 12/1 £97,034
T: Henry Candy, Kingstone Warren,
Berkshire B: W. and R. Barnett Ltd
Sire: Saritamer 2. Slightly Dangerous
3. Last Feather 1l, 1½l 2:34.21
13 ran
1983 Sir Michael Sobell's b f **Sun
Princess** J: Willie Carson 6/1
£99,788 T: Dick Hern, West Ilsley,
Berkshire B: Ballymacoll Stud Farm
Ltd Sire: English Prince 2. Acclimatise
3. New Coins 12l, 2½l 2:40.98
15 ran
1984 Sir Robin McAlpine's b f **Circus
Plume** J: Lester Piggott 4/1
£122,040 T: John Dunlop, Arundel,
Sussex B: Mrs Camilla Drake Sire:
High Top 2. Media Luna 3. Poquito
Queen neck, 3l 2:38.97 16 ran (Out
of Shot finished third, disqualified)

RECORDS FOR WINNING HORSES

Greatest margins
12 lengths — Sun Princess (1983)
10 lengths — Formosa (1868), Noblesse
(1963)
8 lengths — Saucy Sue (1925)
7 lengths — Blue Wind (1981)
6 lengths — Cap and Bells (1901),
Masaka (1948), Sun Cap (1954),
Meld (1955).

Smallest margins
dead-heat — Governess and Gildermire
(1858), Enguerrande and Camélia
(1876)
short head — La Flèche (1892),
Quashed (1935), Sun Stream (1945),
Carrozza (1957), Monade (1962), Fair
Salinia (1978).

Grey
Scotia (1802), Sun Cap (1954), Petite
Etoile (1959), Sleeping Partner (1969).

Black
L'Abbesse de Jouarre (1889),
Charlebelle (1920).

Longest odds
50/1 — Vespa (1833)
40/1 — Queen Bertha (1863)
33/1 — Jenny Howlet (1880), Mirska
(1912), Quashed (1935), Lovely
Rosa (1936), Neasham Belle (1951)
30/1 — Poison (1843)
28/1 — Variation (1830)
25/1 — Turquoise (1828), Refraction
(1845), Glass Doll (1907),
Cherimoya (1911), Châtelaine (1933).

Shortest odds
8/100 — Pretty Polly (1904)
1/4 — Sun Chariot (1942)
30/100 — Saucy Sue (1925)
1/3 — Crucifix (1840), Wheel of Fortune
(1879)
4/11 — Noblesse (1963)

Dead-heat run off
In 1858 Governess beat Gildermire by
three-quarters of a length in a run-off
after the pair had dead-heated for first
place. In 1876, on the occasion of
the only other dead-heat, the owners
of Enguerrande and Camélia divided
the stakes.

Winner on disqualification
In 1918 Stony Ford finished first, beating
My Dear by a length, but was
disqualified following an objection by
the rider of My Dear, on the grounds
of bumping and boring.

Trained in Ireland
Noblesse (1963), Long Look (1965),
Valoris (1966), Blue Wind (1981)

Trained in France
Enguerrande (1876), Camélia (1876),
Brulette (1931), Imprudence (1947),
Asmena (1950), Sun Cap (1954),
Sicarelle (1956), Bella Paola (1958),
Never Too Late (1960), Monade
(1962), La Lagune (1968),
Pawneese (1976).

Bred in France
Fille de l'Air (1864), Reine (1872),
Enguerrande (1876), Camélia
(1876), Brulette (1931), Galatea
(1939), Imprudence (1947), Asmena
(1950), Sun Cap (1954), Sicarelle
(1956), Bella Paola (1958), Monade
(1962), Valoris (1966), La Lagune
(1968), Pawneese (1976).

Bred in USA
Never Too Late (1960), Long Look
(1965)

Siblings
Music (1813) and Minuet (1815), and
Memoir (1890) and La Flèche (1892)
were sisters.
Rhedycina (1850) and Governess
(1858), Spinaway (1875) and Wheel
of Fortune (1879), and Juliette Marny
(1975) and Scintillate (1979) were
half-sisters.

Winners who produced winners
Briseïs (1807) produced Corinne (1818)
Medora (1814) produced Gulnare (1827)
Industry (1838) produced Lady Evelyn
(1849)
Cyprian (1836) produced Songstress
(1852)
Fille de l'Air (1864) produced Reine
(1872)
Queen Bertha (1863) produced
Spinaway (1875) and Wheel of
Fortune (1879)
Spinaway (1875) produced Busybody
(1884)
Musa (1899) produced Mirska (1912).

Unnamed at time of victory
Yellow Filly (1786), Nightshade (1788)

Pregnant at time of victory
The Princess was in foal to Voltaire
when she won in 1844. The resultant
colt was called The Great Unknown,
who did not race but became a minor
stallion

Raced under two names
The filly who won as Lilias in 1826 was
renamed Babel before her next race,
at Newmarket five months later.

Winners in two countries
Fille de l'Air (1864) and Pawneese
(1976) also won the corresponding
French classic, the Prix de Diane.
Masaka (1948), Altesse Royale (1971),
Juliette Marny (1975), Fair Salinia
(1978) and Blue Wind (1981) also
won the Irish Oaks.

Oldest and youngest sires
Matchem sired Tetotum (1780) when 28
years old.
Mieuxcé (Commotion, 1941), Sicambre
(Sicarelle, 1956) and Grundy
(Bireme, 1980) sired winners at the
age of four.

Oldest and youngest dams
Miss Wasp produced Vespa (1833) and
Anonyma produced Lonely (1885)
when 23 years old. A total of 13 mares
have produced winners at the age of
five — the dams of Augusta (1821),
Mincemeat (1854), Queen Bertha
(1863), Geheimniss (1882), Bonny
Jean (1883), Short Story (1926), Sun
Chariot (1942), Frieze (1952), Bella
Paola (1958), Never Too Late
(1960), Mysterious (1973), Polygamy
(1974) and Pawneese (1976).

RECORDS FOR PLACED HORSES

Grey

Dandizette (1823), Fille de Joie (1824), Yasmin (1956), Silken Glider (1957).

Black

Black Puss (1793), Wowski (1800), Zaïda (1809), Barricade (1844), Bird on the Wing (1852), Sneeze (1857), Vivid (1863), Verne (1909)

Longest odds

100/1 — Cypria (1893), Regal Exception (1972)
66/1 — Media Luna (1984)
50/1 — Teleta (1840), Lady Primrose (1891), Sabrinetta (1901), Windmill Girl (1964), New Coins (1983).
40/1 — Welfare (1840), Miss Sarah (1845), Lady Ripon (1861), Mirella (1866), Romping Girl (1867), Adventure (1879), St Helen (1887), Fortalice (1897), Corposant (1899), Arctic Wave (1970).

Trained in Ireland

Attraction (1848), Lady Hasty (1907), Silken Glider (1957), Tender Annie (1962), Glad One (1968), Myastrid (1969), Where You Lead (1973)

Trained in France

White Fox (1939), Folie (1948), Coronation (1949), Plume (1950), Noémi (1953), Altana (1954), Philante (1954), Janiari (1956), Yasmin (1956), Rose Royale (1957), Paimpont (1960), Imberline (1960), Anne la Douce (1961), La Bamba (1964), Arctic Wave (1970), La Manille (1971), Matuta (1974), Dancing Maid (1978).

Bred in France

Clementine (1878), Malibran (1883), Mesa (1935), White Fox (1939), Silverlace (1940), Turkana (1941), Folie (1948), Coronation (1949), Vice Versa (1949), Altana (1954), Philante (1954), Janiari (1956), Yasmin (1956), Mother Goose (1958), Paimpont (1960), Imberline (1960), Anna la Douce (1961), La Bamba (1964), La Manille (1971), Aureoletta (1973), Moonlight Night (1975), Dancing Maid (1978), The Dancer (1980).

Bred in USA

Sibola (1899), Regal Exception (1972), Arkadina (1972), Where You Lead (1973), Matuta (1974), Val's Girl (1975), Roses for the Star (1976), Freeze the Secret (1977), Vaguely Deb (1977), Leap Lively (1981), Slightly Dangerous (1982), Last Feather (1982), New Coins (1983).

Bred in Canada

Poquito Queen (1984)

Placed horses disqualified

Dibidale finished third in 1974, but was disqualified when her rider failed to draw the correct weight.
Out of Shot finished third in 1984, but was disqualified for having interfered with the fourth- and fifth-placed finishers.

MISCELLANEOUS RECORDS

Fastest times

2:34.21 — Time Charter (1982)
2:34.33 — Bireme (1980)
2:34.6 — Beam (1927)
2:35.2 — Light Brocade (1934)
2:35.25 — Pawneese (1976)
In substitute races at Newmarket:
2:29.4 — Godiva (1940)
2:30.0 — Sun Stream (1945)

Largest entry

749 — 1974

Smallest entry

16 — 1781 (12 for substitute races 1915, 1917).

Largest fields

26 — 1848
25 — 1844, 1948
24 — 1846

Smallest fields

4 — 1799, 1904
5 — 1797, 1882
6 — 1781, 1801, 1802, 1888, 1891

Richest first prizes

£122,040 — 1984
£99,788 — 1983
£97,034 — 1982

Smallest first prizes

£551 — 1802
£577 — 1801
£603 — 1788, 1789.

Hottest losing favourite

1/3 — Achievement dead-heated for 2nd in 1867

Most consecutive winning favourites

4 — 1786 to 1789, 1937 to 1940

Most consecutive losing favourites

11 — 1825 to 1835

Race venue switched

The 1940 New Oaks was to have been run at Newbury on 13 June, but the course became unavailable, so the race was switched to Newmarket.

Earliest date

5 May — 1780

Latest date

2 August — 1917

Latest peacetime date

10 June — 1791

Run on

Thursday: 1786, 1915–18, 1940–41, 1947–50, 1953
Friday: 1779–85, 1787–1914, 1919–39, 1942–46, 1951–52, 1954–68
Saturday: from 1969

Run before Derby

1942–45, 1947–50, 1953

Foreign-bred and -trained horses placed 1, 2, 3

In 1954 (Sun Cap, Altana, Philante) and 1956 (Sicarelle, Janiari, Yasmin), winner, 2nd and 3rd were all bred and trained in France.
In 1960 winner Never Too Late was US-bred, and 2nd and 3rd (Paimpont and Imberline) French-bred. All three were trained in France.

Most successful owners

6 wins — 4th Duke of Grafton: 1813, 1815, 1822, 1823, 1828, 1831.
5 wins — 1st Earl Grosvenor: 1781, 1782, 1783, 1797, 1799
3rd Earl of Egremont: 1788, 1789, 1795, 1800, 1820
2nd Viscount Astor: 1917, 1922, 1925, 1926, 1929
4 wins — 6th Viscount Falmouth: 1863, 1875, 1878, 1879
6th Duke of Portland: 1890, 1893, 1894, 1900
Jack Joel: 1903, 1907, 1913, 1914
3 wins — 5th Duke of Bedford: 1790, 1791, 1793
2nd Marquis of Exeter: 1821, 1829, 1832
William Graham: 1865, 1868, 1870
2 wins — 1st Earl of Clermont: 1785, 1792
12th Earl of Derby: 1779, 1794
Sir Frank Standish: 1786, 1796
3rd Duke of Grafton: 1804, 1808
5th Duke of Rutland: 1811, 1814
John Leveson Gower: 1809, 1816
Thomas Grosvenor: 1807, 1825
1st Marquis of Westminster: 1805, 1841
5th Duke of Richmond: 1827, 1845
6th Earl of Chesterfield: 1838, 1849
John Scott: 1836, 1852
Harry Hill: 1848, 1856
Baron Meyer de Rothschild: 1867, 1871
Comte Frédéric de Lagrange: 1864, 1876
16th Earl of Derby: 1896, 1906
Sir Edward Hulton: 1916, 1924
17th Earl of Derby: 1928, 1945
HH Aga Khan III: 1932, 1948
HM Queen Elizabeth II: 1957, 1977
James Morrison: 1975, 1979

Owned winner and 2nd

1st Earl of Clermont: 1792

2nd Marquis of Exeter: 1829
6th Viscount Falmouth: 1875
2nd Viscount Astor: 1925

Most successful breeders

6 wins — 1st Earl Grosvenor: 1781,
    1782, 1783, 1797, 1799, 1805
    3rd Earl of Egremont: 1788, 1789,
    1790, 1795, 1800, 1820
    6th Viscount Falmouth: 1863, 1870,
    1875, 1878, 1879, 1884
    2nd Viscount Astor: 1917, 1922,
    1925, 1926, 1929, 1953 (one in
    partnership).
5 wins — 4th Duke of Grafton: 1815,
    1822, 1823, 1828, 1831
    James Cookson: 1854, 1865, 1868,
    1869, 1880.
4 wins — Jack Joel: 1903, 1907, 1913,
    1914
3 wins — 12th Earl of Derby: 1779,
    1794, 1798
    3rd Duke of Grafton: 1804, 1808,
    1813
    6th Earl of Chesterfield: 1838, 1840,
    1849
    6th Duke of Portland: 1893, 1894,
    1900
    HH Aga Khan III: 1932, 1948, 1959
    (one in partnership).
2 wins — Richard Tattersall: 1786, 1792
    5th Duke of Bedford: 1791, 1793
    John Leveson Gower: 1809, 1816
    Thomas Grosvenor: 1818, 1825
    2nd Marquis of Exeter: 1829, 1832
    Alexander Nowell: 1830, 1833
    5th Earl of Jersey: 1824, 1844
    Isaac Sadler: 1839, 1847
    John Scott: 1836, 1852
    Baron Meyer de Rothschild: 1867,
    1871
    HM Queen Victoria: 1890, 1892
    Caroline, Duchess of Montrose: 1888,
    1896
    Douglas Baird: 1899, 1912
    Lady James Douglas: 1919, 1930
    Edith, Lady Sykes: 1924, 1933
    17th Earl of Derby: 1928, 1945
    National Stud: 1942, 1957
    Robert Forget: 1954, 1966
    Fonthill Stud: 1975, 1979

Bred winner, 2nd and 3rd

3rd Duke of Grafton: 1813

Bred winner and 2nd

Richard Tattersall: 1786
1st Baron Boringdon: 1787
2nd Marquis of Exeter: 1829
6th Viscount Falmouth: 1875
2nd Viscount Astor: 1925

Most successful trainers

12 wins — Robert Robson: 1802, 1804,
    1805, 1807, 1808, 1809, 1813,
    1815, 1818, 1822, 1823, 1825.
8 wins — John Scott: 1836, 1838, 1841,
    1844, 1851, 1852, 1855, 1863
    Alec Taylor: 1910, 1917, 1918, 1919,
    1921, 1922, 1925, 1926

7 wins — John Pratt: 1781, 1782, 1783,
    1785, 1792, 1797, 1799
6 wins — Frank Butters: 1927, 1928,
    1932, 1934, 1946, 1948
5 wins — Mat Dawson: 1853, 1875,
    1878, 1879, 1891
    Noel Murless: 1957, 1959, 1970,
    1971, 1973
4 wins — Frank Neale: 1788, 1789,
    1795, 1800
    Dixon Boyce: 1806, 1811, 1814, 1817
    Charles Morton: 1903, 1907, 1913,
    1914
3 wins — Matt Stephenson: 1790, 1791,
    1793
    Richard Prince: 1786, 1796, 1798
    Robert Stephenson: 1820, 1828,
    1831
    John Porter: 1882, 1892, 1900
    George Dawson: 1890, 1893, 1894
    Joe Lawson: 1929, 1937, 1939
    Dick Hern: 1978, 1980, 1983
2 wins — Saunders: 1779, 1794
    Bill Peirse: 1810, 1812
    Charles Marson: 1829, 1832
    John Barham Day: 1840, 1846
    William Goodwin: 1850, 1854
    John Day, jr: 1848, 1856
    Tom Taylor: 1849, 1859
    Henry Woolcott: 1868, 1870
    Joe Hayhoe: 1867, 1871
    Tom Jennings: 1864, 1872
    Alec Taylor, sr: 1881, 1887
    George Lambton: 1896, 1906
    Tom Jennings, jr: 1897, 1912
    Peter Gilpin: 1904, 1915
    Dick Dawson: 1916, 1923
    Fred Darling: 1941, 1942
    Charles Elsey: 1949, 1952
    Cecil Boyd-Rochfort: 1944, 1955
    François Mathet: 1956, 1958
    Joseph Lieux: 1947, 1962
    Vincent O'Brien: 1965, 1966
    Jeremy Tree: 1975, 1979

Trained winner, 2nd and 3rd

Robert Robson: 1813

Trained winner and 2nd

Robert Robson: 1805
Dixon Boyce: 1806
Charles Marson: 1829
Mat Dawson: 1875, 1891
William I'Anson, jr: 1880
Alec Taylor: 1925
Noel Murless: 1971
In 1918 Alec Taylor trained winner My
    Dear and Silver Bullet, one of the
    dead-heaters for 2nd place.

Most successful jockeys

9 wins — Frank Buckle: 1797, 1798,
    1799, 1802, 1803, 1805, 1817,
    1818, 1823.
6 wins — Frank Butler: 1843, 1844,
    1849, 1850, 1851, 1852
    Lester Piggott: 1957, 1959, 1966,
    1975, 1981, 1984.
5 wins — Sam Chifney, jr: 1807, 1811,
    1816, 1819, 1825

John Barham Day: 1828, 1831, 1834,
    1839, 1840
    George Fordham: 1859, 1868, 1870,
    1872, 1881
4 wins — Sam Chifney: 1782, 1783,
    1789, 1790
    Dennis Fitzpatrick: 1787, 1788, 1795,
    1800
    Tom Cannon: 1869, 1873, 1882, 1884
    Fred Archer: 1875, 1878, 1879, 1885
    Jack Watts: 1883, 1886, 1890, 1893
    Joe Childs: 1912, 1916, 1919, 1921
    Harry Wragg: 1938, 1941, 1945, 1946
3 wins — Bill Scott: 1836, 1838, 1841
    Tommy Lye: 1826, 1835, 1842
    Sim Templeman: 1847, 1848, 1855
    Walter Bradford: 1894, 1897, 1898
    Tommy Weston: 1927, 1928, 1936
    Rae Johnstone: 1947, 1950, 1954
    Willie Carson: 1978, 1980, 1983.
2 wins — Charles Hindley: 1784, 1792
    John Singleton, jr: 1791, 1793
    Bill Clift: 1804, 1808
    Bill Peirse: 1810, 1812
    Tom Goodisson: 1813, 1815
    Harry Edwards: 1820, 1822
    Jem Robinson: 1821, 1824
    Jack Charlton: 1854, 1857
    Jim Snowden: 1860, 1880
    Fred Rickaby: 1891, 1896
    Morny Cannon: 1900, 1903
    Bert Randall: 1902, 1907
    Otto Madden: 1899, 1917
    Henri Jelliss: 1929, 1935
    Steve Donoghue: 1918, 1937
    Bobby Jones: 1926, 1939
    Gordon Richards: 1930, 1942
    Charlie Elliott: 1931, 1943
    Edgar Britt: 1949, 1952
    Geoff Lewis: 1971, 1973
    Yves Saint-Martin: 1962, 1976
    Greville Starkey: 1964, 1978
    Pat Eddery: 1974, 1979

Successful owner-breeder-trainers

John Scott — Cyprian (1836),
    Songstress (1852)
William I'Anson — Blink Bonny (1857)
Odoardo Ginistrelli — Signorinetta
    (1908)

Successful trainer-riders

Bill Peirse — Oriana (1810), Manuella
    (1812)
John Barham Day — Crucifix (1840)
Tom Cannon — Busybody (1884)

Successful owner-trainers

John Forth — Lilias (1826)
Joseph Saxon — Brown Duchess (1861)
Bob Sievier — Sceptre (1902)

Successful as breeder and trainer

Tom Jennings trained Fille de l'Air
    (1864) and Reine (1872), bred Limasol
    (1897).

*Successful as both jockey and
trainer*

James Edwards rode Yellow Filly
    (1786), trained Cobweb (1824).

Continued on page 56

NORTHERN DANCER

Argument over the identity of the most successful or most influential sire in the history of the Thoroughbred is both fascinating and frustrating. Herod, Eclipse and Highflyer would be natural candidates from the 18th century, Stockwell and St Simon would figure from the 19th, and in our own century Phalaris, Hyperion, Nearco and Nasrullah would all attract nominations. But to reduce the list to one would be an impossible task.

But it is contrastingly easy to name the horse who dominates the world of breeding in the 1980s. He is Northern Dancer, the little Canadian-bred whose progress from nonentity to 'super-stud' is well illustrated by the market's view of him in 1962 and 1985. As a yearling Northern Dancer went to auction and would have been sold to anyone who cared to bid $25,000; there were no takers. When he was 24 years old, at an age when most stallions have outlived their usefulness, one right to have a mare covered by Northern Dancer in the 1985 breeding season changed hands for $1 million. What came in between those two events was obviously significant.

Northern Dancer was bred at Windfields Farm, Ontario, by Eddie Taylor, the most prominent owner and breeder in Canadian racing since the early 1950s, and since 1960 the most prolific breeder of winners throughout North America. He came from the first crop of his sire Nearctic (himself a son of Nearco out of a Hyperion mare), and he was the first foal of Natalma, a good race-filly whose career was brought to an abrupt end by injury. By the time Natalma was taken out of training, the 1960 breeding season was almost over, but there was just enough time in which to get her in foal by Nearctic, and Northern Dancer arrived on 27 May 1961.

The colt's failure to find a buyer as a yearling was probably due, in roughly equal measures, to the facts that (a) he was small and seemed unlikely to grow much and (b) neither of his parents had a stud reputation. He did not grow appreciably, and at the end of his career he stood well below average height at 15.1¾ hands. But his late foaling date and lack of size proved inconsequential. He was well balanced and muscular, and he was endowed with a fierce competitive spirit. He won 7 of his 9 starts at two, establishing himself as easily the best of his crop in Canada while also making an impression in New York, where he trounced the Futurity winner Bupers in an allowance race and scored an easy win in the Remsen Stakes.

Northern Dancer again won 7 out of 9 races as a 3-year-old, the best of 6 stakes victories coming in the classic Kentucky Derby (in record time) and Preakness Stakes. He apparently failed to stay 12 furlongs when third in the Belmont Stakes, and he was taken out of training when a bowed tendon followed his easy victory in Canada's top prestige event, the Queen's Plate.

Northern Dancer started at stud in Canada at a fee of $10,000. After 4 seasons there he switched to the Maryland branch of the Windfields operation and in the summer of 1970 he was syndicated at a valuation of $2.4 million. By then he was already world-renowned as the sire of Nijinsky, the English Triple Crown victor who assured Northern Dancer of the 1970 British sires' championship. In 1971 the stallion completed a unique double when he became champion sire in North America — the only instance of those titles being won by the same horse in consecutive years.

The flow of top-class performers from Northern Dancer has never abated, with the inevitable result that the demand both for his stud services and his produce offered at auction became insatiable. His appearance in a pedigree came to be regarded as a virtual guarantee of high class, and the proof that his potency endured came with the immediate success of numerous stallion sons, among them a number who had themselves shown little distinction as runners.

As a result of Nijinsky's exploits, many of Northern Dancer's later progeny were sent to Europe, and such was their class that he was credited with further sires' championships in Britain in 1977, 1983 and 1984. He was also runner-up in the French list in 1984. His outstanding runners in Europe after Nijinsky include The Minstrel (Derby, Irish Derby, King George VI and Queen Elizabeth Stakes), Lomond (2000 Guineas), Shareef Dancer (Irish Derby), El Gran Senor (2000 Guineas, Irish Derby), Secreto (Derby), Sadler's Wells (Eclipse Stakes), Northern Trick (Prix de Diane, Prix Vermeille), Lyphard, Northern Taste, Broadway Dancer, Far North, Be My Guest, Try My Best, Northern Baby, Nureyev, Storm Bird, Woodstream and Danzatore.

In 1982 Be My Guest became Britain's champion sire and Nijinsky became the sire of an unbeaten Derby winner in Golden Fleece. The Minstrel, though based in Maryland, became a leading sire with his runners in Europe, while Northern Taste became champion in Japan. Sons of Northern Dancer are also prominent in Australia, and his influence promises to prove as significant and as widely spread as was that of Nearco and Hyperion 30 years ago.

As is frequently the case with phenomenally successful sires, Northern Dancer's importance is more readily recognised than explained. The derivation of his merit, both as runner and sire, remains something of a mystery. In physique he resembles neither of his parents, nor any of their other offspring; in addition, neither stallion nor mare produced anything else which both displayed and transmitted a remotely comparable measure of class. In that respect Northern Dancer must be regarded as a freak, representing a fortuitous combination of genes.

At stud Northern Dancer surpassed his racetrack achievements by gaining recognition as the world's most influential sire. At the age of 19 (when this photo was taken) he sired Secreto and El Gran Senor, the principals in Epsom's 1984 Derby.

John Barham Day rode Turquoise (1828), Oxygen (1831), Pussy (1834), Deception (1839) and Crucifix (1840), trained Crucifix (1840) and Mendicant (1846).

Tom Cannon rode Brigantine (1869), Marie Stuart (1873), Geheimniss (1882) and Busybody (1884), trained Busybody (1884).

Jack Robinson rode Seabreeze (1888), trained Cherry Lass (1905).

Most successful sires

5 wins — St Simon: Memoir (1890), La Flèche (1892), Mrs Butterwick (1893), Amiable (1894), La Roche (1900)

4 wins — Hyperion: Godiva (1940), Sun Chariot (1942), Hycilla (1944), Sun Stream (1945).

3 wins — Herod: Bridget (1779), Faith (1781), Maid of the Oaks (1783)
Sorceror: Morel (1808), Maid of Orleans (1809), Sorcery (1811)
Waxy: Music (1813), Minuet (1815), Corinne (1818)
Priam: Miss Letty (1837), Industry (1838), Crucifix (1840)
Melbourne: Cymba (1848), Marchioness (1855), Blink Bonny (1857)
King Tom: Tormentor (1866), Hippia (1867), Hannah (1871)

Macaroni: Spinaway (1875), Camélia (1876), Bonny Jean (1883)
Persimmon: Sceptre (1902), Keystone (1906), Perola (1909)

2 wins — Volunteer: Portia (1791), Caelia (1793)
Mercury: Hippolyta (1790), Platina (1795)
Sir Peter Teazle: Hermione (1794), Parisot (1796)
Delpini: Scotia (1802), Theophania (1803)
Whiskey: Eleanor (1801), Pelisse (1804)
Beningbrough: Briseïs (1807), Oriana (1810)
Rubens: Landscape (1816), Pastille (1822)
Woful: Augusta (1821), Zinc (1823)
Selim: Medora (1814), Turquoise (1828)
Sultan: Green Mantle (1829), Galata (1832)
Sweetmeat: Mincemeat (1854), Mincepie (1856)
Buccaneer: Formosa (1868), Brigantine (1869)
Adventurer: Apology (1874), Wheel of Fortune (1879)
Hermit: Thebais (1881), Lonely (1885)
Petrarch: Busybody (1884), Miss Jummy (1886)

Ayrshire: Airs and Graces (1898), Our Lassie (1903)
Isinglass: Cherry Lass (1905), Glass Doll (1907)
St Frusquin: Rosedrop (1910), Mirska (1912)
Martagon: Musa (1899), Snow Marten (1915)
Hurry On: Toboggan (1928), Pennycomequick (1929)
Galloper Light: Beam (1927), Light Brocade (1934)
Felstead: Rockfel (1938), Steady Aim (1946)
Nearco: Masaka (1948), Neasham Belle (1951)
Alycidon: Meld (1955), Homeward Bound (1964).

Sired winner, 2nd and 3rd

Waxy (1813)
Irish Birdcatcher (1852)

Sired winner and 2nd

Eclipse (1787)
Rubens (1822)
Sultan (1829)
Priam (1840)
Bran (1842)
Melbourne (1855)
Hermit (1885)
St Simon (1890, 1892)
St Frusquin (1912)
Lemberg (1922)

St Leger

Title

'a sweepstakes' 1776–77
St Leger's Stakes 1778–85
St Leger Stakes 1786–1820
Great St Leger Stakes 1821–31
St Leger Stakes 1832–33
Great St Leger Stakes 1834–38
St Leger Stakes 1839
Great St Leger Stakes 1840–45
St Leger Stakes 1846–1914
September Stakes 1915–18
St Leger Stakes 1919–38
Yorkshire St Leger Stakes 1940
New St Leger Stakes 1941–44
St Leger Stakes 1945–83
Holsten Pils St Leger Stakes from 1984

Venue

Cantley Common, Doncaster, Yorkshire 1776–77
Town Moor, Doncaster, Yorkshire 1778–1914
Rowley Mile Course, Newmarket, Suffolk 1915–18
Town Moor, Doncaster, Yorkshire 1919–38
Thirsk, Yorkshire 1940
Manchester, Lancashire 1941
Summer Course, Newmarket, Cambridgeshire 1942–44

York, Yorkshire 1945
Town Moor, Doncaster, Yorkshire from 1946

Distances

2 miles 1776–1812
1 mile 6 furlongs 193 yards 1813–25
1 mile 6 furlongs 132 yards 1826–1914
1 mile 6 furlongs 1915–18
1 mile 6 furlongs 132 yards 1919–38
1 mile 7 furlongs 1940
1 mile 6 furlongs 1941
1 mile 6 furlongs 150 yards 1942–44
1 mile 6 furlongs 1945
1 mile 6 furlongs 132 yards 1946–69
1 mile 6 furlongs 127 yards from 1970

Weights

Colts/geldings 8 st 0 lb, fillies 7 st 12 lb 1776–89
Colts/geldings 8 st 2 lb, fillies 8 st 0 lb 1790–1825
Colts/geldings 8 st 6 lb, fillies 8 st 3 lb 1826–38
Colts/geldings 8 st 7 lb, fillies 8 st 2 lb 1839–61
Colts/geldings 8 st 10 lb, fillies 8 st 5 lb 1862–83
Colts/geldings 9 st 0 lb, fillies 8 st 11 lb 1884–1905

Colts 9 st 0 lb, fillies 8 st 11 lb from 1906

1776 2nd Marquis of Rockingham's br f **Allabaculia** J: John Singleton 1/2 Fav £131 2. Emma 3. Orestes 5 ran

1777 William Sotheron's b c **Bourbon** J: John Cade 3/1 £288 2. Ballad Singer 3. Armida 10 ran

1778 Sir Thomas Gascoigne's gr f **Hollandaise** J: George Herring 5/2 £393 2. Young Sir Harry 3. Trincalo 8 ran

1779 Thomas Stapleton's ch c **Tommy** J: George Lowry Evens Fav £367 2. br f by Tantrum 3. Moses 10 ran

1780 William Bethell's b c **Ruler** J: John Mangle 5/2 £420 2. Antagonist 3. b c by Omnium 7 ran

1781 William Radcliffe's b f **Serina** J: Richard Foster no odds recorded £315 2. Wisdom 3. Temperance 9 ran

1782 Henry Goodricke's ch f **Imperatrix** J: George Searle no odds recorded £210 2. Monk 3. Haphazard 5 ran

1783 Sir John Lister Kaye's ch c **Phoenomenon** J: Anthony Hall 4/5 Fav £210 2. Pacolet 3. Myrtle 4 ran

1784 John Coates's b f **Omphale**
J: John Kirton no odds recorded
£288 2. Harlequin Junior 3. b c by
Alfred 7 ran

1785 Richard Hill's b f **Cowslip**
J: George Searle Fav £131 2. Matron
3. Verjuice 4 ran

1786 Lord Archibald Hamilton's b c
Paragon J: John Mangle 20/1 £315
2. Trojan 3. Carlton 8 ran

1787 Lord Archibald Hamilton's b c
Spadille J: John Mangle 2/1 £210
2. Edmund 3. Prince Lee Boo 6 ran

1788 Lord Archibald Hamilton's b f
Young Flora J: John Mangle 2/1
£236 2. Thistle 3. b c by Tandem
5 ran

1789 4th Earl Fitzwilliam's b f **Pewett**
J: William Wilson Fav £210
2. Bellona 3. Ostrich 6 ran (Zanga
finished first, disqualified)

1790 Henry Goodricke's b c
Ambidexter J: George Searle 5/1
£367 2. Fortitude 3. Spanker 8 ran

1791 John Hutchinson's ch c **Young
Traveller** J: John Jackson 3/1 £341
2. Huby 3. Trimmer 8 ran

1792 Lord Archibald Hamilton's ch c
Tartar J: John Mangle 25/1 £525
2. Skypeeper 3. Adonis 11 ran

1793 John Clifton's b c **Ninety-three**
J: Bill Peirse 15/1 £393 2. Foreigner
3. Hornet 8 ran

1794 John Hutchinson's b c
Beningbrough J: John Jackson 2/1
£472 2. Prior 3. Brilliant 8 ran

1795 Sir Charles Turner's b c
Hambletonian J: Dixon Boyce
4/6 Fav £288 2. Disraeli 3. Whynot
5 ran

1796 Joseph Cookson's b c **Ambrosio**
J: John Jackson 4/5 Fav £367
2. Cardinal 3. Rosolio 7 ran

1797 Henry Goodricke's b c **Lounger**
J: John Shepherd no odds recorded
£288 2. Stamford 3. Bottisham
8 ran

1798 Sir Thomas Gascoigne's gr c
Symmetry J: John Jackson 4/1
£341 2. Barnaby 3. Honeycomb
10 ran

1799 Sir Harry Tempest Vane's br c
Cockfighter J: Tom Fields 4/6 Fav
£288 2. Expectation 3. Slapbang
7 ran

1800 Christopher Wilson's b c
Champion J: Frank Buckle
2/1 Jt-Fav £398 2. Rolla 3. Richmond
10 ran

1801 Henry Goodricke's ch c **Quiz**
J: John Shepherd 7/1 £262
2. Belleisle 3. Miracle 8 ran

1802 4th Earl Fitzwilliam's b c **Orville**
J: John Singleton, jr 5/1 £367 2. Pipylin
3. Sparrowhawk 7 ran

1803 10th Earl of Strathmore's b c
Remembrancer J: Ben Smith
5/2 Fav £577 2. Macmanus 3. Sir
Oliver 8 ran

1804 Harry Mellish's b c **Sancho**
J: Frank Buckle 2/1 Fav £603

2. Master Betty 3. Young Chariot
11 ran

1805 Harry Mellish's b c **Staveley**
J: John Jackson 5/1 and 6/1 £650
2. Caleb Quot'Em 3. Sir Paul 10 ran

1806 John Clifton's b c **Fyldener** J: Tom
Carr 7/4 Fav £997 2. Cassio
3. Shuttlecock 15 ran

1807 4th Earl Fitzwilliam's b f **Paulina**
J: Bill Clift 8/1 £1,050 2. Scud 3. Eaton
16 ran

1808 9th Duke of Hamilton's b c
Petronius J: Ben Smith 20/1 £708
2. Clinker 3. Easton 12 ran

1809 9th Duke of Hamilton's b c
Ashton J: Ben Smith 15/8 Fav
£1,312 2. Middlethorpe 3. Lisette
14 ran

1810 6th Duke of Leeds's ch c
Octavian J: Bill Clift 12/1 £1,023
2. Recollection 3. Oriana 8 ran

1811 Richard Oliver Gascoigne's ch c
Soothsayer J: Ben Smith 6/1 £1,627
2. Amadis de Gaul 3. Scamp 24 ran

1812 Mr Rob's b c **Otterington** J: Bob
Johnson 100/1 £1,470 2. Benedick
3. Herrington 24 ran

1813 Richard Watt's ch f **Altisidora**
J: John Jackson 5/2 Fav £1,286
2. Camelopard 3. Tiger 17 ran

1814 9th Duke of Hamilton's b c
William J: John Shepherd 7/1
£1,365 2. Heart of Oak 3. Arabella
12 ran

1815 Sir William Maxwell's br c **Filho da
Puta** J: John Jackson Evens Fav
£1,522 2. Dinmont 3. Fulford 15 ran

1816 Sir Bellingham Graham's b f **The
Duchess** J: Ben Smith 12/1 £1,181
2. Captain Candid 3. Rasping 13 ran

1817 Henry Peirse's b c **Ebor** J: Bob
Johnson 20/1 £1,338 2. Blacklock
3. Restless 18 ran

1818 Henry Peirse's b c **Reveller** J: Bob
Johnson 7/2 and 4/1 £1,312 2. Ranter
3. The Marshal 21 ran

1819 James Ferguson's b c **Antonio**
J: Tom Nicholson 33/1 £1,286
2. Wrangler 3. Archibald 19 ran

1820 Sir Edward Smith's ch c **St Patrick**
J: Bob Johnson 7/1 £1,916
2. Copeland 3. Locksley 27 ran

1821 Thomas Orde-Powlett's br c **Jack
Spigot** J: Bill Scott 6/1 £1,260
2. Fortuna 3. Coronation 13 ran

1822 Edward Petre's b c **Theodore**
J: John Jackson 200/1 £1,890
2. Violet 3. Professor 23 ran

1823 Richard Watt's ch c **Barefoot**
J: Tom Goodisson 4/1 £2,178
2. Sherwood 3. Comte d'Artois 12 ran

1824 Richard Oliver Gascoigne's bl c
Jerry J: Ben Smith 9/1 £1,995
2. Canteen 3. Miller of Mansfield
23 ran

1825 Richard Watt's b c **Memnon** J: Bill
Scott 3/1 Fav £2,175 2. The
Alderman 3. Actaeon 30 ran

1826 6th Earl of Scarbrough's b c
Tarrare J: George Nelson 20/1
£2,350 2. Mulatto 3. Bedlamite 27 ran

1827 Edward Petre's b f **Matilda** J: Jem
Robinson 9/1 and 10/1 £2,225
2. Mameluke 3. Laurel 26 ran

1828 Edward Petre's ch c **The Colonel**
J: Bill Scott 5/2 and 3/1 Fav £1,975
2. Belinda 3. Velocipede 19 ran

1829 Edward Petre's ch c **Rowton**
J: Bill Scott 7/2 Fav £2,400
2. Voltaire 3. Sir Hercules 19 ran

1830 John Beardsworth's br c
Birmingham J: Patrick Conolly 15/1
£1,675 2. Priam 3. Emancipation
28 ran

1831 1st Marquis of Cleveland's b c
Chorister J: John Barham Day 20/1
£2,115 2. The Saddler 3. La Fille Mal
Gardée 24 ran

1832 John Gully's ch c **Margrave**
J: Jem Robinson 8/1 £2,200
2. Birdcatcher 3. gr f by Figaro 17 ran

1833 Richard Watt's b c **Rockingham**
J: Sam Darling 7/1 £2,325
2. Mussulman 3. Carnaby 20 ran

1834 1st Marquis of Westminster's br c
Touchstone J: George Calloway
50/1 £2,000 2. Bran 3. General
Chassé 11 ran

1835 Edward Lloyd Mostyn's br f **Queen
of Trumps** J: Tommy Lye 8/11 Fav
£1,800 2. Hornsea 3. Sheet Anchor
11 ran

1836 Lord George Bentinck's ch c **Elis**
J: John Barham Day 7/2 £2,075
2. Scroggins 3. Beeswing 14 ran

1837 Charles Greville's br c **Mango**
J: Sam Day, jr 13/2 £1,825
2. Abraham Newland 3. The Doctor
13 ran

1838 6th Earl of Chesterfield's b c **Don
John** J: Bill Scott 13/8 Fav £1,675
2. Ion 3. Lanercost 7 ran

1839 Mr Yarburgh's br c **Charles the
Twelfth** J: Bill Scott 4/6 Fav £2,875
2. Euclid 3. The Provost 14 ran

1840 1st Marquis of Westminster's br c
Launcelot J: Bill Scott 7/4 Fav
£2,925 2. Maroon 3. Gibraltar 11 ran

1841 1st Marquis of Westminster's br c
Satirist J: Bill Scott 6/1 £3,500
2. Coronation 3. The Squire 11 ran

1842 13th Earl of Eglinton's b f **The
Blue Bonnet** J: Tommy Lye 8/1
£3,600 2. Seahorse 3. Priscilla
Tomboy 17 ran

1843 Samuel Wrather's b c **Nutwith**
J: Job Marson 100/6 £3,070
2. Cotherstone 3. Prize-fighter 9 ran

1844 E. J. Irwin's br c **Foig a Ballagh**
J: Henry Bell 7/2 £2,525 2. The Cure
3. The Princess 9 ran

1845 George Watts's ch c **The Baron**
J: Frank Butler 10/1 £2,500 2. Miss
Sarah 3. Pantasa 15 ran

1846 Bill Scott's b c **Sir Tatton Sykes**
J: Bill Scott 3/1 Jt-Fav £2,875 2. Iago
3. Brocardo 12 ran

1847 13th Earl of Eglinton's br c **Van
Tromp** J: Job Marson 4/1 £3,175
2. Cossack 3. Eryx 8 ran

1848 3rd Viscount Clifden's b c
Surplice J: Nat Flatman 9/4 £2,975

2. Canezou 3. Flatcatcher 9 ran

1849 13th Earl of Eglinton's br c **The Flying Dutchman** J: Charlie Marlow 4/9 Fav £3,200 2. Nunnykirk 3. Vatican 10 ran

1850 2nd Earl of Zetland's br c **Voltigeur** J: Job Marson 8/13 Fav £2,000 2. Russsborough 3. Bolingbroke 8 ran

1851 Anthony Nichol's b c **Newminster** J: Sim Templeman 12/1 £2,700 2. Aphrodite 3. Hook'em Snivvey 18 ran

1852 2nd Marquis of Exeter's ch c **Stockwell** J: John Norman 7/4 Fav £2,625 2. Harbinger 3. Daniel O'Rourke 6 ran

1853 John Bowes's b c **West Australian** J: Frank Butler 6/4 Fav £2,025 2. The Reiver 3. Rataplan 10 ran

1854 J. B. Morris's b c **Knight of St George** J: Robert Basham 11/1 £3,700 2. Ivan 3. Arthur Wellesley 18 ran

1855 Tom Parr's b c **Saucebox** J: John Wells 40/1 £2,650 2. Rifleman 3. Lady Tatton 12 ran

1856 Anthony Nichol's b c **Warlock** J: Nat Flatman 12/1 £3,050 2= Bonnie Scotland and Artillery 9 ran

1857 John Scott's b f **Impérieuse** J: Nat Flatman 100/6 £3,675 2. Commotion 3. Tournament 11 ran

1858 James Merry's b f **Sunbeam** J: Luke Snowden 15/1 £3,150 2. The Hadji 3. Blanche of Middlebie 18 ran

1859 Sir Charles Monck's br c **Gamester** J: Tom Aldcroft 20/1 £3,925 2. Defencer 3. Magnum 11 ran

1860 2nd Marquis of Ailesbury's ch c **St Albans** J: Luke Snowden 8/1 £3,925 2. High Treason 3. The Wizard 15 ran

1861 William I'Anson's br f **Caller Ou** J: Tom Chaloner 1000/15 £4,150 2. Kettledrum 3. Kildonan 18 ran

1862 Stanhope Hawke's b c **The Marquis** J: Tom Chaloner 100/30 £4,225 2. Buckstone 3. Clarissimus 15 ran

1863 3rd Viscount St Vincent's b c **Lord Clifden** J: John Osborne 100/30 Fav £4,825 2. Queen Bertha 3. Borealis 19 ran

1864 William I'Anson's ch c **Blair Athol** J: Jim Snowden 2/1 Fav £5,150 2. General Peel 3. Cambuscan 10 ran

1865 Comte Frédéric de Lagrange's b c **Gladiateur** J: Harry Grimshaw 8/13 Fav £5,800 2. Regalia 3. Archimedes 14 ran

1866 Richard Sutton's b c **Lord Lyon** J: Harry Custance 4/7 Fav £5,825 2. Savernake 3. Knight of the Crescent 11 ran

1867 Mark Pearson's br f **Achievement** J: Tom Chaloner 75/40 £5,275 2. Hermit 3. Julius 12 ran

1868 William Graham's ch f **Formosa** J: Tom Chaloner 100/30 Jt-Fav £5,825 2. Paul Jones 3. Mercury 12 ran

1869 Sir Joseph Hawley's br c **Pero Gomez** J: John Wells 3/1 £5,525 2. Martyrdom 3. George Osbaldeston 11 ran

1870 Thomas Vaughan Morgan's b c **Hawthornden** J: Jemmy Grimshaw 1000/35 £5,475 2. Kingcraft 3. Wheat-ear 19 ran

1871 Baron Meyer de Rothschild's b f **Hannah** J: Charlie Maidment 9/4 Fav

£4,800 2. Albert Victor 3. Ringwood 10 ran

1872 2nd Earl of Wilton's b c **Wenlock** J: Charlie Maidment 8/1 £4,450 2. Prince Charlie 3. Vanderdecken 17 ran

1873 James Merry's ch f **Marie Stuart** J: Tom Osborne 9/4 £4,400 2. Doncaster 3. Kaiser 8 ran

1874 John King's ch f **Apology** J: John Osborne 4/1 Fav £4,625 2. Leolinus 3. Trent 13 ran

1875 William Stirling Crawfurd's ch c **Craig Millar** J: Tom Chaloner 7/1 £4,150 2. Balfe 3. Earl of Dartrey 13 ran

1876 Viscount Dupplin's b c **Petrarch** J: Jem Goater 5/1 £4,825 2. Wild Tommy 3. Julius Caesar 9 ran

1877 6th Viscount Falmouth's b c **Silvio** J: Fred Archer 65/40 Fav £5,025 2. Lady Golightly 3. Manoeuvre 14 ran

1878 6th Viscount Falmouth's b f **Jannette** J: Fred Archer 5/2 Fav £5,750 2. Childeric 3. Master Kildare 14 ran

1879 Comte Frédéric de Lagrange's ch c **Rayon d'Or** J: Jem Goater 3/1 Jt-Fav £6,525 2. Ruperra 3. Exeter 17 ran

1880 Charles Brewer's b c **Robert the Devil** J: Tom Cannon 4/1 £6,025 2. Cipollata 3. The Abbot 12 ran

1881 Pierre Lorillard's br c **Iroquois** J: Fred Archer 2/1 Fav £5,450 2. Geologist 3. Lucy Glitters 15 ran

1882 6th Viscount Falmouth's br f **Dutch Oven** J: Fred Archer 40/1 £4,500 2. Geheimniss 3. Shotover 14 ran

1883 12th Duke of Hamilton's b c

West Australian, whose victory in the 1853 St Leger made him racing's first Triple Crown winner. He lost only the first of his ten career starts.

Sceptre, whose St Leger win in 1902 would have completed a clean sweep of the Classics had she been ridden competently in the Derby.

Ossian J: Jack Watts 9/1 £4,700
2. Chislehurst 3. Highland Chief 9 ran
1884 Robert Vyner's b c **The Lambkin**
J: Jack Watts 9/1 £4,300
2. Sandiway 3. Superba 13 ran
1885 20th Baron Hastings's b c **Melton**
J: Fred Archer 40/95 Fav £4,800
2. Isobar 3. Lonely 10 ran
1886 1st Duke of Westminster's b c
Ormonde J: Fred Archer 1/7 Fav
£4,450 2. St Mirin 3. Exmoor 7 ran
1887 7th Baron Rodney's br c **Kilwarlin**
J: Jack Robinson 4/1 Jt-Fav £4,050
2. Merry Hampton 3. Timothy 9 ran
1888 5th Baron Calthorpe's ch f
Seabreeze J: Jack Robinson 5/2
£4,350 2. Chillington 3. Zanzibar
16 ran
1889 6th Duke of Portland's b c
Donovan J: Fred Barrett 8/13 Fav
£4,800 2. Miguel 3. Davenport 12 ran
1890 6th Duke of Portland's br f
Memoir J: Jack Watts 10/1 £5,125
2. Blue Green 3. Gonsalvo 15 ran
1891 Sir Frederick Johnstone's br c
Common J: George Barrett 4/5 Fav
£4,300 2. Révérend 3. St Simon of
the Rock 9 ran
1892 Baron Maurice de Hirsch's br f **La**

Flèche J: Jack Watts 7/2 £5,400
2. Sir Hugo 3. Watercress 11 ran
1893 Harry McCalmont's b c **Isinglass**
J: Tommy Loates 40/95 Fav £5,300
2. Ravensbury 3. Le Nicham 7 ran
1894 1st Baron Alington's b f **Throstle**
J: Morny Cannon 50/1 £4,705
2. Ladas 3. Matchbox 8 ran
1895 5th Earl of Rosebery's b c **Sir
Visto** J: Sam Loates 9/4 Fav £4,575
2. Telescope 3. Butterfly 11 ran
1896 HRH Prince of Wales's b c
Persimmon J: Jack Watts 2/11 Fav
£5,050 2. Labrador 3. Rampion 7 ran
1897 John Gubbins's b c **Galtee More**
J: Charlie Wood 1/10 Fav £5,425
2. Chélandry 3. St Cloud 5 ran
1898 Henry Greer's ch c **Wildfowler**
J: Charlie Wood 10/1 £5,000
2. Jeddah 3. Bridegroom 12 ran
1899 1st Duke of Westminster's b c
Flying Fox J: Morny Cannon 2/7 Fav
£4,050 2. Caiman 3. Scintillant 6 ran
1900 HRH Prince of Wales's b c
Diamond Jubilee J: Herbert Jones
2/7 Fav £5,125 2. Elopement
3. Courlan 11 ran
1901 Leopold de Rothschild's br c
Doricles J: Kempton Cannon 40/1

£5,400 T: Alfred Hayhoe, Newmarket
B: Owner Sire: Florizel
2. Volodyovski 3. Revenue neck, 3l
3:08.4 13 ran
1902 Bob Sievier's b f **Sceptre** J: Fred
Hardy 100/30 Fav £5,275 T: Owner,
Shrewton, Wiltshire B: 1st Duke of
Westminster Sire: Persimmon
2. Rising Glass 3. Friar Tuck 3l, 2l
3:12.4 12 ran
1903 Sir James Miller's br c **Rock Sand**
J: Danny Maher 2/5 Fav £4,775
T: George Blackwell, Newmarket
B: Owner Sire: Sainfoin 2. William
Rufus 3. Mead 4l, ½l 3:09.4 5 ran
1904 Eustace Loder's ch f **Pretty Polly**
J: Willie Lane 2/5 Fav £4,625
T: Peter Gilpin, Newmarket B: Owner
Sire: Gallinule 2. Henry the First
3. Almscliff 3l, 6l 3:05.8 6 ran
1905 Washington Singer's b c
Challacombe J: Otto Madden 100/6
£4,400 T: Alec Taylor, Manton,
Wiltshire B: F. W. Dunn Sire: St Serf
2. Polymelus 3. Cherry Lass 3l, 3l
3:05.4 8 ran
1906 2nd Duke of Westminster's b c
Troutbeck J: George Stern 5/1
£4,275 T: Willie Waugh, Kingsclere,
Berkshire B: Owner Sire: Ladas
2. Prince William 3. Beppo
head, head 3:04.2 12 ran
1907 Ned Baird's b c **Wool Winder**

J: Bill Halsey 11/10 Fav £4,125
T: Harry Enoch, Newmarket
B: Owner Sire: Martagon
2. Baltinglass 3. Acclaim 6l, ½l 3:05.6
12 ran
1908 Jack Joel's b c **Your Majesty**
J: Walter Griggs 11/8 Fav £6,450
T: Charles Morton, Wantage,
Berkshire B: Owner Sire:
Persimmon 2. White Eagle 3. Santo
Strato ½l, 4l 3:06.0 10 ran
1909 Alfred Cox's b c **Bayardo**
J: Danny Maher 10/11 Fav £6,450
T: Alec Taylor, Manton, Wiltshire
B: Owner Sire: Bay Ronald 2. Valens
3. Mirador 1½l, ½l 3:08.6 7 ran
1910 17th Earl of Derby's br c
Swynford J: Frank Wootton 9/2
£6,450 T: George Lambton,
Newmarket B: 16th Earl of Derby
Sire: John o' Gaunt 2. Bronzino
3. Lemberg head, 1½l 3:04.0 11 ran
1911 Thomas Pilkington's br c **Prince
Palatine** J: Frank O'Neill 100/30
£6,450 T: Henry Beardsley,
Whatcombe, Berkshire B: William Hall
Walker Sire: Persimmon 2. Lycaon
3. King William 6l, 3l 3:06.0 8 ran
1912 August Belmont, jr's br c **Tracery**
J: George Bellhouse 8/1 £6,450
T: John Watson, Newmarket
B: Owner Sire: Rock Sand 2. Maiden
Erlegh 3. Hector 5l, ¾l 3:11.8 14 ran
1913 William Hall Walker's b c **Night
Hawk** J: Elijah Wheatley 50/1 £6,450
T: Jack Robinson, Foxhill, Wiltshire
B: Owner Sire: Gallinule 2. White
Magic 3. Seremond 2l, 3l 3:03.6
12 ran
1914 Jack Joel's br c **Black Jester**
J: Walter Griggs 10/1 £6,450
T: Charles Morton, Wantage,
Berkshire B: Owner Sire: Polymelus
2. Kennymore 3. Cressingham 5l, 3l
3:02.6 18 ran
1915 Solly Joel's b c **Pommern** J: Steve
Donoghue 1/3 Fav £1,250 T: Charley
Peck, Newmarket B: Owner Sire:
Polymelus 2. Snow Marten 3. Achtoi
2l, 6l 2:55.6 7 ran
1916 James Buchanan's ch c **Hurry On**
J: Charlie Childs 11/10 Fav £1,650
T: Fred Darling, Beckhampton,
Wiltshire B: William Murland Sire:
Marcovil 2. Clarissimus 3. Atheling
3l, 5l 2:59.6 5 ran
1917 Alfred Cox's b c **Gay Crusader**
J: Steve Donoghue 2/11 Fav £1,625
T: Alec Taylor, Manton, Wiltshire
B: Owner Sire: Bayardo 2. Kingston
Black 3. Dansellon 6l, bad 2:59.6
3 ran
1918 Lady James Douglas's b c
Gainsborough J: Joe Childs
4/11 Fav £3,350 T: Alec Taylor,
Manton, Wiltshire B: Owner Sire:
Bayardo 2. My Dear 3. Prince Chimay
3l, 4l 3:04.0 5 ran
1919 17th Earl of Derby's br f **Keysoe**
J: Brownie Carslake 100/8 £6,450
T: George Lambton, Newmarket

B: Owner Sire: Swynford 2. Dominion
3. Buchan 6l, 2l 3:06.8 10 ran
1920 Mathradas Goculdas's gr c
Caligula J: Arthur Smith 100/6
£6,450 T: Jack Leader, Newmarket
B: James Maher Sire: The Tetrarch
2. Silvern 3. Manton ½l, 3l 3:07.4
14 ran
1921 7th Marquis of Londonderry's ch c
Polemarch J: Joe Childs 50/1
£6,450 T: Tom Green, Newmarket
B: Owner Sire: The Tetrarch
2. Franklin 3. Westward Ho 1½l, 3l
3:06.8 9 ran
1922 5th Earl of Lonsdale's b c **Royal
Lancer** J: Bobby Jones 33/1 £10,310
T: Alf Sadler, Newmarket B: National
Stud Sire: Spearmint 2. Silurian
3. Ceylonese 2l, 2l 3:14.2 24 ran
1923 17th Earl of Derby's b f **Tranquil**
J: Tommy Weston 100/9 £10,015
T: Charles Morton, Wantage,
Berkshire B: Owner Sire: Swynford
2. Papyrus 3. Teresina 2l, 1½l 3:05.0
13 ran
1924 HH Aga Khan III's b c **Salmon-
Trout** J: Brownie Carslake 6/1
£10,085 T: Dick Dawson,
Whatcombe, Berkshire B: 1st
Viscount Furness Sire: The Tetrarch
2. Santorb 3. Polyphontes 2l, ½l
3:13.2 17 ran
1925 Sir John Rutherford's b c **Solario**
J: Joe Childs 7/2 Jt-Fav £9,555
T: Reg Day, Newmarket B: 5th Earl
of Dunraven Sire: Gainsborough
2. Zambo 3. Warden of the Marches
3l, 3l 3:04.4 15 ran
1926 1st Baron Woolavington's ch c
Coronach J: Joe Childs 8/15 Fav
£12,010 T: Fred Darling,
Beckhampton, Wiltshire B: Owner
Sire: Hurry On 2. Caissot 3. Foliation
2l, 6l 3:01.6 12 ran
1927 2nd Viscount Astor's b f **Book Law**
J: Henri Jelliss 7/4 Fav £13,280
T: Alec Taylor, Manton, Wiltshire
B: Owner Sire: Buchan 2. Hot Night
3. Son and Heir 3l, 5l 3:14.4 16 ran
1928 17th Earl of Derby's b c **Fairway**
J: Tommy Weston 7/4 Fav T: Frank
Butters, Newmarket B: Owner Sire:
Phalaris 2. Palais Royal 3. Cyclonic
1½l, 1l 3:03.0 13 ran
1929 William Barnett's b c **Trigo**
J: Michael Beary 5/1 £11,281 T: Dick
Dawson, Whatcombe, Berkshire
B: Owner Sire: Blandford 2. Bosworth
3. Horus short head, ¾l 3:03.4
14 ran
1930 1st Baron Glanely's b c **Singapore**
J: Gordon Richards 4/1 Jt-Fav
£11,226 T: Tommy Hogg,
Newmarket B: Sir Alec Black Sire:
Gainsborough 2. Parenthesis
3. Rustom Pasha 1½l, ¾l 3:09.2
13 ran
1931 6th Earl of Rosebery's b c
Sandwich J: Harry Wragg 9/1
£12,339 T: Jack Jarvis, Newmarket
B: James Maher Sire: Sansovino

2. Orpen 3. Sir Andrew 4l, 1l 3:11.2
10 ran
1932 H H Aga Khan III's ch c **Firdaussi**
J: Freddie Fox 20/1 £10,805
T: Frank Butters, Newmarket
B: Owner Sire: Pharos 2. Dastur
3. Silvermere neck, 4l 3:04.4 19 ran
1933 17th Earl of Derby's ch c **Hyperion**
J: Tommy Weston 6/4 Fav £9,573
T: George Lambton, Newmarket
B: Owner Sire: Gainsborough
2. Felicitation 3. Scarlet Tiger 3l, neck
3:06.8 14 ran
1934 Martin Benson's b c **Windsor Lad**
J: Charlie Smirke 4/9 Fav £10,401
T: Marcus Marsh, Lambourn,
Berkshire B: Dan Sullivan Sire:
Blandford 2. Tiberius 3. Lo Zingaro
2l, 2l 3:01.6 10 ran
1935 HH Aga Khan III's b c **Bahram**
J: Charlie Smirke 4/11 Fav £9,543
T: Frank Butters, Newmarket
B: Owner Sire: Blandford 2. Solar
Ray 3. Buckleigh 5l, 3l 3:01.8 8 ran
1936 William Woodward's br c **Boswell**
J: Pat Beasley 20/1 £10,554 T: Cecil
Boyd-Rochfort, Newmarket B: Owner
Sire: Bosworth 2. Fearless Fox
3. Mahmoud ¾l, 3l 3:08.6 13 ran
1937 1st Baron Glanely's b c
Chulmleigh J: Gordon Richards 18/1
£10,197 T: Tommy Hogg,
Newmarket B: Owner Sire: Singapore
2. Fair Copy 3. Mid-day Sun ½l, ¾l
3:07.4 15 ran
1938 Jimmy Rank's b c **Scottish Union**
J: Brownie Carslake 7/1 £10,465
T: Noel Cannon, Middle Woodford,
Wiltshire B: Executors of Lady Sykes
Sire: Cameronian 2. Challenge
3. Pasch neck, 4l 3:11.4 9 ran
1939 no race.
1940 HH Aga Khan III's b c **Turkhan**
J: Gordon Richards 4/1 £980
T: Frank Butters, Newmarket
B: Owner Sire: Bahram 2. Stardust
3. Hippius ¾l, ¾l 3:32.4 6 ran
1941 1st Viscount Portal's b c **Sun
Castle** J: George Bridgland 10/1
£3,550 T: Cecil Boyd-Rochfort,
Newmarket B: Enid, Countess of
Chesterfield Sire: Hyperion
2. Château Larose 3. Dancing Time
head, 1l 3:04.0 16 ran
1942 HM King George VI's b f **Sun
Chariot** J: Gordon Richards 9/4
£2,623 T: Fred Darling,
Beckhampton, Wiltshire B: National
Stud Sire: Hyperion 2. Watling Street
3. Hyperides 3l, 5l 3:08.4 8 ran
1943 17th Earl of Derby's b f
Herringbone J: Harry Wragg 100/6
£3,478 T: Walter Earl, Newmarket
B: Owner Sire: King Salmon
2. Ribbon 3. Straight Deal short head,
¾l 3:05.0 12 ran
1944 HH Aga Khan III's b c **Tehran**
J: Gordon Richards 9/2 £5,467
T: Frank Butters, Newmarket
B: Prince Aly Khan Sire: Bois
Roussel 2. Borealis 3. Ocean Swell

Never Say Die sets the record for the greatest margin of victory in the St Leger, breezing home by a dozen lengths in 1954. He was ridden by Charlie Smirke in place of the suspended Lester Piggott.

1½l, 1l 3:06.6 17 ran

1945 Stanhope Joel's ch c
Chamossaire J: Tommy Lowrey
11/2 £10,120 T: Dick Perryman,
Newmarket B: National Stud Sire:
Precipitation 2. Rising Light 3. Stirling
Castle 2l, ¾l 2:55.8 10 ran

1946 John Ferguson's gr c **Airborne**
J: Tommy Lowrey 3/1 Fav £9,750
T: Dick Perryman, Newmarket
B: Harold Boyd-Rochfort Sire:
Precipitation 2. Mürren 3. Fast and
Fair 1½l, 3l 3:10.2 11 ran

1947 HH Maharaja of Baroda's br c
Sayajirao J: Edgar Britt 9/2 £11,160
T: Sam Armstrong, Newmarket B: Sir
Eric Ohlson Sire: Nearco 2. Arbar
3. Migoli head, 3l 3:07.8 11 ran

1948 William Woodward's br c **Black
Tarquin** J: Edgar Britt 15/2 £15,268
T: Cecil Boyd-Rochfort, Newmarket
B: Belair Stud Sire: Rhodes Scholar
2. Alycidon 3. Solar Slipper 1½l, 5l
3:08.8 14 ran

1949 Geoffrey Smith's br c **Ridge
Wood** J: Michael Beary 100/7
£14,996 T: Noel Murless,
Beckhampton, Wiltshire B: Sledmere
Stud Sire: Bois Roussel 2. Dust Devil
3. Lone Eagle 3l, ¾l 3:08.2 16 ran

1950 Marcel Boussac's ch c **Scratch**
J: Rae Johnstone 9/2 £13,959
T: Charles Semblat, Chantilly, France
B: Owner Sire: Pharis 2. Vieux
Manoir 3. Sanlinea 1l, 5l 3:08.8 15 ran

1951 Marcel Boussac's ch c **Talma**
J: Rae Johnstone 7/1 £14,481
T: Charles Semblat, Chantilly, France
B: Owner Sire: Pharis 2. Fraise du
Bois 3. Medway 10l, 4l 3:13.8 18 ran

1952 HH Aga Khan III's br c **Tulyar**
J: Charlie Smirke 10/11 Fav £15,820
T: Marcus Marsh, Newmarket
B: Owner and Prince Aly Khan Sire:
Tehran 2. Kingsford 3. Alcinus 3l, 4l
3:07.8 12 ran

1953 Wilfrid Wyatt's b c **Premonition**
J: Eph Smith 10/1 £14,146 T: Cecil
Boyd-Rochfort, Newmarket
B: Dunchurch Lodge Stud Sire:
Precipitation 2. Northern Light
3. Aureole 3l, 3l 3:06.8 11 ran

1954 Robert Sterling Clark's ch c **Never
Say Die** J: Charlie Smirke
100/30 Fav £13,372 T: Joe Lawson,
Newmarket B: Owner Sire:
Nasrullah 2. Elopement
3. Estremadur 12l, 4l 3:10.6 16 ran

1955 Lady Zia Wernher's b f **Meld**
J: Harry Carr 10/11 Fav £13,457
T: Cecil Boyd-Rochfort, Newmarket
B: Someries Stud Sire: Alycidon

2. Nucleus 3. Beau Prince ¾l, 3l
3:14.6 8 ran

1956 Ralph Strassburger's ch c
Cambremer J: Freddie Palmer 8/1
£13,321 T: George Bridgland,
Chantilly, France B: Owner Sire:
Chamossaire 2. Hornbeam 3. French
Beige ¾l, 1½l 3:12.2 13 ran

1957 John McShain's ch c **Ballymoss**
J: Tommy Burns 8/1 £14,575
T: Vincent O'Brien, Cashel, Co
Tipperary, Ireland B: Richard Ball
Sire: Mossborough 2. Court Harwell
3. Brioche 1l, ¾l 3:15.6 16 ran

1958 Sir Humphrey de Trafford's b c
Alcide J: Harry Carr 4/9 Fav £15,195
T: Cecil Boyd-Rochfort, Newmarket
B: Owner Sire: Alycidon 2. None
Nicer 3. Nagami 8l, ¾l 3:06.4 8 ran

1959 William Hill's b f **Cantelo**
J: Edward Hide 100/7 £28,636
T: Charles Elsey, Malton, Yorkshire
B: Owner Sire: Chanteur 2. Fidalgo
3. Pindari 1½l, 1l 3:04.6 11 ran

1960 Sir Victor Sassoon's b c **St Paddy**
J: Lester Piggott 4/6 Fav £30,378
T: Noel Murless, Newmarket B: Eve
Stud Ltd Sire: Aureole 2. Die Hard
3. Vienna 3l, 1½l 3:13.2 9 ran

1961 Mrs Vera Lilley's b c **Aurelius**
J: Lester Piggott 9/2 £29,817 T: Noel
Murless, Newmarket B: Tally Ho Stud
Sire: Aureole 2. Bounteous 3. Dicta
Drake ¾l, ¾l 3:06.6 13 ran

1962 Lionel Holliday's b c **Hethersett**

J: Harry Carr 100/8 £31,407 T: Dick Hern, Newmarket B: Owner Sire: Hugh Lupus 2. Monterrico 3. Miralgo 4l, 1l 3:10.8 15 ran

1963 Jim Mullion's b c **Ragusa**
J: Garnie Bougoure 2/5 Fav £32,338 T: Paddy Prendergast, The Curragh, Co Kildare, Ireland B: Harry Guggenheim Sire: Ribot 2. Star Moss 3. Fighting Ship 6l, short head 3:05.4 7 ran

1964 Charles Engelhard's b c **Indiana**
J: Jimmy Lindley 100/7 £43,558 T: Jack Watts, Newmarket B: Frank Tuthill Sire: Sayajirao 2. Patti 3. Soderini head, 4l 3:05.0 15 ran

1965 Jakie Astor's b c **Provoke** J: Joe Mercer 28/1 £42,389 T: Dick Hern, West Ilsley, Berkshire B: Astor Studs Sire: Aureole 2. Meadow Court 3. Solstice 10l, 5l 3:18.6 11 ran

1966 Radha Sigtia's b c **Sodium**
J: Frankie Durr 7/1 £41,177 T: George Todd, Manton, Wiltshire B: Kilcarn Stud Sire: Psidium 2. Charlottown 3. David Jack head, 1½l 3:09.8 9 ran

1967 Charles Engelhard's b c **Ribocco**
J: Lester Piggott 7/2 Jt-Fav £42,695 T: Fulke Johnson Houghton, Blewbury, Berkshire B: Mrs Julian Rogers Sire: Ribot 2. Hopeful Venture 3. Ruysdael 1½l, ½l 3:05.4 9 ran

1968 Charles Engelhard's b c **Ribero**
J: Lester Piggott 100/30 £33,437 T: Fulke Johnson Houghton, Blewbury, Berkshire B: Mrs Julian Rogers Sire: Ribot 2. Canterbury 3. Cold Storage short head, 6l 3:19.8 8 ran

1969 Gerry Oldham's b c **Intermezzo**
J: Ron Hutchinson 7/1 £37,705 T: Harry Wragg, Newmarket B: Citadel Stud Establishment Sire: Hornbeam 2. Ribofilio 3. Prince Consort 1½l, 2l 3:11.8 11 ran

1970 Charles Engelhard's b c **Nijinsky**
J: Lester Piggott 2/7 Fav £37,082 T: Vincent O'Brien, Cashel, Co Tipperary, Ireland B: Eddie Taylor Sire: Northern Dancer 2. Meadowville 3. Politico 1l, ½l 3:06.4 9 ran

1971 Mrs Eileen Rogerson's b c **Athens Wood** J: Lester Piggott 5/2 £35,742 T: Tom Jones, Newmarket B: Kilcarn Stud Sire: Celtic Ash 2. Homeric 3. Falkland neck, head 3:14.9 8 ran

1972 Ogden Phipps's ch c **Boucher**
J: Lester Piggott 3/1 £35,708 T: Vincent O'Brien, Cashel, Co Tipperary, Ireland B: Owner Sire: Ribot 2. Our Mirage 3. Ginevra ½l, 4l 3:28.71 7 ran

1973 Bill Behrens's b c **Peleid**
J: Frankie Durr 28/1 £42,298 T: Bill Elsey, Malton, Yorkshire B: Owner Sire: Derring-Do 2. Buoy 3. Duke of Ragusa 2½l, neck 3:08.21 13 ran

1974 Lady Beaverbrook's b c **Bustino**
J: Joe Mercer 11/10 Fav £56,766 T: Dick Hern, West Ilsley, Berkshire

B: Edgar Cooper Bland Sire: Busted 2. Giacometti 3. Riboson 3l, 4l 3:09.02 10 ran

1975 Charles St George's gr c **Bruni**
J: Tony Murray 9/1 £52,131 T: Ryan Price, Findon, Sussex B: Barrettstown Estates Sire: Sea Hawk 2. King Pellinore 3. Libra's Rib 10l, 1½l 3:05.31 12 ran

1976 Daniel Wildenstein's ch c **Crow**
J: Yves Saint-Martin 6/1 Co-Fav £53,638 T: Angel Penna, Chantilly, France B: Dayton Ltd Sire: Exbury 2. Secret Man 3. Scallywag 2l, neck 3:13.17 15 ran

1977 HM Queen Elizabeth II's b f **Dunfermline** J: Willie Carson 10/1 £52,867 T: Dick Hern, West Ilsley, Berkshire B: Owner Sire: Royal Palace 2. Alleged 3. Classic Example 1½l, 10l 3:05.17 13 ran

1978 Marcos Lemos's b c **Julio Mariner**
J: Edward Hide 28/1 £50,630 T: Clive Brittain, Newmarket B: Fonthill Stud Sire: Blakeney 2. Le Moss 3. M-Lolshan 1½l, head 3:04.94 14 ran

1979 Alexis Rolland's ch c **Son of Love**
J: Alain Lequeux 20/1 £55,060 T: Robert Collet, Chantilly, France B: Haras du Hoguenet Sire: Jefferson 2. Soleil Noir 3. Niniski short head, 2½l 3:09.02 17 ran

1980 Jim Joel's b c **Light Cavalry**
J: Joe Mercer 3/1 £71,256 T: Henry Cecil, Newmarket B: Owner Sire: Brigadier Gerard 2. Water Mill 3. World Leader 4l, 4l 3:11.48 7 ran

1981 Sir Jakie Astor's b c **Cut Above**
J: Joe Mercer 28/1 £76,190 T: Dick Hern, West Ilsley, Berkshire B: Owner Sire: High Top 2. Glint of Gold 3. Bustomi 2½l, 4l 3:11.60 7 ran

1982 Maktoum al Maktoum's b c **Touching Wood** J: Paul Cook 7/1 £80,120 T: Tom Jones, Newmarket B: Pin Oak Farm Sire: Roberto 2. Zilos 3. Diamond Shoal 1½l, 2½l 3:03.53 15 ran

1983 Sir Michael Sobell's b f **Sun Princess** J: Willie Carson 11/8 Fav £81,980 T: Dick Hern, West Ilsley, Berkshire B: Ballymacoll Stud Farm Sire: English Prince 2. Esprit du Nord 3. Carlingford Castle ¾l, short head 3:16.65 10 ran

1984 Ivan Allan's b c **Commanche Run**
J: Lester Piggott 7/4 Fav £110,700 T: Luca Cumani, Newmarket B: Majors Racing International Ltd Sire: Run the Gantlet 2. Baynoun 3. Alphabatim neck, 1½l 3:09.93 11 ran

RECORDS FOR WINNING HORSES

Greatest margins

12 lengths — Never Say Die (1954)
10 lengths — Stockwell (1852), Talma (1951), Provoke (1965), Bruni (1975)

8 lengths — Alcide (1958)
6 lengths — Melton (1885), Wool Winder (1907), Prince Palatine (1911), Gay Crusader (1917), Keysoe (1919), Ragusa (1963)
5 lengths — Don John (1838), Wenlock (1872), Rayon d'Or (1879), Tracery (1912), Black Jester (1914), Bahram (1935)

Smallest margins

dead-heat — Charles the Twelfth and Euclid (1839), Voltigeur and Russborough (1850)
short head — Trigo (1929), Herringbone (1943), Ribero (1968), Son of Love (1979)
half a head — Phoenomenon (1783), Otterington (1812), Altisidora (1813)
head — Chorister (1831), Charles the Twelfth (1839), Nutwith (1843), Knight of St George (1854), Caller Ou (1861), The Marquis (1862), Lord Lyon (1866), Marie Stuart (1873), Troutbeck (1906), Swynford (1910), Sun Castle (1941), Sayajirao (1947), Indiana (1964), Sodium (1966).

Fillies

Allabaculia (1776), Hollandaise (1778), Serina (1781), Imperatrix (1782), Omphale (1784), Cowslip (1785), Young Flora (1788), Pewett (1789), Paulina (1807), Altisidora (1813), The Duchess (1816), Matilda (1827), Queen of Trumps (1835), The Blue Bonnet (1842), Impérieuse (1857), Sunbeam (1858), Caller Ou (1861), Achievement (1867), Formosa (1868), Hannah (1871), Marie Stuart (1873), Apology (1874), Jannette (1878), Dutch Oven (1882), Seabreeze (1888), Memoir (1890), La Flèche (1892), Throstle (1894), Sceptre (1902), Pretty Polly (1904), Keysoe (1919), Tranquil (1923), Book Law (1927), Sun Chariot (1942), Herringbone (1943), Meld (1955), Cantelo (1959), Dunfermline (1977), Sun Princess (1983).

Grey

Hollandaise (1778), Symmetry (1798), Caligula (1920), Airborne (1946), Bruni (1975).

Black

Jerry (1824).

Longest odds

200/1 — Theodore (1822)
100/1 — Otterington (1812)
1000/15 — Caller Ou (1861)
50/1 — Touchstone (1834), Throstle (1894), Night Hawk (1913), Polemarch (1921)
40/1 — Saucebox (1855), Dutch Oven (1882), Doricles (1901)
33/1 — Antonio (1819), Royal Lancer (1922)

Shortest odds

1/10 — Galtee More (1897)
1/7 — Ormonde (1886)
2/11 — Persimmon (1896), Gay Crusader (1917)
2/7 — Flying Fox (1899), Diamond Jubilee (1900), Nijinsky (1970)
1/3 — Pommern (1915)
4/11 — Gainsborough (1918), Bahram (1935)
2/5 — Rock Sand (1903), Pretty Polly (1904), Ragusa (1963).

No odds recorded

Serina (1781), Imperatrix (1782), Omphale (1784), Lounger (1797)

Dead-heats run off

In 1839 Charles the Twelfth beat Euclid by a head in a run-off after the pair had dead-heated for first place.
In 1850, after a dead-heat between Voltigeur and Russborough, the run-off was won by Voltigeur by a length.

Winner carrying overweight

Dutch Oven (1882) carried 1lb overweight at 8 st 6 lb.

Winner on disqualification

Pewett was awarded the 1789 race after the disqualification of Zanga, who finished first, but whose jockey was found guilty of jostling.

Trained in Ireland

Ballymoss (1957), Ragusa (1963), Nijinsky (1970), Boucher (1972).

Trained in France

Scratch (1950), Talma (1951), Cambremer (1956), Crow (1976), Son of Love (1979)

Bred in France

Gladiateur (1865), Rayon d'Or (1879), Scratch (1950), Talma (1951), Cambremer (1956), Crow (1976), Son of Love (1979)

Bred in USA

Iroquois (1881), Tracery (1912), Black Tarquin (1948), Never Say Die (1954), Ribocco (1967), Ribero (1968), Boucher (1972), Touching Wood (1982)

Bred in Canada

Nijinsky (1970)

Siblings

Touchstone (1834) and Launcelot (1840), Persimmon (1896) and Diamond Jubilee (1900), and Ribocco (1967) and Ribero (1968) were brothers.
Memoir (1890) and La Flèche (1892) were sisters.
Spadille (1787) and Young Flora (1788), and Lord Lyon (1866) and

Achievement (1867) were brothers and sisters.
Van Tromp (1847) and The Flying Dutchman (1849) were half-brothers.
Common (1891) and Throstle (1894) were half-brother and half-sister.

Unnamed at time of victory

Allabaculia (1776), Bourbon (1777), Tommy (1779), Ruler (1780), Paragon (1786), Spadille (1787), Young Flora (1788), Young Traveller (1791), Tartar (1792), Remembrancer (1803), Soothsayer (1811)

Raced under two names

The 1786 winner ran unnamed at Doncaster, was called St Leger when he raced next at Newcastle in the following June, and competed for the first time under the name Paragon at Carlisle in July 1787.
The 1791 winner ran unnamed, became Young Traveller at the end of his three-year-old season, and was re-named Lauderdale midway through his four-year-old campaign.
The Duchess, winner in 1816, won as Duchess of Leven at Pontefract only 12 days before her Doncaster victory.

Raced and covered under different names

The 1844 winner was known as Foig a Ballagh during his racing career, but became Faugh a Ballagh when he retired to stud.

Winners in two countries

Royal Lancer (1922), Trigo (1929) and Touching Wood (1982) also won the Irish St Leger.

Oldest and youngest sires

Sampson was 27 years old when he got Allabaculia (1776).
Bahram sired Turkhan (1940) and Psidium sired Sodium (1966) at the age of four.

Oldest and youngest dams

Nutwith (1843) was out of a 25-year-old unnamed mare by Comus. The dams of Tommy (1779), Ashton (1809), Otterington (1812) and The Baron (1845) were all four years old.

RECORDS FOR PLACED HORSES

Fillies

Emma (1776), Ballad Singer (1777), Armida (1777), Tantrum filly (1779), Temperance (1781), Haphazard (1782), Matron (1785), Bellona (1789), Skypeeper (1792), Hornet (1793), Lisette (1809), Oriana (1810), Arabella (1814), Fortuna (1821), Violet (1822), Belinda (1828), La Fille Mal Gardée (1831), Figaro filly (1832), Beeswing (1836), Priscilla

Tomboy (1842), The Princess (1844), Miss Sarah (1845), Canezou (1848), Aphrodite (1851), Lady Tatton (1855), Blanche of Middlebie (1858), Queen Bertha (1863), Borealis (1863), Regalia (1865), Wheat-ear (1870), Lady Golightly (1877), Manoeuvre (1877), Cipollata (1880), Lucy Glitters (1881), Geheimniss (1882), Shotover (1882), Sandiway (1884), Superba (1884), Lonely (1885), Zanzibar (1888), Butterfly (1895), Chélandry (1897), Cherry Lass (1905), Snow Marten (1915), My Dear (1918), Teresina (1923), Foliation (1926), Dancing Time (1941), Ribbon (1943), Sanlinea (1950), None Nicer (1958), Patti (1964), Cold Storage (1968), Ginevra (1972)

Gelding

Courlan (1900)

Grey

Pacolet (1783), Prior (1794), Brilliant (1794), Whynot (1795), Lisette (1809), The Marshal (1818), Professor (1822), Figaro filly (1832), The Squire (1841), Son and Heir (1927), Mahmoud (1936), Migoli (1947), Scallywag (1976), Soleil Noir (1979)

Black

Sir Hercules (1829), The Doctor (1837), Nunnykirk (1851). Le Nicham (1893) was described as brown or black.

Longest odds

300/1 — Scintillant (1899)
200/1 — Gonsalvo (1890), Rampion (1896)
100/1 — Copeland (1820), Belinda (1828), Carnaby (1833), Wild Tommy (1876), Exmoor (1886), Cressingham (1914), Riboson (1974)
1000/15 — Arthur Wellesley (1854)
66/1 — Lucy Glitters (1881), Kingsfold (1952), Cold Storage (1968)
50/1 — Priscilla Tomboy (1842), Clarissimus (1862), St Simon of the Rock (1891), Henry the First (1904)

Trained in Ireland

Russborough (1850), Die Hard (1960), Patti (1964), Meadow Court (1965), Canterbury (1968), King Pellinore (1975), Alleged (1977)

Trained in France

Révérend (1891), Palais Royal (1928), Arbar (1947), Vieux Manoir (1950), Alcinus (1952), Northern Light (1953), Estremadur (1954), Beau Prince (1955), Dicta Drake (1961), Secret Man (1976), Soleil Noir (1979), Esprit du Nord (1983)

Trained in Italy

Ruysdael (1967)

Bred in France

Prince Charlie (1872), Révérend (1891), Le Nicham (1893), Palais Royal (1928), Mahmoud (1936), Arbar (1947), Vieux Manoir (1950), Fraise du Bois (1951), Alcinus (1952), Northern Light (1953), Estremadur (1954), Dicta Drake (1961), Secret Man (1976), Soleil Noir (1979), World Leader (1980).

Bred in USA

St Cloud (1897), Bridegroom (1898), Caiman (1899), Lone Eagle (1949), Solstice (1965), Ribofilio (1969), Politico (1970), King Pellinore (1975), Libra's Rib (1975), Alleged (1977), Niniski (1979), Esprit du Nord (1983), Alphabatim (1984)

MISCELLANEOUS RECORDS

Fastest times

3:01.6 — Coronach (1926), Windsor Lad (1934)
3:01.8 — Bahram (1935)
3:02.6 — Black Jester (1914)
3:03.0 — Fairway (1928)
3:03.4 — Trigo (1929)
3:03.53 — Touching Wood (1982)

Largest entry

662 — 1974

Smallest entry

6 — 1776, 1785

Largest fields

30 — 1825
28 — 1830
27 — 1820, 1826

Smallest fields

3 — 1917
4 — 1783, 1785
5 — 1776, 1782, 1788, 1795, 1897, 1903, 1916, 1918

Richest first prizes

£110,700 — 1984
£81,980 — 1983
£80,120 — 1982

Smallest first prizes

£131 — 1776, 1785
£210 — 1782, 1783, 1787, 1789
£236 — 1788

Hottest losing favourites

1/4 — Craig an Eran was 4th in 1921
4/11 — Meadow Court was 2nd in 1965
4/9 — Shergar was 4th in 1981
1/2 — Coronation was 2nd in 1841, Kisber was 4th in 1876

Most consecutive winning favourites

4 — 1863 to 1866, 1915 to 1918, 1925 to 1928 (one joint)

Most consecutive losing favourites

9 — 1816 to 1824; 1854 to 1862; 1936 to 1945

Race abandoned

The 1939 race, scheduled for 6 September, was cancelled because of the outbreak of World War II on 3 September.

Earliest dates

5 September — 1945 (at York)
6 September — 1893, 1899, 1941 (at Manchester)

Latest date

23 November — 1940 (at Thirsk)

Latest peacetime date

28 September — 1779, 1784, 1790, 1802

Run on

Monday: 1807–24
Tuesday: 1776–79, 1782–93, 1795–1806, 1825–44
Wednesday: 1780–81, 1794, 1845–1938, 1945–46, 1955–57, 1962–69
Saturday: 1940–44, 1947–54, 1958–61, from 1970.

Fillies placed 1, 2, 3

In 1882 the first three home were all fillies — Dutch Oven, Geheimniss and Shotover.

Most successful owners

7 wins — 9th Duke of Hamilton: 1786, 1787, 1788, 1792, 1808, 1809, 1814
6 wins — 17th Earl of Derby: 1910, 1919, 1923, 1928, 1933, 1943
   HH Aga Khan III: 1924, 1932, 1935, 1940, 1944, 1952
4 wins — Henry Goodricke: 1782, 1790, 1797, 1801
   Edward Petre: 1822, 1827, 1828, 1829
   Richard Watt: 1813, 1823, 1825, 1833
   Charles Engelhard: 1964, 1967, 1968, 1970
3 wins — 4th Earl Fitzwilliam: 1789, 1802, 1807
   1st Marquis of Westminster: 1834, 1840, 1841
   13th Earl of Eglinton: 1842, 1847, 1849
   6th Viscount Falmouth: 1877, 1878, 1882
2 wins — John Hutchinson: 1791, 1794
   Sir Thomas Gascoigne: 1778, 1798
   Harry Mellish: 1804, 1805
   John Clifton: 1793, 1806
   Henry Peirse: 1817, 1818
   Richard Oliver Gascoigne: 1811, 1824
   Anthony Nichol: 1851, 1856
   William I'Anson: 1861, 1864
   James Merry: 1858, 1873
   Comte Frédéric de Lagrange: 1865, 1879
   6th Duke of Portland: 1889, 1890
   1st Duke of Westminster: 1886, 1899
   HM King Edward VII: 1896, 1900
   Jack Joel: 1908, 1914
   Alfred Cox: 1909, 1917
   1st Baron Woolavington: 1916, 1926
   1st Baron Glanely: 1930, 1937
   William Woodward: 1936, 1948
   Marcel Boussac: 1950, 1951
   Sir Jakie Astor: 1965, 1981

Owned winner and 2nd

9th Duke of Hamilton: 1809
Henry Peirse: 1818
1st Marquis of Westminster: 1840
6th Viscount Falmouth: 1877, 1878
HH Aga Khan III: 1932, 1940
In 1932 the Aga Khan's four runners finished 1st (Firdaussi), 2nd (Dastur), 4th (Udaipur) and 5th (Taj Kasra).

Most successful breeders

6 wins — 9th Duke of Hamilton: 1786, 1787, 1788, 1808, 1809, 1814
5 wins — 17th Earl of Derby: 1919, 1923, 1928, 1933, 1943
4 wins — HH Aga Khan III: 1932, 1935, 1940, 1952 (one in partnership)
3 wins — John Hutchinson: 1791, 1794, 1795
   Henry Goodricke: 1790, 1797, 1801
   4th Earl Fitzwilliam: 1789, 1802, 1807
   Sir Thomas Gascoigne: 1778, 1798, 1811
   1st Marquis of Westminster: 1834, 1840, 1841
   6th Viscount Falmouth: 1877, 1878, 1882
   HM Queen Victoria: 1857, 1890, 1892
   1st Duke of Westminster: 1886, 1899, 1902
   National Stud: 1922, 1942, 1945
2 wins — Henry Peirse: 1817, 1818
   Richard Watt: 1813, 1825
   William Allen: 1829, 1833
   Henry Vansittart: 1847, 1849
   William I'Anson: 1861, 1864
   Mark Pearson: 1866, 1867
   James Merry: 1858, 1873
   1st Baron Alington: 1891, 1894
   HM King Edward VII: 1896, 1900
   William Hall Walker: 1911, 1913
   Jack Joel: 1908, 1914
   Alfred Cox: 1909, 1917
   James Maher: 1920, 1931
   William Woodward/Belair Stud: 1936, 1948
   Marcel Boussac: 1950, 1951
   Mrs Julian Rogers: 1967, 1968
   Kilcarn Stud: 1966, 1971
   Astor Studs/Sir Jakie Astor: 1965, 1981

Bred winner and 2nd

John Hutchinson: 1795
Henry Peirse: 1818
1st Marquis of Westminster: 1840, 1841
6th Viscount Falmouth: 1877, 1878

Eclipse, who was never beaten, nor even extended, is still recognised after two centuries as the paragon of racing excellence. He is shown here in the famous Stubbs portrait, reproduced by kind permission of the Stewards of the Jockey Club.

Crucifix, depicted by Harry Hall with John Barham Day in the saddle, was foaled in 1837, the year Queen Victoria came to the throne. Day, who was also her trainer, kept her sound just long enough to enable her to win the 1840 Oaks, her third Classic triumph, and remain unbeaten.

Sun Princess set a record margin of victory for the Oaks when Willie Carson brought her home 12 lengths clear of Acclimatise in 1983.

The 1975 King George VI and Queen Elizabeth Stakes was dubbed England's "Race of the Century". Grundy beat Bustino by half a length, and the distant third, Dahlia, also beat the previous course record.

HH Aga Khan III: 1932 (winner, 2nd, 4th and 5th)

Most successful trainers

16 wins — John Scott: 1827, 1828, 1829, 1832, 1834, 1838, 1839, 1840, 1841, 1845, 1851, 1853, 1856, 1857, 1859, 1862

6 wins — Mat Dawson: 1877, 1878, 1882, 1884, 1885, 1895

John Porter: 1869, 1886, 1891, 1892, 1894, 1899

Cecil Boyd-Rochfort: 1936, 1941, 1948, 1953, 1955, 1958

Dick Hern: 1962, 1965, 1974, 1977, 1981, 1983

5 wins — George Searle: 1782, 1785, 1790, 1797, 1801

Alec Taylor: 1905, 1909, 1917, 1918, 1927

Frank Butters: 1928, 1932, 1935, 1940, 1944

4 wins — John Mangle: 1786, 1787, 1788, 1792

Christopher Scaife: 1776, 1789, 1802, 1807

John Lonsdale: 1817, 1818, 1819, 1820

James Croft: 1815, 1816, 1822, 1824

3 wins — John Hutchinson: 1791, 1794, 1795

William Theakston: 1808, 1809, 1814

Richard Shepherd: 1823, 1825, 1833

James Jewitt: 1887, 1888, 1893

Richard Marsh: 1883, 1896, 1900

Charles Morton: 1908, 1914, 1923

George Lambton: 1910, 1919, 1933

Fred Darling: 1916, 1926, 1942

Noel Murless: 1949, 1960, 1961

Vincent O'Brien: 1957, 1970, 1972

2 wins — Joseph Rose: 1778, 1779

Bartle Atkinson: 1804, 1805

Tommy Sykes: 1811, 1813

Sam King: 1798, 1826

John Fobert: 1847, 1849

William I'Anson: 1861, 1864

James Dover: 1866, 1867

Alec Taylor, sr: 1860, 1875

Tom Jennings: 1865, 1879

George Dawson: 1889, 1890

Sam Darling: 1897, 1898

Dick Dawson: 1924, 1929

Tommy Hogg: 1930, 1937

Dick Perryman: 1945, 1946

Marcus Marsh: 1934, 1952

Charles Semblat: 1950, 1951

Fulke Johnson Houghton: 1967, 1968

Tom Jones: 1971, 1982

Trained first 4 to finish

In 1822, the four runners (in a field of 23) saddled by James Croft finished 1st (Theodore), 2nd (Violet), 3rd (Professor) and 4th (Corinthian).

Frank Butters trained 1st, 2nd, 4th and 5th, all owner-bred by the HH Aga Khan III, in 1932.

Trained winner, 2nd and 3rd

Alec Taylor: 1918

Trained winner and 2nd

William Theakston: 1809

John Lonsdale: 1818, 1819

John Scott: 1840

Mat Dawson: 1877, 1878

Dick Perryman: 1946

Most successful jockeys

9 wins — Bill Scott: 1821, 1825, 1828, 1829, 1838, 1839, 1840, 1841, 1846

8 wins — John Jackson: 1791, 1794, 1796, 1798, 1805, 1813, 1815, 1822

Lester Piggott: 1960, 1961, 1967, 1968, 1970, 1971, 1972, 1984

6 wins — Ben Smith: 1803, 1808, 1809, 1811, 1816, 1824

Fred Archer: 1877, 1878, 1881, 1882, 1885, 1886

5 wins — John Mangle: 1780, 1786, 1787, 1788, 1792

Tom Chaloner: 1861, 1862, 1867, 1868, 1875

Jack Watts: 1883, 1884, 1890, 1892, 1896

Gordon Richards: 1930, 1937, 1940, 1942, 1944

4 wins — Bob Johnson: 1812, 1817, 1818, 1820

Joe Childs: 1918, 1921, 1925, 1926

Charlie Smirke: 1934, 1935, 1952, 1954

Joe Mercer: 1965, 1974, 1980, 1981

3 wins — George Searle: 1782, 1785, 1790

John Shepherd: 1797, 1801, 1814

Job Marson: 1843, 1847, 1850

Nat Flatman: 1848, 1856, 1857

Tommy Weston: 1923, 1928, 1933

Brownie Carslake: 1919, 1924, 1938

Harry Carr: 1955, 1958, 1962

2 wins — Frank Buckle: 1800, 1804

Bill Clift: 1807, 1810

Jem Robinson: 1827, 1832

John Barham Day: 1831, 1836

Tommy Lye: 1835, 1842

Frank Butler: 1845, 1853

Luke Snowden: 1858, 1860

John Wells: 1855, 1869

Charlie Maidment: 1871, 1872

John Osborne: 1863, 1874

Jem Goater: 1876, 1879

Jack Robinson: 1887, 1888

Charlie Wood: 1897, 1898

Morny Cannon: 1894, 1899

Danny Maher: 1903, 1909

Walter Griggs: 1908, 1914

Steve Donoghue: 1915, 1917

Harry Wragg: 1931, 1943

Tommy Lowrey: 1945, 1946

Edgar Britt: 1947, 1948

Michael Beary: 1929, 1949

Rae Johnstone: 1950, 1951

Frankie Durr: 1966, 1973

Edward Hide: 1959, 1978

Willie Carson: 1977, 1983

Successful owner-breeder-trainers

John Hutchinson — Young Traveller (1791), Beningbrough (1794)

William I'Anson — Caller Ou (1861), Blair Athol (1864)

Successful owner-rider

Bill Scott — Sir Tatton Sykes (1846)

Successful trainer-riders

George Searle — Imperatrix (1782), Cowslip (1785), Ambidexter (1790)

John Mangle — Paragon (1786), Spadille (1787), Young Flora (1788), Tartar (1792)

Tom Fields — Cockfighter (1799)

Successful breeder-trainers

John Hutchinson — Hambletonian (1795)

John Smith — Chorister (1831)

Successful owner-trainers

Tom Parr — Saucebox (1855)

John Scott — Impérieuse (1857)

Bob Sievier — Sceptre (1902)

Successful as both jockey and trainer

John Mangle rode Ruler (1780) in addition to riding and training Paragon (1786), Spadille (1787), Young Flora (1788) and Tartar (1792).

George Searle trained Lounger (1797) and Quiz (1801) in addition to Imperatrix (1782), Cowslip (1785) and Ambidexter (1790), all of whom he trained and rode.

Bob Johnson rode Otterington (1812), Ebor (1817), Reveller (1818) and St Patrick (1820), trained Nutwith (1843).

Jack Robinson rode Kilwarlin (1887) and Seabreeze (1888), trained Night Hawk (1913).

George Bridgland rode Sun Castle (1941), trained Cambremer (1956).

Harry Wragg rode Sandwich (1931) and Herringbone (1943); trained Intermezzo (1969).

Most successful sires

6 wins — Stockwell: St Albans (1860), Caller Ou (1861), The Marquis (1862), Blair Athol (1864), Lord Lyon (1866), Achievement (1867)

4 wins — Highflyer: Omphale (1784), Cowslip (1785), Spadille (1787), Young Flora (1788)

Sir Peter Teazle: Ambrosio (1796), Fyldener (1806), Paulina (1807), Petronius (1808)

Lord Clifden: Hawthornden (1870), Wenlock (1872), Petrarch (1876), Jannette (1878)

St Simon: Memoir (1890), La Flèche (1892), Persimmon (1896), Diamond Jubilee (1900)

Ribot: Ragusa (1963), Ribocco (1967), Ribero (1968), Boucher (1972)

3 wins — King Fergus: Young Traveller (1791), Beningbrough (1794), Hambletonian (1795)

Touchstone: The Blue Bonnet (1842), Surplice (1848), Newminster (1851)

Irish Birdcatcher: The Baron (1845), Knight of St George (1854), Warlock (1856)

Isonomy: Seabreeze (1888), Common (1891), Isinglass (1893)

Gallinule: Wildfowler (1898), Pretty Polly (1904), Night Hawk (1913)

Persimmon: Sceptre (1902), Your Majesty (1908), Prince Palatine (1911)

The Tetrarch: Caligula (1920), Polemarch (1921), Salmon-Trout (1924)

Gainsborough: Solario (1925), Singapore (1930), Hyperion (1933)

Blandford: Trigo (1929), Windsor Lad (1934), Bahram (1935)

Aureole: St Paddy (1960), Aurelius (1961), Provoke (1965).

2 wins — Florizel: Tartar (1792), Ninety-three (1793)

Comus: Reveller (1818), Matilda (1827)

Whisker: Memnon (1825), The Colonel (1828)

Camel: Touchstone (1834), Launcelot (1840)

Voltaire: Charles the Twelfth (1839), Voltigeur (1850)

Melbourne: Sir Tatton Sykes (1846), West Australian (1853)

Blair Athol: Craig Millar (1875), Silvio (1877)

Polymelus: Black Jester (1914), Pommern (1915)

Bayardo: Gay Crusader (1917), Gainsborough (1918)

Swynford: Keysoe (1919), Tranquil (1923)

Hyperion: Sun Castle (1941), Sun Chariot (1942)

Bois Roussel: Tehran (1944), Ridge Wood (1949)

Pharis: Scratch (1950), Talma (1951)

Alycidon: Meld (1955), Alcide (1958)

Sired winner, 2nd and 3rd

Comus — 1818

Sired winner and 2nd

Le Sang — 1777
Highflyer — 1788
Phoenomenon — 1790
King Fergus — 1795
Sir Peter Teazle — 1806, 1808
Catton — 1826
Velocipede — 1835
Stockwell — 1866
Buccaneer — 1868
Isonomy — 1893
Florizel — 1901

Classic Summary

MOST SUCCESSFUL OWNERS

		2000	1000	Derby	Oaks	Leger	Total
4th Duke of Grafton	1813–1831	5	8	1	6	0	20
17th Earl of Derby	1910–1945	2	7	3	2	6	20
HH Aga Khan III	1924–1957	3	1	5	2	6	17
6th Viscount Falmouth	1862–1883	3	4	2	4	3	16
5th Earl of Jersey	1824–1837	5	2	3	1	0	11
1st Duke of Westminster	1880–1899	4	1	4	0	2	11
6th Duke of Portland	1888–1900	1	2	2	4	2	11
Jack Joel	1903–1921	1	2	2	4	2	11
5th Earl of Rosebery	1883–1924	3	3	3	1	1	11
2nd Viscount Astor	1910–1945	3	2	0	5	1	11
3rd Earl of Egremont	1782–1826	0	0	5	5	0	10
2nd Marquis of Exeter	1821–1852	4	1	0	3	1	9
Sir Victor Sassoon	1937–1960	1	2	4	1	1	9
1st Earl Grosvenor	1781–1799	0	0	3	5	0	8
John Bowes	1835–1853	3	0	4	0	1	8
Sir Joseph Hawley	1847–1869	1	1	4	1	1	8
Comte Frédéric de Lagrange	1864–1879	2	1	1	2	2	8
William Stirling Crawfurd	1859–1882	2	3	1	1	1	8
HM King Edward VII	1896–1909	2	1	3	0	2	8

MOST SUCCESSFUL BREEDERS

		2000	1000	Derby	Oaks	Leger	Total
4th Duke of Grafton	1815–1831	5	8	1	5	0	19
6th Viscount Falmouth	1863–1884	3	4	3	6	3	19
17th Earl of Derby	1916–1945	2	7	3	2	5	19
HH Aga Khan III	1929–1959	3	3	3	3	4	16
3rd Earl of Egremont	1788–1831	0	0	6	6	0	12
5th Earl of Jersey	1824–1847	5	3	2	2	0	12
1st Duke of Westminster	1880–1902	3	2	3	1	3	12
5th Earl of Rosebery	1883–1924	4	3	3	1	1	12
2nd Viscount Astor	1910–1953	3	2	0	6	1	12
James Cookson	1854–1880	2	2	1	5	1	11
HM Queen Victoria	1857–1892	2	3	1	2	3	11
Jack Joel	1903–1921	1	2	2	4	2	11
1st Earl Grosvenor	1781–1805	0	0	3	6	0	9
6th Duke of Portland	1888–1900	1	2	2	3	1	9
National Stud	1919–1957	2	1	0	2	3	8

N.B. HH Aga Khan III's total includes 6 winners bred in partnership with his son, Prince Aly Khan. The total for the 2nd Viscount Astor includes one bred in the name of his Cliveden Stud and one bred in partnership with his sons.

MOST SUCCESSFUL TRAINERS

		2000	1000	Derby	Oaks	Leger	Total
John Scott	1827–1863	7	4	5	8	16	40
Robert Robson	1793–1827	6	9	7	12	0	34
Mat Dawson	1853–1895	5	6	6	5	6	28
John Porter	1868–1900	5	2	7	3	6	23
Alec Taylor	1905–1927	4	1	3	8	5	21
Fred Darling	1916–1947	5	2	7	2	3	19
Noel Murless	1948–1973	2	6	3	5	3	19
Dixon Boyce	1805–1829	5	3	5	4	0	17
Vincent O'Brien	1957–1984	4	1	6	2	3	17
Frank Butters	1927–1948	1	1	2	6	5	15
James Edwards	1811–1837	6	2	5	1	0	14
Richard Marsh	1883–1909	3	2	4	1	3	13
Cecil Boyd-Rochfort	1933–1959	1	3	1	2	6	13
Dick Hern	1962–1983	1	1	2	3	6	13
John Day, jr	1847–1869	4	4	2	2	0	12
Charles Morton	1903–1923	1	2	2	4	3	12
George Lambton	1896–1933	1	4	1	2	3	12
Joe Lawson	1929–1954	4	3	4	3	1	12

MOST SUCCESSFUL TRAINERS (CONTINUED)

		2000	1000	Derby	Oaks	Leger	Total
John Pratt	1781–1799	0	0	6	7	0	11
Alec Taylor, sr	1851–1887	2	3	2	2	2	11
Frank Neale	1782–1804	0	0	5	4	0	10
Richard Prince	1786–1819	1	1	1	3	0	10
John Barham Day	1837–1854	3	4	2	2	0	10
George Dawson	1888–1894	1	2	2	3	2	10
Peter Gilpin	1904–1927	1	4	2	2	1	10
Jack Jarvis	1923–1953	3	3	2	0	1	9
Joe Hayhoe	1864–1879	0	2	3	2	1	8
Tom Jennings	1864–1879	2	1	1	2	2	8
Dick Dawson	1916–1930	1	0	3	2	2	8

MOST SUCCESSFUL JOCKEYS

		2000	1000	Derby	Oaks	Leger	Total
Lester Piggott	1954–1984	3	2	9	6	8	28
Frank Buckle	1792–1827	5	6	5	9	2	27
Jem Robinson	1817–1848	9	5	6	2	2	24
Fred Archer	1874–1886	4	2	5	4	6	21
Bill Scott	1821–1846	3	0	4	3	9	19
Jack Watts	1883–1897	2	4	4	4	5	19
John Barham Day	1826–1841	4	5	0	5	2	16
George Fordham	1859–1883	3	7	1	5	0	16
Joe Childs	1912–1933	2	2	3	4	4	15
Frank Butler	1843–1853	2	2	2	6	2	14
Steve Donoghue	1915–1937	3	1	6	2	2	14
Charlie Elliott	1923–1949	5	4	3	2	0	14
Gordon Richards	1930–1953	3	3	1	2	5	14
Bill Clift	1793–1819	2	2	5	2	2	13
Tom Cannon	1866–1889	4	3	1	4	1	13
Harry Wragg	1928–1946	1	3	3	4	2	13
John Osborne	1856–1888	6	2	1	1	2	12
Rae Johnstone	1934–1956	1	3	3	3	2	12
Tommy Weston	1923–1946	2	1	2	3	3	11
Charlie Smirke	1934–1958	2	1	4	0	4	11
Nat Flatman	1835–1857	3	3	1	0	3	10
Tom Chaloner	1861–1875	3	0	1	1	5	10
Charlie Wood	1880–1898	1	3	3	1	2	10
Bill Arnull	1804–1832	3	3	3	0	0	9
Sam Chifney, jr	1807–1843	1	1	2	5	0	9
Danny Maher	1901–1912	2	1	3	1	2	9
Willie Carson	1972–1983	2	0	2	3	2	9
John Jackson	1791–1822	0	0	0	0	8	8
John Wells	1854–1869	1	2	3	0	2	8
Herbert Jones	1900–1909	4	0	2	1	1	8
Joe Mercer	1953–1981	1	2	0	1	4	8

MOST SUCCESSFUL SIRES

		2000	1000	Derby	Oaks	Leger	Total
Stockwell	1860–1873	4	3	3	1	6	17
St Simon	1890–1900	2	4	2	5	4	17
Touchstone	1842–1855	4	1	3	1	3	12
Melbourne	1846–1857	2	2	2	3	2	11
Blandford	1929–1938	2	1	4	1	3	11
Hyperion	1940–1946	0	4	1	4	2	11
Sir Peter Teazle	1794–1808	0	0	4	2	4	10
Sultan	1829–1837	5	2	1	2	0	10
Highflyer	1784–1789	0	0	3	1	4	8
Sorceror	1808–1813	3	0	1	3	1	8
Waxy	1809–1818	0	1	4	3	0	8
Emilius	1830–1843	1	3	2	1	1	8
Isonomy	1888–1893	2	0	2	1	3	8
Persimmon	1902–1911	1	1	0	3	3	8
Polymelus	1914–1921	1	1	3	1	2	8
Swynford	1918–1925	0	4	1	1	2	8
Hurry On	1922–1929	0	2	3	2	1	8

MULTIPLE CLASSIC-WINNING HORSES

2000 Guineas, 1000 Guineas, Oaks, St Leger

Formosa (1868, one dead-heat), Sceptre (1902)

2000 Guineas, Derby, St Leger

West Australian (1853), Gladiateur (1865), Lord Lyon (1866), Ormonde (1886), Common (1891), Isinglass (1893), Galtee More (1897), Flying Fox (1899), Diamond Jubilee (1900), Rock Sand (1903), Pommern (1915), Gay Crusader (1917), Gainsborough (1918), Bahram (1935), Nijinsky (1970)

1000 Guineas, Oaks, St Leger

Hannah (1871), Apology (1874), La Flèche (1892), Pretty Polly (1904), Sun Chariot (1942), Meld (1955)

2000 Guineas, 1000 Guineas, Oaks

Crucifix (1840)

2000 Guineas, 1000 Guineas

Pilgrimage (1878)

2000 Guineas, Derby

Smolensko (1813), Cadland (1828), Bay Middleton (1836), Cotherstone (1843), Macaroni (1863), Pretender (1869), Shotover (1882), Ayrshire (1888), Ladas (1894), St Amant (1904), Minoru (1909), Sunstar (1911), Manna (1925), Cameronian (1931), Blue Peter (1939), Nimbus (1949), Crepello (1957), Royal Palace (1967), Sir Ivor (1968)

2000 Guineas, Oaks

Pastille (1822)

2000 Guineas, St Leger

Sir Tatton Sykes (1846), Stockwell (1852), The Marquis (1862), Petrarch (1876)

1000 Guineas, Derby

Tagalie (1912)

1000 Guineas, Oaks

Neva (1817), Corinne (1818), Zinc (1823), Cobweb (1824), Galata (1832), Mendicant (1846), Governess (1858), Reine (1872), Spinaway (1875), Camélia (1876, one dead-heat), Wheel of Fortune (1879), Thebais (1881), Busybody (1884), Miss Jummy (1886), Rêve d'Or (1887), Mimi (1891), Amiable (1894), Cherry Lass (1905), Jest (1913), Princess Dorrie (1914), Saucy Sue (1925), Exhibitionnist (1937), Rockfel (1938), Galatea (1939), Godiva (1940), Sun Stream (1945), Imprudence (1947), Musidora (1949), Bella Paola (1958), Petite Etoile (1959), Never Too Late (1960), Sweet Solera

(1961), Altesse Royale (1971), Mysterious (1973)

1000 Guineas, St Leger

Impérieuse (1857), Achievement (1867), Tranquil (1923), Herringbone (1943)

Derby, Oaks

Eleanor (1801), Blink Bonny (1857),

Signorinetta (1908), Fifinella (1916)

Derby, St Leger

Champion (1800), Surplice (1848), The Flying Dutchman (1849), Voltigeur (1850), Blair Athol (1864), Silvio (1877), Iroquois (1881), Melton (1885), Donovan (1889), Sir Visto (1895), Persimmon (1896), Coronach (1926), Trigo (1929), Hyperion (1933), Windsor

Lad (1934), Airborne (1946), Tulyar (1952), Never Say Die (1954), St Paddy (1960)

Oaks, St Leger

Queen of Trumps (1835), Marie Stuart (1873), Jannette (1878), Seabreeze (1888), Memoir (1890), Dunfermline (1977), Sun Princess (1983)

Supreme Court and Charlie Elliott beat Zucchero and 15-year-old Lester Piggott in the inaugural King George VI and Queen Elizabeth Stakes on 21 July 1951. At the time the race was usually referred to as the Festival of Britain Stakes.

King George VI and Queen Elizabeth Stakes

The King George VI and Queen Elizabeth Stakes, now recognised as one of the two most important weight-for-age races in the European calendar, was instituted in 1951. It was staged at the Ascot July meeting as part of the celebrations for that summer's Festival of Britain and was designed to replace the Queen Elizabeth Stakes and incorporate the King George VI Stakes, both former features of Ascot programmes. It immediately assumed far greater importance than either of its predecessors, largely because the prizemoney was the highest ever offered for a race in Great Britain. Its place in the calendar and the distance (a mile and a half) made it a natural target for classic horses.

Title

King George VI and Queen Elizabeth Festival of Britain Stakes 1951
King George VI and Queen Elizabeth Stakes 1952–74
King George VI and Queen Elizabeth Diamond Stakes from 1975

Venue

Ascot Heath, Berkshire from 1951

Distance

1 mile 4 furlongs from 1951

Weights

3-year-old colts 8 st 7 lb, fillies 8 st 4 lb, 4-year-old and up males 9 st 7 lb, females 9 st 4 lb 1951–75.
3-year-old colts 8 st 8 lb, fillies 8 st 5 lb, 4-year-old and up males 9 st 7 lb, females 9 st 4 lb from 1976.

1951 Mrs Vera Lilley's br c **Supreme Court** 3yr J: Charlie Elliott 100/9 £25,322 T: Evan Williams, Kingsclere, Berkshire B: Tom Lilley Sire: Precipitation 2. Zucchero 3yr 3. Tantième 4yr ¾l, 6l 2:29.4 19 ran
1952 HH Aga Khan III's br c **Tulyar** 3yr J: Charlie Smirke 3/1 Fav £23,302 T: Marcus Marsh, Newmarket B: Owner and Prince Aly Khan Sire: Tehran 2. Gay Time 3yr 3. Worden 3yr neck, 1½l 2:33.0 15 ran
1953 Sir Victor Sassoon's b c **Pinza** 3yr J: Sir Gordon Richards 2/1 Fav £23,175 T: Norman Bertie, Newmarket B: Fred Darling Sire: Chanteur 2. Aureole 3yr 3. Worden 4yr 3l, 3l 2:34.0 13 ran
1954 HM Queen Elizabeth II's ch c **Aureole** 4yr J: Eph Smith 9/2 Fav £23,302 T: Cecil Boyd-Rochfort, Newmarket B: HM King George VI Sire: Hyperion 2. Vamos 5yr 3. Darius 3yr ¾l, 2l 2:44.0 17 ran
1955 Pierre Wertheimer's b c **Vimy** 3yr J: Roger Poincelet 10/1 £23,430 T: Alec Head, Chantilly, France B: Owner Sire: Wild Risk 2. Acropolis 3yr 3. Elopement 4yr head, 3l 2:33.76 10 ran

1956 Marchese Mario Incisa della Rocchetta's b c **Ribot** 4yr J: Enrico Camici 2/5 Fav £23,727 T: Ugo Penco, Milan, Italy B: Razza Dormello-Olgiata Sire: Tenerani 2. High Veldt 3yr 3. Todrai 3yr 5l, 2l 2:40.24 9 ran
1957 Ralph Strassburger's b c **Montaval** 4yr J: Freddie Palmer 20/1 £23,090 T: George Bridgland, Chantilly, France B: Owner Sire: Norseman 2. Al Mabsoot 3yr 3. Tribord 6yr short head, 2l 2:41.02 12 ran
1958 John McShain's ch c **Ballymoss** 4yr J: Scobie Breasley 7/4 Fav £23,642 T: Vincent O'Brien, Cashel, Co Tipperary, Ireland B: Richard Ball Sire: Mossborough 2. Almeria 4yr 3. Doutelle 4yr 3l, ¾l 2:36.33 8 ran
1959 Sir Humphrey de Trafford's b c **Alcide** 4yr J: Harry Carr 2/1 Fav £23,642 T: Cecil Boyd-Rochfort, Newmarket B: Owner Sire: Alycidon 2. Gladness 6yr 3. Balbo 5yr 2l, ¾l 2:31.39 11 ran
1960 Sir Harold Wernher's b h **Aggressor** 5yr J: Jimmy Lindley 100/8 £23,345 T: Jack Gosden, Lewes, Sussex B: Someries Stud Sire: Combat 2. Petite Etoile 4yr 3. Kythnos 3yr ½l, 4l 2:35.21 8 ran
1961 Mme Elisabeth Couturié's b c **Right Royal** 3yr J: Roger Poincelet 6/4 £23,090 T: Etienne Pollet, Chantilly, France B: Owner Sire: Owen Tudor 2. St Paddy 4yr 3. Rockavon 3yr 3l, 4l 2:40.34 4 ran
1962 François Dupré's br c **Match** 4yr J: Yves Saint-Martin 9/2 Jt-Fav £23,515 T: François Mathet, Chantilly, France B: Owner Sire: Tantième 2. Aurelius 4yr 3. Arctic Storm 3yr ¾l, neck 2:37.02 11 ran
1963 Jim Mullion's b c **Ragusa** 3yr J: Garnie Bougoure 4/1 £28,742 T: Paddy Prendergast, The Curragh, Co Kildare, Ireland B: Harry Guggenheim Sire: Ribot 2. Miralgo 4yr 3. Tarqogan 4yr 4l, 5l 2:33.80 10 ran
1964 Mrs Howell Jackson's b c **Nasram** 4yr J: Bill Pyers 100/7 £30,740

T: Ernie Fellows, Chantilly, France B: Bull Run Stud Sire: Nasrullah 2. Santa Claus 3yr 3. Royal Avenue 6yr 2l, 4l 2:33.15 4 ran
1965 Max Bell's ch c **Meadow Court** 3yr J: Lester Piggott 6/5 Fav £31,207 T: Paddy Prendergast, The Curragh, Co Kildare, Ireland B: Mrs Pansy Parker Poe Sire: Court Harwell 2. Soderini 4yr 3. Oncidium 4yr 2l, 3l 2:33.27 12 ran
1966 John Hornung's ch f **Aunt Edith** 4yr J: Lester Piggott 7/2 £29,167 T: Noel Murless, Newmarket B: West Grinstead Stud Sire: Primera 2. Sodium 3yr 3. Prominer 4yr ½l, 2l 2:35.06 5 ran
1967 Stanhope Joel's b c **Busted** 4yr J: George Moore 4/1 £24,389 T: Noel Murless, Newmarket B: Snailwell Stud Sire: Crepello 2. Salvo 4yr 3. Ribocco 3yr 3l, neck 2:33.64 9 ran
1968 Jim Joel's b c **Royal Palace** 4yr J: Sandy Barclay 4/7 Fav £24,020 T: Noel Murless, Newmarket B: Owner Sire: Ballymoss 2. Felicio 3yr 3. Topyo 4yr ½l, short head 2:33.22 7 ran
1969 11th Duke of Devonshire's b m **Park Top** 5yr J: Lester Piggott 9/4 Jt-Fav £31,122 T: Bernard van Cutsem, Newmarket B: Mrs Joan Scott Sire: Kalydon 2. Crozier 6yr 3. Hogarth 4yr 1½l, neck 2:32.46 9 ran
1970 Charles Engelhard's b c **Nijinsky** 3yr J: Lester Piggott 40/85 Fav £31,993 T: Vincent O'Brien, Cashel, Co Tipperary, Ireland B: Eddie Taylor Sire: Northern Dancer 2. Blakeney 4yr 3. Crepellana 4yr 2l, 4l 2:36.16 6 ran
1971 Paul Mellon's b c **Mill Reef** 3yr J: Geoff Lewis 8/13 Fav £31,558 T: Ian Balding, Kingsclere, Berkshire B: Owner Sire: Never Bend 2. Ortis 4yr 3. Acclimatization 3yr 6l, 3l 2:32.56 10 ran
1972 Mrs Jean Hislop's b c **Brigadier Gerard** 4yr J: Joe Mercer 8/13 Fav £60,202 T: Dick Hern, West Ilsley, Berkshire B: John Hislop Sire:

Queen's Hussar 2. Parnell 4yr
3. Riverman 3yr 1½l, 5l 2:32.91
9 ran

1973 Nelson Bunker Hunt's ch f **Dahlia**
3yr J: Bill Pyers 10/1 £79,230
T: Maurice Zilber, Chantilly, France
B: Owner Sire: Vaguely Noble
2. Rheingold 4yr 3. Our Mirage 4yr 6l,
2l 2:30.43 12 ran

1974 Nelson Bunker Hunt's ch f **Dahlia**
4yr J: Lester Piggott 15/8 Fav
£81,240 T: Maurice Zilber, Chantilly,
France B: Owner Sire: Vaguely
Noble 2. Highclere 3yr 3. Dankaro
3yr 2½l, 1l 2:33.03 10 ran

1975 Carlo Vittadini's ch c **Grundy** 3yr
J: Pat Eddery 4/5 Fav £81,910
T: Peter Walwyn, Lambourn,
Berkshire B: Overbury Stud Sire:
Great Nephew 2. Bustino 4yr
3. Dahlia 5yr ½l, 5l 2:26.98 11 ran

1976 Daniel Wildenstein's b f
Pawneese 3yr J: Yves Saint-Martin
9/4 £81,508 T: Angel Penna,
Chantilly, France B: Dayton Ltd Sire:
Carvin 2. Bruni 4yr 3. Orange Bay
4yr 1l, short head 2:29.36 10 ran

1977 Robert Sangster's ch c **The
Minstrel** 3yr J: Lester Piggott
7/4 Fav £88,355 T: Vincent O'Brien,
Cashel, Co Tipperary, Ireland
B: Eddie Taylor Sire: Northern Dancer
2. Orange Bay 5yr 3. Exceller 4yr
short head, 1½l 2:30.48 11 ran

1978 David McCall's br c **Ile de
Bourbon** 3yr J: John Reid 12/1
£98,120 T: Fulke Johnson Houghton,
Blewbury, Berkshire B: Mrs Jane
Engelhard Sire: Nijinsky 2. Hawaiian
Sound 3yr 3. Montcontour 4yr
1¾l, 1½l 2:30.53 14 ran (Acamas
finished second, disqualified)

1979 Sir Michael Sobell's b c **Troy** 3yr
J: Willie Carson 2/5 Fav £94,460
T: Dick Hern, West Ilsley, Berkshire
B: Ballymacoll Stud Farm Sire:
Petingo 2. Gay Mécène 4yr 3. Ela-
Mana-Mou 3yr 1½l, 3l 2:33.75 7 ran

1980 Simon Weinstock's b c **Ela-Mana-
Mou** 4yr J: Willie Carson 11/4
£124,696 T: Dick Hern, West Ilsley,
Berkshire B: Patrick Clarke Sire:
Pitcairn 2. Mrs Penny 3yr
3. Gregorian 4yr ¾l, 5l 2:35.39
10 ran

1981 HH Aga Khan IV's b c **Shergar**
3yr J: Walter Swinburn 2/5 Fav
£119,206 T: Michael Stoute,
Newmarket B: Owner Sire: Great
Nephew 2. Madam Gay 3yr
3. Fingal's Cave 4yr 4l, short head
2:35.40 7 ran

1982 Anthony Ward's gr c **Kalaglow**
4yr J: Greville Starkey 13/2 £126,472
T: Guy Harwood, Pulborough, Sussex
B: Someries Stud Sire: Kalamoun
2. Assert 3yr 3. Glint of Gold 4yr
neck, 3l 2:31.88 9 ran

1983 Robert Barnett's b f **Time Charter**
4yr J: Joe Mercer 5/1 £133,851
T: Henry Candy, Kingstone Warren,

*It's Mill Reef first, the rest nowhere in the 1971 'King George' as the American-bred
sets the record for the greatest winning margin in England's premier weight-for-age
contest.*

Berkshire B: W. and R. Barnett Ltd
Sire: Saritamer 2. Diamond Shoal 4yr
3. Sun Princess 3yr ¾l, 1l 2:30.79
9 ran

1984 Eric Moller's b c **Teenoso** 4yr
J: Lester Piggott 13/2 £141,247
T: Geoffrey Wragg, Newmarket
B: Owner Sire: Youth 2. Sadler's Wells
3yr 3. Tolomeo 4yr 2½l, 1½l 2:27.95
13 ran

RECORDS FOR WINNING HORSES

Dual winner
Dahlia (1973, 1974)

Greatest margins
6 lengths — Mill Reef (1971), Dahlia
   (1973)
5 lengths — Ribot (1956)
4 lengths — Ragusa (1963), Shergar
   (1981)

Smallest margins
short head — Montaval (1957), The
   Minstrel (1977)
head — Vimy (1955)

Females
Aunt Edith (1966), Park Top (1969),
   Dahlia (1973, 1974), Pawneese
   (1976), Time Charter (1983)

Grey
Kalaglow (1982)

Longest odds
20/1 — Montaval (1957)
100/7 — Nasram (1964)
100/8 — Aggressor (1960)
12/1 — Ile de Bourbon (1978)
100/9 — Supreme Court (1951)

Shortest odds
2/5 — Ribot (1956), Troy (1979),
   Shergar (1981)
40/85 — Nijinsky (1970)
4/7 — Royal Palace (1968)
8/13 — Mill Reef (1971), Brigadier
   Gerard (1972)

Winner carrying overweight
Tulyar (1952) carried 2 lb overweight at
   8 st 6 lb.

Oldest
Aggressor (1960) and Park Top (1969)
were five-year-olds. The other 32
races to 1984 have been equally
divided between three-year-old and
four-year-old winners.

Trained in Ireland

Ballymoss (1958), Ragusa (1963), Meadow Court (1965), Nijinsky (1970), The Minstrel (1977)

Trained in France

Vimy (1955), Montaval (1957), Right Royal (1961), Match (1962), Nasram (1964), Dahlia (1973, 1974), Pawneese (1976)

Trained in Italy

Ribot (1956)

Bred in France

Vimy (1955), Montaval (1957), Right Royal (1961), Match (1962), Pawneese (1976)

Bred in USA

Nasram (1964), Mill Reef (1971), Dahlia (1973, 1974), Ile de Bourbon (1978), Teenoso (1984)

Bred in Canada

The Minstrel (1977)

Never beaten

Ribot (1956)

RECORDS FOR PLACED HORSES

Females

Almeria (1958), Gladness (1959), Petite Etoile (1960), Crepellana (1970), Highclere (1974), Dahlia (1975), Mrs Penny (1980), Madam Gay (1981), Sun Princess (1983)

Grey

Petite Etoile (1960), Bruni (1976)

Longest odds

40/1 — Acclimatization (1971), Madam Gay (1981), Fingal's Cave (1981).
33/1 — Todrai (1956), Balbo (1959).
28/1 — Felicio (1968), Crozier (1969), Parnell (1972).
25/1 — Worden (1952), Elopement (1955), Tarqogan (1963), Our Mirage (1973), Montcontour (1978), Gregorian (1980).

Oldest

Tribord (1957), Gladness (1959), Royal Avenue (1964) and Crozier (1969) were six-year-olds.

Trained in Scotland

Rockavon (1961)

Trained in Ireland

Gladness (1959), Kythnos (1960), Arctic Storm (1962), Tarqogan (1963), Santa Claus (1964), Prominer (1966), Gregorian (1980), Assert (1982), Sadler's Wells (1984)

Trained in France

Tantième (1951), Worden (1952, 1953), Vamos (1954), Al Mabsoot (1957), Tribord (1957), Balbo (1959), Felicio (1968), Topyo (1968), Crepellana (1970), Acclimatization (1971), Riverman (1972), Dankaro (1974), Dahlia (1975), Exceller (1977), Montcontour (1978), Gay Mécène (1979)

Trained in Italy

Hogarth (1969)

Trained in Belgium

Todrai (1956)

Bred in France

Worden (1952, 1953), Vamos (1954), Al Mabsoot (1957), Tribord (1957), Balbo (1959), Felicio (1968), Topyo (1968), Crepellana (1970), Dankaro (1974), Montcontour (1978)

Bred in Italy

Hogarth (1969), Ortis (1971)

Bred in Belgium

Todrai (1956)

Bred in USA

Salvo (1967), Ribocco (1967), Acclimatization (1971), Riverman (1972), Dahlia (1975), Exceller (1977), Hawaiian Sound (1978), Gay Mécène (1979), Mrs Penny (1980), Sadler's Wells (1984)

Placed horse disqualified

Acamas finished 2nd, beaten 1½ lengths by Ile de Bourbon, in 1978, but was subsequently disqualified and relegated to last place after returning a positive test.

MISCELLANEOUS RECORDS

Fastest times

2:26.98 — Grundy (1975)
2:27.95 — Teenoso (1984)
2:29.4 — Supreme Court (1951)

Largest entry

184 — 1977

Smallest entry

66 — 1953

Largest fields

19 — 1951
17 — 1954
15 — 1952

Smallest fields

4 — 1961, 1964
5 — 1960
6 — 1970

Richest first prizes

£141,247 — 1984
£133,851 — 1983
£126,472 — 1982

Hottest losing favourite

2/13 — Santa Claus (1964)

Most consecutive winning favourites

5 — 1968 to 1972 (one joint)

Most consecutive losing favourites

3 — 1982 to 1984

Foreign-trained horses dominant

In 1957 nine of the 12 runners were trained overseas, the English-trained trio finishing 5th, 11th and 12th. The first four (Montaval, Al Mabsoot, Tribord and Saint Raphael) were all bred and trained in France.

Foreign-bred horses placed 1, 2, 3, 4

In addition to 1957, foreign-bred horses filled the first four places in 1978, after the disqualification of Acamas from 2nd. Winner (Ile de Bourbon) and 2nd (Hawaiian Sound) were US-bred, the 3rd (Montcontour) was French-bred, and the 4th (Balmerino) was bred in New Zealand.

Foreign-bred horses placed 1, 2, 3

In 1971 winner (Mill Reef) and 3rd (Acclimatization) were US-bred and the 2nd (Ortis) was Italian-bred.

Most successful owner

2 wins — Nelson Bunker Hunt: 1973, 1974

Most successful breeders

2 wins — Nelson Bunker Hunt: 1973, 1974
Eddie Taylor: 1970, 1977

Most successful trainers

3 wins — Noel Murless: 1966, 1967, 1968
Vincent O'Brien: 1958, 1970, 1977
Dick Hern: 1972, 1979, 1980
2 wins — Cecil Boyd-Rochfort: 1954, 1959
Paddy Prendergast: 1963, 1965
Maurice Zilber: 1973, 1974

Most successful jockeys

7 wins — Lester Piggott: 1965, 1966, 1969, 1970, 1974, 1977, 1984
2 wins — Roger Poincelet: 1955, 1961
Bill Pyers: 1964, 1973
Yves Saint-Martin: 1962, 1976
Willie Carson: 1979, 1980
Joe Mercer: 1972, 1983

Most successful sires

2 wins — Vaguely Noble: Dahlia (1973, 1974)
Northern Dancer: Nijinsky (1970), The Minstrel (1977)
Great Nephew: Grundy (1975), Shergar (1981)

Prix de l'Arc de Triomphe

The Prix de l'Arc de Triomphe was instituted in 1920, with the objective of establishing an international test at the end of the season over the Classic distance of 2400 metres (a mile and a half). The idea produced an excellent and immediate response, but within a few years foreign countries reverted to their old insular ways and challenges from abroad became rarer. But almost from the outset, the 'Arc' was the natural end-of-term target for all the best French horses, and in time connec-tions of foreign horses came to realise that if they wanted to establish an international reputation for their animals, Longchamp on the first Sunday in October provided the natural occasion. Since World War II, more especially since the victories in the mid-1950s by the great Italian champion, Ribot, the Prix de l'Arc de Triomphe has been regarded as the top inter-age contest in the world of Thoroughbred racing.

Title

Prix de l'Arc de Triomphe 1920–81. Trusthouse Forte Prix de l'Arc de Triomphe from 1982.

Venue

Longchamp, Bois de Boulogne, Paris 1920–42.
Le Tremblay, Paris 1943–44.
Longchamp, Bois de Boulogne, Paris from 1945.

Distance

2400 metres 1920–42
2300 metres 1943–44
2400 metres from 1945

Weights

3-year-old colts 55 kg, fillies 53½ kg, 4-year-old and up males 60 kg, females 58½ kg 1920–29.
3-year-old colts 55½ kg, fillies 54 kg, 4-year-old and up males 60 kg females 58½ kg 1930–75.
3-year-old colts 56 kg, fillies 54½ kg, 4-year-old and up males 59 kg, females 57½ kg from 1976.

1920 Evremond de Saint-Alary's bl c **Comrade** 3yr J: Frank Bullock 69/20 Fr 172,425 T: Peter Gilpin, Newmarket, England B: Ludwig Neumann Sire: Bachelor's Double 2. King's Cross 6yr 3. Pleurs 3yr 1*l*, head 2:39.0 13 ran

1921 Mme Edmond Blanc's ch c **Ksar** 3yr J: George Stern 23/20 Fav Fr 345,675 T: William Walton, Saint-Cloud B: Evremond de Saint-Alary Sire: Brûleur 2. Fléchois 3yr 3. Square Measure 6yr 2*l*, 1½*l* 2:32.96 12 ran

1922 Mme Edmond Blanc's ch c **Ksar** 4yr J: Frank Bullock 3/10 Fav Fr 343,375 T: William Walton, Saint-Cloud B: Evremond de Saint-Alary Sire: Brûleur 2. Fléchois 4yr 3. Relapse 3yr 2½*l*, neck 2:38.78 11 ran

1923 A. Kingsley Macomber's b c **Parth** 3yr J: Frank O'Neill 35/4 Fr 343,250 T: James Crawford, Ogbourne, Wiltshire, England B: Dan Leahy Sire: Polymelus 2. Massine 3yr 3. Filibert de Savoie 3yr neck, neck 2:38.26 13 ran

1924 Henry Ternynck's b c **Massine** 4yr J: Fred Sharpe 23/20 Fav Fr 336,000 T: Elijah Cunnington, Chantilly B: Vicomte du Pontavice de Heussey Sire: Consols 2. Isola Bella 3yr 3. Cadum 3yr 1½*l*, 1*l* 2:40.98 9 ran

1925 Comte Gérard de Chavagnac's b c **Priori** 3yr J: Marcel Allemand 797/20 Fr 447,400 T: Percy Carter, Chantilly B: Georges Delaplace Sire: Brûleur 2. Cadum 4yr 3. Tras los Montes 3yr 1*l*, ½*l* 2:33.96 15 ran (Cadum finished first, relegated to second)

1926 Simon Guthmann's gr c **Biribi** 3yr J: Domingo Torterolo 5/2 Fav Fr 453,700 T: Juan Torterolo, Chantilly B: Jean Stern Sire: Rabelais 2. Dorina 3yr 3. Ptolemy 4yr 2½*l*, neck 2:32.96 16 ran

1927 Miguel Martinez de Hoz's b c **Mon Talisman** 3yr J: Charles Semblat 24/10 Fav Fr 544,450 T: Frank Carter, Chantilly B: Guillermo Ham Sire: Craig an Eran 2. Niño 4yr 3. Felton 4yr 2*l*, 2½*l* 2:32.90 10 ran

1928 Ogden Mills's b c **Kantar** 3yr J: Arthur Esling 32/10 Fr 551,350 T: Dick Carver, Chantilly B: Evremond de Saint-Alary Sire: Alcantara 2. Rialto 5yr 3. Finglas 5yr ¾*l*, 1*l* 2:38.98 11 ran

1929 Giuseppe de Montel's ch c **Ortello** 3yr J: Paolo Caprioli 13/1 Fr 656,950 T: Willy Carter, Milan, Italy B: Owner Sire: Teddy 2. Kantar 4yr 3. Oleander 5yr ½*l*, ½*l* 2:42.94 13 ran

1930 Vicomte Max de Rivaud's b h **Motrico** 5yr J: Marcel Fruhinsholtz 83/10 Fr 648,950 T: Maurice d'Okhuysen, Maisons-Laffitte B: Maurice Labrouche Sire: Radamès 2. Hotweed 4yr 3. Filarete 3yr 2*l*, 3*l* 2:44.98 10 ran

1931 Miss Diana Esmond's b f **Pearl Cap** 3yr J: Charles Semblat 32/10 Fr 600,000 T: Frank Carter, Chantilly B: Edward Esmond Sire: Le Capucin 2. Amfortas 4yr 3. Prince Rose 3yr 1½*l*, 1*l* 2:38.96 10 ran

1932 Vicomte Max de Rivaud's b h **Motrico** 7yr J: Charles Semblat 38/10 Fav Fr 500,000 T: Maurice d'Okhuysen, Maisons-Laffitte B: Maurice Labrouche Sire: Radamès 2. Goyescas 4yr 3. Macaroni 3yr ½*l*, ½*l* 2:44.66 15 ran

1933 Mario Crespi's b c **Crapom** 3yr J: Paolo Caprioli 22/10 Fav Fr 403,350 T: Federico Regoli, Milan, Italy B: Razza Bellotta Sire: Cranach 2. Casterari 3yr 3. Pantalon 3yr ½*l*, short head 2:41.76 15 ran

1934 Baron Edouard de Rothschild's b c **Brantôme** 3yr J: Charles Bouillon 11/10 Fav Fr 400,750 T: Lucien Robert, Chantilly B: Owner Sire: Blandford 2. Assuérus 4yr 3. Felicitation 4yr 2½*l*, 1½*l* 2:41.82 13 ran

1935 Evremond de Saint-Alary's b f **Samos** 3yr J: Wally Sibbritt 189/10 Fr 402,000 T: Frank Carter, Chantilly B: Owner Sire: Brûleur 2. Péniche 3yr 3. Corrida 3yr neck, neck 2:42.64 12 ran

1936 Marcel Boussac's ch f **Corrida** 4yr J: Charlie Elliott 4/5 Fav Fr 500,000 T: John Watts, Chantilly B: Owner Sire: Coronach 2. Cousine 3yr 3. Fantastic 3yr 1½*l*, neck 2:38.72 10 ran

1937 Marcel Boussac's ch m **Corrida** 5yr J: Charlie Elliott Evens Fav Fr 1,000,000 T: John Watts, Chantilly B: Owner Sire: Coronach 2. Tonnelle 3yr 3. Mousson 3yr short head, 1½*l* 2:33.88 12 ran

1938 Baron Edouard de Rothschild's br c **Eclair au Chocolat** 3yr J: Charles Bouillon 26/10 Fav Fr 1,031,600 T: Lucien Robert, Chantilly B: Owner Sire: Bubbles 2. Antonym 3yr 3. Canot 3yr 2*l*, ½*l* 2:39.82 10 ran

1939 no race
1940 no race

1941 Philippe Gund's b c **Le Pacha** 3yr J: Paul Francolon 18/10 Fr 600,000 T: John Cunnington, Chantilly B: André Schwob Sire: Biribi 2. Nepenthe 3yr 3. Djebel 4yr short head, 2*l* 2:36.26 7 ran

1942 Marcel Boussac's b h **Djebel** 5yr J: Jacko Doyasbère 18/10

Fr 1,043,2000 T: Charles Semblat, Chantilly B: Owner Sire: Tourbillon 2. Tornado 3yr 3. Breughel 3yr 2*l*, 1½*l* 2:37.96 9 ran

1943 Comte de Chambure's b c **Verso** 3yr J: Guy Duforez 12/10 Fav Fr 1,072,250 T: Charles Clout, Chantilly B: Henri Bernet Sire: Pinceau 2. Esméralda 4yr 3. Norseman 3yr 3*l*, short neck 2:23.20 13 ran

1944 Marcel Boussac's b c **Ardan** 3yr J: Jacko Doyasbère 6/4 Fav Fr 1,259,800 T: Charles Semblat, Chantilly B: Owner Sire: Pharis 2. Un Gaillard 6yr 3. Deux pour Cent 3yr 1*l*, 1½*l* 2:35.00 11 ran

1945 Mme Robert Patureau's b f **Nikellora** 3yr J: Rae Johnstone 10/1 Fr 1,264,400 T: René Pelat, Maisons-Laffitte B: Henri Tambareau Sire: Vatellor 2. Ardan 4yr 3. Chanteur 3yr ¾*l*, short neck 2:34.82 11 ran

1946 Marcel Boussac's b c **Caracalla** 4yr J: Charlie Elliott 3/10 Fav Fr 2,111,000 T: Charles Semblat, Chantilly B: Owner Sire: Tourbillon 2. Prince Chevalier 3yr 3. Pirette 3yr head, 1½*l* 2:33.32 9 ran

1947 Mme L. Aurousseau's b h **Le Paillon** 5yr J: Fernand Rochetti 23/2 Fr 5,242,000 T: Willie Head, Maisons-Laffitte B: Comte A. de Foucher de Careil Sire: Fastnet 2. Goyama 4yr 3. Madelon 3yr 1½*l*, ¾*l* 2:33.42 12 ran

1948 HH Aga Khan III's gr c **Migoli** 4yr J: Charlie Smirke 10/1 Fr 5,209,500 T: Frank Butters, Newmarket, England B: Owner Sire: Bois Roussel 2. Nirgal 5yr 3. Bey 3yr 1½*l*, 1½*l* 2:31.60 14 ran

1949 Marcel Boussac's b f **Coronation** 3yr J: Roger Poincelet 37/10 Fr 29,855,000 T: Charles Semblat, Chantilly B: Owner Sire: Djebel 2. Double Rose 3yr 3. Amour Drake 3yr 4*l*, 1*l* 2:33.22 28 ran

1950 François Dupré's b c **Tantième** 3yr J: Jacko Doyasbère 5/2 Fr 27,810,000 T: François Mathet, Chantilly B: Owner Sire: Deux pour Cent 2. Alizier 3yr 3. L'Amiral 3yr 1½*l*, 2*l* 2:34.22 12 ran

1951 François Dupré's b c **Tantième** 4yr J: Jacko Doyasbère 17/10 Fav Fr 29,450,000 T: François Mathet, Chantilly B: Owner Sire: Deux pour Cent 2. Nuccio 3yr 3. Le Tyrol 3yr 2*l*, 1*l* 2:32.84 19 ran

1952 HH Aga Khan III's b c **Nuccio** 4yr J: Roger Poincelet 74/10 Fr 29,110,000 T: Alec Head, Chantilly B: Scuderia Val Cervo Sire: Traghetto 2. La Mirambule 3yr 3. Dynamiter 4yr 3*l*, head 2:39.84 18 ran

1953 Paul Duboscq's b f **La Sorellina** 3yr J: Maurice Larraun 65/4 Fr 30,575,000 T: Etienne Pollet,

Chantilly B: Owner and Marquis du Vivier Sire: Sayani 2. Silnet 4yr 3. Worden 4yr head, 3*l* 2:31.82 25 ran

1954 Mme Jean Cochery's b c **Sica Boy** 3yr J: Rae Johnstone 41/10 Fav Fr 29,925,000 T: Pierre Pelat, Maisons-Laffitte B: R. Johner Sire: Sunny Boy 2. Banassa 4yr 3. Philante 3yr 1*l*, 1*l* 2:36.34 21 ran

1955 Marchese Mario Incisa della Rocchetta's b c **Ribot** 3yr J: Enrico Camici 88/10 Fr 30,365,000 T: Ugo Penco, Milan, Italy B: Razza Dormello-Olgiata Sire: Tenerani 2. Beau Prince 3yr 3. Picounda 3yr 3*l*, 2½*l* 2:35.68 23 ran

1956 Marchese Mario Incisa della Rocchetta's b c **Ribot** 4yr J: Enrico Camici 6/10 Fav Fr 29,515,000 T: Ugo Penco, Milan, Italy B: Razza Dormello-Olgiata Sire: Tenerani 2. Talgo 3yr 3. Tanerko 3yr 6*l*, 2*l* 2:34.76 20 ran

1957 Raoul Meyer's br c **Oroso** 4yr J: Serge Boullenger 52/1 Fr 50,055,000 T: Daniel Lescalle, Maisons-Laffitte B: Owner and René Leroy Sire: Tifinar 2. Denisy 3yr 3. Balbo 3yr ½*l*, 2½*l* 2:33.42 24 ran

1958 John McShain's ch c **Ballymoss** 4yr J: Scobie Breasley 39/10 Fr 45,510,700 T: Vincent O'Brien, Cashel, Co Tipperary, Ireland B: Richard Ball Sire: Mossborough 2. Fric 6yr 3. Cherasco 3yr 2*l*, 2½*l* 2:37.91 17 ran

1959 Prince Aly Khan's ch c **Saint Crespin** 3yr J: George Moore 17/1 Fr 48,240,700 T: Alec Head, Chantilly B: Owner and HH Aga Khan III Sire: Aureole 2. Midnight Sun 3yr 3. Le Loup Garou 3yr dead-heat, short head 2:33.30 25 ran (Midnight Sun finished equal first, relegated to second)

1960 Henry Aubert's ch c **Puissant Chef** 3yr J: Max Garcia 14/1 Fr 569,342 T: Mick Bartholomew, Chantilly B: Owner Sire: Djéfou 2. Hautain 3yr 3. Point d'Amour 3yr 3*l*, 3*l* 2:43.96 17 ran

1961 Egidio Verga's br c **Molvedo** 3yr J: Enrico Camici 18/10 Fr 675,894 T: Arturo Maggi, Milan, Italy B: Razza Ticino Sire: Ribot 2. Right Royal 3yr 3. Misti 3yr 2*l*, ½*l* 2:38.44 19 ran

1962 Mme Simone Cino Del Duca's b c **Soltikoff** 3yr J: Marcel Depalmas 40/1 Fr 847,539 T: René Pelat, Maisons-Laffitte B: Enrique Cruz-Valer Sire: Prince Chevalier 2. Monade 3yr 3. Val de Loir 3yr 1*l*, neck 2:30.94 24 ran

1963 Baron Guy de Rothschild's ch c **Exbury** 4yr J: Jean Deforge 36/10 Fr 961,974 T: Geoff Watson, Chantilly B: Owner Sire: Le Haar 2. Le Mesnil 3yr 3. Misti 5yr 2*l*, neck 2:34.98 15 ran

1964 Rex Ellsworth's b c **Prince Royal**

3yr J: Roger Poincelet 16/1 Fr 1,094,126 T: George Bridgland, Lamorlaye B: Charles H. Wacker III Sire: Ribot 2. Santa Claus 3yr 3. La Bamba 3yr ¾*l*, head 2:35.50 22 ran

1965 Jean Ternynck's ch c **Sea-Bird** 3yr J: Pat Glennon 12/10 Fav Fr 1,084,747 T: Etienne Pollet, Chantilly B: Owner Sire: Dan Cupid 2. Reliance 3yr 3. Diatome 3yr 6*l*, 5*l* 2:35.52 20 ran

1966 Walter Burmann's ch c **Bon Mot** 3yr J: Freddy Head 53/10 Fr 1,095,862 T: Willie Head, Maisons-Laffitte B: Owner Sire: Worden 2. Sigebert 5yr 3. Lionel 3yr ½*l*, 2*l* 2:39.8 24 ran

1967 Mme Suzy Volterra's b c **Topyo** 3yr J: Bill Pyers 82/1 Fr 1,119,788 T: Mick Bartholomew, Chantilly B: Owner Sire: Fine Top 2. Salvo 4yr 3. Ribocco 3yr neck, short head 2:38.2 30 ran

1968 Mrs Wilma Franklyn's b c **Vaguely Noble** 3yr J: Bill Williamson 5/2 Fav Fr 1,156,600 T: Etienne Pollet, Chantilly B: Lionel Holliday Sire: Vienna 2. Sir Ivor 3yr 3. Carmarthen 4yr 3*l*, 4*l* 2:35.2 17 ran

1969 Seamus McGrath's b c **Levmoss** 4yr J: Bill Williamson 52/1 Fr 1,181,000 T: Owner, Sandyford, Co Dublin, Ireland B: McGrath Trust Co Sire: Le Levanstell 2. Park Top 5yr 3. Grandier 5yr ¾*l*, 3*l* 2:29.0 24 ran

1970 Arpad Plesch's b c **Sassafras** 3yr J: Yves Saint-Martin 19/1 Fr 1,379,800 T: François Mathet, Chantilly B: Dollanstown Stud Sire: Sheshoon 2. Nijinsky 3yr 3. Miss Dan 3yr head, 2*l* 2:29.7 15 ran

1971 Paul Mellon's b c **Mill Reef** 3yr J: Geoff Lewis 7/10 Fav Fr 1,399,150 T: Ian Balding, Kingsclere, Berkshire, England B: Owner Sire: Never Bend 2. Pistol Packer 3yr 3. Cambrizzia 3yr 3*l*, 1½*l* 2:28.3 18 ran

1972 Gräfin Margit Batthyany's b f **San San** 3yr J: Freddy Head 37/2 Fr 1,415,250 T: Angel Penna, Chantilly B: Harry Guggenheim Sire: Bald Eagle 2. Rescousse 3yr 3. Homeric 4yr 1½*l*, ½*l* 2:28.3 19 ran

1973 Henry Zeisel's b c **Rheingold** 4yr J: Lester Piggott 77/10 Fr 1,497,000 T: Barry Hills, Lambourn, Berkshire, England B: Jim Russell Sire: Fabergé 2. Allez France 3yr 3. Hard to Beat 4yr 2½*l*, 4*l* 2:35.8 27 ran

1974 Daniel Wildenstein's b f **Allez France** 4yr J: Yves Saint-Martin 1/2 Fav Fr 1,412,000 T: Angel Penna, Chantilly B: Bieber-Jacobs Stable Sire: Sea-Bird 2. Comtesse de Loir 3yr 3. Margouillat 4yr head, ¾*l* 2:36.9 20 ran

1975 Waldemar Zeitelhack's b h **Star Appeal** 5yr J: Greville Starkey 119/1 Fr 1,468,150 T: Theo Grieper,

Cologne, West Germany B: Gestüt
Röttgen Sire: Appiani 2. On My Way
5yr 3. Comtesse de Loir 4yr 3l, 2½l
2:33.6 24 ran

1976 Jacques Wertheimer's b f **Ivanjica**
4yr J: Freddy Head 71/10
Fr 1,200,000 T: Alec Head, Chantilly
B: Claiborne Farm Sire: Sir Ivor
2. Crow 3yr 3. Youth 3yr 2l, 3l 2:39.4
20 ran

1977 Robert Sangster's b c **Alleged** 3yr
J: Lester Piggott 39/10 Fav
Fr 1,200,000 T: Vincent O'Brien,
Cashel, Co Tipperary, Ireland B: Mrs
June McKnight Sire: Hoist the Flag
2. Balmerino 5yr 3. Crystal Palace
3yr 1½l, 2l 2:30.6 26 ran

1978 Robert Sangster's b c **Alleged** 4yr
J: Lester Piggott 14/10 Fav
Fr 1,200,000 T: Vincent O'Brien,
Cashel, Co Tipperary, Ireland B: Mrs
June McKnight Sire: Hoist the Flag
2. Trillion 4yr 3. Dancing Maid 3yr 2l,
2l 2:36.1 18 ran

1979 Mme Ghislaine Head's b f **Three
Troikas** 3yr J: Freddy Head 88/10
Fr 1,200,000 T: Mme Criquette Head,
Chantilly B: Artur Pfaff Sire: Lyphard
2. Le Marmot 3yr 3. Troy 3yr 3l, 1l
2:28.9 22 ran

1980 Robert Sangster's br f **Detroit** 3yr
J: Pat Eddery 67/10 Fr 1,200,000
T: Olivier Douieb, Chantilly B: Société
Aland Sire: Riverman 2. Argument
3yr 3. Ela-Mana-Mou 4yr ½l, short
head 2:28.0 20 ran

1981 Jacques Wertheimer's ch f **Gold
River** 4yr J: Gary Moore 53/1
Fr 2,000,000 T: Alec Head, Chantilly
B: Owner Sire: Riverman 2. Bikala
3yr 3. April Run 3yr ¾l, nose 2:35.2
24 ran

1982 HH Aga Khan IV's br f **Akiyda** 3yr
J: Yves Saint-Martin 43/4
Fr 2,000,000 T: François Mathet,
Chantilly B: Owner Sire: Labus
2. Ardross 6yr 3. Awaasif 3yr
head, ½l 2:37.0 17 ran

1983 Daniel Wildenstein's b f **All Along**
4yr J: Walter Swinburn 173/10
Fr 2,500,000 T: Patrick Biancone,
Chantilly B: Dayton Ltd Sire:
Targowice 2. Sun Princess 3yr
3. Luth Enchantée 3yr 1l, short neck
2:28.1 26 ran

1984 Daniel Wildenstein's b c **Sagace**
4yr J: Yves Saint-Martin 29/10
Fr 2,500,000 T: Patrick Biancone,
Chantilly B: Dayton Ltd Sire: Luthier
2. Northern Trick 3yr 3. All Along 5yr
2l, 6l 2:39.1 22 ran

RECORDS FOR WINNING HORSES

Dual winners
Ksar (1921, 1922), Motrico (1930,
1932), Corrida (1936, 1937), Tantième
(1950, 1951), Ribot (1955, 1956),
Alleged (1977, 1978)

Greatest margins
6 lengths — Ribot (1956), Sea-Bird
(1965)
4 lengths — Coronation (1949)

Smallest margins
dead-heat — Saint Crespin and Midnight
Sun (1959)
short head — Corrida (1937), Le Pacha
(1941)
head — Caracalla (1946), La Sorellina
(1953), Sassafras (1970), Akiyda
(1982)

Females
Pearl Cap (1931), Samos (1935),
Corrida (1936, 1937), Nikellora
(1945), Coronation (1949), La
Sorellina (1953), San San (1972),
Allez France (1974), Ivanjica (1976),
Three Troikas (1979), Detroit (1980),
Gold River (1981), Akiyda (1982), All
Along (1983)

Grey
Biribi (1926), Migoli (1948)

Black
Comrade (1920)

Longest odds
119/1 — Star Appeal (1975)
82/1 — Topyo (1967)
53/1 — Gold River (1981)
52/1 — Oroso (1957), Levmoss (1969)

Shortest odds
3/10 — Ksar (1922), Caracalla (1946)
1/2 — Allez France (1974)
6/10 — Ribot (1956)
7/10 — Mill Reef (1971)
4/5 — Corrida (1936)

Winner carrying overweight
Kantar (1928) carried ½ kg overweight
at 55½ kg.

Oldest
7 years — Motrico (1932)
5 years — Motrico (1930), Corrida
(1937), Djebel (1942), Le Paillon
(1947), Star Appeal (1975)
The other 57 races to 1984 have been
won by 38 three-year-olds and 19
four-year-olds.

Winners on disqualification
In 1925 Cadum finished first, beating
Priori by a length, but the order was
reversed by the stewards, who found
that Cadum had hampered Priori in
the straight.
Midnight Sun dead-heated with Saint
Crespin in 1959, but was relegated
to 2nd place for having hampered
Saint Crespin several times.

Trained in England
Comrade (1920), Parth (1923), Migoli
(1948), Mill Reef (1971), Rheingold
(1973)

Trained in Ireland
Ballymoss (1958), Levmoss (1969),
Alleged (1977, 1978)

*Alleged and Lester Piggott win the 1978 'Arc', dominating their rivals for the second
successive year. The colt's only defeat in a ten-race career came in the 1977 St Leger.*

Trained in Italy

Ortello (1929), Crapom (1933), Ribot (1955, 1956), Molvedo (1961)

Trained in West Germany

Star Appeal (1975)

Bred in England

Comrade (1920), Parth (1923), Migoli (1948), Ribot (1955, 1956), Ballymoss (1958), Saint Crespin (1959), Prince Royal (1964), Akiyda (1982)

Bred in Ireland

Vaguely Noble (1968), Levmoss (1969), Rheingold (1973), Star Appeal (1975)

Bred in Italy

Ortello (1929), Crapom (1933), Nuccio (1952), Molvedo (1961)

Bred in USA

Mill Reef (1971), San San (1972), Allez France (1974), Ivanjica (1976), Alleged (1977, 1978)

Never beaten

Caracalla (1946), Ribot (1955, 1956)

RECORDS FOR PLACED HORSES

Females

Isola Bella (1924), Tras los Montes (1925), Dorina (1926), Péniche (1935), Corrida (1935), Cousine (1936), Tonnelle (1937), Esméralda (1943), Pirette (1946), Madelon (1947), Double Rose (1949), La Mirambule (1952), Banassa (1954), Philante (1954), Picounda (1955), Denisy (1957), Monade (1962), La Bamba (1964), Park Top (1969), Miss Dan (1970), Pistol Packer (1971), Cambrizzia (1971), Rescousse (1972), Allez France (1973), Comtesse de Loir (1974, 1975), Trillion (1978), Dancing Maid (1978), April Run (1981), Awaasif (1982), Sun Princess (1983), Luth Enchantée (1983), Northern Trick (1984), All Along (1984)

Grey

Filibert de Savoie (1923), Péniche (1935), Nepenthe (1941), Crystal Palace (1977)

Longest odds

100/1 — Talgo (1956)
90/1 — Carmarthen (1968), Awaasif (1982)
79/1 — On My Way (1975)
74/1 — Argument (1980)
73/1 — Breughel (1942)
72/1 — Margouillat (1974)
70/1 — Grandier (1969)
66/1 — Tras los Montes (1925)

60/1 — Double Rose (1949), Picounda (1955)
53/1 — Comtesse de Loir (1974).

Oldest

King's Cross (1920), Square Measure (1921), Un Gaillard (1944), Fric (1958) and Ardross (1982) were all six-year-olds.

Trained in England

Square Measure (1921), Felicitation (1934), Talgo (1956), Salvo (1967), Ribocco (1967), Park Top (1969), Balmerino (1977), Troy (1979), Ela-Mana-Mou (1980), Ardross (1982), Awaasif (1982), Sun Princess (1983)

Trained in Ireland

Santa Claus (1964), Sir Ivor (1968), Nijinsky (1970)

Trained in Italy

Filarete (1930)

Trained in Germany

Oleander (1929)

Trained in Belgium

Prince Rose (1931)

Bred in England

Square Measure (1921), Prince Rose (1931), Felicitation (1934), Beau Prince (1955), Park Top (1969), Homeric (1972), Hard to Beat (1973), Troy (1979), Sun Princess (1983)

Bred in Ireland

Filarete (1930), Talgo (1956), Santa Claus (1964), Ela-Mana-Mou (1980), Bikala (1981), April Run (1981), Ardross (1982)

Bred in Italy

Nuccio (1952)

Bred in Germany

Oleander (1929)

Bred in USA

Salvo (1967), Ribocco (1967), Sir Ivor (1968), Pistol Packer (1971), Allez France (1973), On My Way (1975), Youth (1976), Trillion (1978), Northern Trick (1984)

Bred in Canada

Nijinsky (1970), Awaasif (1982)

Bred in New Zealand

Balmerino (1977)

MISCELLANEOUS RECORDS

Fastest times

2:28.0 — Detroit (1980)
2:28.1 — All Along (1983)

2:28.3 — Mill Reef (1971), San San (1972)
2:28.9 — Three Troikas (1979).

Largest fields

30 — 1967
28 — 1949
27 — 1973
26 — 1977, 1983

Smallest fields

7 — 1941
9 — 1924, 1942, 1946
10 — 1927, 1930, 1931, 1936, 1938

Richest first prizes

Fr 2,500,000 — 1983, 1984
Fr 2,000,000 — 1981, 1982

Hottest losing favourites

1/10 — Ardan, Coaraze and Micipsa (grouped) in 1945.

Most consecutive winning favourites

3 — 1932 to 1934, 1936 to 1938

Most consecutive losing favourites

8 — 1957 to 1964

Females dominant

In 1983 the first four places were filled by fillies (All Along, Sun Princess, Luth Enchantée and Time Charter). Other females finished sixth, eighth and tenth in the 26-runner field.

Samos, Péniche and Corrida, the only three-year-old fillies in the 1935 race, finished 1st, 2nd and 3rd.

Siblings winner and 2nd

La Sorellina and Silnet, winner and 2nd in 1953, were half-sister and half-brother.

Race not run

There was no race in 1940 and 1941 on account of World War II.

Most successful owners

6 wins — Marcel Boussac: 1936, 1937, 1942, 1944, 1946, 1949
3 wins — Robert Sangster: 1977, 1978, 1980
Daniel Wildenstein: 1974, 1983, 1984
2 wins — Mme Edmond Blanc: 1921, 1922
Vicomte Max de Rivaud: 1930, 1932
Evremond de Saint-Alary: 1929, 1935
Baron Edouard de Rothschild: 1934, 1938
François Dupré: 1950, 1951
HH Aga Khan III: 1948, 1952
Marchese Mario Incisa della Rocchetta: 1955, 1956
Jacques Wertheimer: 1976, 1981

Owned winner and 2nd

Paul Duboscq — 1953

Most successful breeders

6 wins — Marcel Boussac: 1936, 1937,

1942, 1944, 1946, 1949
4 wins — Evremond de Saint-Alary:
   1921, 1922, 1928, 1935
2 wins — Maurice Labrouche: 1930,
   1932
   Baron Edouard de Rothschild: 1934,
   1938
   François Dupré: 1951, 1952
   Razza Dormello-Olgiata: 1955, 1956
   HH Aga Khan III: 1948, 1959 (one in
      partnership)
   Mrs June McKnight: 1977, 1978
   Dayton Ltd: 1983, 1984.

Bred winner and 2nd

Paul Duboscq and Marquis du Vivier:
   1953

Most successful trainers

4 wins — Charles Semblat: 1942, 1944,
   1946, 1949
   Alec Head: 1952, 1959, 1976, 1981
   François Mathet: 1950, 1951, 1970,
   1982
3 wins — Frank Carter: 1927, 1931,
   1935
   Etienne Pollet: 1953, 1965, 1968
   Vincent O'Brien: 1958, 1977, 1978
2 wins — William Walton: 1921, 1922

Maurice d'Okhuysen: 1930, 1932
John Watts: 1936, 1937
Lucien Robert: 1934, 1938
Ugo Penco: 1955, 1956
René Pelat: 1945, 1962
Willie Head: 1947, 1966
Mick Bartholomew: 1960, 1967
Patrick Biancone: 1983, 1984

Trained winner and 2nd

Etienne Pollet: 1953

Most successful jockeys

4 wins — Jacko Doyasbère: 1942,
   1944, 1950, 1951
   Freddy Head: 1966, 1972, 1976, 1979
   Yves Saint-Martin: 1970, 1974, 1982,
   1984
3 wins — Charles Semblat: 1927, 1931,
   1932
   Charlie Elliott: 1936, 1937, 1946
   Enrico Camici: 1955, 1956, 1961
   Roger Poincelet: 1949, 1952, 1964
   Lester Piggott: 1973, 1977, 1978
2 wins — Frank Bullock: 1920, 1922
   Paolo Caprioli: 1929, 1933
   Charles Bouillon: 1934, 1938
   Rae Johnstone: 1945, 1954
   Bill Williamson: 1968, 1969

Successful as both jockey and trainer

Charles Semblat rode Mon Talisman
   (1927), Pearl Cap (1931) and Motrico
   (1932), trained Djebel (1942), Ardan
   (1944), Caracalla (1946), and
   Coronation (1949).

Successful woman trainer

Mme Criquette Head — 1979

Most successful sires

4 wins — Brûleur: Ksar (1921, 1922),
   Priori (1925), Samos (1935)
2 wins — Radamès: Motrico (1930,
   1932)
   Coronach: Corrida (1936, 1937)
   Tourbillon: Djebel (1942), Caracalla
   (1946)
   Deux pour Cent: Tantième (1950,
   1951)
   Tenerani: Ribot (1955, 1956) Prince
   Royal
   Ribot: Molvedo (1961, 1964)
   Hoist the Flag: Alleged (1977, 1978)
   Riverman: Detroit (1980), Gold River
   (1981)

Sired winner and 2nd

Tourbillon — 1942

Champion Hurdle

The Champion Hurdle is England's championship race for hurdlers. It was inaugurated in 1927, at a time when hurdling was a minor branch of the sport, and most of the early runnings were weakly contested, but since the war it has been a true test of champions and has nearly always been won by the best hurdler in the British Isles.

Title

Champion Hurdle Challenge Cup
   1927–42
Champion Hurdle 1945
Champion Hurdle Challenge Cup
   1946–77
Waterford Crystal Champion Hurdle
   Challenge Trophy from 1978

Venue

Prestbury Park, Cheltenham,
   Gloucestershire from 1927

Distance

2 miles 1927–28
2 miles and a few yards 1929–57
2 miles 1958
2 miles 125 yards 1959–60
2 miles 100 yards 1961–64
2 miles 200 yards 1965–79
2 miles from 1980, run over 8 flights of
   hurdles

Weights

1927–49: 4-year-olds 11 st 0 lb,
   5-year-olds 11 st 10 lb, older horses
   12 st 0 lb.
1950–74: 4-year-olds 11 st 4 lb,
   5-year-olds 11 st 12 lb, older horses
   12 st 0 lb.

from 1975: 4-year-olds 11 st 6 lb, older
   horses 12 st 0 lb.
A 5 lb allowance for mares was
   introduced in 1984.

1927 Mrs H. M. Hollins's b g **Blaris** 6yr
   J: George Duller 11/10 Fav £365
   T: Bill Payne, Epsom, Surrey
   B: Barney Parr Sire: Achtoi 2. Boddam
   8yr 3. Harpist 6yr 8*l*, 1*l* 4:13.6 4 ran
1928 Harold Wernher's br g **Brown
   Jack** 4yr J: Bilbie Rees 4/1 £680
   T: Aubrey Hastings, Wroughton,
   Wiltshire B: George Webb Sire:
   Jackdaw 2. Peace River 5yr 3. Blaris
   7yr 1½*l*, 6*l* 4:05.0 6 ran
1929 Miss Victoria Williams-Bulkeley's
   ch h **Royal Falcon** 6yr J: Dick Rees
   11/2 £675 T: Bob Gore, Findon,
   Sussex B: National Stud Sire: White
   Eagle 2. Rolie 8yr 3. Clear Cash 4yr
   4*l*, 5*l* 4:01.2 6 ran
1930 Mrs J. de Selincourt's br g **Brown
   Tony** 4yr J: Tommy Cullinan 7/2
   £670 T: Jack Anthony, Letcombe
   Regis, Berkshire B: S. Slocock Sire:
   Jackdaw 2. Clear Cash 5yr 3. Peertoi
   5yr head, short head 4:20.2 5 ran
1931 no race
1932 Miss Dorothy Paget's b g
   Insurance 5yr J: Ted Leader

4/5 Fav £670 T: Basil Briscoe,
   Longstowe, Cambridgeshire B: E. J.
   Hope Sire: Achtoi 2. Song of Essex
   6yr 3. Jack Drummer 4yr 12*l*, bad
   4:14.2 3 ran
1933 Miss Dorothy Paget's b g
   Insurance 6yr J: Billy Stott
   10/11 Fav £670 T: Basil Briscoe,
   Exning, Suffolk B: E. J. Hope Sire:
   Achtoi 2. Windermere Laddie 9yr
   3. Indian Salmon 4yr ¾*l*, 8*l* 4:37.6
   5 ran
1934 Pete Bostwick's b g **Chenango**
   7yr J: Danny Morgan 4/9 Fav £670
   T: Ivor Anthony, Wroughton, Wiltshire
   B: Charles Prior Sire: Hapsburg
   2. Pompelmoose 4yr 3. Black
   Duncan 4yr 5*l*, 6*l* 4:17.0 5 ran
1935 R. Fox-Carlyon's b or br g **Lion
   Courage** 7yr J: Gerry Wilson 100/8
   £670 T: Frank Brown, Bourton-on-
   the-Hill, Gloucestershire B: M. J.
   Gleeson Sire: Jackdaw 2. Gay Light
   9yr 3. Hill Song ½*l*, ¾*l* 4:00.2
   11 ran
1936 Mrs Michael Stephens's gr g
   Victor Norman 5yr J: Frenchie
   Nicholson 4/1 £670 T: Morgan Blair,
   Ewhurst, Surrey B: W. J. Peek Sire:
   King Sol 2. Free Fare 8yr 3. Cactus
   6yr 3*l*, 1½*l* 4:14.4 8 ran

1937 Ben Warner's ch g **Free Fare** 9yr
J: Georges Pellerin 2/1 Fav £670
T: Ted Gwilt, Lambourn, Berkshire
B: Albert Lowry Sire: Werwolf 2. Our
Hope 8yr 3. Menton 5yr 2*l*, short head
4:19.2 7 ran

1938 Roderic Gubbins's gr g **Our Hope**
9yr J: Captain Perry Harding 5/1
£745 T: Owner, Lambourn, Berkshire
B: W. E. Robinson Sire: Son and Heir
2. Chuchoteur 6yr 3. Lobau 6yr
1½*l*, 10*l* 4:04.8 5 ran

1939 Horace Brueton's ch m **African
Sister** 7yr J: Keith Piggott 10/1 £720
T: Charlie Piggott, Cheltenham,
Gloucestershire B: A. Baker Sire:
Prester John 2. Vitement 6yr 3. Apple
Peel 9yr 3*l*, ½*l* 4:13.6 13 ran

1940 Miss Dorothy Paget's b g **Solford**
9yr J: Sean Magee 5/2 Fav £410
T: Owen Anthony, Letcombe Bassett,
Berkshire B: Paddy Hartigan Sire:
Soldennis 2. African Sister 8yr
3. Carton 5yr 1½*l*, 4*l* 4:13.4 8 ran

1941 Sir Malcolm McAlpine's ch c
Seneca 4yr J: Ron Smyth 7/1 £410
T: Vic Smyth, Epsom, Surrey
B: Owner Sire: Calígula 2. Anarchist
4yr 3. Ephorus 5yr head, 2*l* 4:09.0
6 ran

1942 Vic Smyth's b g **Forestation** 4yr
J: Ron Smyth 10/1 £495 T: Owner,
Epsom, Surrey B: Sir Woodman
Burbidge Sire: Felicitation 2. Anarchist
5yr 3. Southport 6yr 3*l*, 3*l* 4:10.4
20 ran

1943 no race

1944 no race

1945 F. Blakeway's ch g **Brains Trust**
5yr J: Fred Rimell 9/2 £340 T: Gerry
Wilson, Andoversford,
Gloucestershire B: Miss Dorothy
Paget Sire: Rhodes Scholar 2. Vidi
4yr 3. Red April 8yr ¾*l*, ¾*l* 4:09.4
16 ran

1946 Miss Dorothy Paget's b g **Distel**
5yr J: Bobby O'Ryan 4/5 Fav £980
T: Maxie Arnott, Clonsilla, Co Dublin,
Ireland B: Arthur and Isidore Blake
Sire: Rosewell 2. Carnival Boy 5yr
3. Robin o' Chantry 6yr 4*l*, ½*l* 4:05.0
8 ran

1947 Len Abelson's ch g **National
Spirit** 6yr J: Danny Morgan 7/1
£1,035 T: Vic Smyth, Epsom, Surrey
B: Owner Sire: Scottish Union 2. Le
Paillon 5yr 3. Freddy Fox 8yr 1*l*, 2*l*
4:03.8 14 ran

1948 Len Abelson's ch g **National
Spirit** 7yr J: Ron Smyth 6/4 Fav
£2,068 T: Vic Smyth, Epsom, Surrey
B: Owner Sire: Scottish Union
2. D.U.K.W. 5yr 3. Encoroli 5yr
2*l*, ¾*l* 3:54.8 12 ran

1949 Mrs Moya Keogh's b g **Hatton's
Grace** 9yr J: Aubrey Brabazon
100/7 £2,299 T: Vincent O'Brien,
Churchtown, Co Cork, Ireland
B: John Harris Sire: His Grace
2. Vatelys 9yr 3. Captain Fox 4yr
6*l*, 1*l* 4:00.6 14 ran

1950 Mrs Moya Keogh's b g **Hatton's
Grace** 10yr J: Aubrey Brabazon
5/2 Fav £2,427 T: Vincent O'Brien,
Churchtown, Co Cork, Ireland
B: John Harris Sire: His Grace
2. Harlech 5yr 3. Speciality 5yr 1½*l*,
2*l* 3:59.6 12 ran

1951 Mrs Moya Keogh's b g **Hatton's
Grace** 11yr J: Tim Molony 4/1 £3,615
T: Vincent O'Brien, Churchtown, Co
Cork, Ireland B: John Harris Sire: His
Grace 2. Pyrrhus 8yr 3. Prince
Hindou 5yr 5*l*, ½*l* 4:11.2 8 ran

1952 Maurice Kingsley's b g **Sir Ken** 5yr
J: Tim Molony 3/1 Fav £3,632 T: Willie
Stephenson, Royston, Hertfordshire
B: Marcel Chenorio Sire: Laëken
2. Noholme 5yr 3. Approval 6yr 2*l*, 4*l*
4:03.2 16 ran

1953 Maurice Kingsley's b g **Sir Ken** 6yr
J: Tim Molony 2/5 Fav £3,479 T: Willie
Stephenson, Royston, Hertfordshire
B: Marcel Chenorio Sire: Laëken
2. Galatian 6yr 3. Teapot 8yr 2*l*, 1½*l*
3:55.4 7 ran

1954 Maurice Kingsley's b g **Sir Ken** 7yr
J: Tim Molony 4/9 Fav £3,657 T: Willie
Stephenson, Royston, Hertfordshire

*In March 1951 Hatton's Grace (left) is about to become the first triple Champion
Hurdle winner as National Spirit, champion in 1947 and 1948, falls at the final flight.*

B: Marcel Chenorio Sire: Laëken
2. Impney 5yr 3. Galatian 7yr 1l, 3l
4:11.0 13 ran

1955 Gerry Judd's br g **Clair Soleil** 6yr
J: Fred Winter 5/2 Fav £3,717 T: Ryan
Price, Findon, Sussex B: François
Dupré Sire: Maravédis 2. Stroller 7yr
3. Cruachan 7yr head, 4l 4:12.8
21 ran

1956 Clifford Nicholson's ch g
Doorknocker 8yr J: Harry Sprague
100/9 £3,300 T: Charlie Hall, Towton,
Yorkshire B: P. Mangan Sire:
Caçador 2. Quita Que 7yr 3. Baby
Don 6yr ¾l, 4l 4:02.2 14 ran

1957 Arthur Jones's b g **Merry Deal** 7yr
J: Grenville Underwood 28/1 £3,729
T: Owner, Oswestry, Shropshire
B: Miss Dorothy Paget Sire: Straight
Deal 2. Quita Que 8yr 3. Tout ou Rien
5yr 5l, 5l 4:07.4 16 ran

1958 Mrs Dorothy Wright's b g
Bandalore 7yr J: George Slack
20/1 £4,812 T: Stan Wright,
Leintwardine, Shropshire B: Mrs
A. Warman Sire: Tambourin
2. Tokoroa 7yr 3. Retour de Flamme
5yr 2l, 3l 3:56.0 18 ran

1959 Gerry Judd's b g **Fare Time** 6yr
J: Fred Winter 13/2 £4,587 T: Ryan
Price, Findon, Sussex B: Mrs
Catherine Macdonald-Buchanan Sire:
Thoroughfare 2. Ivy Green 9yr
3. Prudent King 7yr 4l, 1l 4:07.8
14 ran

1960 John Byrne's b g **Another Flash**
6yr J: Bobby Beasley 11/4 Fav
£4,290 T: Paddy Sleator, Grange
Con, Co Wicklow, Ireland B: Tony
Duncan Sire: Roi d'Egypte 2. Albergo
6yr 3. Saffron Tartan 9yr 2l, 3l 3:55.0
12 ran

1961 Burjor Pajgar's b h **Eborneezer**
6yr J: Fred Winter 4/1 £5,211
T: Ryan Price, Findon, Sussex
B: Owner Sire: Ocean Swell 2. Moss
Bank 5yr 3. Farmer's Boy 8yr
3l, 1½l 4:10.0 17 ran

1962 Sir Thomas Ainsworth's ro g
Anzio 5yr J: Willie Robinson 11/2
£5,143 T: Fulke Walwyn, Lambourn,
Berkshire B: Harwood Stud Sire: Vic
Day 2. Quelle Chance 7yr 3. Another
Flash 8yr 3l, 1½l 4:00.2 14 ran

1963 George Spencer's bl or br g
Winning Fair 8yr J: Mr Alan
Lillingston 100/9 £5,585 T: Owner,
Thurles, Co Tipperary, Ireland
B: Paddy Finn Sire: Fun Fair
2. Farrney Fox 8yr 3. Quelle Chance
8yr 3l, neck 4:15.5 21 ran

1964 James McGhie's br g **Magic
Court** 6yr J: Pat McCarron 100/6
£8,161 T: Tommy Robson,
Greystoke, Cumberland B: Tom
Lilley Sire: Supreme Court 2. Another
Flash 10yr 3. Kirriemuir 4yr 4l, ¾l
4:08.0 24 ran

1965 Mrs Doreen Beddington's br g
Kirriemuir 5yr J: Willie Robinson
50/1 £8,042 T: Fulke Walwyn,

Lambourn, Berkshire B: Mrs F. B.
Watkins Sire: Tangle 2. Spartan
General 6yr 3. Worcran 7yr 1l, 1½l
4:06.6 19 ran

1966 Mrs Eileen Rogerson's ch g
Salmon Spray 8yr J: Johnny Haine
4/1 £7,921 T: Bob Turnell, Ogbourne
Maisey, Wiltshire B: Bill Corry Sire:
Vulgan 2. Sempervivum 8yr
3. Flyingbolt 7yr 3l, ¾l 4:10.2 17 ran

1967 Kenneth Alder's b h **Saucy Kit** 6yr
J: Roy Edwards 100/6 £8,857
T: Peter Easterby, Great Habton,
Yorkshire B: Sassoon Studs Sire:
Hard Sauce 2. Makaldar 7yr 3. Talgo
Abbess 8yr 5l, 1½l 4:11.2 23 ran
(Aurelius finished second,
disqualified)

1968 Henry Alper's b g **Persian War** 5yr
J: Jimmy Uttley 4/1 £7,798 T: Colin
Davies, Chepstow, Monmouthshire
B: Astor Studs Sire: Persian Gulf
2. Chorus 7yr 3. Black Justice 6yr 4l,
5l 4:03.8 16 ran

1969 Henry Alper's b g **Persian War** 6yr
J: Jimmy Uttley 6/4 Fav £7,876
T: Colin Davies, Chepstow,
Monmouthshire B: Astor Studs Sire:
Persian Gulf 2. Drumikill 8yr 3. Privy
Seal 5yr 4l, 2½l 4:41.8 17 ran

1970 Henry Alper's b g **Persian War** 7yr
J: Jimmy Uttley 5/4 Fav £7,739
T: Colin Davies, Chepstow,
Monmouthshire B: Astor Studs Sire:
Persian Gulf 2. Major Rose 8yr
3. Escalus 5yr 1½l, 1½l 4:13.8
14 ran

1971 Bill Edwards-Heathcote's br g
Bula 6yr J: Paul Kelleway 15/8 Fav
£7,466 T: Fred Winter, Lambourn,
Berkshire B: Charles Purcell Sire:
Raincheck 2. Persian War 8yr

3. Major Rose 9yr 4l, 1l 4:22.3 9 ran

1972 Bill Edwards-Heathcote's br g
Bula 7yr J: Paul Kelleway 8/11 Fav
£15,648 T: Fred Winter, Lambourn,
Berkshire B: Charles Purcell Sire:
Raincheck 2. Boxer 5yr 3. Lyford Cay
8yr 8l, 3l 4:25.3 12 ran

1973 Ted Wheatley's br g **Comedy of
Errors** 6yr J: Bill Smith 8/1 £14,563
T: Fred Rimell, Kinnersley,
Worcestershire B: Miss Elizabeth
Sykes Sire: Goldhill 2. Easby Abbey
6yr 3. Captain Christy 6yr 1½l, 2l
4:07.7 8 ran

1974 9th Baron Howard de Walden's
br g **Lanzarote** 6yr J: Richard
Pitman 7/4 £14,023 T: Fred Winter,
Lambourn, Berkshire B: Owner Sire:
Milesian 2. Comedy of Errors 7yr
3. Yenisei 7yr 3l, 8l 4:17.7 7 ran

1975 Ted Wheatley's br g **Comedy of
Errors** 8yr J: Ken White 11/8 Fav
£14,459 T: Fred Rimell, Kinnersley,
Worcestershire B: Miss Elizabeth
Sykes Sire: Goldhill 2. Flash Imp 6yr
3. Tree Tangle 6yr 8l, head 4:28.5
13 ran

1976 Reg Spencer's b g **Night Nurse**
5yr J: Paddy Broderick 2/1 Fav
£14,530 T: Peter Easterby, Great
Habton, Yorkshire B: Cloghran Stud
Farm Sire: Falcon 2. Birds Nest 6yr
3. Flash Imp 7yr 2½l, 8l 4:05:9 8 ran

1977 Reg Spencer's b g **Night Nurse**
6yr J: Paddy Broderick 15/2 £18,147
T: Peter Easterby, Great Habton,
Yorkshire B: Cloghran Stud Farm
Sire: Falcon 2. Monksfield 5yr
3. Dramatist 6yr 2l, 2l 4:24.0 10 ran

1978 Michael Mangan's b h **Monksfield**
6yr J: Tommy Kinane 11/2 £21,332
T: Des McDonogh, Moynalty, Co

*Sir Ken displays his fluent jumping technique at the final flight in the 1953 Champion
Hurdle, the second of his three consecutive wins in the race.*

Meath, Ireland B: Peter Ryan Sire: Gala Performance 2. Sea Pigeon 8yr 3. Night Nurse 7yr 2*l*, *l* 4:12.7 13 ran

1979 Michael Mangan's b h **Monksfield** 7yr J: Dessie Hughes 9/4 Fav £22,730 T: Des McDonogh, Moynalty, Co Meath, Ireland B: Peter Ryan Sire: Gala Performance 2. Sea Pigeon 9yr 3. Beacon Light 8yr ¾*l*, 15*l* 4:27.9 10 ran

1980 Pat Muldoon's br g **Sea Pigeon** 10yr J: Jonjo O'Neill 13/2 £24,972 T: Peter Easterby, Great Habton, Yorkshire B: Greentree Stud Sire: Sea-Bird 2. Monksfield 8yr 3. Birds Nest 10yr 7*l*, 1½*l* 4:06.0 9 ran

1981 Pat Muldoon's br g **Sea Pigeon** 11yr J: John Francome 7/4 Fav £32,260 T: Peter Easterby, Great Habton, Yorkshire B: Greentree Stud Sire: Sea-Bird 2. Pollardstown 6yr 3. Daring Run 6yr 1½*l*, neck 4:11.4 14 ran

1982 Danno Heaslip's b g **For Auction** 6yr J: Mr Colin Magnier 40/1 £37,043 T: Michael Cunningham, Kildalkey, Co Meath, Ireland B: Mrs Paul Finegan Sire: Royal Trip 2. Broadsword 5yr 3. Ekbalco 6yr 7*l*, 1½*l* 4:12.4 14 ran

1983 Sheikh Ali Abu Khamsin's b g **Gaye Brief** 6yr J: Richard Linley 7/1 £34,865 T: Mrs Mercy Rimell, Kinnersley, Worcestershire B: Phil Sweeney Sire: Lucky Brief 2. Boreen Prince 6yr 3. For Auction 7yr 3*l*, 7*l* 3:57.8 17 ran

1984 Mrs Charmian Hill's b m **Dawn Run** 6yr J: Jonjo O'Neill 4/5 Fav £36,680 T: Paddy Mullins, Goresbridge, Co Kilkenny, Ireland B: John Riordan Sire: Deep Run 2. Cima 6yr 3. Very Promising 6yr ¾*l*, 4*l* 3:52.6 14 ran

1985 Stype Wood Stud's br g **See You Then** 5yr J: Steve Smith Eccles 16/1 £38,030 T: Nick Henderson, Lambourn, Berkshire B: Ribblesdale Stud Sire: Royal Palace 2. Robin Wonder 7yr 3. Stans Pride 8yr 7*l*, 3*l* 3:51.7 14 ran

RECORDS FOR WINNING HORSES

Triple champions

Hatton's Grace (1949, 1950, 1951) Sir Ken (1952, 1953, 1954) Persian War (1968, 1969, 1970) When trying for a fourth title, Hatton's Grace came fifth in 1952, Sir Ken fourth in 1955 and Persian War second in 1971.

Double champions

Insurance (1932, 1933, his only 2 starts in the Champion Hurdle) National Spirit (1947, 1948) Bula (1971, 1972) Comedy of Errors (1973, 1975)

Night Nurse (1976, 1977) Monksfield (1978, 1979) Sea Pigeon (1980, 1981)

Greatest margins

12 lengths — Insurance (1932) 8 lengths — Blaris (1927), Bula (1972), Comedy of Errors (1975) 7 lengths — Sea Pigeon (1980), For Auction (1982), See You Then (1985)

Smallest margins

head — Brown Tony (1930), Seneca (1941), Clair Soleil (1955) ½ length — Lion Courage (1935)

Oldest

11 years — Hatton's Grace (1951), Sea Pigeon (1981) 10 years — Hatton's Grace (1950), Sea Pigeon (1980) 9 years — Free Fare (1937), Our Hope (1938), Solford (1940), Hatton's Grace (1949)

Youngest

4 years — Brown Jack (1928), Brown Tony (1930), Seneca (1941), Forestation (1942)

Mares

African Sister (1939), Dawn Run (1984)

Entires

Royal Falcon (1929), Seneca (1941, later gelded), Eborneezer (1961), Saucy Kit (1967), Monksfield (1978, 1979).

Grey or roan

Victor Norman (1936), Our Hope (1938), Anzio (1962)

Black

Winning Fair (1963) was described as black or brown

Longest odds

50/1 — Kirriemuir (1965) 40/1 — For Auction (1982) 28/1 — Merry Deal (1957)

Shortest odds

2/5 — Sir Ken (1953) 4/9 — Chenango (1934), Sir Ken (1954) 8/11 — Bula (1972) 4/5 — Insurance (1932), Distel (1946), Dawn Run (1984) 10/11 — Insurance (1933)

Led all the way

Blaris (1927), Victor Norman (1936), Night Nurse (1976)

Trained in Ireland

Distel (1946), Hatton's Grace (1949, 1950, 1951), Another Flash (1960), Winning Fair (1963), Monksfield (1978, 1979), For Auction (1982), Dawn Run (1984).

Bred in France

Sir Ken (1952, 1953, 1954), Clair Soleil (1955)

Bred in USA

Sea Pigeon (1980, 1981).

Champion when still unbeaten

Bula's first Champion Hurdle (1971) was the 12th race and 12th win of his career. Seneca (1941) and Clair Soleil (1955) won the title when still unbeaten over hurdles but both had lost races on the Flat.

Won at the fourth attempt

Sea Pigeon (1980)

Won at the third attempt

Salmon Spray (1966)

Novices

Brown Jack (1928), Brown Tony (1930), Seneca (1941) Forestation (1942), Brains Trust (1945) and Doorknocker (1956) won the title in the same season as their first victory over hurdles. Seneca did so in only his second race over hurdles and Brown Tony in his fourth.

Juvenile and senior champions

Clair Soleil (1955) and Persian War (1968, 1969, 1970) had previously won the Triumph Hurdle for 4-year-olds

Champion in England and France

Irish mare Dawn Run also won the Grande Course de Haies d'Auteuil in 1984

Champion over hurdles and fences

No horse has been versatile enough to win both the Champion Hurdle and the Cheltenham Gold Cup, though dual champion hurdler Night Nurse (1976, 1977) came second in the 1981 Gold Cup. Chenango (1934) had been America's leading steeplechaser of 1931, when his victories included the Temple Gwathmey Memorial Chase.

RECORDS FOR PLACED HORSES

Placed twice without winning

Clear Cash (1929, 1930), Anarchist (1941, 1942), Galatian (1953, 1954), Quita Que (1956, 1957), Quelle Chance (1962, 1963), Major Rose (1970, 1971), Flash Imp (1975, 1976), Birds Nest (1976, 1980).

Oldest

10 years — Another Flash (1964), Birds Nest (1980).

Mares

African Sister (1940), Ivy Green (1959), Stans Pride (1985).

Entires

Boddam (1927), Peace River (1928), Clear Cash (1929, 1930), Indian Salmon (1933), Pompelmoose (1934), Gay Light (1935), Chuchoteur (1938), Lobau (1938), Anarchist (1941, 1942), Vidi (1945), Carnival Boy (1946), Le Paillon (1947), Vatelys (1949), Captain Fox (1949), Harlech (1950), Speciality (1950), Prince Hindou (1951), Tout ou Rien (1957), Retour de Flamme (1958), Spartan General (1965), Worcran (1965), Privy Seal (1969), Escalus (1970), Monksfield (1977, 1980), Broadsword (1982).

Grey

Our Hope (1937), Chuchoteur (1938), Vitement (1939), Southport (1942), Yenisei (1974).

Black

Black Duncan (1934), Black Justice (1968), Flash Imp (1975, 1976)

Longest odds

100/1 — Yenisei (1974), Stans Pride (1985).
66/1 — Lyford Cay (1972), Cima (1984), Robin Wonder (1985).

Trained in Ireland

Galatian (1953, 1954), Teapot (1953), Stroller (1955), Quita Que (1956, 1957), Ivy Green (1959), Prudent King (1959), Albergo (1960), Moss Bank (1961), Farrney Fox (1963), Flyingbolt (1966), Talgo Abbess (1967), Captain Christy (1973), Yenisei (1974), Monksfield (1977, 1980), Daring Run (1981), Boreen Prince (1983), For Auction (1983).

Trained in France

Chuchoteur (1938), Le Paillon (1947), Pyrrhus (1951), Prince Hindou (1951), Tout ou Rien (1957).

Bred in France

Chuchoteur (1938), Lobau (1938), Le Paillon (1947), Freddy Fox (1947), Encoroli (1948), Vatelys (1949), Pyrrhus (1951), Prince Hindou (1951), Teapot (1953), Tout ou Rien (1957) Retour de Flamme (1958), Worcran (1965), Makaldar (1967).

Bred in USA

Sea Pigeon (1978, 1979), Broadsword (1982)

Bred in New Zealand

Yenisei (1974)

Disqualification

Aurelius finished second in 1967 but was disqualified and placed last for hampering the third finisher, Makaldar, soon after the final flight.

MISCELLANEOUS RECORDS

Fastest times

3:51.7 for two miles — See You Then (1985)
3:52.6 for two miles — Dawn Run (1984)
3:55.0 for two miles 125 yards — Another Flash (1960)

Largest fields

24 — 1964
23 — 1967
21 — 1955, 1963

Smallest fields

3 — 1932
4 — 1927
5 — 1930, 1933, 1934, 1938

Richest first prizes

£38,030 — 1985
£37,043 — 1982
£36,680 — 1984

Smallest first prizes

£340 — 1945
£365 — 1927
£410 — 1940, 1941

Most appearances

6 times — National Spirit (1947 to 1952) Birds Nest (1976 to 1981)
5 times — Hatton's Grace (1948 to 1952) Merry Deal (1957 to 1961) Sea Pigeon (1977 to 1981)

Most often in first 3

4 times — Persian War (1968, 1969, 1970, 1971) Monksfield (1977, 1978, 1979, 1980) Sea Pigeon (1978, 1979, 1980, 1981)
3 times — Hatton's Grace (1949, 1950, 1951) Sir Ken (1952, 1953, 1954) Another Flash (1960, 1962, 1964) Comedy of Errors (1973, 1974, 1975) Night Nurse (1976, 1977, 1978)

Most champions in one field

5 — Another Flash, Winning Fair, Magic Court, Kirriemuir and Salmon Spray in 1964

Champions placed 1, 2, 3

Magic Court, Another Flash, Kirriemuir (1964)
Monksfield, Sea Pigeon, Night Nurse (1978)

Foreign-trained horses placed 1, 2, 3

Hatton's Grace (Ireland), Pyrrhus (France), Prince Hindou (France) (1951)

Oldest runner

12 years — Hatton's Grace (1952)

Most recent 4-year-old runners

Kirriemuir and Sun Hat (1964)

Hottest losing favourites

1/2 — Free Fare (1938)
4/7 — Solford (1941)
4/6 — Comedy of Errors (1974), Browne's Gazette (1985)
5/6 — Bula (1973).

Longest-priced favourite

6/1 — Another Flash (1964)

Favourite most often

3 times — Free Fare (1936, 1937, 1938) Sir Ken (1952, 1953, 1954) Another Flash (1960, 1962, 1964) Bula (1971, 1972, 1973).

Most consecutive winning favourites

4 — 1952 to 1955, 1969 to 1972.

Most consecutive losing favourites

8 — 1961 to 1968

Race not run

1931 because of frost
1943 and 1944 because of World War II

Race postponed

1929, 1937, 1947, 1955

Earliest dates

1 March — 1932
2 March — 1948, 1954
3 March — 1953, 1959

Latest dates

12 April — 1947
31 March — 1945
20 March — 1968

Run on

Tuesday: 1929–39, 1946, 1948–54, 1956–60, from 1980
Wednesday: 1927, 1940–41, 1955, 1961–63, 1965–79
Thursday: 1928
Friday: 1964
Saturday: 1942, 1945, 1947

Most successful owners

4 wins — Miss Dorothy Paget: 1932, 1933, 1940, 1946
3 wins — Mrs Moya Keogh: 1949, 1950, 1951
Maurice Kingsley: 1952, 1953, 1954
Henry Alper: 1968, 1969, 1970

Most successful breeders

3 wins — John Harris: 1949, 1950, 1951
Marcel Chenorio: 1952, 1953, 1954
Astor Studs: 1968, 1969, 1970
2 wins with different horses — Miss Dorothy Paget: 1945, 1957

Most successful trainers

5 wins—Peter Easterby: 1967, 1976, 1977, 1980, 1981.

4 wins—Vic Smyth: 1941, 1942, 1947, 1948

3 wins—Vincent O'Brien: 1949, 1950, 1951
Willie Stephenson: 1952, 1953, 1954
Ryan Price: 1955, 1959, 1961
Colin Davies: 1968, 1969, 1970
Fred Winter: 1971, 1972, 1974

Successful woman trainer

Mrs Mercy Rimell: 1983

Most successful jockeys

4 wins—Tim Molony: 1951, 1952, 1953, 1954

3 wins—Ron Smyth: 1941, 1942, 1948

Fred Winter: 1955, 1959, 1961
Jimmy Uttley: 1968, 1969, 1970

Successful amateur riders

Perry Harding (1938), Alan Lillingston (1963), Colin Magnier (1982)

Successful owner-breeders

Sir Malcolm McAlpine (1941), Len Abelson (1947, 1948), Burjor Pajgar (1961), 9th Baron Howard de Walden (1974)

Successful owner-trainers

Roderic Gubbins (1938), Vic Smyth (1942), Arthur Jones (1957), George Spencer (1963). Stan Wright (1958) trained Bandalore for his wife Dorothy.

Successful as both jockey and trainer

Fred Winter has won 3 times both as a jockey and as a trainer (*see above*)
Gerry Wilson rode Lion Courage (1935) and trained Brains Trust (1945),
Fred Rimell rode Brains Trust (1945) and trained Comedy of Errors (1973, 1975).

Most successful sires

3 wins—Achtoi: Blaris (1927), Insurance (1932, 1933).
Jackdaw: Brown Jack (1928), Brown Tony (1930), Lion Courage (1935).
His Grace: Hatton's Grace (1949, 1950, 1951).
Laëken: Sir Ken (1952, 1953, 1954).
Persian Gulf: Persian War (1968, 1969, 1970).

Cheltenham Gold Cup

The Cheltenham Gold Cup is England's championship race for steeplechasers. Inaugurated in 1924, it was at first no more than a trial for the Grand National, but it grew steadily in importance and became in the immediate post-war years the main objective of the best staying steeplechasers in the British Isles.

Title

Cheltenham Gold Cup from 1924, with the addition of sponsors' names from 1975.
Sponsored by the Horserace Totalisator Board from 1980.

Venue

Prestbury Park, Cheltenham, Gloucestershire from 1924.

Distance

about 3¼ miles 1924–28
about 3 miles 3 furlongs 1929–35
about 3¼ miles 1936–39
3 miles 1940–45
about 3¼ miles 1946–58
about 3¼ miles 130 yards 1959–64
about 3¼ miles 76 yards 1965–76
about 3¼ miles from 1977, run over 22 fences

Weights

12 stone (level weights) except 5-year-olds who are allowed 10 lb (9 lb before 1975).
A 5 lb allowance for mares was introduced in 1984.

1924 Humphrey Wyndham's ch g **Red Splash** 5yr J: Dick Rees 5/1 £685 T: Fred Withington, Bicester, Oxfordshire B: Owner Sire: Copper Ore 2. Conjuror 12yr 3. Gerald L. 10yr head, neck 9 ran
1925 Christopher Bentley's ch m **Ballinode** 9yr J: Ted Leader 3/1 £880 T: Frank Morgan, The Curragh, Co Kildare, Ireland B: H. B. Warren Sire: Machakos 2. Alcazar 9yr 3. Patsey 11yr 5*l*, bad 7:29.6 4 ran

1926 Frank Barbour's b g **Koko** 8yr J: Tim Hamey 10/1 £880 T: Alfred Bickley, Tarporley, Cheshire B: Owner Sire: Santoi 2. Old Tay Bridge 12yr 3. Ruddyglow 8yr 4*l*, 5*l* 7:10.4 8 ran
1927 2nd Baron Stalbridge's ch g **Thrown In** 11yr J: Mr Hugh Grosvenor 10/1 £780 T: Owen Anthony, Lambourn, Berkshire B: G. C. Sharpe Sire: Beau Bill 2. Grakle 5yr 3. Silvo 11yr 2*l*, 1½*l* 7:28.0 8 ran
1928 F. W. Keen's br g **Patron Saint** 5yr J: Dick Rees 7/2 £780 T: Stanley Harrison, Bangor-on-Dee, Denbighshire B: A. B. Barrow Sire: St Girons 2. Vive 13yr 3. Koko 10yr 4*l*, 2*l* 7:29.6 7 ran
1929 Jock Whitney's ch g **Easter Hero** 9yr J: Dick Rees 7/4 Fav £776 T: Jack Anthony, Letcombe Regis, Berkshire B: Larry King Sire: My Prince 2. Lloydie 7yr 3. Grakle 7yr 20*l*, 2*l* 6:57.0 10 ran
1930 Jock Whitney's ch g **Easter Hero** 10yr J: Tommy Cullinan 8/11 Fav £670 T: Jack Anthony, Letcombe Regis, Berkshire B: Larry King Sire: My Prince 2. Grakle 8yr 3. Gib 7yr 20*l*, bad 7:06.0 4 ran
1931 no race
1932 Miss Dorothy Paget's b g **Golden Miller** 5yr J: Ted Leader 13/2 £670 T: Basil Briscoe, Longstowe, Cambridgeshire B: Julius Solomon Sire: Goldcourt 2. Inverse 6yr 3. Aruntius 11yr 4*l*, bad 7:33.4 6 ran
1933 Miss Dorothy Paget's b g **Golden Miller** 6yr J: Billy Stott 4/7 Fav £670

T: Basil Briscoe, Exning, Suffolk B: Julius Solomon Sire: Goldcourt 2. Thomond 7yr 3. Delaneige 8yr 10*l*, 5*l* 7:33.0 7 ran
1934 Miss Dorothy Paget's b g **Golden Miller** 7yr J: Gerry Wilson 6/5 Fav £670 T: Basil Briscoe, Exning, Suffolk B: Julius Solomon Sire: Goldcourt 2. Avenger 5yr 3. Kellsboro' Jack 8yr 6*l*, 6*l* 7:04.6 7 ran
1935 Miss Dorothy Paget's b g **Golden Miller** 8yr J: Gerry Wilson 1/2 Fav £670 T: Basil Briscoe, Exning, Suffolk B: Julius Solomon Sire: Goldcourt 2. Thomond 9yr 3. Kellsboro' Jack 9yr ¾*l*, 5*l* 6:30.0 5 ran
1936 Miss Dorothy Paget's b g **Golden Miller** 9yr J: Evan Williams 21/20 Fav £670 T: Owen Anthony, Letcombe Bassett, Berkshire B: Julius Solomon Sire: Goldcourt 2. Royal Mail 7yr 3. Kellsboro' Jack 10yr 12*l*, 2*l* 7:05.2 6 ran
1937 no race
1938 Dealtry Part's b g **Morse Code** 9yr J: Danny Morgan 13/2 £720 T: Ivor Anthony, Wroughton, Wiltshire B: Owner Sire: The Pilot 2. Golden Miller 11yr 3. Macaulay 7yr 2*l*, 3*l* 6:35.2 6 ran
1939 Mrs Jean Smith-Bingham's b g **Brendan's Cottage** 9yr J: George Owen 8/1 £1,120 T: George Beeby, Compton, Berkshire B: M. Cunningham Sire: Cottage 2. Morse Code 10yr 3. Embarrassed 6yr 5*l*, bad 7:34.2 5 ran
1940 Miss Dorothy Paget's b g **Roman Hackle** 7yr J: Evan Williams Evens Fav £495 T: Owen Anthony,

Continued on page 86

ARKLE

Who was the greatest steeplechaser of all time? Exact comparisons are impossible between champions of different eras but Arkle, the brilliant Irish performer of the 1960s, did enough to convince most observers that he had reached the pinnacle of equine achievement in his sphere.

This bay gelding, three times winner of the Cheltenham Gold Cup, displayed outstanding pace, stamina, jumping ability, intelligence and courage under crushing burdens in handicaps, never falling and always giving his best. No other steeplechaser has even come close to matching his margin of superiority over his contemporaries, yet until he put Mill House in his place the latter had been widely regarded as the best Gold Cup winner since Golden Miller.

Arkle was bred by Mrs Mary Baker of Malahow, Co Dublin, Ireland and was foaled at Ballymacoll Stud, Co Meath on 19 April 1957. His sire, Archive, had been a complete failure as a racehorse but his dam, Bright Cherry, was a good steeplechase winner from a prominent jumping family.

In August 1960 he was bought for 1,150 guineas by Anne, Duchess of Westminster at Goff's Sales. She named her new purchase after a Scottish mountain and sent him in due course to Tom Dreaper of Kilsallaghan, a master of the trainer's profession who had already guided the fortunes of one champion in Prince Regent.

By no means prepossessing as a youngster, Arkle was given plenty of time to mature and did not see a racecourse until December 1961, when he was nearly five. He won two hurdle races that winter and in 1962/63 switched to fences, proving himself the best novice in the British Isles by triumphing in the Broadway Chase at Cheltenham and the Power Gold Cup at Fairyhouse.

That season's Cheltenham Gold Cup victor, Mill House, looked set for a long reign and in the Hennessy Gold Cup at Newbury in November 1963 he gave Arkle weight and an apparently emphatic beating. Few realised that Arkle had plenty of improvement left in him, but in his four subsequent races against Mill House that initial defeat was handsomely avenged each time.

Their second and decisive meeting came in the 1964 Cheltenham Gold Cup, when the Irish challenger drew clear up the final hill to prevail by five lengths. Thereafter his progress was one of almost unbroken triumph. He won that season's Irish Grand National at Fairyhouse under top weight and

Arkle (far side) is about to head Mill House on the second circuit of the 1965 Cheltenham Gold Cup.

Tom Dreaper patiently guided Arkle's uniquely successful career.

in the autumn trounced Mill House in the Hennessy Gold Cup, leading for most of the way under 12 st 7 lb and winning by ten lengths.

A week later even this magnificent performer found 12 st 10 lb a shade too much in the Massey-Ferguson Gold Cup but in March 1965 he led throughout in his second Cheltenham Gold Cup with Mill House finishing 20 lengths in arrears. The following month he carried 12 st 7 lb in the Whitbread Gold Cup at Sandown Park and, conceding at least 35 lb all round, made most of the running to collect the most valuable prize of his career.

In 1965/66 not even the full range of the handicap could bring Arkle back to his rivals as he added to his tally the Gallaher Gold Cup in record time at Sandown; his second Hennessy Gold Cup under 12 st 7 lb, this time by a record 15 lengths; the King George VI Chase by a distance; his third Leopardstown Chase; and his third Cheltenham Gold Cup, cantering home in this championship event by a record 30 lengths at odds of 1/10.

In the autumn of 1966 he reappeared in the Hennessy but found the task of conceding 35 lb to the fitter Stalbridge Colonist just beyond him; his conqueror nearly won the Cheltenham Gold Cup later in the season. Arkle then took the SGB Handicap Chase at Ascot under 12 st 7 lb by 15 lengths but in the last race of his career, the King George VI Chase at Kempton Park on 27 December 1966, he fractured the pedal bone of his off-fore hoof, though he still battled on to finish second.

He eventually recovered soundness but in October 1968 came the announcement that he would race no more. He suffered increasingly from stiffness and was put down at Bryanstown, his owner's estate in Co Kildare, on 31 May 1970.

Altogether Arkle won 27 of his 35 races over six seasons; he lost both his 'bumper' events (National Hunt Flat races), but won four of his six starts over hurdles and was successful on his only appearance in a regular Flat race. His remaining 26 races were over fences; he won 22 of them and was second twice and third twice. The six horses who finished in front of him in a steeplechase were:

- Mill House (gave 5 lb) and Happy Spring (received 23 lb) by 8 lengths and ¾ length in the 1963 Hennessy Gold Cup.
- Flying Wild (received 32 lb) and Buona notte (received 26 lb) by a short head and a length in the 1964 Massey-Ferguson Gold Cup.
- Stalbridge Colonist (received 35 lb) by half a length in the 1966 Hennessy Gold Cup.
- Dormant (received 21 lb) by a length in the 1966 King George VI Chase.

Arkle, who never carried less than 12 stone in his last 19 races, set a new earnings record of £78,464 5s 6d for a jumper in the British Isles. In every one of his races over fences he was ridden by Pat Taaffe.

Had he not been injured in his prime he would have eclipsed Golden Miller's record sequence of victories in the Cheltenham Gold Cup, but that would merely have altered the wording of his story, not its magnitude.

Arkle set the standard by which all other steeplechasers are measured, and in addition he became a British public hero to an extent matched only by Red Rum among racehorses. Let the final word lie with Timeform, whose authoritative jumping 'black book' stated unequivocally in late 1966, just before the champion's injury, that he 'has proved himself the greatest chaser ever'.

Letcombe Bassett, Berkshire
B: Captain and Mrs G. L. Hastings
Sire: Yutoi 2. Black Hawk 9yr
3. Royal Mail 11yr 10*l*, 2*l* 6:46.4 7 ran
1941 David Sherbrooke's ch g **Poet Prince** 9yr J: Roger Burford 7/2 £495
T: Ivor Anthony, Wroughton, Wiltshire
B: James Sherrard Sire: Milton
2. Savon 9yr 3. Red Rower 7yr 3*l*,
short head 6:15.6 10 ran
1942 7th Earl of Sefton's b g **Médoc** 8yr
J: Frenchie Nicholson 9/2 £495
T: Reg Hobbs, Lambourn, Berkshire
B: L. Goubert Sire: Van 2. Red
Rower 8yr 3. Asterabad 11yr 8*l*, 4*l*
6:38.0 12 ran
1943 no race
1944 no race
1945 2nd Baron Stalbridge's b g **Red Rower** 11yr J: Davy Jones 11/4 Fav
£340 T: Owner, Eastbury, Berkshire
B: Owner Sire: Rameses the Second
2. Schubert 11yr 3. Paladin 11yr
3*l*, 1½*l* 6:16.0 16 ran
1946 Jimmy Rank's b g **Prince Regent** 11yr J: Tim Hyde 4/7 Fav £1,130
T: Tom Dreaper, Kilsallaghan, Co
Dublin, Ireland B: A. H. Maxwell Sire:
My Prince 2. Poor Flame 8yr 3. Red
April 9yr 5*l*, 4*l* 6:47.5 6 ran
1947 3rd Baron Grimthorpe's ch h
Fortina 6yr J: Mr Dick Black 8/1
£1,140 T: Hector Christie, Milton
Marlborough, Wiltshire B: Baron
Dutacq Sire: Formor 2. Happy Home
8yr 3. Prince Blackthorn 9yr 10*l*, 6*l*
6:41.2 12 ran
1948 Frank Vickerman's b or br g
Cottage Rake 9yr J: Aubrey
Brabazon 10/1 £1,911 T: Vincent
O'Brien, Churchtown, Co Cork,
Ireland B: Otto Vaughan Sire: Cottage
2. Happy Home 9yr 3. Coloured
School Boy 8yr 1½*l*, 10*l* 6:56.4 12 ran
1949 Frank Vickerman's b or br g
Cottage Rake 10yr J: Aubrey
Brabazon 4/6 Fav £2,817 T: Vincent
O'Brien, Churchtown, Co Cork,
Ireland B: Otto Vaughan Sire: Cottage
2. Cool Customer 10yr 3. Coloured
School Boy 9yr 2*l*, 6*l* 6:38.0 6 ran
1950 Frank Vickerman's b or br g
Cottage Rake 11yr J: Aubrey
Brabazon 5/6 Fav £2,936 T: Vincent
O'Brien, Churchtown, Co Cork,
Ireland B: Otto Vaughan Sire: Cottage
2. Finnure 9yr 3. Garde Toi 9yr
10*l*, 8*l* 7:01.6 6 ran
1951 1st Baron Bicester's ch g **Silver Fame** 12yr J: Martin Molony 6/4 Fav
£2,783 T: George Beeby, Compton,
Berkshire B: J. W. Osborne and
Eustace Mansfield Sire: Werwolf
2. Greenogue 9yr 3. Mighty Fine 9yr
short head, 2*l* 6:23.4 6 ran
1952 Miss Dorothy Paget's ch g **Mont Tremblant** 6yr J: Dave Dick 8/1
£3,232 T: Fulke Walwyn, Lambourn,
Berkshire B: Maurice Hennessy
Sire: Gris Perle 2. Shaef 8yr
3. Galloway Braes 7yr 10*l*, 4*l* 7:01.0

13 ran
1953 Mrs Moya Keogh's ch g **Knock Hard** 9yr J: Tim Molony 11/2 £3,258
T: Vincent O'Brien, Cashel, Co
Tipperary, Ireland B: T. J. Sheahan
Sire: Domaha 2. Halloween 8yr
3. Galloway Braes 8yr 5*l*, 2*l* 6:28.0
12 ran
1954 Alan Strange's b g **Four Ten** 8yr
J: Tommy Cusack 100/6 £3,576
T: John Roberts, Cheltenham,
Gloucestershire B: Messrs L. Strange
and Sons Sire: Blunderbuss
2. Mariner's Log 7yr 3. Halloween 9yr
4*l*, 4*l* 7:12.2 9 ran
1955 Philip Burt's b g **Gay Donald** 9yr
J: Tony Grantham 33/1 £3,775
T: Jim Ford, Cholderton, Wiltshire
B: Harry Frank Sire: Gay Light
2. Halloween 10yr 3. Four Ten 9yr
10*l*, 8*l* 6:59.8 9 ran
1956 James Davey's ch g **Limber Hill** 9yr J: Jimmy Power 11/8 Fav £3,750
T: Bill Dutton, Malton, Yorkshire
B: Owner Sire: Bassam 2. Vigor 8yr
3. Halloween 11yr 4*l*, 1½*l* 6:42.0
11 ran
1957 David Brown's br g **Linwell** 9yr
J: Michael Scudamore 100/9 £3,996
T: Ivor Herbert, Cadmore End,
Buckinghamshire B: James Delany
Sire: Rosewell 2. Kerstin 7yr 3. Rose
Park 11yr 1*l*, 5*l* 6:55.8 13 ran
1958 George Moore's br m **Kerstin** 8yr
J: Stan Hayhurst 7/1 £5,788 T: Verly
Bewicke, Glanton, Northumberland
B: Cornelius Burke Sire: Honor's
Choice 2. Polar Flight 8yr 3. Gay
Donald 12yr ½*l*, bad 6:55.8 9 ran
1959 12th Earl of Fingall's b g **Roddy Owen** 10yr J: Bobby Beasley 5/1
£5,363 T: Danny Morgan, Newbridge,
Co Kildare, Ireland B: Andy Nolan
Sire: Owenstown 2. Linwell 11yr
3. Lochroe 11yr 3*l*, 10*l* 7:28.4 11 ran
1960 John Rogerson's b or br g **Pas Seul** 7yr J: Bill Rees 6/1 £5,414
T: Bob Turnell, Ogbourne Maisey,
Wiltshire B: Harry Frank Sire: Erin's
Pride 2. Lochroe 12yr 3. Zonda 9yr 1*l*,
5*l* 7:00.0 12 ran
1961 Guy Westmacott's b or br g
Saffron Tartan 10yr J: Fred Winter
2/1 Fav £6,043 T: Don Butchers,
Epsom, Surrey B: C. C. Thompson
Sire: Tartan 2. Pas Seul 8yr
3. Mandarin 10yr 1½*l*, 3*l* 6:49.6 11 ran
1962 Mme Peggy Hennessy's b g
Mandarin 11yr J: Fred Winter 7/2
£5,720 T: Fulke Walwyn, Lambourn,
Berkshire B: Kilian Hennessy Sire:
Deux pour Cent 2. Fortria 10yr
3. Cocky Consort 9yr 1*l*, 10*l* 6:39.8
9 ran
1963 Bill Gollings's b g **Mill House** 6yr
J: Willie Robinson 7/2 Fav £5,958
T: Fulke Walwyn, Lambourn,
Berkshire B: Mrs B. M. Lawlor Sire:
King Hal 2. Fortria 11yr 3. Duke of
York 8yr 12*l*, 4*l* 7:08.4 12 ran
1964 Anne, Duchess of Westminster's

b g **Arkle** 7yr J: Pat Taaffe 7/4
£8,004 T: Tom Dreaper, Kilsallaghan,
Co Dublin, Ireland B: Mrs Mary
Baker Sire: Archive 2. Mill House 7yr
3. Pas Seul 11yr 5*l*, 25*l* 6:45.6 4 ran
1965 Anne, Duchess of Westminster's
b g **Arkle** 8yr J: Pat Taaffe
30/100 Fav £7,986 T: Tom Dreaper,
Kilsallaghan, Co Dublin, Ireland
B: Mrs Mary Baker Sire: Archive
2. Mill House 8yr 3. Stoney Crossing
7yr 20*l*, 30*l* 6:41.2 4 ran
1966 Anne, Duchess of Westminster's
b g **Arkle** 9yr J: Pat Taaffe 1/10 Fav
£7,674 T: Tom Dreaper, Kilsallaghan,
Co Dublin, Ireland B: Mrs Mary
Baker Sire: Archive 2. Dormant 9yr
3. Snaigow 7yr 30*l*, 10*l* 6:54.2 5 ran
1967 Harry Collins's b g **Woodland Venture** 7yr J: Terry Biddlecombe
100/8 £7,999 T: Fred Rimell,
Kinnersley, Worcestershire B: Owner
Sire: Eastern Venture 2. Stalbridge
Colonist 8yr 3. What a Myth 10yr ¾*l*,
2*l* 6:59.8 8 ran
1968 John Thomson's b g **Fort Leney** 10yr J: Pat Taaffe 11/2 £7,713
T: Tom Dreaper, Kilsallaghan, Co
Dublin, Ireland B: Owner Sire:
Fortina 2. The Laird 7yr 3. Stalbridge
Colonist 9yr neck, 1*l* 6:51.0 5 ran
1969 Lady Weir's ch g **What a Myth**
12yr J: Paul Kelleway 8/1 £8,129
T: Ryan Price, Findon, Sussex B: Ian
Muir Sire: Coup de Myth
2. Domacorn 7yr 3. Playlord 8yr
1½*l*, 20*l* 7:30.8 11 ran
1970 Raymond Guest's ch g
L'Escargot 7yr J: Tommy Carberry
33/1 £8,103 T: Dan Moore, The
Curragh, Co Kildare, Ireland B: Mrs
Barbara O'Neill Sire: Escart 2. French
Tan 8yr 3. Spanish Steps 7yr
1½*l*, 10*l* 6:47.5 12 ran
1971 Raymond Guest's ch g
L'Escargot 8yr J: Tommy Carberry
7/2 Co-Fav £7,995 T: Dan Moore,
The Curragh, Co Kildare, Ireland
B: Mrs Barbara O'Neill Sire: Escart
2. Leap Frog 7yr 3. The Dikler 8yr
10*l*, 15*l* 8:00.7 8 ran
1972 Pat Doyle's ch m **Glencaraig Lady** 8yr J: Frank Berry 6/1 £15,255
T: Francis Flood, Grange Con, Co
Wicklow, Ireland B: Jim Hogan Sire:
Fortina 2. Royal Toss 10yr 3. The
Dikler 9yr ¾*l*, head 7:18.0 12 ran
1973 Mrs Peggy August's b g **The Dikler** 10yr J: Ron Barry 9/1 £15,125
T: Fulke Walwyn, Lambourn,
Berkshire B: Joseph Moorhead Sire:
Vulgan 2. Pendil 8yr 3. Charlie
Potheen 8yr short head, 6*l* 6:37.2
8 ran
1974 Mrs Jane Samuel's b g **Captain Christy** 7yr J: Bobby Beasley 7/1
£14,572 T: Pat Taaffe, Straffan, Co
Kildare, Ireland B: George Williams
Sire: Mon Capitaine 2. The Dikler
11yr 3. Game Spirit 8yr 5*l*, 20*l* 7:05.5
7 ran

Captain Christy, the 1974 Cheltenham Gold Cup victor, on his way to a 30–length victory in the 1975 King George VI Chase at Kempton Park. This is the best performance by any steeplechaser in England since the days of Arkle.

1975 Anne, Duchess of Westminster's br g **Ten Up** 8yr J: Tommy Carberry 2/1 £17,757 T: Jim Dreaper, Kilsallaghan, Co Dublin, Ireland B: Joe Osborne Sire: Raise You Ten 2. Soothsayer 8yr 3. Bula 10yr 6l, ½l 7:51.4 8 ran

1976 Sir Edward Hanmer's b g **Royal Frolic** 7yr J: John Burke 14/1 £18,134 T: Fred Rimell, Kinnersley, Worcestershire B: John Seymour Sire: Royal Buck 2. Brown Lad 10yr 3. Colebridge 12yr 5l, 5l 6:40.1 11 ran

1977 Mrs Anne-Marie McGowan's b g **Davy Lad** 7yr J: Dessie Hughes 14/1 £21,990 T: Mick O'Toole, Maddenstown, Co Kildare, Ireland B: Mrs K. Westropp-Bennett Sire: David Jack 2. Tied Cottage 9yr 3. Summerville 11yr 6l, 20l 7:13.8 13 ran

1978 Mrs Olive Jackson's b g **Midnight Court** 7yr J: John Francome 5/2 £23,827 T: Fred Winter, Lambourn, Berkshire B: Airlie Stud Sire: Twilight Alley 2. Brown Lad 12yr 3. Master H. 9yr 7l, 1l 6:57.3 10 ran

1979 Snailwell Stud's ch g **Alverton** 9yr J: Jonjo O'Neill 5/1 Jt-Fav £30,293 T: Peter Easterby, Great Habton, Yorkshire B: George Pratt Sire: Midsummer Night 2. Royal Mail 9yr 3. Aldaniti 9yr 25l, 20l 7:01.0 14 ran

1980 Arthur Barrow's ch g **Master Smudge** 8yr J: Richard Hoare 14/1 £35,997 T: Owner, Bridgwater, Somerset B: H. J. Radford Sire: Master Stephen 2. Mac Vidi 15yr 3. Approaching 9yr 5l, 2½l 7:14.2 15 ran (Tied Cottage finished first, disqualified)

1981 Robin Wilson's b g **Little Owl** 7yr J: Mr Jim Wilson 6/1 £44,258 T: Peter Easterby, Great Habton, Yorkshire B: Mrs J. Ferris Sire: Cantab 2. Night Nurse 10yr 3. Silver Buck 9yr 1½l, 10l 7:09.9 15 ran

1982 Mrs Christine Feather's br g **Silver Buck** 10yr J: Robert Earnshaw 8/1 £48,386 T: Michael Dickinson, Harewood, Yorkshire B: Mrs Edith Booth Sire: Silver Cloud 2. Bregawn 8yr 3. Sunset Cristo 8yr 2l, 12l 7:11.2 22 ran

1983 James Kennelly's ch g **Bregawn** 9yr J: Graham Bradley 100/30 Fav £45,260 T: Michael Dickinson, Harewood, Yorkshire B: J. Fitzgerald Sire: Saint Denys 2. Captain John 9yr 3. Wayward Lad 8yr 5l, 1½l 6:57.6 11 ran

1984 Stan Riley's br g **Burrough Hill Lad** 8yr J: Phil Tuck 7/2 £47,375 T: Mrs Jenny Pitman, Lambourn, Berkshire B: Owner Sire: Richboy 2. Brown Chamberlin 9yr 3. Drumlargan 10yr 3l, 8l 6:41.4 12 ran

1985 T. Kilroe & Sons Ltd's ch g **Forgive'n Forget** 8yr J: Mark Dwyer 7/1 £52,560 T: Jimmy FitzGerald, Malton, Yorkshire B: Thomas Walsh Sire: Precipice Wood 2. Righthand Man 8yr 3. Earls Brig 10yr 1½l, 2½l 6:48.3 15 ran

RECORDS FOR WINNING HORSES

5-times champion
Golden Miller (1932 to 1936)

Triple champions
Cottage Rake (1948, 1949, 1950)
Arkle (1964, 1965, 1966)

Double champions
Easter Hero (1929, 1930)
L'Escargot (1970, 1971)

Greatest margins
30 lengths—Arkle (1966)
25 lengths—Alverton (1979)
20 lengths—Easter Hero (1929, 1930), Arkle (1965).

Smallest margins
short head—Silver Fame (1951), The Dikler (1973)
head—Red Splash (1924)
neck—Fort Leney (1968)

Oldest
12 years—Silver Fame (1951), What a Myth (1969)

Youngest
5 years—Red Splash (1924), Patron Saint (1928), Golden Miller (1932)

Mares
Ballinode (1925), Kerstin (1958), Glencaraig Lady (1972)

Entire
Fortina (1947)

Longest odds
33/1—Gay Donald (1955), L'Escargot (1970)

Shortest odds
1/10—Arkle (1966)
30/100—Arkle (1965)
1/2—Golden Miller (1935)

Led all the way
Koko (1926), Easter Hero (1929, 1930),

Arkle (1965), Tied Cottage (1980, disqualified).

Trained in Wales
Patron Saint (1928)

Trained in Ireland
Ballinode (1925), Prince Regent (1946), Cottage Rake (1948, 1949, 1950), Knock Hard (1953), Roddy Owen (1959), Arkle (1964, 1965, 1966), Fort Leney (1968), L'Escargot (1970, 1971), Glencaraig Lady (1972), Captain Christy (1974), Ten Up (1975), Davy Lad (1977).

Bred in France
Médoc (1942), Fortina (1947), Mont Tremblant (1952), Mandarin (1962).

Siblings
Gay Donald (1955) and Pas Seul (1960) were half-brothers.

Won at the fourth attempt
The Dikler (1973).

Won at the third attempt
Red Rower (1945), Mandarin (1962)

Novices
Red Splash (1924), Golden Miller (1932), Mont Tremblant (1952) and Captain Christy (1974) won the title in the same season as their first victory over fences.

Champion in England and France
Mandarin also won the Grand Steeple-Chase de Paris in 1962.

Champion in England and USA
L'Escargot (1970, 1971) was voted America's champion steeplechaser in 1969, when he won the Meadow Brook Chase.

Also won Grand National
Golden Miller in 1934 is the only horse to triumph in the Gold Cup and the Grand National in the same season. L'Escargot (1970, 1971) won the Grand National in 1975.

Most successful at stud
Fortina (1947) became an outstanding sire of jumpers, and his offspring included Gold Cup winners Fort Leney and Glencaraig Lady.

Disqualification
Tied Cottage was first past the post by 8 lengths in 1980 but was disqualified when traces of the prohibited substance theobromine were found in his post-race urine sample; the blame lay with foodstuffs that had been accidentally contaminated. Chinrullah, fifth in the same race, was disqualified for the same reason.

RECORDS FOR PLACED HORSES

Placed 4 times
Halloween (1953, 1954, 1955, 1956).

Placed 3 times
Grakle (1927, 1929, 1930), Kellsboro' Jack (1934, 1935, 1936), The Dikler (1971, 1972, 1974)

Fell and remounted
Gib (1930)

Oldest
15 years — Mac Vidi (1980)
13 years — Vive (1928).

Youngest
5 years — Grakle (1927), Avenger (1934).

Mare
Kerstin (1957)

Entire
Alcazar (1925)

Grey
Stalbridge Colonist (1967, 1968).

Black
Royal Mail (1936, 1940)

Longest odds
100/1 — Garde Toi (1950), Stoney Crossing (1965), Sunset Cristo (1982)
66/1 — Galloway Braes (1952), Mac Vidi (1980).

Trained in Ireland
Zonda (1960), Fortria (1962, 1963), French Tan (1970), Leap Frog (1971), Brown Lad (1976, 1978), Colebridge (1976), Tied Cottage (1977), Drumlargan (1984).

Trained in France
Garde Toi (1950).

Bred in France
Garde Toi (1950), Vigor (1956), Mandarin (1961).

Bred in USA
Soothsayer (1975).

Bred in Australia
Stoney Crossing (1965).

Bred in New Zealand
Royal Mail (1979).

MISCELLANEOUS RECORDS

Fastest times
6:23.4 for 3¼ miles — Silver Fame (1951)
6:28.0 for 3¼ miles — Knock Hard (1953)
6:15.6 for 3 miles — Poet Prince (1941)

Largest fields
22 — 1982
16 — 1945
15 — 1980, 1981, 1985

Smallest fields
4 — 1925, 1930, 1964, 1965
5 — 1935, 1939, 1966, 1968

Richest first prizes
£52,560 — 1985
£48,386 — 1982
£47,375 — 1984.

Smallest first prizes
£340 — 1945
£495 — 1940, 1941, 1942

Most appearances
7 times — The Dikler (1970 to 1976)
6 times — Golden Miller (1932 to 1936, 1938)
5 times — Pas Seul (1959, 1960, 1961, 1962, 1964)
Mill House (1963, 1964, 1965, 1967, 1968)
Tied Cottage (1977, 1979, 1980, 1981, 1982)

Most often in first 3
6 times — Golden Miller (1932 to 1936, 1938)
4 times — Halloween (1953, 1954, 1955, 1956)
The Dikler (1971, 1972, 1973, 1974)
3 times — Grakle (1927, 1929, 1930)
Kellsboro' Jack (1934, 1935, 1936)
Red Rower (1941, 1942, 1945)
Cottage Rake (1948, 1949, 1950)
Pas Seul (1960, 1961, 1964)
Mill House (1963, 1964, 1965)
Arkle (1964, 1965, 1966)

Most champions in one field
5 — Gay Donald, Limber Hill, Linwell, Kerstin and Mandarin in 1958

Champions placed 1, 2, 3
1961 — Saffron Tartan, Pas Seul, Mandarin
1964 — Arkle, Mill House, Pas Seul

Grand National winners placed 1, 2, 3
1936 — Golden Miller, Royal Mail, Kellsboro' Jack

Oldest runners
15 years — Rightun (1945), Mac Vidi (1980)
14 years — Tied Cottage (1982), Drumroan (1982)

Most recent 5-year-old runner
Hobgoblin (1940)

Hottest losing favourites
4/7 — Morse Code (1939)
8/13 — Alcazar (1925), Pendil (1974)
4/6 — Pendil (1973)
4/5 — Koko (1928)
10/11 — Grakle (1932)

Longest-priced favourites
6/1 — Kerstin and Pointsman (1957)

Favourite most often
5 times — Golden Miller (1933 to 1936, 1938)
3 times — Mill House (1963, 1964, 1968)

Most consecutive winning favourites
4 — 1933 to 1936

Most consecutive losing favourites
7 — 1972 to 1978

Race not run
1931 because of frost
1937 because of snow
1943 and 1944 because of World War II

Race postponed
1929, 1940, 1947, 1949, 1951, 1978

Earliest dates
1 March — 1932
4 March — 1948, 1954
5 March — 1953, 1959

Latest dates
25 April — 1951
12 April — 1947, 1978
11 April — 1949

Run before the Champion Hurdle
1927, 1928, 1945, 1947

Run the same day as the Champion Hurdle
1929, 1930, 1932, 1933, 1934, 1947.

Run on
Monday: 1949
Tuesday: 1926–34

Wednesday: 1924–25, 1940, 1951, 1978
Thursday: 1935–39, 1941, 1946, 1948, 1950, 1952–63, 1965–77, from 1979
Saturday: 1942, 1945, 1947, 1964.

Most successful owners
7 wins — Miss Dorothy Paget: 1932 to 1936, 1940, 1952
4 wins — Anne, Duchess of Westminster: 1964, 1965, 1966, 1975
3 wins — Frank Vickerman: 1948, 1949, 1950

Most successful breeders
5 wins — Julius Solomon: 1932 to 1936
3 wins — Otto Vaughan: 1948, 1949, 1950
   Mrs Mary Baker: 1964, 1965, 1966
2 wins with different horses — Harry Frank: 1955, 1960

Most successful trainers
5 wins — Tom Dreaper: 1946, 1964, 1965, 1966, 1968.
4 wins — Basil Briscoe: 1932, 1933, 1934, 1935
   Vincent O'Brien: 1948, 1949, 1950, 1953
   Fulke Walwyn: 1952, 1962, 1963, 1973
3 wins — Owen Anthony: 1927, 1936, 1940

Trained first 5 to finish
In 1983 Michael Dickinson trained each of the first 5 horses to finish, namely Bregawn (ridden by Graham Bradley), Captain John (David Goulding), Wayward Lad (Jonjo O'Neill), Silver Buck (Robert Earnshaw) and Ashley House (Mr Dermot Browne).

Trained winner and second
Peter Easterby trained Little Owl and Night Nurse in 1981, and Michael Dickinson trained Silver Buck and Bregawn in 1982.

Successful woman trainer
Mrs Jenny Pitman: 1984.

Most successful jockeys
4 wins — Pat Taaffe: 1964, 1965, 1966, 1968
3 wins — Dick Rees: 1924, 1928, 1929
   Aubrey Brabazon: 1948, 1949, 1950
   Tommy Carberry: 1970, 1971, 1975

Successful amateur riders
Hugh Grosvenor (1927), Dick Black (1947), Jim Wilson (1981).

Successful owner-breeder-trainer
2nd Baron Stalbridge (1945).

Successful owner-breeders
Humphrey Wyndham (1924), Frank Barbour (1926), Dealtry Part (1938), James Davey (1956), Harry Collins (1967), John Thomson (1968), Stan Riley (1984).

Successful owner-trainer
Arthur Barrow (1980)

Successful as both jockey and trainer
Danny Morgan rode Morse Code (1938) and trained Roddy Owen (1959)
Pat Taaffe rode Arkle (1964, 1965, 1966) and Fort Leney (1968) and trained Captain Christy (1974)
Fred Winter rode Saffron Tartan (1961) and Mandarin (1962) and trained Midnight Court (1978).

Most successful sires
5 wins — Goldcourt: Golden Miller (1932 to 1936).
4 wins — Cottage: Brendan's Cottage (1939), Cottage Rake (1948, 1949, 1950).
3 wins — My Prince: Easter Hero (1929, 1930), Prince Regent (1946).
   Archive: Arkle (1964, 1965, 1966).

Sired winner and second
Cottage (1948).

Grand National

The Grand National, run over a double circuit of the uniquely demanding Aintree fences, is the most famous steeplechase in the world. Since its early days the race has been a handicap with chance playing a large part in the outcome, but because of its generous prize money and the lack of a true championship contest, it long reigned supreme as the ultimate goal of all steeplechasers. Many of the winners have been moderate horses, though a few were genuine champions. After the last war the Grand National lost its primacy among British steeplechases to the Cheltenham Gold Cup, but it retains its popular appeal thanks to its tradition and the spectacle which it provides.

Many details of the early Grand Nationals were never recorded and in some cases it is not even possible to determine the age of the winner.

Title

Grand Liverpool Steeple Chase
    1839–42
Liverpool and National Steeple Chase
    1843–46
Grand National Steeple Chase from
    1847, with the addition of sponsors'
    names from 1975. Sponsored by
    Seagram Ltd from 1984.

Venue

Aintree, Liverpool from 1839, except for
    the two war periods.

Distance

over 4 miles 1839–50
about 4 miles 1851–62
about 4¼ miles 1863–71
about 4½ miles 1872–75
nearly 4½ miles 1876–86
4 miles 1000 yards 1887
4½ miles 1888
about 4 miles 856 yards 1889–1975
about 4½ miles from 1976, run over 30
    fences.

Weights

12 stone (level weights) 1839–42
    except Lottery, who carried 7lb extra
    in 1840 and 18lb extra in 1841 and
    1842. The race became a handicap
    in 1843.
In 1930 qualifying conditions were
    introduced and 5-year-olds were
    barred.

The following 3 steeplechases were run
at Liverpool but not over the Aintree
course:
    1836 The Duke
    1837 The Duke
    1838 Sir William

1839 John Elmore's br g **Lottery** 9yr
    J: Jem Mason 5/1 Fav £590
    2. Seventy-four 3. Paulina 17 ran
1840 Mr Villebois's b g **Jerry** J: Mr B.
    Bretherton 12/1 £630 2. Arthur 6 yr
    3. Valentine 13 ran
1841 2nd Earl of Craven's b g **Charity**
    11yr J: H. N. Powell 14/1 £430
    2. Cigar 3. Peter Simple 7yr 11 ran
1842 John Elmore's b g **Gaylad** 8yr
    J: Tom Oliver 7/1 £515 2. Seventy-
    four 3. Peter Simple 8yr 15 ran
1843 6th Earl of Chesterfield's b g
    Vanguard a–11–10 J: Tom Oliver
    12/1 £565 2. Nimrod a–11–0
    3. Dragsman a–11–3 16 ran
1844 Mr Quartermaine's ch g **Discount**
    a–10–12 J: H. Crickmere
    5/1 Jt-Fav £535 2. The Returned
    a–12–0 3. Tom Tug a–10–7 15 ran
1845 William Loft's br g **Cure-all**
    a–11–5 J: Owner unquoted £585
    2. Peter Simple 11–11–12 3. The
    Exquisite a–11–0 15 ran
1846 Mr Adam's b g **Pioneer** 6–11–12
    J: W. Taylor unquoted £695
    2. Culverthorpe a–11–4 3. Switcher
    5–12–4 22 ran

1847 John Courtenay's b g **Mathew**
    9–10–6 J: Denny Wynne
    10/1 Jt-Fav £840 2. St Leger a–12–3
    3. Jerry a–11–6 28 ran
1848 Josey Little's br g **Chandler**
    12–11–12 J: Owner 12/1 £1,015
    2. The Curate a–11–12 3. British
    Yeoman 8–11–4 29 ran
1849 Finch Mason's b g **Peter Simple**
    11–11–0 J: Tom Cunningham
    20/1 £825 2. The Knight of Gwynne
    a–10–7 3. Prince George a–10–10
    24 ran
1850 Joseph Osborne's b g **Abd-el-
    Kader** 8–9–12 J: Chris Green
    unquoted £950 2. The Knight of
    Gwynne a–11–8 3. Sir John a–11–8
    32 ran
1851 Joseph Osborne's b g **Abd-el-
    Kader** 9–10–4 J: T. Abbott 7/1 £750
    2. Maria Day a–10–5 3. Sir John
    a–11–12 21 ran
1852 J. P. Mason's b m **Miss Mowbray**
    a–10–4 J: Mr Alec Goodman 12/1
    £790 2. Maurice Daley a–9–6 3. Sir
    Peter Laurie a–11–2 24 ran
1853 Josey Little's b g **Peter Simple**
    15–10–10 J: Tom Oliver 9/1 £750
    2. Miss Mowbray a–10–12 3. Oscar
    a–10–2 21 ran
1854 William Moseley's b g **Bourton**
    a–11–12 J: Tasker 4/1 Fav £795
    2. Spring 6–9–10 3. Crabbs a–9–2
    20 ran
1855 Mr Dunn's b h **Wanderer** a–9–8
    J: J. Hanlon 25/1 £730 2. Freetrader
    6–9–4 3. Maurice Daley a–9–6
    20 ran
1856 W. Barnett's br h **Freetrader**
    7–9–6 J: George Stevens 25/1 £720
    2. Minerva 6–9–10 3. Minos a–9–4
    21 ran
1857 George Hodgman's b g **Emigrant**
    a–9–10 J: Charlie Boyce 10/1 £945
    2. Weathercock 6–8–12
    3. Treachery 5–9–0 28 ran
1858 Christopher Capel's b g **Little
    Charley** 10–10–7 J: William Archer
    100/6 £730 2. Weathercock 7–11–7
    3. Xanthus a–11–0 16 ran
1859 Mr Willoughby's br h **Half Caste**
    6–9–7 J: Chris Green 7/1 £820
    2. Jean du Quesne a–9–9
    3. Huntsman 6–11–2 20 ran
1860 Christopher Capel's b m **Anatis**
    10–9–10 J: Mr Tommy Pickernell
    7/2 Fav £750 2. Huntsman 7–11–8
    3. Xanthus a–10–0 19 ran
1861 J. Bennett's br m **Jealousy**
    7–9–12 J: Joe Kendall 5/1 £985
    2. The Dane 5–10–0 3. Old Ben Roe
    a–10–7 24 ran
1862 Vicomte de Namur's b h
    Huntsman 9–11–0 J: Harry
    Lamplugh 3/1 Fav £910
    2. Bridegroom a–10–3 3. Romeo
    a–8–12 13 ran
1863 9th Earl of Coventry's ch m
    Emblem 7–10–10 J: George
    Stevens 4/1 £855 2. Arbury a–11–2
    3. Yaller Gal a–10–13 16 ran

1864 9th Earl of Coventry's ch m
    Emblematic 6–10–6 J: George
    Stevens 10/1 £1,035 2. Arbury
    a–11–12 3. Chester a–10–0 25 ran
1865 Cherry Angell's ch h **Alcibiade**
    5–11–4 J: Captain Bee Coventry
    100/6 £1,105 2. Hall Court 6–11–0
    3. Emblematic 7–11–10 23 ran
1866 Edward Studd's b or br g
    Salamander 7–10–7 J: Mr Alec
    Goodman 40/1 £1,600 2. Cortolvin
    7–11–6 3. Creole a–10–10 30 ran
1867 12th Duke of Hamilton's br g
    Cortolvin 8–11–13 J: John Page
    16/1 £1,660 2. Fan 5–10–3
    3. Shangarry 6–10–13 23 ran
1868 6th Earl Poulett's gr h **The Lamb**
    6–10–7 J: Mr George Ede 9/1
    £1,570 2. Pearl Diver a–10–12
    3. Alcibiade 8–11–10 21 ran
1869 John Weyman's br h **The Colonel**
    6–10–7 J: George Stevens 100/7
    £1,760 2. Hall Court 10–10–12
    3. Gardener 7–10–7 22 ran
1870 Executors of John Weyman's br h
    The Colonel 7–11–12 J: George
    Stevens 7/2 Fav £1,465 2. The Doctor
    9–11–7 3. Primrose 6–10–12 23 ran
1871 6th Earl Poulett's gr h **The Lamb**
    9–11–5 J: Mr Tommy Pickernell
    11/2 £1,665 2. Despatch a–10–0
    3. Scarrington 8–11–4 25 ran
1872 E. Brayley's ch m **Casse Tête**
    7–10–0 J: John Page 20/1 £1,455
    2. Scarrington 9–11–2 3. Despatch
    a–10–4 25 ran
1873 James Machell's b h **Disturbance**
    6–11–11 J: Mr Maunsell Richardson
    20/1 £1,960 2. Ryshworth 7–11–8
    3. Columbine a–10–9 28 ran
1874 James Machell's ch h **Reugny**
    6–10–12 J: Mr Maunsell Richardson
    5/1 Fav £1,890 2. Chimney Sweep
    a–10–2 3. Merlin a–10–7 22 ran
1875 Hubert Bird's b g **Pathfinder**
    8–10–11 J: Mr Tommy Pickernell
    100/6 £1,940 2. Dainty 9–11–0 3. La
    Veine 5–11–12 19 ran
1876 James Machell's bl g **Regal**
    5–11–3 J: Joe Cannon 25/1 £1,485
    2. Congress 10–11–8 3. Shifnal
    7–10–13 19 ran
1877 Fred Hobson's ch h **Austerlitz**
    5–10–8 J: Owner 15/1 £1,290
    2. Congress 11–12–7 3. The
    Liberator 8–10–12 16 ran
1878 John Nightingall's br h **Shifnal**
    9–10–12 J: Jack Jones 7/1 £1,665
    2. Martha 7–10–9 3. Pride of Kildare
    7–11–7 12 ran
1879 Garrett Moore's b or br g **The
    Liberator** 10–11–4 J: Owner 5/1
    £1,695 2. Jackal 11–11–0 3. Martha
    8–10–13 18 ran
1880 P. Ducrot's ch m **Empress**
    5–10–7 J: Mr Tommy Beasley 8/1
    £1,145 2. The Liberator 11–12–7
    3. Downpatrick 6–10–7 14 ran
1881 T. W. Kirkwood's ch g
    Woodbrook 7–11–3 J: Mr Tommy
    Beasley 11/2 Jt-Fav £925 2. Regal

10–11–12 3. Thornfield 5–10–9 13 ran

1882 3rd Baron Manners's b g **Seaman** 6–11–6 J: Owner 10/1 £1,000 2. Cyrus 5–10–9 3. Zoëdone 5–10–0 12 ran

1883 Graf Karl Kinsky's ch m **Zoëdone** 6–11–0 J: Owner 100/7 £925 2. Black Prince 11–10–4 3. Mohican 6–12–1 10 ran

1884 H. F. Boyd's br g **Voluptuary** 6–10–5 J: Mr Ted Wilson 10/1 £1,035 2. Frigate 6–11–3 3. Roquefort 5–10–5 15 ran

1885 Arthur Cooper's br g **Roquefort** 6–11–0 J: Mr Ted Wilson 100/30 Fav £1,035 2. Frigate 7–11–10 3. Black Prince 13–10–5 19 ran

1886 A. J. Douglas's b g **Old Joe** 7–10–9 J: Tom Skelton 25/1 £1,380 2. Too Good 7–11–12 3. Gamecock 7–10–12 23 ran

1887 E. Jay's b g **Gamecock** 8–11–0 J: Bill Daniels 20/1 £1,206 2. Savoyard 9–10–13 3. Johnny Longtail 9–10–6 16 ran

1888 Ned Baird's bl g **Playfair** 7–10–7 J: George Mawson 40/1 £1,175 2. Frigate 10–11–2 3. Ballot Box 9–12–4 20 ran

1889 Mat Maher's b m **Frigate** 11–11–4 J: Mr Tommy Beasley 8/1 £1,234 2. Why Not 8–11–5 3. M.P. 8–10–9 20 ran

1890 George Masterman's ch g **Ilex** 6–10–5 J: Arthur Nightingall 4/1 Fav £1,680 2. Pan 7–10–5 3. M.P. 9–11–5 16 ran

1891 William Jameson's b g **Come Away** 7–11–12 J: Mr Harry Beasley 4/1 Fav £1,680 2. Cloister 7–11–7 3. Ilex 7–12–3 21 ran

1892 Gordon Wilson's b g **Father O'Flynn** 7–10–5 J: Captain Roddy Owen 20/1 £1,680 2. Cloister 8–12–3 3. Ilex 8–12–7 25 ran

1893 Charles Duff's b g **Cloister** 9–12–7 J: Bill Dollery 9/2 Fav £1,975 2. Aesop 7–10–4 3. Why Not 12–11–12 15 ran

1894 C. H. Fenwick's b g **Why Not** 13–11–13 J: Arthur Nightingall 5/1 Jt-Fav £1,975 2. Lady Ellen 6–9–10 3. Wild Man from Borneo 6–10–9 14 ran

1895 John Widger's ch g **Wild Man from Borneo** 7–10–11 J: Mr Joe Widger 10/1 £1,975 2. Cathal 6–10–9 3. Van der Berg 9–9–13 19 ran

1896 William Hall Walker's b g **The Soarer** 7–9–13 J: Mr David Campbell 40/1 £1,975 2. Father O'Flynn 11–10–12 3. Biscuit 8–10–0 28 ran

1897 Harry Dyas's b g **Manifesto** 9–11–3 J: Terry Kavanagh 6/1 Fav £1,975 2. Filbert 7–9–7 3. Ford of Fyne 6–10–7 28 ran

1898 C. G. Adam's b g **Drogheda** 6–10–12 J: John Gourley 25/1 £1,975 2. Cathal 9–11–5 3. Gauntlet 7–10–13 25 ran

1899 John Bulteel's b g **Manifesto** 11–12–7 J: George Williamson 5/1 £1,975 2. Ford of Fyne 8–10–10 3. Elliman 8–10–1 10 ran

1900 HRH Prince of Wales's br g **Ambush** 6–11–3 J: Algy Anthony 4/1 £1,975 2. Barsac 8–9–12 3. Manifesto 12–12–13 16 ran

1901 Bernard Bletsoe's b h **Grudon** 11–10–0 J: Arthur Nightingall 9/1 £1,975 T: Owner, Denton, Northamptonshire B: Owner Sire: Old

Buck 2. Drumcree 7–10–0 3. Buffalo Bill 7–9–7 4l, 6l 9:47.8 24 ran

1902 Ambrose Gorham's b or br m **Shannon Lass** 7–10–1 J: David Read 20/1 £2,000 T: James Hackett, Telscombe, Sussex B: J. Reidy Sire: Butterscotch 2. Matthew 6–9–12 3. Manifesto 14–12–8 3l, 3l 10:03.0 21 ran

1903 John Morrison's b g **Drumcree** 9–11–3 J: Percy Woodland 13/2 Fav £2,000 T: Sir Charles Nugent, Cranborne, Dorset B: C. Hope Sire: Ascetic 2. Detail 7–9–13 3. Manifesto 15–12–3 3l, 20l 10:09.4 23 ran

1904 Spencer Gollan's br g **Moifaa** 8–10–7 J: Arthur Birch 25/1 £2,000 T: W. Hickey, Epsom, Surrey B: in New Zealand Sire: Natator 2. Kirkland 8–10–10 3. The Gunner 7–10–4 8l, neck 9:58.6 26 ran

1905 Frank Bibby's ch g **Kirkland** 9–11–5 J: Tich Mason 6/1 £2,025 T: E. Thomas, Lawrenny, Pembrokeshire B: E. Clifford Sire: Kirkham 2. Napper Tandy 8–10–0 3. Buckaway 7–9–11 3l, 4l 9:48.8 27 ran

1906 Prinz Franz von Hatzfeldt's ch g **Ascetic's Silver** 9–10–9 J: Mr Aubrey Hastings 20/1 £2,175 T: Aubrey Hastings, Wroughton, Wiltshire B: P. J. Dunne Sire: Ascetic 2. Red Lad 6–10–2 3. Aunt May 10–11–2 10l, 2l 9:34.4 23 ran

1907 Stanley Howard's b g **Eremon** 7–10–1 J: Alf Newey 8/1 £2,400 T: Tom Coulthwaite, Hednesford, Staffordshire B: James Cleary Sire: Thurles 2. Tom West 8–9–12 3. Patlander 11–10–7 6l, bad 9:47.2 23 ran

1908 Frank Douglas-Pennant's ch g **Rubio** 10–10–5 J: Henry Bletsoe 66/1 £2,400 T: Fred Withington, Danebury, Hampshire B: James Haggin Sire: Star Ruby 2. Mattie Macgregor 6–10–6 3. The Lawyer 11–10–3 10l, 6l 10:33.2 24 ran

1909 James Hennessy's ch g **Lutteur** 5–10–11 J: Georges Parfrement 100/9 Jt-Fav £2,400 T: Harry Escott, Lewes, Sussex B: M. Gaston-Dreyfus Sire: St Damien 2. Judas 8–10–10 3. Caubeen 8–11–7 2l, bad 9:33.8 32 ran

1910 Stanley Howard's b g **Jenkinstown** 9–10–5 J: Bob Chadwick 100/8 £2,400 T: Tom Coulthwaite, Hednesford, Staffordshire B: P. Leonard Sire: Hackler 2. Jerry M. 7–12–7 3. Odor 9–9–8 3l, 3l 10:04.8 25 ran

1911 Frank Bibby's b g **Glenside** 9–10–3 J: Mr Jack Anthony 20/1 £2,500 T: Robert Collis, Kinlet, Worcestershire B: W. G. Peareth Sire: St Gris 2. Rathnally 6–11–0 3. Shady Girl 10–10–5 20l, 3l 10:35.0 26 ran

1912 Sir Charles Assheton-Smith's b g

Manifesto, the Grand National hero of 1897 and 1899, was the hardiest perennial in the race's history. He put in the last of his record eight appearances at the age of 16 in 1904.

Jerry M. 9–12–7 J: Ernie Piggott 4/1 Jt-Fav £3,200 T: Bob Gore, Findon, Sussex B: C. F. Hartigan Sire: Walmsgate 2. Bloodstone 10–11–6 3. Axle Pin 8–10–4 6/, 4/ 10:13.4 24 ran

1913 Sir Charles Assheton-Smith's b g **Covertcoat** 7–11–6 J: Percy Woodland 100/9 £3,170 T: Bob Gore, Findon, Sussex B: James Maher Sire: Hackler 2. Irish Mail 6–11–4 3. Carsey 10–12–0 distance, distance 10:19.0 22 ran

1914 Tom Tyler's b g **Sunloch** 8–9–7 J: William Smith 100/6 £3,515 T: Owner, Loughborough, Leicestershire B: Henry Black Sire: Sundorne 2. Trianon 9–11–9 3. Lutteur 10–12–6 8/, 8/ 9:58.8 20 ran

1915 Lady Nelson's b or br g **Ally Sloper** 6–10–6 J: Mr Jack Anthony 100/9 £3,515 T: Aubrey Hastings, Wroughton, Wiltshire B: C. J. C. Hill Sire: Travelling Lad 2. Jacobus 8–11–0 3. Father Confessor 6–9–10 2/, 8/ 9:47.8 20 ran

3 war-time substitute races were run at Gatwick:
  1916 Vermouth 6–11–10
  1917 Ballymacad 10–9–12
  1918 Poethlyn 8–11–6

1919 Mrs Gwladys Peel's b g **Poethlyn** 9–12–7 J: Ernie Piggott 11/4 Fav £3,590 T: Harry Escott, Lewes, Sussex B: Hugh Peel Sire: Rydal Head 2. Ballyboggan 8–11–10 3. Pollen 10–11–4 8/, 6/ 10:08.4 22 ran

1920 Thomas Gerrard's br g **Troytown** 7–11–9 J: Mr Jack Anthony 6/1 £4,425 T: Algy Anthony, The Curragh, Co Kildare, Ireland B: Owner Sire: Zria 2. The Turk 10–9–8 3. The Bore 9–10–1 12/, 6/ 10:20.4 24 ran

1921 Malcolm McAlpine's b g **Shaun Spadah** 10–11–7 J: Dick Rees 100/9 £7,060 T: George Poole, Lewes, Sussex B: Patrick McKenna Sire: Easter Prize 2. The Bore 10–11–8 3. All White 7–10–13 distance, distance 10:26.0 35 ran

1922 Hugh Kershaw's b g **Music Hall** 9–11–8 J: Bilbie Rees 100/9 £7,075 T: Owen Anthony, Lambourn, Berkshire B: Mrs Freddie Blacker Sire: Cliftonhall 2. Drifter 8–10–0 3. Taffytus 9–11–0 12/, 6/ 9:55.8 32 ran

1923 Stephen Sanford's ch g **Sergeant Murphy** 13–11–3 J: Captain Tuppy Bennet 100/6 £7,850 T: George Blackwell, Newmarket B: G. L. Walker Sire: General Symons 2. Shaun Spadah 12–12–7 3. Conjuror 11–11–0 3/, 6/ 9:36.0 28 ran

1924 12th Earl of Airlie's ch g **Master Robert** 11–10–5 J: Bob Trudgill 25/1 £8,240 T: Aubrey Hastings, Wroughton, Wiltshire B: Robert McKinlay Sire: Moorside 2. Fly Mask

10–10–12 3. Silvo 8–12–2 4/, 6/ 9:40.0 30 ran

1925 David Goold's ch g **Double Chance** 9–10–9 J: Major Jack Wilson 100/9 £8,120 T: Fred Archer, Newmarket B: Leopold de Rothschild Sire: Day Comet 2. Old Tay Bridge 11–11–12 3. Fly Mask 11–11–11 4/, 6/ 9:42.6 33 ran

1926 Charlie Schwartz's ch g **Jack Horner** 9–10–5 J: Billy Watkinson 25/1 £7,635 T: Jack Leader, Exning, Suffolk B: Melton Stud Sire: Cyllius 2. Old Tay Bridge 12–12–3 3. Bright's Boy 7–11–8 3/, 1/ 9:36.0 30 ran

1927 Mrs Mary Partridge's ch g **Sprig** 10–12–4 J: Ted Leader 8/1 Fav £8,215 T: Tom Leader, Newmarket B: Richard Partridge Sire: Marco 2. Bovril 9–10–12 3. Bright's Boy 8–12–7 1/, 1/ 10:20.2 37 ran

1928 Harold Kenyon's br g **Tipperary Tim** 10–10–0 J: Mr Bill Dutton 100/1 £11,255 T: Joseph Dodd, Whitchurch, Shropshire B: Jack Ryan Sire: Cipango 2. Billy Barton 10–10–11 distance, only 2 finished 10:23.6 42 ran

1929 Mrs M. A. Gemmell's ch g **Gregalach** 7–11–4 J: Bob Everett 100/1 £13,000 T: Tom Leader, Newmarket B: Michael Finlay Sire: My Prince 2. Easter Hero 9–12–7 3. Richmond 6–10–6 6/, bad 9:47.4 66 ran

1930 Walter Midwood's ch g **Shaun Goilin** 10–11–7 J: Tommy Cullinan 100/8 £9,805 T: Frank Hartigan, Weyhill, Hampshire B: John Edwards Sire: probably Shaun Aboo 2. Melleray's Belle 11–10–0 3. Sir Lindsay 9–10–6 neck, 1½/ 9:40.6 41 ran

1931 Cecil Taylor's b g **Grakle** 9–11–7 J: Bob Lyall 100/6 £9,385 T: Tom Coulthwaite, Rugeley, Staffordshire B: Messrs Slocock Sire: Jackdaw 2. Gregalach 9–12–0 3. Annandale 9–10–7 1½/, 10/ 9:32.8 43 ran

1932 William Parsonage's br g **Forbra** 7–10–7 J: Tim Hamey 50/1 £8,165 T: Tom Rimell, Kinnersley, Worcestershire B: H. Glover Sire: Foresight 2. Egremont 8–10–7 3. Shaun Goilin 12–12–4 3/, bad 9:44.6 36 ran

1933 Mrs Florence Clark's b g **Kellsboro' Jack** 7–11–9 J: Dudley Williams 25/1 £7,345 T: Ivor Anthony, Wroughton, Wiltshire B: H. Hutchinson Sire: Jackdaw 2. Really True 9–10–12 3. Slater 8–10–7 3/, neck 9:28.0 34 ran

1934 Miss Dorothy Paget's b g **Golden Miller** 7–12–2 J: Gerry Wilson 8/1 £7,265 T: Basil Briscoe, Exning, Suffolk B: Julius Solomon Sire: Goldcourt 2. Delaneige 9–11–6 3. Thomond 8–12–4 5/, 5/ 9:20.4 30 ran

1935 Noel Furlong's bl or br g

Reynoldstown 8–11–4 J: Mr Frank Furlong 22/1 £6,545 T: Owner, Skeffington, Leicestershire B: Richard Ball sr Sire: My Prince 2. Blue Prince 7–10–7 3. Thomond 9–11–13 3/, 8/ 9:20.2 27 ran

1936 Noel Furlong's bl or br g **Reynoldstown** 9–12–2 J: Mr Fulke Walwyn 10/1 £7,095 T: Owner, Skeffington, Leicestershire B: Richard Ball sr Sire: My Prince 2. Ego 9–10–8 3. Bachelor Prince 9–10–9 12/, 6/ 9:37.8 35 ran

1937 Hugh Lloyd Thomas's bl g **Royal Mail** 8–11–13 J: Evan Williams 100/6 £6,645 T: Ivor Anthony, Wroughton, Wiltshire B: Charlie Rogers Sire: My Prince 2. Cooleen 9–11–4 3. Pucka Belle 11–10–7 3/, 10/ 9:59.8 33 ran

1938 Mrs Marion Scott's ch h **Battleship** 11–11–6 J: Bruce Hobbs 40/1 £7,598 T: Reg Hobbs, Lambourn, Berkshire B: Walter Salmon Sire: Man o' War 2. Royal Danieli 7–11–3 3. Workman 8–10–2 head, bad 9:27.0 36 ran

1939 Sir Alexander Maguire's br g **Workman** 9–10–6 J: Tim Hyde 100/8 £7,284 T: Jack Ruttle, Celbridge, Co Dublin, Ireland B: P. J. O'Leary Sire: Cottage 2. MacMoffat 7–10–3 3. Kilstar 8–10–3 3/, 15/ 9:42.2 37 ran

1940 2nd Baron Stalbridge's br g **Bogskar** 7–10–4 J: Mervyn Jones 25/1 £4,225 T: Owner, Eastbury, Berkshire B: Christopher Roche Sire: Werwolf 2. MacMoffat 8–10–10 3. Gold Arrow 8–10–3 4/, 6/ 9:20.6 30 ran

1941 to 1945 no race.

1946 John Morant's b g **Lovely Cottage** 9–10–8 J: Captain Bobby Petre 25/1 £8,805 T: Tommy Rayson, Headbourne Worthy, Hampshire B: M. J. Hyde Sire: Cottage 2. Jack Finlay 7–10–2 3. Prince Regent 11–12–5 4/, 3/ 9:38.2 34 ran

1947 Jack McDowell's br g **Caughoo** 8–10–0 J: Eddie Dempsey 100/1 £10,007 T: Herbie McDowell, Malahide, Co Dublin, Ireland B: Patrick Power Sire: Within-the-Law 2. Lough Conn 11–10–1 3. Kami 10–10–13 20/, 4/ 10:03.8 57 ran

1948 John Procter's b m **Sheila's Cottage** 9–10–7 J: Arthur Thompson 50/1 £9,103 T: Neville Crump, Middleham, Yorkshire B: Mrs P. Daly Sire: Cottage 2. First of the Dandies 11–10–4 3. Cromwell 7–10–11 1/, 6/ 9:25.4 43 ran

1949 Fearnie Williamson's b g **Russian Hero** 9–10–8 J: Leo McMorrow 66/1 £9,528 T: George Owen, Malpas, Cheshire B: Owner Sire: Peter the Great 2. Roimond 8–11–12 3. Royal Mount 10–10–12 8/, 1/ 9:24.2 43 ran

1950 Mrs Lurline Brotherton's b g **Freebooter** 9–11–11 J: Jimmy Power 10/1 Jt-Fav £9,314 T: Bobby Renton, Ripon, Yorkshire B: W. F. Phelan Sire: Steel-point 2. Wot No Sun 8–11–8 3. Acthon Major 10–11–2 15l, 10l 9:24.2 49 ran

1951 Jeffrey Royle's b m **Nickel Coin** 9–10–1 J: Johnny Bullock 40/1 £8,815 T: Jack O'Donoghue, Reigate, Surrey B: Richard Corbett Sire: Pay Up 2. Royal Tan 7–10–13 3. Derrinstown 11–10–0 6l, bad 9:48.8 36 ran

1952 Harry Lane's b g **Teal** 10–10–12 J: Arthur Thompson 100/7 £9,268 T: Neville Crump, Middleham, Yorkshire B: Gerald Carroll Sire: Bimco 2. Legal Joy 9–10–4 3. Wot No Sun 10–11–7 5l, bad 9:21.5 47 ran

1953 Joe Griffin's ch g **Early Mist** 8–11–2 J: Bryan Marshall 20/1 £9,330 T: Vincent O'Brien, Cashel, Co Tipperary, Ireland B: D. J. Wrinch Sire: Brumeux 2. Mont Tremblant 7–12–5 3. Irish Lizard 10–10–6 20l, 4l 9:22.8 31 ran

1954 Joe Griffin's ch g **Royal Tan** 10–11–7 J: Bryan Marshall 8/1 £8,571 T: Vincent O'Brien, Cashel, Co Tipperary, Ireland B: James Toppin Sire: Tartan 2. Tudor Line 9–10–7 3. Irish Lizard 11–10–5 neck, 10l 9:32.8 29 ran

1955 Mrs Cecily Welman's b g **Quare Times** 9–11–0 J: Pat Taaffe 100/9 £8,934 T: Vincent O'Brien, Cashel, Co Tipperary, Ireland B: Phil Sweeney Sire: Artist's Son 2. Tudor Line 10–11–3 3. Carey's Cottage 8–10–11 12l, 4l 10:19.2 30 ran

1956 Mrs Stella Carver's b or br g **E.S.B.** 10–11–3 J: Dave Dick 100/7 £8,695 T: Fred Rimell, Kinnersley, Worcestershire B: Miss S. Burke Sire: Bidar 2. Gentle Moya 10–10–2 3. Royal Tan 12–12–1 10l, 10l 9:21.4 29 ran

1957 Mrs Geoffrey Kohn's ch g **Sundew** 11–11–7 J: Fred Winter 20/1 £8,868 T: Frank Hudson, Henley-in-Arden, Warwickshire B: N. McArdle Sire: Sun King 2. Wyndburgh 7–10–7 3. Tiberetta 9–10–0 8l, 6l 9:42.6 35 ran

1958 David Coughlan's b g **Mr What** 8–10–6 J: Arthur Freeman 18/1 £13,719 T: Tom Taaffe, Rathcoole, Co Dublin, Ireland B: Mrs Barbara O'Neill Sire: Grand Inquisitor 2. Tiberetta 10–10–6 3. Green Drill 8–10–10 30l, 15l 9:59.8 31 ran

1959 John Bigg's b g **Oxo** 8–10–13 J: Michael Scudamore 8/1 £13,646 T: Willie Stephenson, Royston, Hertfordshire B: A. C. Wyatt Sire: Bobsleigh 2. Wyndburgh 9–10–12 3. Mr What 9–11–9 1½l, 8l 9:37.8 34 ran

1960 Miss Winifred Wallace's b g **Merryman** 9–10–12 J: Gerry Scott 13/2 Fav £13,134 T: Neville Crump, Middleham, Yorkshire B: 2nd Marquess of Linlithgow Sire: Carnival Boy 2. Badanloch 9–10–9 3. Clear Profit 10–10–1 15l, 12l 9:27.0 26 ran

1961 Jeremy Vaughan's gr g **Nicolaus Silver** 9–10–1 J: Bobby Beasley 28/1 £20,020 T: Fred Rimell, Kinnersley, Worcestershire B: James Heffernan Sire: Nicolaus 2. Merryman 10–11–12 3. O'Malley Point 10–11–4 5l, neck 9:22.6 35 ran

1962 Nat Cohen's b g **Kilmore** 12–10–4 J: Fred Winter 28/1 £20,238 T: Ryan Price, Findon, Sussex B: Gilbert Webb Sire: Zalophus 2. Wyndburgh 12–10–9 3. Mr What 12–10–9 10l, 10l 9:49.6 32 ran

1963 Pierre Raymond's ch g **Ayala** 9–10–0 J: Pat Buckley 66/1 £21,315 T: Keith Piggott, Lambourn, Berkshire B: Jim Philipps Sire: Supertello 2. Carrickbeg 7–10–3 3. Hawa's Song 10–10–0 ¾l, 5l 9:35.8 47 ran

1964 Jack Goodman's b g **Team Spirit** 12–10–3 J: Willie Robinson 18/1 £20,280 T: Fulke Walwyn, Lambourn, Berkshire B: P. J. Coonan Sire: Vulgan 2. Purple Silk 9–10–4 3. Peacetown 10–10–1 ½l, 6l 9:46.8 33 ran

1965 Mrs Mary Stephenson's b g **Jay Trump** 8–11–5 J: Mr Tommy Smith 100/6 £22,041 T: Fred Winter, Lambourn, Berkshire B: Jay Sensenich Sire: Tonga Prince 2. Freddie 8–11–10 3. Mr Jones 10–11–5 ¾l, 20l 9:31.8 47 ran

1966 Stuart Levy's ch g **Anglo** 8–10–0 J: Tim Norman 50/1 £22,334 T: Fred Winter, Lambourn, Berkshire B: William Kennedy Sire: Greek Star 2. Freddie 9–11–7 3. Forest Prince 8–10–8 20l, 5l 9:53.0 47 ran

1967 Cyril Watkins's br g **Foinavon** 9–10–0 J: John Buckingham 100/1 £17,630 T: John Kempton, Compton, Berkshire B: T. H. Ryan Sire: Vulgan 2. Honey End 10–10–4 3. Red Alligator 8–10–0 15l, 3l 9:49.4 44 ran

1968 John Manners's ch g **Red Alligator** 9–10–0 J: Brian Fletcher 100/7 £17,848 T: Denys Smith, Bishop Auckland, Co Durham B: William Kennedy Sire: Magic Red 2. Moidore's Token 11–10–8 3. Different Class 8–11–5 20l, neck 9:29.0 45 ran

1969 Tom McKoy's br g **Highland Wedding** 12–10–4 J: Eddie Harty 100/9 £17,849 T: Toby Balding, Weyhill, Hampshire B: John Caldwell Sire: Question 2. Steel Bridge 11–10–0 3. Rondetto 13–10–6 12l, 1l 9:29.8 30 ran

1970 Tony Chambers's b g **Gay Trip** 8–11–5 J: Pat Taaffe 15/1 £14,804 T: Fred Rimell, Kinnersley, Worcestershire B: Frank Farmer Sire: Vulgan 2. Vulture 8–10–0 3. Miss Hunter 9–10–0 20l, ½l 9:38.0 28 ran

1971 Fred Pontin's br g **Specify** 9–10–13 J: John Cook 28/1 £15,500 T: John Sutcliffe, sr, Epsom, Surrey B: Alec Parker Sire: Specific 2. Black Secret 7–11–5 3. Astbury 8–10–0 neck, 2½l 9:34.2 38 ran

1972 Tim Forster's ch g **Well To Do** 9–10–1 J: Graham Thorner 14/1 £25,765 T: Owner, Letcombe Bassett, Berkshire B: Mrs Aline Lloyd Thomas Sire: Phébus 2. Gay Trip 10–11–9 3= Black Secret 8–11–2 and General Symons 9–10–0 2l, 3l 10:08.4 42 ran

1973 Noel Le Mare's b g **Red Rum** 8–10–5 J: Brian Fletcher 9/1 Jt-Fav £25,486 T: Donald McCain, Southport, Lancashire B: Martyn McEnery Sire: Quorum 2. Crisp 10–12–0 3. L'Escargot 10–12–0 ¾l, 25l 9:01.9 38 ran

1974 Noel Le Mare's b g **Red Rum** 9–12–0 J: Brian Fletcher 11/1 £25,102 T: Donald McCain, Southport, Lancashire B: Martyn McEnery Sire: Quorum 2. L'Escargot 11–11–13 3. Charles Dickens 10–10–0 7l, short head 9:20.3 42 ran

1975 Raymond Guest's ch g **L'Escargot** 12–11–3 J: Tommy Carberry 13/2 £38,005 T: Dan Moore, The Curragh, Co Kildare, Ireland B: Mrs Barbara O'Neill Sire: Escart 2. Red Rum 10–12–0 3. Spanish Steps 12–10–3 15l, 8l 9:31.1 31 ran

1976 Pierre Raymond's ch g **Rag Trade** 10–10–12 J: John Burke 14/1 £37,420 T: Fred Rimell, Kinnersley, Worcestershire B: Ian Williams Sire: Menelek 2. Red Rum 11–11–10 3. Eyecatcher 10–10–7 2l, 8l 9:20.9 32 ran

1977 Noel Le Mare's b g **Red Rum** 12–11–8 J: Tommy Stack 9/1 £41,140 T: Donald McCain, Southport, Lancashire B: Martyn McEnery Sire: Quorum 2. Churchtown Boy 10–10–0 3. Eyecatcher 11–10–1 25l, 6l 9:30.3 42 ran

1978 Mrs Fiona Whitaker's b g **Lucius** 9–10–9 J: Bob Davies 14/1 £39,092 T: Gordon Richards, Greystoke, Cumbria B: Dr Margaret Lloyd Sire: Perhapsburg 2. Sebastian 10–10–1 3. Drumroan 10–10–0 ½l, neck 9:33.9 37 ran

1979 John Douglas's br g **Rubstic** 10–10–0 J: Maurice Barnes 25/1 £40,506 T: John Leadbetter, Denholm, Roxburghshire B: Mrs Robert Digby Sire: I Say 2. Zongalero 9–10–5 3. Rough and Tumble 9–10–7 1½l, 5l 9:52.9 34 ran

1980 Redmond Stewart's ch g **Ben Nevis** 12–10–12 J: Mr Charlie Fenwick 40/1 £45,595 T: Tim Forster,

Letcombe Bassett, Oxfordshire
B: A. S. Pattenden Ltd Sire: Casmiri
2. Rough and Tumble 10–10–11
3. The Pilgarlic 12–10–4 20l, 10l
10:17.4 30 ran
1981 Nick Embiricos's ch g **Aldaniti**
11–10–13 J: Bob Champion 10/1
£51,324 T: Josh Gifford, Findon,
Sussex B: Tommy Barron Sire:
Derek H 2. Spartan Missile 9–11–5
3. Royal Mail 11–11–7 4l, 2l 9:47.2
39 ran
1982 Frank Gilman's b g **Grittar**
9–11–5 J: Mr Dick Saunders 7/1 Fav
£52,507 T: Owner, Morcott,
Leicestershire B: Owner Sire: Grisaille
2. Hard Outlook 11–10–1 3. Loving
Words 9–10–11 15l, distance 9:12.6
39 ran
1983 Brian Burrough's ch g **Corbière**
8–11–4 J: Ben de Haan 13/1
£52,949 T: Mrs Jenny Pitman,
Lambourn, Berkshire B: M. Parkhill
Sire: Harwell 2. Greasepaint 8–10–7
3. Yer Man 8–10–0 ¾l, 20l 9:47.4
41 ran
1984 Richard Shaw's b g **Hallo Dandy**
10–10–2 J: Neale Doughty 13/1
£54,769 T: Gordon Richards,
Greystoke, Cumbria B: J. P. Frost
Sire: Menelek 2. Greasepaint
9–11–2 3. Corbière 9–12–0 4l, 1½l
9:21.4 40 ran
1985 Anne, Duchess of Westminster's
br g **Last Suspect** 11–10–5
J: Hywel Davies 50/1 £54,314 T: Tim
Forster, Letcombe Bassett,
Oxfordshire B: Countess of Mount
Charles Sire: Above Suspicion 2. Mr
Snugfit 8–10–0 3. Corbière
10–11–10 1½l, 3l 9:42.7 40 ran

The following records do not take into account the results of the war-time substitute races at Gatwick in 1916, 1917 and 1918 because they were run over a course which bore little resemblance to Aintree.

RECORDS FOR WINNING HORSES

Triple winner
Red Rum (1973, 1974, 1977)

Double winners
Abd-el-Kader (1850, 1851)
Peter Simple (1849, 1853)
The Colonel (1869, 1870)
The Lamb (1868, 1871)
Manifesto (1897, 1899)
Reynoldstown (1935, 1936, his only 2 starts in the Grand National)
Poethlyn (1919), had won a war-time substitute race at Gatwick the previous year.

Highest weights
12st 7lb — Cloister (1893), Manifesto (1899), Jerry M. (1912), Poethlyn (1919).
12st 4lb — Sprig (1927)
12st 2lb — Golden Miller (1934), Reynoldstown (1936)

Lowest weight
9st 6lb — Freetrader (1856)

Carried a penalty
10lb extra — Emblem (1863)
6lb extra — Peter Simple (1849)

Carried overweight
6lb extra — Mr What (1958)
3lb extra — Lovely Cottage (1946), Last Suspect (1985)
1lb extra — Ally Sloper (1915)

Greatest margins
distance — Covertcoat (1913), Shaun Spadah (1921), Tipperary Tim (1928)
40 lengths — Cloister (1893)
30 lengths — Mr What (1958)

Smallest margins
head — Alcibiade (1865), Seaman (1882), Battleship (1938)
short neck — Half Caste (1859)
half a neck — Abd-el-Kader (1851)

Finished alone without mishap
Glenside (1911), Shaun Spadah (1921), Tipperary Tim (1928) and Foinavon (1967) were the only ones not to fall or otherwise be put out of the race, though in each case at least one other horse eventually completed the course.
In 1928 at least half the runners were stopped at the Canal Turn on the first circuit when Easter Hero fell into the ditch in front of the fence. In 1967 a pile-up was caused at the 23rd fence by a loose horse, Popham Down, and Foinavon, who had been towards the rear, was alone in clearing the fence at his first attempt.

Oldest
15 years — Peter Simple (1853)
13 years — Why Not (1894), Sergeant Murphy (1923).

Youngest
5 years — Alcibiade (1865), Regal

Red Rum (left), the only horse to win three Grand Nationals, takes the lead at Becher's Brook on the second circuit in 1974. Charles Dickens (centre) finished third just behind L'Escargot (right), who won the race 12 months later.

(1876), Austerlitz (1877), Empress (1880), Lutteur (1909)

Mares

Miss Mowbray (1852), Anatis (1860), Jealousy (1861), Emblem (1863), Emblematic (1864), Casse Tête (1872), Empress (1880), Zoëdone (1883), Frigate (1889), Shannon Lass (1902), Sheila's Cottage (1948), Nickel Coin (1951).

Entires

Wanderer (1855), Freetrader (1856), Half Caste (1859), Huntsman (1862), Alcibiade (1865), The Lamb (1868, 1871), The Colonel (1869, 1870), Disturbance (1873), Reugny (1874), Austerlitz (1877), Shifnal (1878), Grudon (1901), Battleship (1938).

Grey

The Lamb (1868, 1871), Nicolaus Silver (1961)

Black

Regal (1876), Playfair (1888), Royal Mail (1937). Reynoldstown (1935, 1936) was described as black or brown.

Longest odds

100/1 — Tipperary Tim (1928), Gregalach (1929), Caughoo (1947), Foinavon (1967)
66/1 — Rubio (1908), Russian Hero (1949), Ayala (1963).
Cure-all (1845), Pioneer (1846) and Abd-el-Kader (1850) were not quoted in the betting.

Shortest odds

11/4 — Poethlyn (1919)
3/1 — Huntsman (1862)
100/30 — Roquefort (1885)

Trained in Scotland

Rubstic (1979)

Trained in Wales

Kirkland (1905)

Trained in Ireland

Mathew (1847), Wanderer (1855), The Liberator (1879), Empress (1880), Woodbrook (1881), Frigate (1889), Come Away (1891), Ambush (1900), Troytown (1920), Workman (1939), Caughoo (1947), Early Mist (1953), Royal Tan (1954), Quare Times (1955), Mr What (1958), L'Escargot (1975).

Trained in France

Huntsman (1862), Cortolvin (1867)

Bred in France

Alcibiade (1865), Reugny (1874), Lutteur (1909)

Bred in USA

Rubio (1908), Battleship (1938), Jay Trump (1965)

Bred in New Zealand

Moifaa (1904)

Siblings

Emblem (1863) and Emblematic (1864) were sisters.
Vanguard (1843) and Pioneer (1846) were half-brothers, as were Anglo (1966) and Red Alligator (1968).

Won at the sixth attempt

Frigate (1889)

Won at the fifth attempt

Why Not (1894), Team Spirit (1964)

Least experienced

Alcibiade (1865) and Voluptuary (1884) both won on their début over fences. The last novice to win was Mr What (1958).

Also won Grand Steeple-Chase de Paris

Jerry M. (1912) won France's premier steeplechase in 1910 and Troytown (1920) did so in 1919.

Also won American Grand National

Battleship (1938) won the Grand National at Belmont Park, New York in 1934.

Also won Maryland Hunt Cup

Jay Trump (1965) won America's premier timber race in 1963, 1964 and 1966, and Ben Nevis (1980) did so in 1977 and 1978.

Most successful at stud

Empress (1880) was the dam of Red Prince, who made his mark on the Flat, over fences and at stud; she also became the ancestress of Goodwood Cup winner Old Orkney and Japan Cup heroine Stanerra.
Battleship (1938) sired two champion American steeplechasers, War Battle and Shipboard, of whom the latter won the American Grand National twice.

RECORDS FOR PLACED HORSES

Placed 3 times

Peter Simple (1841, 1842, 1845). This horse was not the Peter Simple who won the race in 1849 and 1853.
Frigate (1884, 1885, 1888).
Manifesto (1900, 1902, 1903).
Wyndburgh (1957, 1959, 1962) — the only horse to come second 3 times without winning.

Placed second twice without winning

Seventy-four (1839, 1842), The Knight

of Gwynne (1849, 1850), Weathercock (1857, 1858), Arbury (1863, 1864), Hall Court (1865, 1869), Congress (1876, 1877), Cathal (1895, 1898), Old Tay Bridge (1925, 1926), MacMoffat (1939, 1940), Tudor Line (1954, 1955), Freddie (1965, 1966), Greasepaint (1983, 1984).

Highest weights

12st 13lb — Manifesto (1900)
12st 8lb — Manifesto (1902)
12st 7lb — Congress (1877), The Liberator (1880), Ilex (1892), Jerry M. (1910), Shaun Spadah (1923), Bright's Boy (1927), Easter Hero (1929).

Lowest weight

8st 12lb — Weathercock (1857), Romeo (1862).

Fell and remounted

Arthur (1840), Rathnally (1911), Shady Girl (1911), Carsey (1913), The Bore (1921), All White (1921), Billy Barton (1928), Derrinstown (1951).

Brought down and remounted

Red Alligator (1967), Loving Words (1982).

Badly balked

Honey End (1967)

Oldest

15 years — Manifesto (1903)
14 years — Manifesto (1902)
13 years — Black Prince (1885), Rondetto (1969).

Youngest

5 years — Switcher (1846), Treachery (1857), The Dane (1861), Fan (1867), La Veine (1875), Thornfield (1881), Cyrus (1882), Zoëdone (1882), Roquefort (1884)

Mares

Paulina (1839), Maria Day (1851), Miss Mowbray (1853), Minerva (1856), Treachery (1857), Yaller Gal (1863), Emblematic (1865), Primrose (1870), Columbine (1873), Dainty (1875), La Veine (1875), Martha (1878, 1879), Pride of Kildare (1878), Zoëdone (1882), Frigate (1884, 1885, 1888), Lady Ellen (1894), Biscuit (1896), Aunt May (1906), Mattie Macgregor (1908), Shady Girl (1911), Melleray's Belle (1930), Cooleen (1937), Pucka Belle (1937), Gentle Moya (1956), Tiberetta (1957, 1958), Miss Hunter (1970), Eyecatcher (1976, 1977)

Entires

Arthur (1840), Valentine (1840), Switcher (1846), Sir Peter Laurie (1852), Freetrader (1855), Jean du Quesne (1859), Huntsman (1859,

1860), The Dane (1861), Bridegroom (1862), Shangarry (1867), Alcibiade (1868), Ryshworth (1873), Shifnal (1876), Downpatrick (1880), Mohican (1883), Elliman (1899), Barsac (1900), The Gunner (1904), Caubeen (1909).

Grey

Arthur (1840), Cigar (1841), Peter Simple (1841, 1842, 1845), Downpatrick (1880), Trianon (1914), Loving Words (1982).

Black

Tom Tug (1844), Gardener (1869), Regal (1881), Black Prince (1883, 1885), Buckaway (1905), Mr Jones (1965).

Longest odds

100/1 — Pan (1890), Filbert (1897), Buckaway (1905), Odor (1910), Bovril (1927), Annandale (1931), Jack Finlay (1946).

Trained in Ireland

Arthur (1840), Valentine (1840), Cigar (1841), Switcher (1846), St Leger (1847), Sir John (1850, 1851), The Liberator (1877, 1880), Martha (1878, 1879), Pride of Kildare (1878), Cyrus (1882), Mohican (1883), Frigate (1884, 1885, 1888), Too Good (1886), Wild Man from Borneo (1894), The Gunner (1904), Red Lad (1906), Ballyboggan (1919), Royal Danieli (1938), Workman (1938), Prince Regent (1946), Lough Conn (1947), Royal Tan (1951, 1956), Derrinstown (1951), Carey's Cottage (1955), Mr What (1959), Vulture (1970), Miss Hunter (1970), Black Secret (1971, 1972), General Symons (1972), L'Escargot (1973, 1974), Drumroan (1978), Greasepaint (1983, 1984), Yer Man (1983).

Trained in France

Jean du Quesne (1859), La Veine (1875), Trianon (1914).

Bred in France

Jean du Quesne (1859), Alcibiade (1868), La Veine (1875), Trianon (1914), Lutteur (1914), Kami (1947), Mont Tremblant (1953).

Bred in USA

The Bore (1920, 1921), Billy Barton (1928).

Bred in Australia

Crisp (1973)

Bred in New Zealand

Royal Mail (1981).

MISCELLANEOUS RECORDS

Fastest times

9:01.9 — Red Rum (1973)
9:12.6 — Grittar (1982)
9:20.2 — Reynoldstown (1935)

Largest fields

66 — 1929
57 — 1947
49 — 1950

Smallest fields

10 — 1883
11 — 1841
12 — 1878, 1882

Richest first prizes

£54,769 — 1984
£54,314 — 1985
£52,949 — 1983

Smallest first prizes

£430 — 1841
£515 — 1842
£535 — 1844

Most appearances

8 times — Manifesto (1895 fourth, 1896 fell, 1897 won, 1899 won, 1900 third, 1902 third, 1903 third, 1904 ninth)
7 times — Hall Court (1865 to 1870, 1872)
The Liberator (1876, 1877, 1879 to 1882, 1886)
Frigate (1884 to 1890)
Gamecock (1885 to 1891)
Why Not (1889 to 1891, 1893 to 1896)
All White (1919 to 1922, 1924, 1925, 1927)

Most often in first 3

5 times — Manifesto (1897, 1899, 1900, 1902, 1903)
Red Rum (1973, 1974, 1975, 1976, 1977)
4 times — Frigate (1884, 1885, 1888, 1889)
3 times — Peter Simple (1841, 1842, 1845)
Huntsman (1859, 1860, 1862)
The Liberator (1877, 1879, 1880)
Ilex (1890, 1891, 1892)
Cloister (1891, 1892, 1893)
Why Not (1889, 1893, 1894)
Royal Tan (1951, 1954, 1956)
Wyndburgh (1957, 1959, 1962)
Mr What (1958, 1959, 1962)
L'Escargot (1973, 1974, 1975)
Corbière (1983, 1984, 1985)

Highest weights ever carried

13st 4lb — Lottery (1841, 1842)
13st 2lb — L'Africain (1866)
13st 1lb — Peter Simple (1843)

Lowest weight ever carried

8st 4lb — Conrad (1858)

Most Grand National winners in one field

7 — Voluptuary, Roquefort, Gamecock, Ilex, Come Away, Cloister and Why Not in 1891.

Grand National winners placed 1, 2, 3, 4

1884 — Voluptuary, Frigate, Roquefort, Zoëdone
1891 — Come Away, Cloister, Ilex, Roquefort

Grand National winners placed 1, 2, 3

1892 — Father O'Flynn, Cloister, Ilex.

Most finishers

23 — 1984
22 — 1963
19 — 1933, 1947
The average number of finishers has increased since the fences were made less formidable in 1961 by being sloped on the take-off side.

Fewest finishers

2 — 1928
3 — 1913, 1951

Hottest favourites

2/1 — Golden Miller (1935)
5/2 — Lottery (1841), Regal (1879), Conjuror (1924).

Longest-priced favourites

100/7 — Flying Wild, Laffy, Pappageno's Cottage and Time (1964).

Favourite most often

3 times — Lottery (1839, 1841, 1842)
Golden Miller (1933 1935, 1937)

Most consecutive winning favourites

2 — 1890–91, 1893–94 (one joint).

Most consecutive losing favourites

17 — 1928 to 1949.

Race not run

1916 to 1918 because of World War I (substitute races were run at Gatwick); 1941 to 1945 because of World War II.

Race postponed

1855, 1858

Earliest dates

26 February — 1839, 1851
27 February — 1850, 1856
28 February — 1844, 1849

Latest dates

9 April — 1983
8 April — 1967, 1972
7 April — 1951

Run on

Tuesday: 1839, 1871
Wednesday: 1841–57, 1859–70

Thursday: 1840, 1872–75
Friday: 1876–1946, 1957
Saturday: 1858, 1947–56, from 1958

Most successful owners

3 wins--James Machell: 1873, 1874,
    1876.
    Sir Charles Assheton-Smith (formerly
        Charles Duff): 1893, 1912, 1913
    Noel Le Mare: 1973, 1974, 1977

Most successful breeders

3 wins—Martyn McEnery: 1973, 1974,
    1977
2 wins with different horses—
    R. Swale: 1863, 1864
    William Kennedy: 1966, 1968
    Mrs Barbara O'Neill: 1958, 1975

Most successful trainers

4 wins—Fred Rimell: 1956, 1961, 1970,
    1976
3 wins—William Holman: 1856, 1858,
    1860
    Willie Moore: 1894, 1896, 1899
    Aubrey Hastings: 1906, 1915, 1924
    Tom Coulthwaite: 1907, 1910, 1931
    Vincent O'Brien: 1953, 1954, 1955
    Neville Crump: 1948, 1952, 1960
    Donald McCain: 1973, 1974, 1977
    Tim Forster: 1972, 1980, 1985

Trained winner and second

Fred Withington trained Rubio and
    Mattie Macgregor in 1908

Successful woman trainer

Mrs Jenny Pitman: 1983

Most successful jockeys

5 wins—George Stevens: 1856, 1863,
    1864, 1869, 1870
3 wins—Tom Oliver: 1842, 1843, 1853
    Mr Tommy Pickernell: 1860, 1871,
        1875
    Mr Tommy Beasley: 1880, 1881,
        1889
    Arthur Nightingall: 1890, 1894, 1901
    Mr Jack Anthony: 1911, 1915, 1920
    Brian Fletcher: 1968, 1973, 1974.

Successful amateur riders

B. Bretherton (1840), William Loft
    (1845), Josey Little (1848), Alec
    Goodman (1852, 1866), Tommy
    Pickernell (1860, 1871, 1875), Bee
    Coventry (1865), George Ede (1868),
    Maunsell Richardson (1873, 1874),
    Fred Hobson (1877), Garrett Moore
    (1879), Tommy Beasley (1880, 1881,
    1889), 3rd Baron Manners (1882),
    Graf Karl Kinsky (1883), Ted Wilson
    (1884, 1885), Harry Beasley (1891),
    Roddy Owen (1892), Joe Widger
    (1895), David Campbell (1896),
    Aubrey Hastings (1906), Jack
    Anthony (1911, 1915, 1920), Tuppy
    Bennet (1923), Jack Wilson (1925),
    Bill Dutton (1928), Frank Furlong
    (1935), Fulke Walwyn (1936), Bobby

Fred Rimell is the only trainer to triumph in four Grand Nationals at Liverpool though his first winner, E.S.B. in 1956, profited from the collapse of the Queen Mother's Devon Loch on the run-in.

Petre (1946), Tommy Smith (1965),
    Charlie Fenwick (1980), Dick
    Saunders (1982).

First woman rider to take part

Miss Charlotte Brew on Barony Fort,
    who refused at the 27th fence in 1977.

First woman rider to complete the course

Mrs Geraldine Rees on Cheers, who
    was last to finish in 1982.

Only jockey to be killed

James Wynne suffered fatal injuries
    when his mount O'Connell fell at the
    Chair fence in 1862.

Successful owner-breeder-trainers

Mat Maher (1889), Bernard Bletsoe
    (1901), Frank Gilman (1982).

Successful breeder-trainer-rider

Harry Beasley (1891)

Successful owner-breeders

John Weyman (1869), Harry Dyas
    (1897), Thomas Gerrard (1920),
    Fearnie Williamson (1949).

Successful owner-trainers

John Courtenay (1847), John Nightingall
    (1878), Tom Tyler (1914), Noel
    Furlong (1935, 1936), 2nd Baron
    Stalbridge (1940), Tim Forster (1972)

Successful owner-riders

William Loft (1845), Josey Little (1848),
    Fred Hobson (1877), Garrett Moore

(1879), 3rd Baron Manners (1882),
    Graf Karl Kinsky (1883).

Successful trainer-riders

Tom Cunningham (1849), Tom Oliver
    (1853), Charlie Boyce (1857), Chris
    Green (1859), Harry Lamplugh
    (1862), Maunsell Richardson (1873,
    1874), Joe Cannon (1876), Aubrey
    Hastings (1906).

Successful as both jockey and trainer

Algy Anthony rode Ambush (1900) and
    trained Troytown (1920).
Fulke Walwyn rode Reynoldstown
    (1936) and trained Team Spirit
    (1964)
Fred Winter rode Sundew (1957) and
    Kilmore (1962) and trained Jay
    Trump (1965) and Anglo (1966).

Most successful sires

4 wins—My Prince: Gregalach (1929),
    Reynoldstown (1935, 1936), Royal
    Mail (1937).
3 wins—Ascetic: Cloister (1893),
    Drumcree (1903), Ascetic's Silver
    (1906).
    Cottage: Workman (1939), Lovely
    Cottage (1946), Sheila's Cottage
    (1948).
    Vulgan: Team Spirit (1964), Foinavon
    (1967), Gay Trip (1970).
    Quorum: Red Rum (1973, 1974,
    1977).

Sired winner and second

Xenophon (1882), My Prince (1929),
    Vulgan (1970).

US Triple Crown Races

Kentucky Derby

3-year-olds, Churchill Downs, Louisville, Kentucky; 1½ miles 1875–95, 1¼ miles from 1896.

In the following list the jockey's name appears last.

1875 H. P. McGrath's ch c **Aristides** O. Lewis
1876 W. Astor's br g **Vagrant** R. Swim
1877 D. Swigert's ch c **Baden Baden** W. Walker
1878 T. J. Nichols's ch c **Day Star** J. Carter
1879 G. W. Darden & Co's b c **Lord Murphy** C Shauer
1880 J. S. Shawhan's ch c **Fonso** G. Lewis
1881 Dwyer Bros' b c **Hindoo** J. McLaughlin
1882 Morris & Patton's ch g **Apollo** B. Hurd
1883 Chinn & Morgan's b c **Leonatus** W. Donohue
1884 W. Cottrill's ch c **Buchanan** I. Murphy
1885 J. T. Williams's ch c **Joe Cotton** E. Henderson
1886 J. B. Haggin's br c **Ben Ali** P. Duffy
1887 Labold Bros' b c **Montrose** I. Lewis
1888 Chicago Stable's br g **Macbeth** G. Covington
1889 N. Armstrong's ch c **Spokane** T. Kiley
1890 E. Corrigan's b c **Riley** I. Murphy
1891 Jacobin Stable's b c **Kingman** I. Murphy
1892 Bashford Manor Farm's b c **Azra** A. Clayton
1893 Cushing & Orth's ch c **Lookout** E. Kunze
1894 Leigh & Rose's b c **Chant** F. Goodale
1895 B. McClelland's bl c **Halma** J. Perkins
1896 M. F. Dwyer's b c **Ben Brush** W. Simms
1897 J. C. Cahn's ch c **Typhoon** F. Garner
1898 J. E. Madden's br c **Plaudit** W. Simms
1899 A. H. & D. H. Morris's b c **Manuel** F. Taral
1900 C. H. Smith's b c **Lieut. Gibson** J. Boland
1901 F. B. Van Meter's b c **His Eminence** J. Winkfield
1902 T. C. McDowell's ch c **Alan-A Dale** J. Winkfield
1903 C. R. Ellison's b c **Judge Himes** H. Booker
1904 Mrs C. E. Durnell's b c **Elwood** F. Prior

1905 S. S. Brown's b c **Agile** J. Martin
1906 G. J. Long's b c **Sir Huon** R. Troxler
1907 J. H. Woodford's b c **Pink Star** A. Minder
1908 C. E. Hamilton's b c **Stone Street** A. Pickens
1909 J. B. Respess's b c **Wintergreen** V. Powers
1910 W. Gerst's b c **Donau** F. Herbert
1911 R. F. Carmen's b c **Meridian** G. Archibald
1912 H. C. Hallenbeck's br c **Worth** C. H. Shilling
1913 T. P. Hayes's b c **Donerail** R. Goose
1914 H. C. Applegate's b g **Old Rosebud** J. McCabe
1915 H. P. Whitney's ch f **Regret** J. Notter
1916 J. Sanford's bl c **George Smith** J. Loftus
1917 Billings & Johnson's ch c **Omar Khayyam** C. Borel
1918 W. S. Kilmer's ch g **Exterminator** W. Knapp
1919 J. K. L. Ross's ch c **Sir Barton** J. Loftus
1920 R. Parr's br g **Paul Jones** T. Rice
1921 E. R. Bradley's b c **Behave Yourself** C. Thompson

1922 B. Block's bl c **Morvich** A. Johnson
1923 Rancocas Stable's br c **Zev** E. Sande
1924 Mrs R. M. Hoots's bl c **Black Gold** J. D. Mooney
1925 G. A. Cochran's bl c **Flying Ebony** E. Sande
1926 Idle Hour Stock Farm's ch c **Bubbling Over** A. Johnson
1927 H. P. Whitney's b c **Whiskery** L. McAtee
1928 Mrs J. D. Hertz's ch c **Reigh Count** C. Lang
1929 H. P. Gardner's ch g **Clyde Van Dusen** L. McAtee
1930 Belair Stud's b c **Gallant Fox** E. Sande
1931 Greentree Stable's b c **Twenty Grand** C. Kurtsinger
1932 E. R. Bradley's ch c **Burgoo King** E. James
1933 E. R. Bradley's br c **Brokers Tip** D. Meade
1934 Brookmeade Stable's br c **Cavalcade** M. Garner
1935 Belair Stud's ch c **Omaha** W. Saunders
1936 M. L. Schwartz's ch c **Bold Venture** I. Hanford
1937 Glen Riddle Farm's br c **War**

Mrs Lucille Markey, owner of Calumet Farm, is flanked by trainers Ben Jones and his son Jimmy Jones as she greets Bill Hartack and Iron Liege after the 1957 Kentucky Derby. Between them they hold most of the records for America's premier Classic.

Brigadier Gerard, out on his own at the end of the 1972 Queen Elizabeth II Stakes at Ascot, as so often in a career which brought 17 wins from 18 starts and recognition as the best British miler since Tudor Minstrel.

Fred Rimell whose score of four Aintree Grand National winners is the record for a trainer, was equally proficient in other branches of the sport. He is seen here with Comedy of Errors, whom he saddled for victories in the Champion Hurdles of 1973 and 1975.

Red Rum's mastery of the Aintree fences is unmatched in history. Here he shows his style on the way to the second of his three Grand National victories, in 1974.

Lester Piggott (left) and the diminutive Bill Shoemaker have dominated the jockey ranks of Britain and the United States respectively since World War II. Piggott has ridden a record 28 English Classic winners, (to the end of 1984), while Shoemaker's world record tally of winners exceeds 8000.

The widest recorded winning margin in Derby history was the 10–length romp by Shergar in 1981, when Glint of Gold was his nearest, but distant, pursuer.

Admiral C. Kurtsinger
1938 Woolford Farm's b c **Lawrin**
E. Arcaro
1939 Belair Stud's b c **Johnstown**
J. Stout
1940 Milky Way Farm's b c
Gallahadion C. Bierman
1941 Calumet Farm's ch c **Whirlaway**
E. Arcaro
1942 Greentree Stable's ch c **Shut Out**
W. D. Wright
1943 Mrs J. D. Hertz's br c **Count Fleet**
J. Longden
1944 Calumet Farm's ch c **Pensive**
C. McCreary
1945 F. W. Hooper's b c **Hoop Jr**
E. Arcaro
1946 King Ranch's ch c **Assault**
W. Mehrtens
1947 Maine Chance Farm's ch c **Jet Pilot** E. Guerin
1948 Calumet Farm's b c **Citation**
E. Arcaro
1949 Calumet Farm's b c **Ponder**
S. Brooks
1950 King Ranch's ch c **Middleground**
W. Boland
1951 J. Amiel's b c **Count Turf**
C. McCreary
1952 Calumet Farm's b c **Hill Gail**
E. Arcaro
1953 Cain Hoy Stable's br c **Dark Star**
H. Moreno
1954 A. J. Crevolin's gr c **Determine**
R. York
1955 R. C. Ellsworth's ch c **Swaps**
W. Shoemaker
1956 D. & H. Stable's b c **Needles**
D. Erb
1957 Calumet Farm's b c **Iron Liege**
W. Hartack
1958 Calumet Farm's b c **Tim Tam**
I. Valenzuela

1959 F. Turner, jr's b c **Tomy Lee**
W. Shoemaker
1960 Sunny Blue Farm's ch c **Venetian Way** W. Hartack
1961 Mrs K. Price's br c **Carry Back**
J. Sellers
1962 El Peco Ranch's gr c **Decidedly**
W. Hartack
1963 Darby Dan Farm's ch c **Chateaugay** B. Baeza
1964 Windfields Farm's b c **Northern Dancer** W. Hartack
1965 Mrs A. L. Rice's b c **Lucky Debonair** W. Shoemaker
1966 Ford Stable's b c **Kauai King**
D. Brumfield
1967 Darby Dan Farm's b c **Proud Clarion** R. Ussery
1968 Calumet Farm's b c **Forward Pass** I. Valenzuela
1969 F. McMahon's ch c **Majestic Prince** W. Hartack
1970 R. E. Lehmann's ch c **Dust Commander** M. Manganello
1971 E. Caibett's b c **Canonero**
G. Avila
1972 Meadow Stable's b c **Riva Ridge**
R. Turcotte
1973 Meadow Stable's ch c **Secretariat**
R. Turcotte
1974 J. M. Olin's b c **Cannonade**
A. Cordero, jr
1975 J. L. Greer's b c **Foolish Pleasure**
J. Vasquez
1976 E. R. Tizol's b c **Bold Forbes**
A. Cordero, jr
1977 Mrs K. Taylor's br c **Seattle Slew**
J. Cruguet
1978 Harbor View Farm's ch c **Affirmed**
S. Cauthen
1979 Hawksworth Farm's gr c
Spectacular Bid R. J. Franklin
1980 Mrs B. R. Firestone's ch f

Genuine Risk J. Vasquez
1981 Buckland Farm's b c **Pleasant Colony** J. Velasquez
1982 Hancock & Peter's gr c **Gato Del Sol** E. Delahoussaye
1983 D. J. Foster's ch c **Sunny's Halo**
E. Delahoussaye
1984 Claiborne Farm's br c **Swale**
L. Pincay, jr

MOST SUCCESSFUL CONNECTIONS

Owners
4 wins — E. R. Bradley (Idle Hour Stock
Farm): 1921, 1926, 1932, 1933
Warren Wright (Calumet Farm): 1941,
1944, 1948, 1949
Mrs Warren Wright/Mrs Gene Markey
(Calumet Farm): 1952, 1957,
1958, 1968.

Breeder
8 wins — Calumet Farm: 1941, 1944,
1948, 1949, 1952, 1957, 1958,
1968.

Trainer
6 wins — Ben Jones: 1938, 1941, 1944,
1948, 1949, 1952

Jockeys
5 wins — Eddie Arcaro: 1938, 1941,
1945, 1948, 1952
Bill Hartack: 1957, 1960, 1962, 1964,
1969

Sires
3 wins — Virgil: 1876, 1881, 1886
Falsetto: 1894, 1901, 1906
Sir Gallahad: 1930, 1940, 1945
Bull Lea: 1948, 1952, 1957.

Preakness Stakes

3-year-olds, Pimlico, Baltimore,
Maryland; 1½ miles 1873–88, 1¼
miles 1889, 1 mile 110 yards
1894–1900 and 1908, 1 mile 70 yards
1901–07, 1 mile 1909–10, 1 mile 1
furlong 1911–24, 1 mile 1½ furlongs
from 1925; run at Gravesend
1894–1908.

*In the following list the jockey's name
appears last.*

1873 J. F. Chamberlain's b c **Survivor**
G. Barbee
1874 H. Gaffney's b c **Culpepper**
M. Donohue
1875 J. F. Chamberlain's b c **Tom Ochiltree** L. Hughes
1876 P. Lorillard's b g **Shirley**
G. Barbee
1877 E. A. Clabaugh's ch c
Cloverbrook C. Holloway

1878 G. L. Lorillard's b c **Duke of Magenta** C. Holloway
1879 G. L. Lorillard's ch c **Harold**
L. Hughes
1880 G. L. Lorillard's b c **Grenada**
L. Hughes
1881 G. L. Lorillard's ch c **Saunterer**
T. Costello
1882 G. L. Lorillard's b c **Vanguard**
T. Costello
1883 J. E. Kelly's b c **Jacobus**
G. Barbee
1884 T. W. Doswell's ch c **Knight of Ellerslie** S. Fisher
1885 W. Donohue's b c **Tecumseh**
J. McLaughlin
1886 A. J. Cassatt's b c **The Bard**
S. Fisher
1887 W. Jennings's b c **Dunboyne**
W. Donohue

1888 R. W. Walden's ch c **Refund**
F. Littlefield
1889 S. S. Brown's b c **Buddhist**
W. Anderson
1890–93 no race

1894 J. R. & F. P. Keene's ch c
Assignee F. Taral
1895 Preakness Stable's gr c **Belmar**
F. Taral
1896 A. Belmont, jr's ch c **Margrave**
H. Griffin
1897 T. P. Hayes's b c **Paul Kauvar**
C. Thorpe
1898 C. F. Dwyer's ch c **Sly Fox**
W. Simms
1899 P. J. Dwyer's ch c **Half Time**
R. Clawson
1900 G. J. Long's b c **Hindus**
H. Spencer

Continued on page 106

MAN O' WAR

To most Americans, Man o' War is the greatest racehorse who ever lived and the single most famous figure in the history of the sport. This high-spirited, charismatic individual won 20 of his 21 races over two seasons and was so overwhelmingly superior to all the other horses of his day in America that he set the standard by which all subsequent champions have been measured.

'Big Red', who derived his nickname from his flaming chestnut coat, was foaled on 29 March 1917 at the Nursery Stud near Lexington, Kentucky owned by his breeder August Belmont, chairman of the Jockey Club of New York. His sire, Fair Play, was a top-class racehorse but his dam, Mahubah, a daughter of English Triple Crown winner Rock Sand, was successful only once. He came up for sale at Saratoga in August 1918

and was bought for $5,000 by Samuel D. Riddle, whose horses raced in the name of Glen Riddle Farm and were trained by young Louis Feustel.

Man o' War, who started at odds-on in every race he contested, made a winning début at Belmont Park in June 1919 and then established himself as the leader of his generation by taking the Keene Memorial, Youthful, Hudson, Tremont and United States Hotel Stakes. However, on 13 August 1919 came the Sanford Memorial Stakes at Saratoga, the only loss and the most controversial race of his career.

He was among the worst sufferers in a straggling start and when John Loftus, who

Man o' War as a three-year-old in 1920. In the saddle is Clarence Kummer, who rode him in most of his races that season.

rode him in all his juvenile outings, moved up on the rail he found himself boxed in. With only a furlong to go he pulled back and switched to the outside, whereupon Upset, who received 15 lb, was sent clear; Man o' War tried valiantly to make up the leeway but was still half a length in arrears at the line. The result was clearly misleading, for Man o' War beat Upset on six other occasions and emphasised his status as champion in his three subsequent races that year — the Grand Union Hotel Stakes, Hopeful Stakes and Belmont Futurity.

During his all-conquering campaign of 11 starts in 1920, Man o' War staked his claim to immortality, outclassing the few horses who dared to oppose him and breaking five world or American time records. He missed the Kentucky Derby because Riddle refused to run a 3-year-old over 10 furlongs so early in the season, and his reappearance was delayed until the Preakness Stakes, in which he beat Upset in his first race outside New York State and his first under his new regular jockey Clarence Kummer. He then won the Withers Stakes, beat a single rival by 20 lengths for the Belmont Stakes and trotted up in the Stuyvesant Handicap, for which he started at odds of 1/100 despite carrying 135 lb.

His next race, the Dwyer Stakes at Aqueduct, was the only one that year in which he looked in danger of defeat. His solitary opponent was the top-class colt John P. Grier, to whom he conceded 18 lb, and the pair galloped stride for stride until John P. Grier edged in front at the furlong-pole. Kummer gave Man o' War one crack with the whip and the champion went away to win by a length and a half.

Man o' War next took the Miller and the Travers Stakes at Saratoga, ridden by Earl Sande and Andy Schuttinger respectively, and when reunited with Kummer he beat his only rival by 100 lengths in the Lawrence Realization Stakes. His odds were 1/100 on that occasion and they were the same for his 15-length victory in the Jockey Club Stakes (now the Jockey Club Gold Cup).

The Potomac Handicap at Havre de Grace was perhaps his finest win, for he carried 138 lb yet easily beat top-class opponents to whom he gave lumps of weight. For his final appearance he travelled to Kenilworth Park, Canada in October 1920 for a match with Sir Barton, who the previous year had become America's first Triple Crown winner. This was the only time Man o' War ever met an older horse and it was no contest; the $80,000 prize, the richest of his career, enabled him to replace Domino as America's leading earner with a total of $249,465.

Man o' War was retired at the peak of his powers. If he had been kept in training at four, he would have had few opportunities outside handicaps so Samuel Riddle asked Walter Vosburgh, the Jockey Club handicapper, how much weight his colt would be given. The answer was, 'If he wins his first race, I will put the heaviest weight on him ever carried by a Thoroughbred.'

The champion stood for his first two stud seasons at Hinata Stock Farm, Lexington and was then moved a couple of miles to Faraway Farm, where he spent the rest of his days. He was a great success in his new rôle, which was a tribute to his own merit rather than the way he was managed. Riddle kept him almost as a private stallion for the benefit of himself and his friends, and seldom made nominations available to outside breeders. He was never bred to more than 25 mares in one season and most of them were of inferior quality, especially in his later years, yet he became America's champion sire in 1926 and was runner-up three times.

His offspring included champions American Flag, Maid at Arms, Crusader, Edith Cavell, Scapa Flow, Bateau and, the best of all, Triple Crown hero War Admiral. He also sired Mars, Clyde Van Dusen, Battleship, War Glory, War Relic and Salaminia, while his daughters proved valuable broodmares. 'Big Red' served his last season in 1942 and died at the age of 30 on 1 November 1947.

Will Harbut, the groom who looked after him for most of his stud career, became part of the Man o' War legend thanks to the lengthy monologue on the subject of the champion's achievements which he devised for the many thousands who visited Faraway Farm each year. Few can have disagreed with Harbut's conclusion that he was 'the mostest hoss that ever was'.

1901 R. T. Wilson, jr's b c **The Parader**
F. Landry

1902 G.B. Morris's b c **Old England**
L. Jackson

1903 M. H. Tichenor's ch f **Flocarline**
W. Gannon

1904 Goughacres Stable's br c **Bryn Mawr** E. Hildebrand

1905 S. Paget's b c **Cairngorm**
W. Davis

1906 T. J. Gaynor's ch f **Whimsical**
W. Miller

1907 A. Belmont, jr's b g **Don Enrique**
G. Mountain

1908 H. P. Whitney's b c **Royal Tourist**
E. Dugan

1909 W. T. Ryan's br c **Effendi**
W. Doyle

1910 E. B. Cassatt's ch g **Layminster**
R. Estep

1911 A. Belmont, jr's b c **Watervale**
E. Dugan

1912 Beverwyck Stable's br c **Colonel Holloway** C. Turner

1913 J. Whalen's b g **Buskin** J Butwell

1914 Mrs A. Barklie's b g **Holiday**
A. Schuttinger

1915 E. F. Whitney's b f **Rhine Maiden**
D. Hoffman

1916 J. K. L. Ross's br c **Damrosch**
L. McAtee

1917 E. R. Bradley's b c **Kalitan**
E. Haynes

1918 A. K. Macomber's b c **War Cloud**
J. Loftus

W. E. Applegate's b c **Jack Hare, Jr**
C. Peak

Run in two divisions

1919 J. K. L. Ross's ch c **Sir Barton**
J. Loftus

1920 Glen Riddle Farm's ch c **Man o' War** C. Kummer

1921 H. P. Whitney's b c **Broomspun**
F. Coltiletti

1922 R. T. Wilson, jr's ch c **Pillory**
L. Morris

1923 W. J. Salmon's ch c **Vigil**
B. Marinelli

1924 H. C. Fisher's b f **Nellie Morse**
J. Merimee

1925 G. A. Cochran's bl c **Coventry**
C. Kummer

1926 W. J. Salmon's b c **Display**
J. Maiben

1927 H. P. Whitney's bl c **Bostonian**
A. Abel

1928 H. P. Whitney's b c **Victorian**
R. Workman

1929 W. J. Salmon's ch c **Dr Freeland**
L. Schaefer

Ron Turcotte checks the teletimer as Secretariat powers to victory by a record 31 lengths in the 1973 Belmont Stakes. This, the most devastating single performance in recent racing history, made the colt America's first Triple Crown hero for 25 years.

1930 Belair Stud's b c **Gallant Fox**
E. Sande

1931 A. C. Bostwick's ch c **Mate**
G. Ellis

1932 E. R. Bradley's b c **Burgoo King**
E. James

1933 Mrs S. B. Mason's ch c **Head Play**
C. Kurtsinger

1934 Brookmeade Stable's b c **High Quest** R. Jones

1935 Belair Stud's ch c **Omaha**
W. Saunders

1936 M. Schwartz's ch c **Bold Venture**
G. Woolf

1937 Glen Riddle Farm's br c **War Admiral** C. Kurtsinger

1938 Foxcatcher Farms's ch c **Dauber**
M. Peters

1939 W. L. Brann's b c **Challedon**
G. Seabo

1940 E. R. Bradley's b c **Bimelech**
F. A. Smith

1941 Calumet Farm's ch c **Whirlaway**
E. Arcaro

1942 Mrs A. Sabath's b c **Alsab**
B. James

1943 Mrs J. D. Hertz's br c **Count Fleet**
J. Longden

1944 Calumet Farm's ch c **Pensive**
C. McCreary

1945 Mrs P. A. B. Widener's br c **Polynesian** W. D. Wright

1946 King Ranch's ch c **Assault**
W. Mehrtens

1947 Calumet Farm's br c **Faultless**
D. Dodson

1948 Calumet Farm's b c **Citation**
E. Arcaro

1949 Greentree Stable's br c **Capot**
T. Atkinson

1950 C. T. Chenery's b c **Hill Prince**
E. Arcaro

1951 Brookmeade Stable's b c **Bold**
E. Arcaro

1952 White Oak Stable's b c **Blue Man**
C. McCreary

1953 A. G. Vanderbilt's gr c **Native Dancer** E. Guerin

1954 Hasty House Farm's b c **Hasty Road** J. Adams

1955 Belair Stud's b c **Nashua**
E. Arcaro

1956 Calumet Farm's br c **Fabius**
W. Hartack

1957 Wheatley Stable's b c **Bold Ruler**
E. Arcaro

1958 Calumet Farm's b c **Tim Tam**
I. Valenzuela

1959 Estate of J. Braunstein's ch c **Royal Orbit** W. Harmatz

1960 Turfland's b c **Bally Ache**
R. Ussery

1961 Mrs K. Price's br c **Carry Back** J. Sellers

1962 Brandywine Stable's ch c **Greek Money** J. Rotz

1963 R. C. Ellsworth's ch c **Candy Spots** W. Shoemaker

1964 Windfields Farm's b c **Northern Dancer** W. Hartack

1965 Powhatan Stable's b c **Tom Rolfe**
R. Turcotte

1966 Ford Stable's b c **Kauai King**
D. Brumfield

1967 Mrs T. Bancroft's b c **Damascus**
W. Shoemaker

1968 Calumet Farm's b c **Forward Pass** I. Valenzuela

1969 F. McMahon's ch c **Majestic Prince** W. Hartack

1970 Mrs E. D. Jacobs's b c **Personality** E. Belmonte

1971 E. Caibett's b c **Canonero**
G. Avila

1972 W. S. Farish III's b c **Bee Bee Bee**
E. Nelson

1973 Meadow Stable's ch c **Secretariat**
R. Turcotte

1974 Darby Dan Farm's ch c **Little Current** M. Rivera

1975 Golden Chance Farm's ch c **Master Derby** D. McHargue

1976 E. C. Cashman's b c **Elocutionist**
J. Lively

1977 Mrs K. Taylor's br c **Seattle Slew**
J. Cruguet

1978 Harbor View Farm's ch c **Affirmed**
S. Cauthen

1979 Hawksworth Farm's gr c **Spectacular Bid** R. J. Franklin

1980 Tartan Stable's ch c **Codex**
A. Cordero, jr

1981 Buckland Farm's b c **Pleasant Colony** J. Velasquez

1982 N. Scherr's b c **Aloma's Ruler**
J. Kaenel

1983 F. P. Sears's b c **Deputed Testamony** D. Miller, jr

1984 K. Opstein's b c **Gate Dancer**
A. Cordero, jr

MOST SUCCESSFUL CONNECTIONS

Owner

5 wins — George Lorillard: 1878, 1879, 1880, 1881, 1882

Breeder

6 wins — Harry Payne Whitney: 1908, 1913, 1914, 1921, 1927, 1928.

Trainer

7 wins — Wyndham Walden: 1875, 1878, 1879, 1880, 1881, 1882, 1888.

Jockey

6 wins — Eddie Arcaro: 1941, 1948, 1950, 1951, 1955, 1957

Sires

3 wins — Lexington: 1875, 1876, 1878
Broomstick: 1914, 1921, 1927

Belmont Stakes

3-year-olds, Belmont Park, Elmont, New York; 1 mile 5 furlongs 1867–73, 1½ miles 1874–89, 1¼ miles 1890–92, 1895, 1904–05, 1 mile 1 furlong 1893–94, 1 mile 3 furlongs 1896–1903, 1906–10, 1913–25, 1½ miles from 1926; run at Jerome Park 1867–89, Morris Park 1890–1904, Aqueduct 1963–67

In the following list the jockeys name appears last.

1867 F. Morris's b f **Ruthless**
J. Gilpatrick

1868 McConnell & Harness's ch c **General Duke** R. Swim

1869 A. Belmont's ch c **Fenian** C. Miller

1870 D. Swigert's b c **Kingfisher**
E. Brown

1871 D. McDaniel's ch c **Harry Bassett**
W. Miller

1872 D. McDaniel's ch c **Joe Daniels**
J. Rowe

1873 D. McDaniel's ch c **Springbok**
J. Rowe

1874 P. Lorillard's br c **Saxon**
G. Barbee

1875 H. P. McGrath's br c **Calvin**
R. Swim

1876 Doswell & Cammacks's b c **Algerine** W. Donohue

1877 E. A. Clabaugh's ch c **Cloverbrook** C. Holloway

1878 G. L. Lorillard's b c **Duke of Magenta** W. Hughes

1879 J. R. Keene's ch c **Spendthrift**
G. Evans

1880 G. L. Lorillard's br c **Grenada**
W. Hughes

1881 G. L. Lorillard's ch c **Saunterer**
T. Costello

1882 Appleby & Johnson's ch c **Forester** J. McLaughlin

1883 Dwyer Bros' b c **George Kinney**
J. Mclaughlin

1884 Dwyer Bros' ch c **Panique**
J. McLaughlin

1885 J. B. Haggin's ch c **Tyrant**
P. Duffy

1886 Dwyer Bros' b c **Inspector B.**
J. McLaughlin

1887 Dwyer Bros' ch c **Hanover**
J. McLaughlin

1888 Dwyer Bros' br c **Sir Dixon**
J. McLaughlin

1889 A. J. Cassatt's b c **Eric**
W. Hayward

1890 Hough Bros' bl c **Burlington** S. Barnes

1891 C. E. Rand's b c **Foxford** E. Garrison

1892 L. Stuart's b c **Patron** W. Hayward

1893 Empire Stable's ch c **Comanche** W. Simms

1894 B. McClelland's ch c **Henry of Navarre** W. Simms

1895 Preakness Stable's gr c **Belmar** F. Taral

1896 A. Belmont, jr's br c **Hastings** H. Griffin

1897 M. Daly's br c **Scottish Chieftain** J. Scherrer

1898 A. H. & D. H. Morris's b c **Bowling Brook** F. Littlefield

1899 S. Paget's b c **Jean Bereaud** R. Clawson

1900 H. E. Leigh's br c **Ildrim** N. Turner

1901 J. R. Keene's b c **Commando** H. Spencer

1902 A. Belmont, jr's ch c **Masterman** J. Bullman

1903 Hampton Stable's b c **Africander** J. Bullman

1904 J. R. Keene's br c **Delhi** G. Odom

1905 H. P. Whitney's ch f **Tanya** E Hildebrand

1906 H. P. Whitney's br c **Burgomaster** L. Lyne

1907 J. R. Keene's b c **Peter Pan** G. Mountain

1908 J. R. Keene's b c **Colin** J. Notter

1909 S. C. Hildreth's ch c **Joe Madden** E. Dugan

1910 J. R. Keene's br c **Sweep** J. Butwell

1911–12 no race

1913 H. P. Whitney's b c **Prince Eugene** R. Troxler

1914 J. W. Schorr's b c **Luke McLuke** M Buxton

1915 H. C. Hallenbeck's bl c **The Finn** G. Byrne

1916 A. Belmont, jr's ch c **Friar Rock** E. Haynes

1917 A. Belmont, jr's br c **Hourless** J. Butwell

1918 H. P. Whitney's b c **Johren** F. Robinson

1919 J. K. L. Ross's ch c **Sir Barton** J. Loftus

1920 Glen Riddle Farm's ch c **Man o' War** C. Kummer

1921 Rancocas Stable's ch c **Grey Lag** E. Sande

1922 R. T. Wilson, jr's ch c **Pillory** C. H. Miller

1923 Rancocas Stable's br c **Zev** E. Sande

1924 Rancocas Stable's ch c **Mad Play** E. Sande

1925 Glen Riddle Farm's ch c **American Flag** A. Johnson

1926 Glen Riddle Farm's ch c **Crusader** A. Johnson

1927 J. E. Widener's b c **Chance Shot** E. Sande

1928 A. H. Cosden's b c **Vito** C. Kummer

1929 E. R. Bradley's b c **Blue Larkspur** M. Garner

1930 Belair Stud's b c **Gallant Fox** E. Sande

1931 Greentree Stable's b c **Twenty Grand** C. Kurtsinger

1932 Belair Stud's b c **Faireno** T. Malley

1933 J. E. Widener's b c **Hurryoff** M. Garner

1934 J. E. Widener's b c **Peace Chance** W. D. Wright

1935 Belair Stud's ch c **Omaha** W. Saunders

1936 Belair Stud's b c **Granville** J. Stout

1937 Glen Riddle Farm's br c **War Admiral** C. Kurtsinger

1938 Mrs W. P. Stewart's ch c **Pasteurized** J. Stout

1939 Belair Stud's b c **Johnstown** J. Stout

1940 E. R. Bradley's b c **Bimelech** F. A. Smith

1941 Calumet Farm's ch c **Whirlaway** E. Arcaro

1942 Greentree Stable's ch c **Shut Out** E. Arcaro

1943 Mrs J. D. Hertz's br c **Count Fleet** J. Longden

1944 W. Ziegler, jr's br c **Bounding Home** G. L. Smith

1945 W. M. Jeffords's br c **Pavot** E. Arcaro

1946 King Ranch's ch c **Assault** W. Mehrtens

1947 C. V. Whitney's b c **Phalanx** R. Donoso

1948 Calumet Farm's b c **Citation** E. Arcaro

1949 Greentree Stable's br c **Capot** T. Atkinson

1950 King Ranch's ch c **Middleground** W. Boland

1951 C. V. Whitney's ch c **Counterpoint** D. Gorman

1952 Mrs W. M. Jeffords's br c **One Count** E. Arcaro

1953 A. G. Vanderbilt's gr c **Native Dancer** E. Guerin

1954 King Ranch's br c **High Gun** E. Guerin

1955 Belair Stud's b c **Nashua** E. Arcaro

1956 D. & H. Stable's b c **Needles** D. Erb

1957 R. Lowe's b c **Gallant Man** W. Shoemaker

1958 J. E. O'Connell's ch c **Cavan** P. Anderson

1959 Brookmeade Stable's ch c **Sword Dancer** W. Shoemaker

1960 J. E. O'Connell's ch c **Celtic Ash** W. Hartack

1961 J. Sher's b c **Sherluck** B. Baeza

1962 G. D. Widener's b c **Jaipur** W. Shoemaker

1963 Darby Dan Farm's ch c **Chateaugay** B. Baeza

1964 Rokeby Stable's b c **Quadrangle** M. Ycaza

1965 Mrs B. Cohen's b c **Hail to All** J. Sellers

1966 R. N. Webster's b c **Amberoid** W. Boland

1967 Mrs T. Bancroft's b c **Damascus** W. Shoemaker

1968 Greentree Stable's ch c **Stage Door Johnny** H. Gustines

1969 Rokeby Stable's ch c **Arts and Letters** B. Baeza

1970 Mrs E. D. Jacob's ro c **High Echelon** J. Rotz

1971 October House Farm's b c **Pass Catcher** W. Blum

1972 Meadow Stable's b c **Riva Ridge** R. Turcotte

1973 Meadow Stable's ch c **Secretariat** R. Turcotte

1974 Darby Dan Farm's ch c **Little Current** M. Rivera

1975 A. A. Seeligson, jr's ch c **Avatar** W. Shoemaker

1976 E. R. Tizol's b c **Bold Forbes** A. Cordero, jr

1977 Mrs K. Taylor's br c **Seattle Slew** J. Cruguet

1978 Harbor View Farm's ch c **Affirmed** S. Cauthen

1979 W. H. Perry's ch c **Coastal** R. Hernandez

1980 Loblolly Stable's b c **Temperence Hill** E. Maple

1981 C. T. Wilson's b c **Summing** G. Martens

1982 H. de Kwiatkowski's b c **Conquistador Cielo** L. Pincay, jr

1983 A. Belmont IV's b c **Caveat** L. Pincay, jr

1984 Claiborne Farm's br c **Swale** L. Pincay, jr

MOST SUCCESSFUL CONNECTIONS

Owners

5 wins—Dwyer Bros: 1883, 1884, 1886, 1887, 1888
James R. Keene: 1901, 1904, 1907, 1908, 1910
William Woodward, sr (Belair Stud): 1930, 1932, 1935, 1936, 1939

Breeder

8 wins—A. J. Alexander: 1871, 1872, 1873, 1878, 1879, 1880, 1890, 1892.

Trainer

8 wins—James Rowe, sr: 1883, 1884, 1901, 1904, 1907, 1908, 1910, 1913

Jockeys

6 wins—Jimmy McLaughlin: 1882, 1883, 1884, 1886, 1887, 1888
Eddie Arcaro: 1941, 1942, 1945, 1948, 1952, 1955

Sire

4 wins—Lexington: 1868, 1870, 1871, 1878

III
EQUINE ACHIEVEMENT

John Henry (centre), ridden by Bill Shoemaker, is about to win the inaugural Arlington Million at Arlington Park, Chicago in August 1981.

Most Successful Horses: Races Won

Most races won in a career

The holder of the world record for races won in a career is Galgo Jr, a Puerto Rican-bred horse, foaled in 1928 on Vieques Island. The product of parents imported from the USA, he did all his racing at the Quintana and Las Monjas tracks in Puerto Rico between 1930 and 1936. He ran 159 times, recording 137 wins, 18 second places, one third and two fourths. He finished 'out of the money' only once, and his earnings of $31,738 constituted a then-record for Puerto Rican racing. Galgo Jr was still in training when he died of a heart attack in his box at Las Monjas Racing Park on 21 December 1936, and at the time of his death he was the holder, or joint-holder, of eight track records for native Puerto Rican-breds, from 5½ furlongs to 9 furlongs. Inevitably, Galgo Jr enjoyed the status of a local hero, but his merit was never tested at international level and the times he achieved suggested that he was not an outstanding runner by comparison with contemporary champions in more prominent racing nations. But if his class was suspect, his consistency and durability made him a worthy record holder.

Most races won in a British career

The record for races won in a career by a British-bred horse is 79, achieved by the mare Catherina between 1832 and 1841. She ran only once against top-class opposition, when unplaced as third favourite for the 1833 Oaks, but thereafter proved markedly successful in lesser company all over the North of England, the Midlands and Wales. In all she contested 176 races, but her record is all the more impressive for the fact that many of those events were run in heats. She actually faced the starter 298 times and came home first on 136 occasions, including two dead-heats, two heats in which she was disqualified from first place, and one walk-over. As a 9-year-old she ran six 2-mile heats in the course of an afternoon at Welshpool, finishing fresh enough to come back and win another race in three 1½-mile heats on the following day.

Catherina, foaled in 1830, was a daughter of 1815 Derby winner Whisker out of a mare called Alecto who was herself tough enough to win three races in an afternoon at Heaton Park as a pregnant 7-year-old.

Confounding the theory that hard-trained mares retain no vitality for their stud careers, Catherina became the dam of two above-average runners in Sweetheart, winner of the 1849 July Stakes at Newmarket, and Phaeton, who won both the 1853 Criterion Stakes at Newmarket and the 1854 Ascot Derby. The mare was destroyed at the age of 28 in 1858.

Most races won in a season

The world record for races won in a single season is 30, registered in 1931 by the Puerto Rican-bred three-year-old Galgo Jr, also holder of the record for most races won in a career. Galgo Jr, whose other seasonal tallies included 25 wins as a 7-year-old and 21 at two, also boasted a winning streak of 39 races, between July 1930 and July 1931.

Most races won in a British season

The record for races won in a British season is 23, attained by the 3-year-old colt Fisherman in 1856.

Trained by his owner, Tom Parr, Fisherman was the unfashionably-bred son of Heron and Mainbrace. He started 34 times between 12 February and 30 October, also notching five second places and three thirds. Many of his races were uncompetitive in terms of numbers of rivals — he walked over three times and had only one or two opponents on eight other occasions — but he did prove victorious over a wide range of distances, from ½-mile to 3 miles, and among his victims were the winners of that season's Derby, Oaks and St Leger.

The nearest approach to Fisherman's 1856 record was the same horse's tally of 22 wins in 1857. He won the Ascot Gold Cups of 1858 and 1859, his score in the former year being 21 wins. In all he won 69 of 119 starts.

The 5-year-old mare Lilian won 21 races in 1874, and in 1844 the 6-year-old mare Alice Hawthorn had 20 outright wins plus a dead-heat.

The record number of wins by a British 2-year-old is 16, set by The Bard (including one walk-over) in 1885 and equalled by Provideo in 1984.

Most wins in one race

The only horse to win the same race 7 consecutive times is Doctor Syntax (foaled 1811), who won the Preston Gold Cup from 1815 to 1821 inclusive. Run over distances between 3 and 4 miles, the race never had more than 4 runners during that period but Doctor Syntax beat some top-class horses in it, notably St Leger winners Filho da Puta, The Duchess and Reveller. In 1822 he attempted an eighth victory at the Lancashire course but the previous year's runner-up, Reveller, reversed the placings with him. Doctor Syntax had a career total of 35 wins and went on to sire champion racemare Beeswing, who was prevented only by one second place (in 1840) from winning the Gold Cup at Newcastle every year from 1836 to 1842. At the age of 9, in 1842, she also won the Ascot Gold Cup.

The only other horse to win the same race 7 times was Franc Picard, the most famous French steeplechaser of the 19th century. He won the Grand Steeple-Chase at Dieppe from 1853 to 1857 inclusive and also in 1859 and 1861; he did not contest the race in 1858 and was beaten in 1860.

The 20th-century record is held by Brown Jack, who won at Royal Ascot every year from 1928 to 1934; on the last 6 occasions he won the Queen Alexandra Stakes (Alexandra Stakes before 1931) over 2¾ miles 85 yards.

The only horses to win the same championship race 5 times are Golden Miller and Kelso. Golden Miller monopolised the Cheltenham Gold Cup from 1932 to 1936, and though the race had not attained its present status, he was certainly the best steeplechaser of his time in England. Kelso was America's Horse of the Year from 1960 to 1964 and each time he clinched the title with victory in the Jockey Club Gold Cup. At the time the race was the most important weight-for-age prize in the country.

Most stake and Pattern wins

The most stake races won in North America is 34 by Exterminator. This remarkable gelding landed the Kentucky Derby in 1918 but did not reach his peak until the age of 7, becoming one of America's greatest and most popular champions. 'Old Bones' usually carried heavy weights in handicaps, but he was almost unbeatable over long distances and won America's premier prize for stayers, the Saratoga Cup, 4 times (1919–22). He was also successful 3 times in the Pimlico Cup (1919–21) and Toronto Autumn Cup (1920–22) and his other triumphs included the Latonia Cup and Brooklyn Handicap. He won exactly half his career total of 100 starts over 8 seasons.

Exterminator's record of 34 stakes is one more than the number achieved by Kingston. The latter won more races than any other horse in American history, with a total of 89 wins from 138 starts in a career of 9 seasons from 1886 to 1894.

The most Pattern races won in Europe is 12 by Brigadier Gerard, who was a 3-year-old when the Pattern-race system was introduced in 1971. This brilliant English miler lost just one of his 18 career starts and gained Group I triumphs in the 2000 Guineas, Sussex Stakes and Champion Stakes in 1971 and the Eclipse Stakes, King George VI and Queen Elizabeth Stakes and Champion Stakes in 1972. He achieved Group II success in the St James's Palace and Queen Elizabeth II Stakes in 1971 and the Lockinge, Prince of Wales's and Queen Elizabeth II Stakes in 1972, when he also won the Group III Westbury Stakes.

Most active careers

The lack of comprehensive information on racing in most parts of the world makes it impossible to determine which horse has run most times in a career or in one season, though America in the late 19th and early 20th centuries boasted some of the busiest campaigners. For instance, the geldings George de Mar (foaled 1922) raced 333 times for 60 wins and Seth's Hope (foaled 1924) 327 times for 62 wins. In 1890 John Jay S. started in 76 races, gaining 4 victories, at a time when some tracks raced all year round. Another American horse, Blitzen, had 18 races in 37 days in 1893; he won 10 of them, came second 6 times and third once, and was only once unplaced. Imp ran 50 times as a 3-year-old in 1897, winning 14, and blossomed in her next 3 seasons to become one of America's greatest racemares. Donau won 15 of his 41 races as a juvenile before triumphing in the Kentucky Derby of 1910.

Most Successful Horses: Money Earned

World record earnings: career

Earnings are a poor guide to a horse's merit, especially in an era of million-dollar prizes, but John Henry is a worthy holder of the world record for the amount of prize money earned in a career. At the age of 9 he was voted America's Horse of the Year for the second time in 1984 and at the end of that season his total stood at $6,591,860 — nearly double the amount won by the next horse, Slew o' Gold.

John Henry, foaled in 1975, is the latest in a long line of champion American geldings. He was sold for $1,100 as a yearling and his present owner, bicycle importer Sam Rubin, bought him for $25,000 as a 3-year-old. He blossomed late in life and took his first Horse of the Year title in 1981 after beating Spectacular Bid's existing career earnings record. His victories include the Arlington Million and Santa Anita Handicap twice each and the Jockey Club Gold Cup, but his richest win came in the Ballantine's Scotch Classic at The Meadowlands, New Jersey on his last start of 1984; he received $740,000 including a bonus for having already won the Turf Classic at Belmont Park. John Henry, trained by Ron McAnally, is renowned for his tenacity and durability rather than for displays of brilliance. He has won top-class races on dirt but is more at home on grass, having been voted America's champion male performer on that surface in 1980, 1981, 1983 and 1984. His earnings each year have been (in dollars):

1977 — 49,380;   1978 — 120,319;   1979 — 129,864;
1980 — 925,217; 1981 — 1,798,030; 1982 — 580,300;
    1983 — 652,100;   1984 — 2,336,650.

The first horse to pass $1 million in earnings was 6-year-old Citation when winning the Hollywood Gold Cup at Hollywood Park, California on 14 July 1951. Despite injury problems the American Triple Crown hero was kept in training solely in order to achieve this target, which had been the ambition of his late owner Warren Wright. Having succeeded, Citation was promptly retired to stud.

World record earnings: season

The record amount of prize money earned in one season is $2,627,944 by 4-year-old Slew o' Gold in America in 1984. He won his first 5 starts of that campaign, notably the Woodward Stakes, Marlboro Cup and Jockey Club Gold Cup at Belmont Park, and in the third of those races he collected a $1-million bonus for having won the other two. After claiming second prize in the inaugural Breeders' Cup Classic he was retired with career earnings of $3,533,534, which place him second only to John Henry in that category.

Below are lists of horses who have held a world or British record for the amount of money earned in a career. In all cases the earnings include place money, and official exchange rates have been used where appropriate. The date on the left is the year in which each horse broke the record but the other figures reflect complete racing careers.

Progressive list of world financial champions

Since Zev surpassed the earnings of English champion Isinglass in 1923, all holders of the world earnings record have been trained in North America.

		Ran	Won	2nd	3rd	$
1923	Zev (1920)	43	23	8	5	313,639
1930	Gallant Fox (1927)	17	11	3	2	328,165
1931	Sun Beau (1925)	74	33	12	10	376,744
1940	Seabiscuit (1933)	89	33	15	13	437,730
1942	Whirlaway (1938)	60	32	15	9	561,161
1947	Assault (1943)	42	18	6	7	675,470
	Armed (1941)	81	41	20	10	817,475
	Stymie (1941)	131	35	33	28	918,485
1950	Citation (1945)	45	32	10	2	1,085,760
1956	Nashua (1952)	30	22	4	1	1,288,565
1958	Round Table (1954)	66	43	8	5	1,749,869
1964	Kelso (1957)	63	39	12	2	1,977,896
1979	Affirmed (1975)	29	22	5	1	2,393,818
1980	Spectacular Bid (1976)	30	26	2	1	2,781,607
1981	*John Henry (1975)	83	39	15	9	6,591,860

*in training in 1985

Female world financial champions

Since 2-year-old Top Flight surpassed the earnings of English champion Sceptre in 1931, all holders of the world earnings record for fillies and mares have raced in North America, though Trinycarol earned all her prize money in her native Venezuela and All Along was trained in France throughout her career.

		Ran	Won	2nd	3rd	$
1931	Top Flight (1929)	16	12	–	–	275,900
1945	Busher (1942)	21	15	3	1	334,035
1947	Gallorette (1942)	72	21	20	13	445,535
1951	Bewitch (1945)	55	20	10	11	462,605
1962	Cicada (1959)	42	23	8	6	783,675
1971	Shuvee (1966)	44	16	10	6	890,445
1974	Dahlia (1970)	48	15	4	6	1,535,443
1982	Trinycarol (1979)	29	18	3	1	2,647,141
1984	All Along (1979)	21	9	4	2	3,018,420

English and Irish financial champions

The following have held the record for the most money earned in a career by a horse trained in the British Isles. Donovan and Isinglass also held the world record.

		Ran	Won	2nd	3rd	£
1889	Donovan (1886)	21	18	2	1	55,443
1895	Isinglass (1890)	12	11	1	–	58,655
1952	Tulyar (1949)	13	9	1	1	76,577
1958	Ballymoss (1954)	17	8	5	1	114,150
1963	Ragusa (1960)	12	7	1	2	148,955
1964	Santa Claus (1961)	7	4	2	–	153,646
1967	Ribocco (1964)	14	5	3	3	155,669
1968	Royal Palace (1964)	11	9	–	1	166,063
1968	Sir Ivor (1965)	13	8	3	1	227,100
1970	Nijinsky (1967)	13	11	2	–	282,223
1972	Mill Reef (1968)	14	12	2	–	314,212
1975	Grundy (1972)	11	8	2	–	326,421
1977	The Minstrel (1974)	9	7	1	1	333,197
1978	Alleged (1974)	10	9	1	–	336,784
1979	Troy (1976)	11	8	2	1	450,428
1982	Glint of Gold (1978)	17	10	6	1	472,760
1984	Time Charter (1979)	20	9	4	1	526,910

Female English and Irish financial champions

The following have held the record for the most money earned by a filly or mare trained in the British Isles. La Flèche and Sceptre also held the world record.

		Ran	Won	2nd	3rd	£
1892	La Flèche (1889)	24	16	3	2	35,003
1903	Sceptre (1899)	25	13	5	3	39,583
1955	Meld (1952)	6	5	1	–	43,162
1959	Petite Etoile (1956)	19	14	5	–	72,624
1969	Park Top (1964)	24	13	6	2	137,414
1978	Dunfermline (1974)	12	3	3	3	138,830
1978	Fair Salinia (1975)	8	4	2	–	139,354
1980	Mrs Penny (1977)	16	5	4	2	281,379
1983	Time Charter (1979)	20	9	4	1	526,910

English and Irish financial champions: geldings on the Flat

		Ran	Won	2nd	3rd	£
1899	Democrat (1897)	17	8	3	–	14,037
1901	Epsom Lad (1897)	8	3	1	–	19,712

1933	Brown Jack (1924)	55	18	8	4	23,526
1959	Morecambe (1953)	33	11	8	6	25,584
1965	Grey of Falloden (1959)	55	13	12	12	31,119
1970	Morris Dancer (1961)	90	25	14	12	38,198
1973	Petty Officer (1967)	44	12	10	3	56,330
1976	Boldboy (1970)	45	14	10	10	131,073
1984	Bedtime (1980)	12	10	1	–	182,221

English and Irish financial champions: jumpers

(The following figures do not include Flat or National Hunt Flat races.)

		Ran	Won	2nd	3rd	£
1950	Freebooter (1941)	61	18	15	7	24,725
1961	Nicolaus Silver (1952)	55	9	9	6	28,973
1962	Mandarin (1951)	52	19	13	5	51,496
1965	Arkle (1957)	32	26	2	2	78,464
1975	Comedy of Errors (1967)	49	23	12	4	111,633
1977	Red Rum (1965)	100	24	14	21	145,234
1981	Night Nurse (1971)	64	32	14	7	181,770
1983	Silver Buck (1972)	48	34	2	3	196,053

Triple Crown Winners

English Triple Crown Champions

For more than a century it has been generally acknowledged that the highest status attainable by a Thoroughbred on the British Turf is that of Triple Crown winner. Few horses are capable of excelling over a variety of courses and distances, and only a truly exceptional athlete possesses all the necessary gifts to achieve dominance over his or her contemporaries over Newmarket's straight mile in the first week in May, around Epsom's switchback mile and a half a month later, and again over the flat, extended mile and three-quarters of the galloping Doncaster course in September.

Only 15 colts have managed to win all three of the Classics open to them, and three of those (Pommern, Gay Crusader and Gainsborough) were not required to display the degree of adaptability shown by the others, recording their trebles in wartime substitute events at Newmarket. There have been eight winners of the Fillies' Triple Crown, including one, Sun Chariot, whose victories were all achieved at Newmarket. As racing becomes ever more competitive and as breeding seems to be increasingly geared to the production of specialists, rather than all-round performers, it is possible that the following list may never be extended.

West Australian, a bay colt bred and raced by John Bowes, became the first horse to collect the 2000 Guineas, the Derby and the St Leger in 1853. Trained at Malton by John Scott, he suffered one surprising reverse at two, but was otherwise unbeaten, his 4-year-old campaign including a victory in the Ascot Gold Cup. He stood at stud in both England and France, but his achievements as a stallion did not match his exceptional merit as a runner.

Gladiateur earned the nickname 'Avenger of Waterloo' when he became the first French-bred winner of the Derby in 1865. He had been a narrow winner of the 2000 Guineas, but his Epsom and Doncaster triumphs were achieved with complete authority, and, unique among Triple Crown winners, he also had victories to his credit in the Grand Prix de Paris and the Ascot Gold Cup. Though bred in France by his owner, Comte Frédéric de Lagrange, he raced from the Newmarket stable of Tom Jennings. His stud career proved extremely disappointing.

Lord Lyon, bred by Mark Pearson and leased for racing purposes to Richard Sutton, had the Triple Crown of 1866 among his 17 career victories. His reputation was never particularly exalted, largely because the rest of his generation appeared to be moderate and in both the Derby and St Leger he could only scrape home by a head. Trained at East Ilsley by James Dover (who always rated the colt in lower esteem than his younger sister, Achievement), he went on to sire two top-class

Unbeaten Triple Crown hero Ormonde with Fred Archer in the saddle – perhaps the greatest racehorse and the greatest jockey ever seen on the English Turf.

runners in Placida (Oaks) and Minting (Grand Prix de Paris), but his overall record at stud was not impressive.

Formosa, who became the first winner of the Fillies' Triple Crown in 1868, set a notable record by racing unbeaten in four Classics. She shared the 2000 Guineas in a desperate finish with Moslem, but took the other three—she did not run in the Derby—by clear-cut margins, including the Oaks by 10 lengths. Bred by James Cookson, she was sold as a yearling for only 700 gns and was trained at Beckhampton by Henry Woolcott. She died at the age of 15 in France, having failed to distinguish herself as a broodmare.

Hannah, bred and raced by Baron Meyer de Rothschild and trained at Newmarket by Joe Hayhoe, was the dominant three-year-old filly of 1871. She scored by three lengths in both the 1000 Guineas and the Oaks, and in the St Leger she had a length to spare over Albert Victor, one of the dead-heaters for second place in the Derby. She

was a stable companion of the Derby winner, Favonius, and many compared her favourably with the colt. Sadly her form tailed off badly at four and she died as a 7-year-old after slipping twins.

Apology, winner of the 1874 Fillies' Triple Crown, was bred and raced by a clergyman, the Rev. John King, who raced under the *nom de course* of 'Mr Launde' in a vain attempt to avoid the censure of his Bishop. The filly may have been a little lucky in that her generation was not conspicuously rich in talent, but she went on to win the Ascot Gold Cup as a 5-year-old, by which time she was the property of King's widow, his former kitchen maid whom he had married when he was 74 and she was 22. Apology left William Osborne's Middleham stable for stud at the end of 1876 and in due course became the dam of winners of the Gimcrack and Craven Stakes.

Ormonde was the first Triple Crown winner to be hailed as such at the time of his success in 1886, the term having gained currency some time after Lord Lyon's feat of 20 years before. Unquestionably one of the true giants of racing history, he was trained at Kingsclere by John Porter for his owner-breeder, the 1st Duke of Westminster, and he raced unbeaten through three campaigns. Unfortunately, he developed a wind infirmity as a three-year-old, and in his second stud season he contracted a severe illness which left him sub-fertile. He served as a stallion in England, Argentina and the USA, his few foals including the dual Eclipse Stakes winner Orme at home and the Futurity winner Ormondale in the States.

Common, winner of the 1891 Triple Crown, was said to have been aptly named in view of his looks, but he was something out of the ordinary as a runner, as he indicated when he won the 2000 Guineas in a canter on his racecourse début. But he was to prove the most lightly-campaigned of all Triple Crown winners, his only other races producing a bloodless victory over a solitary rival in the St James's Palace Stakes and a third place in the Eclipse Stakes behind Surefoot, the previous season's vanquished Derby favourite. Partners Lord Alington and Sir Frederick Johnstone, who bred and raced Common, sold him for £15,000 after his hard-fought neck victory in the St Leger and he left John Porter's stable for an unexciting term at stud.

La Flèche, a record-priced yearling at 5,500 gns, proved a tremendous bargain for Baron Maurice de Hirsch. Bought out of the Hampton Court Stud (and thus officially bred by Queen Victoria), she was undefeated in four starts as a 2-year-old and at three collected eight out of nine, her sole loss coming in the Derby, when she was the victim of an incompetent ride and finished second to Sir Hugo. She settled matters with Sir Hugo decisively in the St Leger in the most conclusive of her Classic triumphs, then proceeded to win the Cambridge-shire under 8 st 10 lb. At the end of her 3-year-old campaign La Flèche moved from John Porter's stable to that of Richard Marsh at Newmarket. She was never quite so dominant again, but she did win the Ascot Gold Cup and the Champion Stakes at five, when carrying her first foal. Her best son was John o' Gaunt, who ran second in the Derby and became the sire of the outstanding Swynford.

Isinglass, bred and raced by sometime Member of Parliament for Newmarket, Harry McCalmont, was more than just the leader of his generation by a wide margin. Having won his Triple Crown in 1893, he proved himself decidedly superior to the following season's 2000 Guineas and Derby victor, Ladas, and at five he ran away with the Ascot Gold Cup. He suffered only one defeat in four seasons, when narrowly failing to give away 10 lb to Derby third Raeburn at Manchester, and when he quit Jimmy Jewitt's Newmarket stable for a successful stud career, he took with him an earnings record unsurpassed in England for 57 years.

Galtee More, who was trained by Sam Darling at Beckhampton, carried the colours of Co Limerick owner-breeder John Gubbins. He compiled a two-season record of 11 wins from 13 starts, failing only when dead-heating for second with Glencally, a short head behind Brigg, in a valuable juvenile contest at Liverpool, and on his final appearance at three, when 'anchored' by 9 st 6 lb in the Cambridgeshire. He consistently overwhelmed Velasquez, himself a thoroughly top-class horse, hinting that he might well have been one of the very best Triple Crown winners. The shame is that apart from Velasquez, there was nothing capable of testing him at anything like level terms. He was sold to Russia at the end of his Classic season (1897) and later moved to Germany; he did well as a sire in both countries.

Flying Fox, who represented the same owner-breeder and trainer as Ormonde and was a grandson of that champion, did not always get his act together as a two-year-old. But all the promises were delivered in 1899, when he proved himself easily the best of his generation. The only moment of doubt came in the straight at Epsom, when Holocauste seemed to be going every bit as well as Flying Fox, but the French-trained challenger then broke a fetlock, leaving the favourite to win at his leisure. On the death of the 1st Duke of Westminster in 1900, Flying Fox was submitted to auction at Kingsclere, where he fetched the unprecedented sum of 37,500 gns. The price seemed outlandish, but the buyer, French breeder Edmond Blanc, eventually profited handsomely from the deal. Flying Fox became an important sire in Blanc's Haras de Jardy, while his sale price remained a British auction record for a horse in training until Vaguely Noble changed hands for 136,000 gns 67 years later.

Diamond Jubilee was, by general consent, nothing like so good a racehorse as his elder brother Persimmon. But whereas Persimmon was slow to come to hand at three, missing the 2000 Guineas (in which, in any case, he might not have beaten St Frusquin), Diamond Jubilee was able to go one better and take the 1900 Triple Crown. Diamond Jubilee had no adversary of St Frusquin's merit to contend with, the chief threat to his Classic campaign coming from his own temperament. The problem was solved by the allocation of race-riding duties to Herbert Jones, his regular work jockey. The partnership flourished to the extent of victories in the Triple Crown, the Newmarket Stakes and the Eclipse Stakes, but after the St Leger his form deteriorated and he did not win again. Diamond Jubilee, bred and owned by the Prince of Wales, was trained by Richard Marsh at Newmarket. He subsequently headed the sires' list in Argentina on four occasions.

Sceptre holds the distinction of being the only outright winner of four Classic races, a feat she achieved in 1902. Like Flying Fox, she was a product of the 1st Duke of Westminster's Eaton Stud and she came up for sale at Newmarket as a result of the Duke's death. Her price, 10,000 gns, constituted a record for an auction yearling, but it proved a good deal less than her value. Her buyer was Bob Sievier, a notoriously heavy gambler, who turned her over to Wantage trainer Charles Morton. She showed abundant promise in her first season, winning the Woodcote and July Stakes, but the accomplished Morton then departed to become private trainer to Jack Joel, and Sievier decided that he would train the filly himself. With an amateur trainer and, for several races, a jockey who had only just turned professional, the filly was patently grossly misused. But she overcame the treatment famously, bouncing back from a narrow defeat in the Lincolnshire Handicap to contest all five Classics. She won the 2000 Guineas in record time, readily added the 1000, finished fourth as even-money favourite for the Derby, then proved easily best in both the Oaks and the St Leger. Sceptre was restored to professional hands after her first start at four, when Sievier sold her to William Bass and she joined Alec Taylor's Manton string. In due course she came into her own with a crushing defeat of the year-younger Triple Crown victor Rock Sand in the Jockey Club Stakes, and she added the Champion Stakes by 10 lengths. Sceptre was evidently 'over the top' at five, when she failed to win in three efforts, but she subsequently became a successful broodmare, each of her first two foals winning a Cheveley Park Stakes.

Rock Sand, who raced for owner-breeder Sir James Miller, was trained at Newmarket by George Blackwell. As a 2-year-old he suffered one surprising defeat in the Middle Park Stakes, but overall his form suggested that he was the best of his crop and a worthy favourite for the 1903 Classics. So it proved. Nothing emerged as a serious challenger to him for the Triple Crown, which he collected with the minimum of fuss. But he was possibly lucky to have avoided competition from Zinfandel, whose Classic entries had been rendered void by the death of his owner. Zinfandel might have proved his match at three; he was more than Rock Sand's match at four in the Coronation Cup. There was also abundant evidence to indicate that Rock Sand's best form was inferior to that of Sceptre and Ard Patrick, leaders of the previous generation. Rock Sand stood in England, the USA and France during a brief stud career which ended with his death at the age of 14. He did quite well as a sire, his best son being Tracery, while one of his daughters produced Man o' War.

Pretty Polly, who raced for owner-breeder Eustace Loder and was trained by Peter Gilpin at Newmarket, burst on the scene with an amazing début display at Sandown Park in 1903. She raced clear of her rivals almost throughout and finished so far in front that many observers imagined there must have been a false start. She became a public idol almost from that moment on, and success piled upon success. Her juvenile performances included easy victories in the Champagne, Cheveley Park and Middle Park Stakes, and at three she collected the 1000 Guineas, Oaks and St Leger, all by emphatic three-length margins. After 15 consecutive wins she carried an air of invincibility, but her triumphant sequence was ended in sensational style when Presto beat her in the Prix du Conseil Municipal at Longchamp. The result did not truly reflect her merit, and she proceeded to provide ample evidence that she had not permanently lost her form. In the following year she won the Coronation Cup in devastating fashion, establishing a course record (2:33.8) for the Epsom mile and a half which has been matched only once — by Mahmoud in the 1936 Derby — and never surpassed in 80 years. Pretty Polly retired after being beaten by Bachelor's Button in the 1906 Ascot Gold Cup — only her second defeat in 24 races. At stud she produced two talented daughters in Molly Desmond (Cheveley Park Stakes) and Polly Flinders (National Breeders' Produce Stakes).

Pommern, first of the 'substitute Triple Crown' winners, was bred and raced by Solly Joel, who bought the dam when she was carrying him for only 500 gns. He was a good, rather than outstanding 2-year-old, but at three proved easily best of a generation which seemed otherwise rather undistinguished. Trained at Newmarket by Charley Peck, he failed to give 15 lb to Rossendale in the Craven Stakes, but thereafter he was unbeaten, his victories in the 2000 Guineas, New Derby and September Stakes all achieved by clear margins. He proved a disappointing sire.

Gay Crusader, bred and raced by Alfred Cox and trained at Manton by Alec Taylor, developed into a formidable 3-year-old in 1917. After failing honourably to give 11 lb to Coq d'Or in the Column Produce Stakes in the spring, he proved invincible, picking up all the substitute Classics open to him, in addition to Newmarket's version of the Gold Cup and the Champion Stakes. He was injured before he could start at four and retired to a stud career which did not come up to expectations.

Gainsborough failed to reach a 2,000 gns reserve when offered for sale as a yearling, so his breeder, Lady James Douglas, opted to put him in training with Alec Taylor. He turned out to be a colt of similar merit to Gay Crusader, and he emulated his year-older stable companion with successes in the substitute Triple Crown and Gold Cup. But he did not dominate his generation to any great extent and lost by a length when asked to concede 3 lb to Prince Chimay in the Jockey Club Stakes. He became champion sire on two occasions, with Solario and Hyperion his most celebrated sons.

Bahram became only the second Triple Crown winner (after Ormonde) to retire undefeated. He was the undisputed champion of his generation at two and three years, and there was general disappointment when his owner-breeder, Aga Khan III, decided to retire him after he had completed his sweep of the Triple Crown events. He looked better than ever when he took the 1935 St Leger (only his ninth start) by five lengths, and his Newmarket trainer Frank Butters would dearly have loved to keep him for a third season. Instead, Bahram went to stud, where he was to sire such as Big Game and Persian Gulf before his controversial sale to America for £40,000. He was not a success in the States and later moved on to Argentina, where his record was equally disappointing.

Sun Chariot, bred at the National Stud and leased for racing purposes to King George VI, was a popular heroine of the Turf during World War II. But for one temperamental lapse in a minor event at Salisbury, she would never have been beaten, and she proved herself manifestly superior to the colts of her generation at both two and three. In 1942 she won the New 1000 Guineas by four lengths, the New Oaks by a length (after losing a lot of ground at the start and again at the turn), and the New St Leger emphatically by three lengths over Watling Street, the New Derby winner. Her career comprised only nine races, but Beckhampton trainer Fred Darling was not totally sorry to see her leave on account of the frequently mulish behaviour, which made her a problem to handle. Her first foal was the highly-gifted, but unsound, unbeaten colt Blue Train, and she produced other good winners in Gigantic, Landau, Persian Wheel and Pindari.

Meld, bred by her owner, Lady Zia Wernher, at the Someries Stud, was trained at Newmarket by Cecil (later Sir Cecil) Boyd-Rochfort. Her career was anything but exacting, as it consisted of only six races, but she won both fillies-only Classics in decisive fashion, then overcame the colts in the St Leger while sickening for the cough. She was never required to tackle the kind of formidable male opposition which such as Sceptre, Pretty Polly and Sun Chariot had to encounter, but she was unquestionably a high-class performer. Her only defeat came on her début, when she started as an unfancied outsider and went under by a length to a stable companion. Her stud career was patchy, but in 1966, 11 years after her own Classic campaign, she became the dam of Derby winner Charlottown. She survived to the grand old age of 31.

Nijinsky became the first Triple Crown-winning colt to have been purchased at auction. Bred in Canada by Eddie Taylor, he was acquired for $84,000 by Charles Engelhard, who put him into training with Vincent O'Brien. Comfortably best of the 1969 two-year-olds in England and Ireland, he proceeded to stride majestically through a second campaign which had many referring to him as 'the horse of the century'. His Triple Crown

Continued on page 120

Nijinsky becomes the first winner of the colts' Triple Crown in Britain for 35 years as he beats Meadowville and Politico in the 1970 St Leger. At the time he was unbeaten, but this was to be the last of his 11 victories.

PHAR LAP

When talk among racing people turns to the identity of the greatest horses of all time, the only Australasian champions to merit serious consideration are Carbine and Phar Lap. Of all the outstanding geldings in racing history none ranks higher than Phar Lap, who achieved unprecedented status as a national hero in Australia before being sent to America and dying in mysterious circumstances.

Phar Lap was bred by Alick Roberts and was foaled on 26 October 1926 at Seadown Stud, near Timaru on New Zealand's South Island. His sire Night Raid (a descendant of Carbine) failed to win at all in England and did not fare much better when exported to Australia, while his dam Entreaty was unplaced on her only start.

The rich chesnut colt had little to commend him on pedigree or looks when offered at Trentham Yearling Sales in January 1928 but Harry Telford, a minor trainer in Sydney, persuaded American David Davis to buy him and the purchase was duly made for 160 guineas. When the big, ungainly youngster arrived in Australia Davis was reluctant to pay to have him in training so Telford took a 3-year lease on him.

Phar Lap, named after the Thai word for lightning, was gelded and took plenty of time to mature. In fact he lost nine of his first ten races, being unplaced in eight of them, but once he found his form he soon asserted his supremacy. As a 3-year-old in 1929–30 he won the premier classics in both Sydney and Melbourne, the AJC and Victoria Derbys, but could finish only third in Australia's greatest race, the two-mile Melbourne Cup. However, he swept unbeaten through his last nine starts of that campaign including the VRC and AJC St Legers. The pattern of his career had been set: classics, handicaps and weight-for-age races all came alike to him and he displayed a remarkable blend of speed and stamina, often crushing top-class opposition in effortless style by a wide margin.

As a 4-year-old in 1930–31, Phar Lap set the seal on his greatness, finishing a close second on his first and last outings of the season but in between running up a sequence of 14 wins including the Melbourne Cup. This, the most celebrated victory of his career, was preceded by an attempt by gunmen, presumably in the pay of underworld bookmakers, to shoot him on his way back to his stable from morning exercise. The shots missed their target and Phar Lap, an exceptionally placid individual, won the Melbourne Stakes that very afternoon. Three days later, on 4 November 1930, came the Cup itself; the champion, despite being handicapped at 9 st 12 lb and conceding at least a stone all round, started at odds-on and turned the race into a procession, winning by three lengths with regular jockey Jim Pike sitting motionless.

His other victories that season included Australia's premier weight-for-age prize, the W. S. Cox Plate at Moonee Valley, and the Futurity Stakes against top sprinters. Among those left toiling in his wake at various times were Amounis and Nightmarch, both of whom were outstanding champions by any standard except his own. Trainer Telford's lease ended in February 1931 but Davis allowed him to buy a half-share in the champion very cheaply.

Phar Lap remained almost invincible in late 1931, winning his first eight races as a 5-year-old including the Spring Stakes, Randwick Plate, W. S. Cox Plate and Melbourne Stakes for the second time and the Craven Plate for the third time. However, he was jaded when the Melbourne Cup came round again and in any case had the impossible burden of 10 st 10 lb, 5 lb more than Carbine's record for the race.

In finishing eighth, conceding 54 lb to the

winner, Phar Lap ran his last race in Australia, for David Davis had already decided to send him to North America for the ten-furlong Agua Caliente Handicap, billed as the richest race in the world. He travelled by ship to California via his native New Zealand, where he had never raced, and arrived in January 1932 in the charge of Tommy Woodcock, the young man who had been his constant attendant throughout his career and was now promoted to trainer.

Betting had been outlawed in California and the race was run at Caliente, just over the border in Mexico, on 20 March. The prize money had been halved, so Phar Lap could not become the world's leading earner as planned, and he had to overcome a hoof injury, but by winning decisively in record time he did enough to persuade some hard-headed judges that he was the greatest Thoroughbred ever to race in North America.

Immediately afterwards the champion was moved to Menlo Park, near San Francisco, where he fell ill on the morning of 5 April

Phar Lap in action with regular partner Jim Pike in the saddle.

1932. His stomach became distended and he died in agony soon after midday, leaving a mystery that has never been explained satisfactorily.

The news was regarded as a national disaster in Australia and there were wild rumours of deliberate poisoning. The generally-accepted explanation was that he had eaten grass accidentally contaminated by arsenic from an insecticide, though another theory blamed swelling of the abdomen caused by eating damp lucerne. The medical evidence was inconclusive and the true cause of his tragic death will never be known for sure.

Phar Lap won 37 of his 51 races over four seasons, including 32 of his last 35; he was campaigned rigorously and it is likely that at his death his best years were already behind him. For toughness, durability and soundness as well as sheer brilliance, few champions of any country or any era can be considered his equal. His mounted hide is on display in the National Museum in Melbourne and still attracts more visitors than any other exhibit, while his skeleton stands in the National Museum, Wellington.

victories were all emphatically achieved, and he took in the Irish Derby and Ascot's King George VI and Queen Elizabeth Stakes (beating the previous year's Derby winner Blakeney with scarcely an effort) along the way. He came to the Prix de l'Arc de Triomphe still unbeaten in 11 races, but Sassafras deprived him of that prize by a head, and on his only subsequent outing Nijinsky turned in a dull effort to finish second to Lorenzaccio in the Champion Stakes. Sent to stud in Kentucky, he swiftly established himself among the world's leading sires, one of his sons being the unbeaten Derby winner Golden Fleece.

US Triple Crown Champions

For many years the nearest American equivalents to the English Triple Crown races were a trio of events at New York's Belmont Park — the Withers Stakes (founded 1874) over a mile in May, the Belmont Stakes (1867) at 1 mile 3 furlongs in June, and the Lawrence Realization Stakes (1889) over 1 mile 5 furlongs in September. This treble was achieved twice, by the celebrated Man o' War in 1920 and three years later by Zev, best-known for his match-race victory over England's Derby winner Papyrus.

However, Americans rightly did not consider themselves bound by English convention, and when the term 'Triple Crown' gained currency in the 1930s, after an article by Turf writer Charles Hatton, the races denoted were the Kentucky Derby, the Preakness Stakes and the Belmont Stakes. They were (and still are) the most important races contested by 3-year-olds in Kentucky, Maryland and New York respectively, but they have little in common with their English counterparts, being closer together both in distance and in the calendar and thus a series which is easier to win. To date there have been 11 US Triple Crown champions.

Sir Barton, first to complete the treble, came into the 1919 Kentucky Derby a maiden after six efforts, there merely to set the pace for his owner's proven performer Billy Kelly. As it happened, Billy Kelly could never get in a blow against Sir Barton, who won by five lengths. Four days later he collected by Preakness by four lengths and within a month he completed his Classic set, establishing a new American record for 11 furlongs as he stormed clear of his only two Belmont rivals. Having won the Kentucky Derby claiming a maiden allowance (though putting up 2½ lb overweight), Sir Barton had rapidly become a champion for trainer Guy Bedwell and owner John Ross. In 1920 he was trounced by Man o' War in a famous match race in Canada, but he accumulated career earnings of $116,857, having won 13 of 31 starts, before becoming a stallion of no repute.

Gallant Fox, bred and raced by William Woodward of Belair Stud and trained by 'Sunny Jim' Fitzsimmons, was nothing special as a 2-year-old, but from the moment he went into training his preparation was geared to fulfilment of his potential at three. He proved unquestionably the best horse around in 1930, when he won nine of ten starts, including the Preakness by three-quarters of a length, the Kentucky Derby by two and the Belmont Stakes by three. His other victories included the Wood Memorial, the Dwyer Stakes and the Jockey Club Gold Cup, and his sole defeat (in the Travers Stakes at Saratoga) is still regarded as one of the shock results of the century. He went to stud at four, having won 11 of his 17 races and earned $328,165, and from his first crop of foals the second Triple Crown winner sired the third to gain that distinction.

Omaha, who represented the same owner-breeder and trainer as Gallant Fox, won only one of his nine races at two in 1934, and only when second in the Sanford Stakes at Saratoga gave a hint of what was to come. Omaha's Triple Crown was remarkable in that after winning the Kentucky Derby handily by a length and a half and the Preakness a week later by six lengths, he got beaten by Rosemont in the Withers Stakes *en route* to the Belmont Stakes. But all came right on the big day, when he left Rosemont toiling in third place, almost 10 lengths in arrears. By the end of July he had added triumphs in the Dwyer Handicap and the Arlington Classic, and he was expected to advance his reputation still further at Saratoga. But when he got there he fell lame, and he never raced in America again. However, when he was restored to fitness, Omaha was sent to England, where Cecil Boyd-Rochfort took charge of him. He won both his prep races for the Ascot Gold Cup, but lost a thrilling battle with Quashed for the Cup itself and afterwards went under narrowly to Taj Akbar in the Princess of Wales's Stakes at Newmarket. Omaha won nine of his 22 career starts and earned $154,755. He was not a success at stud.

War Admiral, the Triple Crown hero of 1937, was remarkable for courage as well as class. Trained by George Conway for owner-breeder Sam Riddle (who had also raced his sire Man o' War), he swept unbeaten through his 3-year-old campaign, notching eight successes. At Churchill Downs he scored comfortably by nearly two lengths from Pompoon, but that rival gave him a far tougher time at Pimlico a week later, so that the Preakness was won by only a head. Pompoon tried again at Belmont Park, but could never get in contention as War Admiral equalled the American record for a mile and a half, stringing his field out impressively. War Admiral was almost as dominant again at four, when he took the Widener Handicap and Jockey Club Gold Cup among nine triumphs. He would have been 'Horse of the Year' for a second time if he had won his match race against Seabiscuit, but the result and the title went the other way. He retired after a solitary (winning) run at five, bringing his record to 21 wins from 26 starts, with earnings of $273,240. He enjoyed a long and quite successful stud career.

Whirlaway, son of Epsom Derby winner Blenheim, was bred and raced by Warren Wright of Calumet Farm and had Ben Jones as trainer. He had toughness and consistency to match his class, as his career record of 32 wins and 14 minor placings from 60 starts testifies. He headed the Experimental Handicap at two in 1940, and he was voted 'Horse of the Year' at both three and four. His domination of the Triple Crown events was total. He ran away with the Kentucky Derby by eight lengths, overcame a sluggish start to take the Preakness by more than five, then toyed with the three no-hopers who dared to challenge him in the Belmont. Although he was beaten almost as often as he won, he was undoubtedly a true champion. Many of his losses resulted from his habit of veering to the right under pressure. He retired with earnings of $561,161 and was a total disaster as a sire.

Count Fleet raced for his breeder, Mrs Frances Hertz, and was trained by a Scotsman, Don Cameron. He was comfortably the best 2-year-old of 1942, when he won 10 of his 15 starts, and

Citation, one of the greatest of American Triple Crown heroes, won 19 of his 20 starts as a three-year-old in 1948. He remained in training until 1951, when this victory over stablemate Bewitch in the Hollywood Gold Cup made him the first horse ever to earn $1 million.

at three he was invincible. Six races brought six victories, all by clear margins, including the Kentucky Derby by three, the Preakness by eight and the Belmont by 25 — a record until Secretariat came along. Unfortunately he suffered an injury in the Belmont which caused his retirement from racing. He had won 16 of 21 races and earned $250,300. He soon became a leading sire and died in December 1973, less than a month before what would have been his 34th official birthday.

Assault, bred and raced by Texan breeder Bob Kleberg of King Ranch, was trained by Max Hirsch. He was not one of the foremost 2-year-olds of 1945, winning only twice that season, once as a 71/1 shot in the Flash Stakes at Saratoga. But he proved altogether more formidable at three, when a campaign of 15 starts brought him eight victories and five minor placings. He streaked home by eight lengths in the Kentucky Derby, held on bravely by a neck when Lord Boswell's late bid threatened him in the Preakness, and impressively put three lengths between himself and Natchez in the last furlong of the Belmont. Assault later won the Dwyer Handicap and beat Stymie in a famous match at Pimlico. At four he collected the Suburban and Brooklyn Handicaps, giving weight to Stymie on both occasions, as he compiled a winning streak of five, but thereafter he was only intermittently sound. He was retired from racing after a single start in 1948, but a routine test on his arrival at stud showed that he was sterile. In due course he was put back into training and he won a second Brooklyn Handicap at six. He finally bowed out of racing at seven, having won 18 of 42 starts and earned $675,470.

Citation, a second Triple Crown winner for owner-breeder Warren Wright, seemed to be the second coming of Man o' War — at least until the

end of his second season in training. He won nine out of ten as a juvenile and 19 out of 20 at three, dominating at all distances from 4½ furlongs to 2 miles. He took the Kentucky Derby by three and a half lengths, the Preakness by five and a half, and the Belmont by eight. He acquired a sky-high reputation early, with the result that he often faced few rivals, and on one occasion at Pimlico he was accorded the honour of a walk-over. But whatever challenged him was ruthlessly shrugged aside as he piled prestige victory on prestige victory. At the end of 1948 he suffered a fetlock injury, tendon trouble followed, and he was away from the races for over a year. He was never so formidable thereafter, but was kept in training with the objective of becoming the first horse in history to earn a million dollars. The target was reached with victory in the 1951 Hollywood Gold Cup Handicap, and Citation went to stud, winner of 32 out of 45 races, with $1,085,760 in the bank. His stud career proved appreciably less successful.

Secretariat became the first Triple Crown winner for 25 years in 1973 and in doing so became a national hero. Much the best of his crop at two, when he finished first in eight consecutive races, he confirmed his status emphatically at three, in spite of three uncharacteristic lapses. There were no mistakes in the Triple Crown. He set a track record time in the Kentucky Derby, just missed the track record in the Preakness, then annihilated the track record in the Belmont, which he won by a record 31 lengths — the most one-sided Classic in history. His subsequent victories included the Marlboro Cup Handicap, the Man o' War Stakes and the Canadian International Championship, after which race he was retired as winner of 16 of 21 starts, with earnings of $1,316,808. He raced throughout in the colours of his breeder, Meadow Stud, though he had already been syndicated for stud duties at the end of his first season. To date he has not come up to expectations as a sire.

Seattle Slew, who fetched only $17,500 as a yearling, became the first horse to complete the Triple Crown series while still unbeaten. He achieved that feat in 1977 and the Belmont was only the ninth start of his career. He was named champion 2-year-old on the strength of an impressive victory in the Champagne Stakes, and his second title was assured by his Classic campaign, which produced authoritative displays in the Kentucky Derby and Preakness and a comprehensive four-length triumph in the Belmont. Surprisingly, Seattle Slew finished only fourth in his next race, but returned to take a third title as a 4-year-old, when he twice beat the year-younger Triple Crown winner, Affirmed. Seattle Slew, trained in his Classic season by Billy Turner for Mrs Karen Taylor, retired with career earnings of $1,208,726 after 14

wins from 17 starts. His stud career started sensationally and he was America's champion sire, with record progeny earnings, in 1984.

Affirmed, the latest Triple Crown hero, was bred and raced by Louis Wolfson's Harbor View Farm and trained by Laz Barrera. He was named the best of his crop at two and repeated the performance at three in 1978 in a season which featured several memorable duels between him and Alydar. To Alydar fell the unique distinction of a Triple Crown runner-up, as he was Affirmed's closest and gamest pursuer in the Kentucky Derby (beaten 1½ lengths), the Preakness (a neck) and the Belmont (a head). Affirmed later went under by three lengths to Seattle Slew in the first-ever encounter between Triple Crown winners in the Marlboro Cup, and was considerably farther behind in their second meeting, when both were beaten by Exceller. But that occasion was marred by the slipping of Affirmed's saddle. After a couple of early defeats as a 4-year-old, Affirmed renewed his winning ways and concluded his career with a seven-victory sequence which included the Santa Anita Handicap, the Hollywood Gold Cup, the Woodward Stakes and the Jockey Club Gold Cup. His final score was 22 wins and six minor placings from 29 starts, with earnings of $2,393,818. The early results of his stud career were rather unexciting.

Other Triple Crown Winners

IRELAND

The Irish Triple Crown consists of the Irish 2000 Guineas (inaugurated 1921) over a mile, the Irish Derby (1866) over 1½ miles and the Irish St Leger (1915) over 1¾ miles, all run at The Curragh. However, these classics contained penalty clauses before 1946 and the Irish St Leger was opened to older horses in 1983. The two Triple Crown winners have been Museum (1935), who also won the Ebor Handicap as a 3-year-old, and unbeaten Windsor Slipper (1942), who started in no other race that year.

JAPAN

The Japanese Triple Crown consists of the Satsuki Shou (2000 Guineas) over 2000 metres at Nakayama, the Tokyo Yuushun (Derby) over 2400 metres in Tokyo and the Kikuka Shou (St Leger) over 3000 metres at Kyoto. The 4 Triple Crown winners have been St Lite (1941), Shinzan (1964), Mr C. B. (1983) and Symboli Rudolf (1984).

CANADA

The Canadian Triple Crown consists of the premier classic, the Queen's Plate over 1¼ miles at Wood-

The only winner to date of Germany's Triple Crown was Königs-stuhl in 1979. He is shown here beating Esclavo to record the first of those triumphs in the Henckel-Rennen.

bine, followed by the Prince of Wales Stakes over 1½ miles at Fort Erie and the Breeders' Stakes over 1½ miles at Woodbine. All three have been won by New Providence (1959) and Canebora (1963).

WEST GERMANY

The West German Triple Crown consists of the Henckel-Rennen (inaugurated 1871) over 1600 metres at Gelsenkirchen, the Deutsches Derby (1869) over 2400 metres at Hamburg and the Deutsches St Leger (1881) over 2800 metres at Dortmund. The only horse to win all 3 races was Königsstuhl in 1979.

FRANCE

There is no such thing as the French Triple Crown, though for many years the nearest French equivalents to the English Triple Crown races were the Poule d'Essai des Poulains (Poule d'Essai before 1883), Prix du Jockey-Club and Prix Royal-Oak (open to older horses from 1979). This treble was achieved by Zut in 1879 and Perth in 1899.

ENGLISH STAYERS

In England the stayers' Triple Crown consists of the 3 principal Cup events: the Ascot Gold Cup (inaugurated 1807) over 2½ miles, the Goodwood Cup (1812) over 2 miles 5 furlongs and the Doncaster Cup (1766) over 2¼ miles. These have been won in the same year by Isonomy (1879), Alycidon

(1949), Souepi (1953) and Le Moss (1979 and 1980), though Souepi could only dead-heat at Doncaster. Rock Roi was first past the post in all 3 races in 1971 but was disqualified in the Ascot Gold Cup.

AMERICAN FILLIES

The American Triple Crown races for fillies were once recognised as the distaff equivalents to the colts' Triple Crown races, namely the Kentucky Oaks over 1 mile 1 furlong at Churchill Downs, the Black-Eyed Susan Stakes (Pimlico Oaks before 1952) over 1 mile 110 yards at Pimlico, and the Coaching Club American Oaks over 1½ miles at Belmont Park. These three have been won by Wistful (1949), Real Delight (1952) and Davona Dale (1979).

A more modern fillies' Triple Crown, established by the New York Racing Association in 1961, consists of the Acorn Stakes over a mile, the Mother Goose Stakes over 1 mile 1 furlong, and the Coaching Club American Oaks over 1½ miles, all at Belmont Park. These three have been won by Dark Mirage (1968), Shuvee (1969), Chris Evert (1974), Ruffian (1975) and Davona Dale (1979).

AMERICAN HANDICAPPERS

The American Handicap Triple Crown consists of the Metropolitan Handicap (inaugurated 1891) over a mile, the Suburban Handicap (1884) over 1¼ miles and the Brooklyn Handicap (1887) over 1½ miles, all run at Belmont Park, though their distances and venues have varied. All three have been won in the same year by Whisk Broom (1913), Tom Fool (1953), Kelso (1961) and Fit to Fight (1984).

Horses of the Year

Great Britain: Flat

From 1959 to 1965 the *Bloodstock Breeders' Review* asked 20 racing journalists to name their Horse of the Year. The champions, with their ages and the number of votes they received, were as follows:-

1959 Petite Etoile (3)	18
1960 St Paddy (3)	11
1961 Right Royal (3)	10
1962 Match (4)	9
1963 Exbury (4)	15
1964 Santa Claus (3)	10
1965 Sea-Bird (3)	19

Since 1965 an official Racehorse of the Year has been elected by a panel of journalists; any horse who has run in Great Britain during the year is eligible. The Racecourse Association presented the award from 1965 to 1977, since when the Race-goers' Club has been responsible. In 1965 and 1966 the 40 voters gave points to their top six horses in order of preference. The champions, with their ages, the number of votes they obtained and the total number of votes cast, have been as follows:

1965 Sea-Bird (3)	228/240
1966 Charlottown (3)	176/240
1967 Busted (4)	18/40
1968 Sir Ivor (3)	26/40
1969 Park Top (5)	20/40
1970 Nijinsky (3)	38/40
1971 Mill Reef (3)	30/37
1972 Brigadier Gerard (4)	40/40
1973 Dahlia (3)	29/39
1974 Dahlia (4)	32/36
1975 Grundy (3)	38/40
1976 Pawneese (3)	21/40
1977 The Minstrel (3)	26/37
1978 Shirley Heights (3)	21/35
1979 Troy (3)	27/32
1980 Moorestyle (3)	23/31
1981 Shergar (3)	22/31
1982 Ardross (6)	17/30
1983 Habibti (3)	23/26
1984 Provideo (2)	17/30

Double champion
Dahlia (1973, 1974)

Elected unanimously
Brigadier Gerard (1972)

Closest decision
Charlottown (1966) received just 2 points more than Sodium, who had twice beaten him on merit

Oldest
6 years—Ardross (1982)
5 years—Park Top (1969)

Youngest
2 years—Provideo (1984)

Fillies and mares
Petite Etoile (1959), Park Top (1969), Dahlia (1973, 1974), Pawneese (1976), Habibti (1983)
In 1983 fillies monopolised the voting through Habibti, Sun Princess and Time Charter.

Grey
Petite Etoile (1959)

Most wins in championship season
16—Provideo (1984)

7—Brigadier Gerard (1972), Moorestyle (1980)

Unbeaten in championship season
6 races—Petite Etoile (1959)
5 races—Exbury (1963), Sea-Bird (1965)
4 races—Busted (1967)

Least successful
Charlottown won only 2 of his 5 races in 1966.

Most active
24 races—Provideo (1984)
10 races—Dahlia (1973, 1974)

Least active
4 races—Busted (1967)
Right Royal (1961), Match (1962), Exbury (1963), Sea-Bird (1965) and Dahlia (1973) won on their only appearance in Great Britain that year.

Earliest retirements
1 July—Shirley Heights (1978)
23 July—The Minstrel (1977)

Trained in Ireland
Santa Claus (1964), Sir Ivor (1968), Nijinsky (1970), The Minstrel (1977)

Trained in France
Right Royal (1961), Match (1962), Exbury (1963), Sea-Bird (1965), Dahlia (1973, 1974), Pawneese (1976).

Most successful owner
2 wins—Nelson Bunker Hunt: Dahlia twice

Most successful breeders
2 wins—Nelson Bunker Hunt: Dahlia twice
Eddie Taylor: Nijinsky, The Minstrel

Most successful trainers
3 wins—Noel Murless: Petite Etoile, St Paddy, Busted
Vincent O'Brien: Sir Ivor, Nijinsky, The Minstrel.

Most successful sires
2 wins—Vaguely Noble: Dahlia twice.
Northern Dancer: Nijinsky, The Minstrel.
Great Nephew: Grundy, Shergar.

Great Britain: jumping

From 1958/59 to 1964/65 the *Bloodstock Breeders' Review* asked 20 racing journalists to name the best steeplechaser and the best hurdler of the season. The champions, with their ages and the number of votes they received, were as follows:

Best steeplechaser

1958/59 Mandarin (8)	5
1959/60 Pas Seul (7)	14
1960/61 Pas Seul (8)	15
1961/62 Mandarin (11)	10
1962/63 Mill House (6)	20
1963/64 Arkle (7)	20
1964/65 Arkle (8)	20

Best hurdler

1958/59 Fare Time (6)	15
1959/60 Another Flash (6)	15
1960/61 Eborneezer (6)	8
1961/62 Anzio (5)	20
1962/63 Anzio (6)	14
1963/64 Magic Court (6)	16
1964/65 Salmon Spray (7)	13

Since 1965/66 an official National Hunt Horse of the Year award for the overall champion jumper has been made along the same lines as the Racehorse of the Year award on the Flat. For the first 2 seasons the 40 voters gave points to their top 6 horses in order of preference. The champions, with their ages, the number of votes they obtained and the total number of votes cast, have been as follows:

1965/66 Arkle (9)	239/240
1966/67 Mill House (10)*	197/240
1967/68 Persian War (5)	36/40
1968/69 Persian War (6)	39/40
1969/70 Persian War (7)	33/38
1970/71 Bula (6)	36/40
1971/72 Bula (7)	37/39
1972/73 Pendil (8)	12/38
1973/74 Red Rum (9)	38/38
1974/75 Comedy of Errors (8)	34/39
1975/76 Night Nurse (5)	37/40
1976/77 Night Nurse (6)	23/39
1977/78 Midnight Court (7)	20/37
1978/79 Monksfield (7)	33/34
1979/80 Sea Pigeon (10)	29/31
1980/81 Sea Pigeon (11)	17/33
1981/82 Silver Buck (10)	25/31
1982/83 Gaye Brief (6)	17/30
1983/84 Dawn Run (6)	14/30

*In 1966/67 some voters mistakenly thought that Arkle's injury had rendered the Irish champion ineligible for the award.

Triple champions
Arkle, Persian War

Elected unanimously
Anzio (1961/62), Mill House (1962/63), Arkle (1963/64 and 1964/65), Red Rum (1973/74)

Closest decisions
Mandarin was elected champion steeplechaser of 1958/59 by one vote. Pendil received just 2 votes more than Crisp in 1972/73.

Oldest
11 years — Mandarin (1961/62), Sea Pigeon (1980/81)

Youngest
5 years — Anzio (1961/62), Persian War (1967/68), Night Nurse (1975/76)

Mare
Dawn Run (1983/84)

Entires
Eborneezer (1960/61), Monksfield (1978/79)

Roan
Anzio (1961/62, 1962/63)

Most wins in championship season
8 — Night Nurse (1975/76)

Unbeaten in championship season
8 races — Night Nurse (1975/76).
7 races — Bula (1970/71), Midnight Court (1977/78).
5 races — Mandarin (1961/62), Arkle (1965/66).

Least successful
Mandarin (1958/59) and Pas Seul

(1959/60) won only one of their 8 races in those championship seasons.

Most active
10 races — Red Rum (1973/74).

Trained in Ireland
Another Flash, Arkle, Monksfield, Dawn Run.

Most successful owners
3 wins — Anne, Duchess of Westminster: Arkle (3 times)
Henry Alper: Persian War (3 times)

Most successful trainers
6 wins — Fulke Walwyn: Mandarin, Anzio and Mill House (twice each)
4 wins — Fred Winter: Bula (twice), Pendil, Midnight Court.
Peter Easterby: Night Nurse and Sea Pigeon (twice each).

Timeform champions

Since 1969 the Timeform organisation in Halifax, Yorkshire has named a Horse of the Year in its *Racehorses of 19—* annual, which contains ratings for all the best horses in Europe. The Timeform champion has always been the horse with the highest rating except in 1969 (Habitat rated 134), 1982 (Assert and Green Forest rated level with Ardross) and 1984 (El Gran Senor rated 136).

Champion	Rating
1969 Levmoss (4)	133
1970 Nijinsky (3)	138
1971 Mill Reef (3)	141
Brigadier Gerard (3)	141
1972 Brigadier Gerard (4)	144
1973 Rheingold (4)	137
Apalachee (2)	137
1974 Allez France (4)	136
1975 Grundy (3)	137
1976 Youth (3)	135

Continued on page 128

SEA-BIRD

It is often (and rightly) said that comparisons between horses of different eras are unfair. Time has wrought tremendous changes in the kind of tests to which horses are subjected, in the manner of their training and riding, and in the way races are run. It seems a reasonable assumption that the likes of Shergar or Secretariat would outpace a St Simon or an Ormonde, and we would be inclined to feel that a St Simon or an Ormonde would have been more than a match for an Eclipse or a Highflyer. But we cannot put them together, to compete under the same conditions, so we cannot be dogmatic about it. It is possible that if there has been significant improvement in racing standards, it has resulted more through improved techniques in the handling of horses rather than through improvement of the breed itself. The best basis for comparisons of merit is inevitably direct confrontation.

However, the science of handicapping has developed to a point where meaningful comparisons can be made between horses of different generations. Granted a balanced racing system, which constantly offers the same opportunities, and commensurate rewards, for high-class horses, it is possible to reach reliable conclusions about the standards attained by individual horses and their merits relative to others of previous or succeeding crops who have competed in the same racing environment.

Such conditions have obtained in Europe's principal racing countries since 1947, the year in which *Timeform* established its handicap of all horses running in Great Britain, along with many of the more prominent horses trained overseas. On the *Timeform* handicap, the best horse rated (at 145 lb) has been Sea-Bird, a French-bred colt by Dan Cupid out of Sicalade, foaled in 1962.

Sea-Bird was bred by Jean Ternynck, who raced him from the Chantilly stable of Etienne Pollet. He raced 3 times as a 2-year-old, beginning with a victory in the Prix de Blaison over 7 furlongs at Chantilly. His lack of experience showed in a tardy start, but he finished fast to prevail by a short neck. A fortnight later he ran an almost identical race with the same result, but the contest was the much more significant Critérium de Maisons-Laffitte and his immediate victim was Blabla, a filly who would win the Prix de Diane (French Oaks) the following summer. In his only subsequent 1964 effort, Sea-Bird was pitted against the best of his contemporaries in France in the Grand Critérium, over a mile at Longchamp. He was not expected to

The judge seemed generous to Sea-Bird when recording a margin of six lengths for his victory over Reliance in the 1965 Arc de Triomphe. But the gap would have been eight lengths or more if Sea-Bird had not veered to the left in the final furlong.

win; in fact he started only as second string to his stable companion Grey Dawn, who had already proved a clearcut winner of the two most prestigious juvenile races of the season so far, the Prix Morny and the Prix de la Salamandre. Grey Dawn duly won, while Sea-Bird came from a long way off the pace to reach second place, beaten by 2 lengths. Many believed that jockey Maurice Larraun had given Sea-Bird too much to do and that the chesnut had been the moral winner, but the argument was futile. Grey Dawn, in any case, had been by no means extended. The official French handicap gave Grey Dawn a 3 lb advantage, and *Timeform* agreed, giving Sea-Bird a rating of 129 lb—the mark of a high-class, but not outstanding 2-year-old.

Things were different in 1965. Sea-Bird's first two races in the spring were both over 10½ furlongs at Longchamp. He won the Prix Greffulhe easily by 3 lengths over unexciting rivals, then stormed home a 6-length winner of the Prix Lupin over Diatome (recent winner of the important Prix Noailles) and Cambremont (who had upset Grey Dawn in the Poule d'Essai des Poulains). That performance had the effect of making Sea-Bird a hot favourite for the Derby.

The Derby performance had to be seen to be believed. In a field of 22 he came to the front, still cantering, 1½ furlongs from home, then was just pushed out for 100 yards before being eased again so that runner-up Meadow Court was flattered by the 2 lengths' deficit. Within a few weeks Meadow Court would become an authoritative winner of both the Irish Derby and the King George VI and Queen Elizabeth Stakes.

Sea-Bird raced only twice more. The competition in the Grand Prix de Saint-Cloud was negligible and he won in a canter. But the Prix de l'Arc de Triomphe promised a sterner test; always Europe's championship race, it was that and more this time, enlivened by the presence of America's top 3-year-old Tom Rolfe, the great Russian champion Anilin (unbeaten in his homeland) and a formidable array of talent from nearer home, including Reliance, unbeaten hero of the Prix du Jockey-Club and Grand Prix de Paris. On paper it promised to be a tremendous contest; it turned out to be the occasion for the most devastating solo *tour de force* ever seen at that level of competition. Sea-Bird and Reliance drew out from the pack together, but as Reliance moved up a gear and swiftly left 18 toiling in his wake, he was himself left for dead by a sprinting Sea-Bird. The champion veered away to the left in the last of the 12 furlongs, but for which his winning margin would have been greater than the official 6 lengths. Reliance had 5 lengths in hand over the third, Diatome, while Anilin and Tom Rolfe came home soundly beaten, fifth and sixth respectively. Little more than a month later Diatome would frank the form impressively, beating American 'Horse of the Year' Roman Brother into third place in the Washington D.C. International.

Sea-Bird went to stud in Kentucky, where he got an 'Arc' winner in Allez France and a dual US Classic winner in Little Current. But his efforts as a stallion never promised to match his status as Europe's greatest racehorse in the post-war era. He returned to France shortly before his untimely death, at the age of 11, as a result of an intestinal blockage.

Champion	Rating
1977 Alleged (3)	137
1978 Alleged (4)	138
1979 Troy (3)	137
1980 Moorestyle (3)	137
1981 Shergar (3)	140
1982 Ardross (6)	134
1983 Habibti (3)	136
1984 Provideo (2)	112

Since 1975/76 the Timeform organisation has named a Champion Jumper in its *Chasers & Hurdlers* annual, which contains ratings for all the best jumpers in the British Isles. The Timeform champion has always been the jumper with the highest rating except in 1975/76 (Captain Christy rated 182) and 1983/84 (Badsworth Boy rated 177).

Champion	Rating
1975/76 Night Nurse (5)	178
1976/77 Night Nurse (6)	182
1977/78 Monksfield (6)	177
1978/79 Monksfield (7)	180
1979/80 Sea Pigeon (10)	175
1980/81 Little Owl (7)	176
1981/82 Silver Buck (10)	175
1982/83 Badsworth Boy (8)	179
1983/84 Dawn Run (6)	173

Five-times American 'Horse of the Year' Kelso, seen here with Eddie Arcaro in the saddle, was the most popular American horse of the early 1960s and holder of the world earnings record for 15 years.

United States

In 1936 Triangle Publications and the magazine *Turf and Sports Digest* started separate Horse of the Year polls among journalists, and in 1950 a third poll was established among racing secretaries at Thoroughbred Racing Associations tracks. The results were usually the same but in some years 2 champions were acclaimed. From 1971 the Thoroughbred Racing Associations, *Daily Racing Form* and the National Turf Writers' Association have conducted their own polls, with the results combined to determine the recipient of the official Eclipse Award as Horse of the Year.

1936 Granville (3)	1940 Challedon (4)	
1937 War Admiral (3)	1941 Whirlaway (3)	
1938 Seabiscuit (5)	1942 Whirlaway (4)	
1939 Challedon (3)	1943 Count Fleet (3)	

1944 Twilight Tear (3)	1964 Kelso (7)
1945 Busher (3)	1965 Roman Brother (4)
1946 Assault (3)	Moccasin (2)
1947 Armed (6)	1966 Buckpasser (3)
1948 Citation (3)	1967 Damascus (3)
1949 Capot (3)	1968 Dr Fager (4)
Coaltown (4)	1969 Arts and Letters (3)
1950 Hill Prince (3)	1970 Fort Marcy (6)
1951 Counterpoint (3)	Personality (3)
1952 One Count (3)	1971 Ack Ack (5)
Native Dancer (2)	1972 Secretariat (2)
1953 Tom Fool (4)	1973 Secretariat (3)
1954 Native Dancer (4)	1974 Forego (4)
1955 Nashua (3)	1975 Forego (5)
1956 Swaps (4)	1976 Forego (6)
1957 Bold Ruler (3)	1977 Seattle Slew (3)
Dedicate (5)	1978 Affirmed (3)
1958 Round Table (4)	1979 Affirmed (4)
1959 Sword Dancer (3)	1980 Spectacular Bid (4)
1960 Kelso (3)	1981 John Henry (6)
1961 Kelso (4)	1982 Conquistador Cielo (3)
1962 Kelso (5)	1983 All Along (4)
1963 Kelso (6)	1984 John Henry (9)

5-times champion
Kelso (1960 to 1964)

Triple champion
Forego (1974, 1975, 1976)

Champion each year he raced
Secretariat (1972, 1973)

Closest decision
One vote for Slew o' Gold instead of John Henry in 1984 would have given him the title.

Oldest
9 years — John Henry (1984)
7 years — Kelso (1964)

Youngest
2 years — Native Dancer (1952), Moccasin (1965), Secretariat (1972)

Fillies
Twilight Tear (1944), Busher (1945), Moccasin (1965), All Along (1983).

Geldings
Armed (1947), Kelso (1960 to 1964), Roman Brother (1965), Fort Marcy (1970), Forego (1974, 1975, 1976), John Henry (1981, 1984).

Grey
Native Dancer (1952, 1954), Spectacular Bid (1980)

Most wins in championship season
19 — Citation (1948)
14 — Twilight Tear (1944), Round Table (1958)

Unbeaten in championship season
10 races — Tom Fool (1953)
9 races — Native Dancer (1952), Spectacular Bid (1980)
8 races — War Admiral (1937), Moccasin (1965)
6 races — Count Fleet (1943)
3 races — Native Dancer (1954)

Least successful
Dedicate won only 4 of his 12 races in 1957.

Most active
22 races — Whirlaway (1942)
20 races — Whirlaway (1941), Citation (1948), Round Table (1958).

Least active
3 races — Native Dancer (1954).

Earliest retirements
5 June — Count Fleet (1943)
3 July — Seattle Slew (1977)

Most versatile
Dr Fager (1968) was also voted champion on grass and champion sprinter.

Campaigned exclusively in California
Ack Ack (1971)

Campaigned exclusively on grass
All Along (1983)

Trained in France
All Along (1983)

Most successful owners
6 wins — Calumet Farm (Warren Wright): Whirlaway (twice), Twilight Tear, Armed, Citation, Coaltown.
5 wins — Bohemia Stable (Mrs Allaire duPont): Kelso (5 times)

Most successful breeders
6 wins — Calumet Farm (Warren Wright): Whirlaway (twice), Twilight Tear, Armed, Citation, Coaltown.
5 wins — Mrs Allaire duPont: Kelso (5 times)

Most successful trainers
5 wins — Carl Hanford: Kelso (5 times)
3 wins — Ben Jones: Whirlaway (twice), Twilight Tear
Jimmy Jones: Armed, Citation, Coaltown
Jim Fitzsimmons: Granville, Nashua, Bold Ruler
Elliott Burch: Sword Dancer, Arts and Letters, Fort Marcy

Most successful sires
5 wins — Your Host: Kelso (5 times)
4 wins — Bull Lea: Twilight Tear, Armed, Citation, Coaltown

France

Since 1979 the French magazine *Courses & Elevage* has held a Horse of the Year poll among racing journalists.

1979 Three Troikas (3)	1982 Saint Cyrien (2)
1980 Detroit (3)	1983 All Along (4)
1981 Bikala (3)	1984 Northern Trick (3)

Long Winning Sequences

56 — Camarero (1951)

The world record for the most wins in succession is held by Camarero, who was unbeaten in the first 56 races of his career in Puerto Rico from April 1953 to August 1955. Owned by José Coll Vidal, he won 18 races as a juvenile in 1953, notably the Clasico Munoz Rivera Memorial, and 19 at 3 years including the local triple crown. Camarero scored on his first 19 outings in 1955, thus breaking Kincsem's record of 54 races without defeat, but finished fourth on his next start. He eventually won 29 out of 32 at the age of four and a further seven out of eight before falling fatally ill in August 1956. Overall, Camarero won 73 of his 77 races at Quintana and Las Casas over distances from 5 to 9 furlongs; he came second twice, fourth once and sixth once. Although both his parents were thoroughbreds imported from America, he was no more than pony-sized and ran only in races for Puerto Rican native-breds. He was too good for his local rivals but not good enough for open competition.

54 — Kincsem (1874)

In many respects the most remarkable career record in Turf history is that of Kincsem, a Hungarian-bred mare who raced 54 times and never knew defeat. She was in training for 4 seasons, winning 10 races as a 2-year-old, 17 at 3 years, 15 at 4 years and 12 at 5 years. A renowned international traveller, she took the train to wherever she could find competition, contesting many of the top races in Hungary, Austria, Germany, Czechoslovakia, France and, on one occasion, England. At the time of her visit to England, in the summer of 1878, she had already won 36 races, including the Austrian versions of the 2000 Guineas and Derby, the Hungarian equivalents of the 2000 Guineas and Oaks, and the top German all-aged race, the Grosser Preis von Baden. In spite of that formidable record, she started as the outsider of three for the Goodwood Cup, but she won easily. On her way home she collected a Grand Prix de Deauville and a second Grosser Preis von Baden, this one after the only close call she ever experienced. She won that by 5 lengths after being taken to a deciding heat by Prince Giles the First. A third victory in the Grosser Preis von Baden provided the feature of her final racing campaign, and she retired with an unblemished record, having been tested at all distances from under 5 furlongs to 2½ miles, with as much as 12 st 1 lb in the saddle.

39 — Galgo Jr (1928)

Galgo Jr, who raced exclusively on two tracks in Puerto Rico, set world records for the number of races won in a season and in a career. Another remarkable feat was his tally of 39 consecutive victories, recorded between July 1930 and July 1931.

23 — Leviathan (1793)

Leviathan was the first gelding to become a champion in America and the grey still holds the record for the longest winning sequence by any American horse. Owned in turn by Edmund Brooke and John Tayloe III, he campaigned almost exclusively in Virginia and swept unchallenged through 23 consecutive races from 1797 to 1801, nine of them in 4-mile heats. In the spring of 1801, at the age of eight, he won a 5-mile match under 180 lb, conceding 70 lb to his rival, but his sequence ended the following autumn. He never scored again, retiring with 24 wins in 30 races.

21 — Meteor (1783)

The record for the most wins in succession by a horse trained in Great Britain is held by Meteor, who won his last 4 races as a 3-year-old in 1786 and was unbeaten in 5 outings in 1787 and 12 in 1788, most of them at Newmarket. Bred and owned by the 1st Earl Grosvenor, this son of Eclipse came second in the Derby but then developed into such an outstanding champion that he scared away nearly all opposition. During his record sequence he walked over 5 times and had a solitary rival on 9 occasions, though most of those were matches against top-class rivals. Sir Peter Teazle was the horse who finally ended his run. Meteor was small in stature, but he won 30 of his 33 starts over 5 seasons and came second in the other three.

21 — Bond's First Consul (1798)

Bond's First Consul was champion of the northern states of America in the early 1800s. From 1801 to 1806 Joshua Bond's horse won the first 21 races of his career, mostly in 4-mile heats and meeting the best horses in training at courses from New York to Maryland, but he lost his remaining 4 races.

21 — Lottery (1803)

Lottery was an outstanding American mare who

lost only the first of her 22 races. Owned by Richard Singleton, she won the Jockey Club purse in 4-mile heats at Charleston, South Carolina in 1808 and 1810, and she also picked up similar prizes over shorter distances at the same venue. She became an influential broodmare.

20 — Filch (1773)

Filch, a grey Irish horse, won his last 9 races of 1778, notably the Jockey Club Purse and a King's Plate at The Curragh. He was unbeaten in 7 outings as a 6-year-old, including a walk-over for his second Jockey Club Purse, and added four more prizes in 1780, among them another King's Plate, before his sequence ended. During that time he had a total of 12 races in heats and 3 walk-overs.

20 — Fashion (1837)

Fashion, perhaps the greatest of all American race-mares, won 32 of her 36 races over 9 seasons and came second in the other four; most of them were run in 4-mile heats. She won her last 3 starts in 1841 and was undefeated in 4 races in 1842, seven in 1843 and six in 1844 at courses from New York to Maryland. For her most famous victory she represented the North in a match with the great but ageing southern champion Boston at the Union Course, Long Island in May 1842.

20 — Kentucky (1861)

Kentucky dominated racing in America at the end of the Civil War together with unbeaten Asteroid and Norfolk; all three were sons of Lexington. Eastern champion Kentucky suffered his only defeat when fourth to Norfolk in the 1864 Jersey Derby. He numbered the Travers Stakes at Saratoga's inaugural meeting and the Jersey St Leger among his 6 victories later that year, and was unbeaten in 7 races in both 1865 and 1866 including the first 2 runnings of the Saratoga Cup. He had 2 walk-overs and 8 races in heats.

19 — Skiff (1821)

Skiff, running only at minor Scottish meetings, won his last 9 races in 1825 and all 11 in 1826, though on the final occasion he was disqualified for carrying too little weight. He picked up Gold Cups at Inverness and Montrose and a King's Plate at Perth; his sequence included 3 walk-overs and 5 races in heats.

19 — Boston (1833)

Boston was perhaps the best horse to race in America before the Civil War and no American champion except Kelso has dominated the sport for so long. He won 40 of his 45 starts over 8 seasons, mostly in 4-mile heats, and in 37 consecutive races from 1836 to 1841 he lost only when unfit on his début in 1839. He won his remaining 8 races that year, all seven (including a walk-over) in 1840 and, after a season at stud, his first four in 1841 at courses from New York to Georgia. Boston became champion sire 3 times and his offspring included Lexington.

19 — Sweetmeat (1842)

Sweetmeat did not contest the Classics but was unbeaten in 19 outings as a 3-year-old in 1845 including the Gold Vase at Ascot, the Doncaster Cup (beating Alice Hawthorn) and 9 races in which he walked over after scaring away all opposition. He won 22 of his 25 career starts and became an influential sire.

19 — The Hero (1843)

The Hero was the first horse to win all three of England's premier Cup events. John Barham Day's colt took his last 11 races in 1846, including the Doncaster Cup, and his first 8 in 1847, notably the Gold Vase, Emperor of Russia's Plate (Ascot Gold Cup) and Goodwood Cup; he also had 5 walk-overs and 2 races in heats.

19 — Desert Gold (1912)

Desert Gold was the greatest racemare ever produced in New Zealand and, together with Gloaming, she holds the Australasian record of 19 consecutive victories. Having won on her last start at 2 years, she swept unbeaten through her 14-race campaign as a 3-year-old in 1915–16 including the New Zealand Derby and Oaks at Riccarton and the Great Northern Derby, Oaks and St Leger at Ellerslie; she also won her first 4 races the following season. Desert Gold usually dominated her rivals from the start, and set several time records.

19 — Gloaming (1915)

Gloaming ranks second only to Phar Lap among New Zealand geldings and he shares with Desert Gold the Australasian record of 19 wins in succession. Having landed 3 Derbys in his first season, this remarkable champion won his last 5 races at 4 years, all 12 as a 5-year-old in 1920–21 including the Islington, Auckland and Kelburn Plates, and his first two at 6 years. Gloaming, who never ran in a handicap or beyond 12 furlongs, retired with 57 wins and 9 seconds from 67 starts over 7 seasons; he fell in his only other race.

18 — Eclipse (1764)

Eclipse was the greatest racehorse of the 18th century and has become almost a legendary figure. He won all his 18 races, nine of them as a 5-year-old in 1769 and 9 in 1770, and though eight of them were walk-overs, that was merely because his overwhelming superiority frightened away nearly all opposition. Seven of his other races were run in heats of up to 4 miles each and he was a frequent competitor in King's Plates, winning 11 of those prestige prizes altogether including two at Newmarket. Bred by William, Duke of Cumberland, Eclipse ran at first in the name of William Wildman but was later bought by Dennis O'Kelly, who had correctly predicted on the champion's début that the result would be 'Eclipse first and the rest nowhere'. Over 90 per cent of all modern Thoroughbreds descend from him in the male line.

18 — Sally Hope (1822)

American racemare Sally Hope won her last 18 races, most of them in heats of up to 4 miles. Running almost exclusively in Virginia, she took her last 7 races in 1827 and all 10 in 1828, including 4 Jockey Club purses, but she broke down when winning another such prize on her reappearance the following spring.

18 — Light (1856)

Light was not a champion but set a French record for consecutive victories which still stands. He won his last 7 races in 1859 and 11 more in 1860 including the Prix Biennal and Prix de Suresnes at Longchamp, though he usually ran in the provinces. He sired Classic winners Bigarreau and Sornette.

18 — Hindoo (1878)

Hindoo, perhaps the greatest American champion of the 19th century, won 30 of his 35 races including the first 18 of a brilliant 3-year-old campaign in 1881. Trained by James Rowe for the brothers Phil and Mike Dwyer, he romped away with the Kentucky Derby before moving to New York and winning the Tidal, Coney Island Derby, Lorillard, Travers, United States Hotel, Kenner, Champion, Jersey St Leger and other stakes. He walked over once and had one race in heats.

18 — Ajax (1934)

Ajax, one of Australia's greatest champions, was a brilliant miler and holds the record for the most consecutive wins in that country. They comprised his last 6 races at 3 years, notably the Newmarket Handicap and All Aged Plate, and his first 12 as a 4-year-old in 1938–39, all but one of them at weight-for-age including the W.S. Cox Plate and the Underwood, Melbourne, Caulfield and L.K.S. Mackinnon Stakes. He retired with 36 wins from 46 starts.

18 — Karayel (1970)

Karayel was the best horse ever to race in Turkey and was never extended in any of his 18 races. Sadik Eliyesil's colt won 5 times as a juvenile and his tally of 11 in 1973 included the Triple Crown — Erkek Tay Deneme Kosusu (2000 Guineas), Gazi Kosusu (Derby) and Ankara Kosusu (St Leger) — as well as Turkey's premier weight-for-age race, the Cumhurbaskanligi Kupasi Kosusu over 2400 metres, by a distance. Karayel, a son of 2000 Guineas runner-up Prince Tudor, won twice more in the spring of 1974 but then fractured a cannon-bone in a training gallop, though he was saved for stud duty.

17 — Careless (1751)

Careless won the first 17 races of his career in England from 1755 to 1758 including 10 King's Plates, the only ones he ever started for. He had 7 walk-overs and 7 races in heats.

17 — Boston (1833)

When American champion Boston won 19 races in succession (see above) he already had a sequence of 17 to his credit. In 1836 this bad-tempered horse refused to race on his first public appearance, but he won his remaining 2 starts that year, all four in 1837 and all 11 in 1838.

17 — Harkaway (1834)

Harkaway disputes with Barcaldine the distinction of being the greatest Irish racehorse of the 19th century. He won on 17 consecutive outings at The Curragh between April 1837 and June 1838, including 7 Royal Plates, and later became the first Irish horse to prove himself a champion in England, winning the Goodwood Cups of 1838 and 1839. He would have achieved even greater glory but for being mismanaged by his owner, Tom Ferguson.

17 — Beeswing (1835)

The American Beeswing, foaled 2 years after her more famous English namesake, won 17 in a row before breaking down at New Orleans in 1840. This was during a race run in heats and the Louisiana mare had to be withdrawn despite winning the first heat.

17 — Alice Hawthorn (1838)

Alice Hawthorn, one of the toughest of English racemares, won her last 16 races as a 6-year-old in 1844 and her first at 7 years. In that time this great stayer recorded her second success in the Doncaster Cup and also picked up the Gold Cups at York and Richmond, and 7 Queen's Plates; she walked over 7 times, had one race in heats and dead-heated once.

17 — Hanover (1884)

Hanover, based in New York, was unbeaten in 3 juvenile starts — the Hopeful, July and Sapling Stakes — and was the best horse in America as a 3-year-old in 1887. He won his first 14 races and 20 in all that year, adding the Brooklyn Derby, Withers, Belmont, Swift, Tidal, Coney Island Derby and Lorillard Stakes to his tally before his first defeat. He became champion sire 4 times.

17 — Dudley (1914)

Dudley was perhaps the best 2-mile steeplechaser of his time in England and this tough, versatile gelding won his first 17 contests as an 11-year-old in 1925, comprising 6 steeplechases, 4 hurdle races, one Flat race and 6 National Hunt Flat races. They included the Victory Chase at Manchester, the Cheltenham Grand Annual Chase (both handicaps) and a walk-over.

17 — Mainbrace (1947)

Mainbrace is one of the very greatest champions in New Zealand racing history. He won 23 of his 25 starts, the last 17 of them consecutively, and his 15 victories as a 3-year-old in 1950–51 constitute a New Zealand record for one season. Among them were 4 Guineas races, the Great Northern Derby and the New Zealand and Great Northern St Legers. He had 2 further races at 4 before injury ended his career.

17 — Sir Ken (1947)

Sir Ken was a great hurdler who failed to win in his native France but was unbeaten in 16 races over

timber and one on the Flat during his first 3 seasons in England. He won the Lancashire Hurdle in 1951 and the Champion Hurdle in each of the next 2 years before his sequence ended. He added a third title in 1954.

17 — Gradisco (1957)

Gradisco won the first 17 races of his career in Venezuela during 1959 and 1960 before fracturing a sesamoid. He attempted a come-back in 1961 but broke down, thus spoiling an unbeaten record.

16 — Master Bagot (1787)

Master Bagot won his last 4 starts in 1790 and was Ireland's leading earner in 1791 thanks to an unbeaten campaign of 11 races (three of them in heats) in which he added two more King's Plates and the Lord Lieutenant's Plate at The Curragh to his score; he also won on his reappearance at 5 years. He became champion sire a record 8 times in Ireland.

16 — Luke Blackburn (1877)

Luke Blackburn was one of the greatest American champions of the 19th century. Based in New York, he won 22 of his 24 races as a 3-year-old in 1880, the last 15 of them in succession including the

Mainbrace, perhaps the greatest racehorse to have run exclusively in New Zealand, won 23 of his 25 starts and had an undefeated sequence of 17 up to the time of his breakdown as a four-year-old.

United States Hotel, Grand Union Prize, Kenner, Champion and Great Challenge Stakes and the Long Island and Kentucky St Legers. He scored on his reappearance in 1881 but his crown then passed to his stablemate Hindoo.

16 — Miss Woodford (1880)

Miss Woodford is probably the greatest filly or mare to race in America since the Civil War and she succeeded stablemate Hindoo as the best horse in the country. Her long sequence of victories included all nine of her starts at the age of four in 1884 and she later became the first horse of either sex to earn $100,000 in America. She was unplaced only twice in a career of 48 races, winning 37 of them.

16 — The Bard (1883)

The Bard set a British record with an unbeaten campaign of 16 races as a 2-year-old including the Brocklesby Stakes at Lincoln, New Biennial Stakes at Ascot, Tattersall Sale Stakes at Doncaster and a walk-over. On his reappearance he came second to mighty Ormonde in the Derby; he later won the Doncaster Cup.

16 — Ormonde (1883)

Ormonde may well have been the greatest of all English champions, for he never looked likely to be beaten in any of his 16 races. This brilliant colt numbered the Criterion Stakes and Dewhurst Plate among his 3 outings as a juvenile and in 1886 his triumphant progress took in the Triple Crown events plus the St James's Palace, Hardwicke, Great Foal and Champion Stakes, the Free Handicap and 2 walk-overs. He then became a roarer but added the Rous Memorial Stakes, Hardwicke Stakes and Imperial Gold Cup (July Cup) to his tally at 4. He died in 1904.

16 — Prestige (1903)

Prestige was easily the best of his generation in France but was not entered for the major 3-year-old events. This unbeaten champion won 7 races as a juvenile, notably the Critérium de Maisons-Laffitte, Grand Critérium and Prix de la Forêt, and nine in 1906, including the Prix Eugène Adam and 2 walk-overs. Trained by William Duke for William K. Vanderbilt, he was far superior to his stablemate and contemporary Maintenon, who won the Prix du Jockey-Club. Prestige sired Sardanapale, one of France's greatest champions, and died in 1924.

16 — Citation (1945)

Citation ranks among the very greatest American champions. During a magnificent 3-year-old campaign in 1948 his sole conqueror was Saggy, and he swept unchallenged through his remaining 15 races (including a walk-over) that season over distances from 6 furlongs to 2 miles and at tracks across the USA, winning the Triple Crown plus the American Derby and Jockey Club Gold Cup. Sidelined by injury throughout 1949, he won on his reappearance at 5 years but the longest winning sequence in North America this century was then ended by Miche. Citation was trained by Jimmy Jones for Calumet Farm and usually ridden by Eddie Arcaro.

16 — Ribot (1952)

Ribot, a product of the Italian breeding genius Federico Tesio, was never beaten in 16 races and disputes with Sea-Bird the distinction of being the greatest middle-distance horse in Europe since World War II. Having taken 3 prizes as a juvenile, including the Gran Criterium, he had 5 races in Italy in 1955, among them the Gran Premio del Jockey Club, and also romped away with the Prix de l'Arc de Triomphe. His 7-race campaign in 1956 featured the Gran Premio di Milano, the King George VI and Queen Elizabeth Stakes and his second Arc by a record margin of 6 lengths. Ribot spent most of his stud career in America and died in 1972.

16 — Minimo (1968)

Turkish champion Minimo lost her first race but won her next 16. Her unblemished 1971 record included the Disi Tay Deneme Kosusu (1000 Guineas), Kisrak Kosusu (Oaks), Gazi Kosusu (Derby), Ankara Kosusu (St Leger) and Turkey's premier weight-for-age prize, the Reisi Cumhur Kupasi Kosusu, all in effortless style.

15 — Rattler (1816)

Rattler, also known as Thornton's Rattler, was an American horse who won his first 15 races including the Jockey Club purse at Charleston, South Carolina in 1820. He was injured when suffering his first defeat.

15 — Thebais (1878)

Thebais, England's champion 2-year-old of 1880, won her last 10 races that season, among them the Ham Produce, Great Challenge and Criterion Stakes and 3 walk-overs, and her first five in 1881,

Allez France, seen here on the way to post before her victory in the 1974 Prix de l'Arc de Triomphe, is generally acknowledged to have been the greatest European racemare at middle distances in the post-war era.

Dawn Run completed a unique double of Champion Hurdle victories at Cheltenham and Auteuil in 1984. Here she is leaving the paddock at Cheltenham, with Jonjo O'Neill in the saddle.

Vincent O'Brien, who abandoned National Hunt racing when there were no fields left to conquer, became the supreme master trainer on the Flat. To the end of 1984 he had won 17 English and 23 Irish Classics.

Peter Easterby (left), the most successful trainer in Champion Hurdle history, celebrates the 1980 victory of Sea Pigeon with jockey Jonjo O'Neill, owner Pat Muldoon and Mrs Muldoon.

including the 1000 Guineas, Oaks, Nassau Stakes and Yorkshire Oaks. Her brother Clairvaux was an unbeaten champion sprinter and her sister St Marguerite won the 1000 Guineas.

15 — Carbine (1885)

Carbine disputes with Phar Lap the distinction of being the greatest horse ever to race in Australasia. Bred in New Zealand but trained in Australia after the age of two by Walter Hickenbotham for Donald Wallace, he won his last 7 races as a 4-year-old in 1889–90, including the Sydney Cup, and his first eight at 5 years, notably the Melbourne Cup under 10 st 5 lb, a weight which is still a record for the winner of Australia's greatest prize. Carbine, who started twice on the same afternoon several times, won 33 of his 43 races and spent most of his successful stud career in England.

15 — Pretty Polly (1901)

Pretty Polly dominated her contemporaries and set the standard by which all English champion fillies are measured. Her 9 victories as a juvenile included the National Breeders' Produce, Champagne, Cheveley Park, Middle Park and Criterion Stakes, and in 1904 she breezed through the 1000 Guineas, Oaks, Coronation Stakes, Nassau Stakes, St Leger and Park Hill Stakes before suffering her first defeat on her only visit to France.

15 — Colin (1905)

Colin is one of a handful of American champions who can be compared with Man o' War. Trained by James Rowe for James R. Keene and racing only in the state of New York, this unbeaten colt swept in brilliant style through his 12 races as a juvenile including the Saratoga Special, Futurity, Matron and Champagne Stakes. In 1908 he won the Withers, Belmont and Tidal Stakes before a leg injury ended his career, though he was sent to trainer Sam Darling in England before his retirement was announced. Colin died in 1932; his male-line descendants include Teenoso.

15 — Bayardo (1906)

Bayardo, the greatest horse of his time in England, was a champion in each of his 3 seasons. He was not fit when unplaced in the 2000 Guineas and Derby of 1909, but won his remaining 11 races that year including the Prince of Wales's, Eclipse, St Leger and Champion Stakes. He also took his first four in 1910, highlighted by a magnificent victory in the Ascot Gold Cup, and retired with 22 wins from 25 starts.

15 — Macon (1922)

Macon was the best horse of his time in Argentina. His 9 wins in 1925 included the Polla de Potrillos (2000 Guineas), Gran Premio Nacional (Derby) and Argentina's premier weight-for-age prize, the Gran Premio Carlos Pellegrini. In 1926 the unbeaten colt won 6 more races, notably the Gran Premio de Honor (stayers' championship) and a second Gran Premio Carlos Pellegrini.

15 — Vander Pool (1928)

Vander Pool, an American colt, won all his 11 races as a juvenile and his first four at 3 years, but on the only occasion he met top-class opposition he was lucky to be awarded the Youthful Stakes (his seventh race) on the disqualification of Equipoise.

15 — Bernborough (1939)

Bernborough was probably the best racehorse ever bred in Australia. Until he was 6 years, controversy over his ownership restricted him to a country meeting in Queensland but at that age, in 1945–46, he entered major competition and won his last 10 races, notably the Newmarket Handicap, Rawson Stakes, All Aged Stakes, Doomben Ten Thousand and Doomben Cup. This great weight-carrier also won his first 5 races at 7 years, including the Melbourne and Caulfield Stakes.

15 — Buckpasser (1963)

Buckpasser was the champion of his generation in America in each of his 3 seasons. In 1966 he won the last 13 races of his brilliant Horse of the Year campaign including the Flamingo, Arlington Classic, Brooklyn Handicap, American Derby, Travers, Woodward and Jockey Club Gold Cup, though injury made him miss the Triple Crown series. He took his first 2 starts in 1967, notably the Metropolitan Handicap, but then lost his only race on grass.

15 — Brigadier Gerard (1968)

Brigadier Gerard won 17 of his 18 races and is rivalled only by Tudor Minstrel as the greatest miler to race in England since World War II. The Middle Park Stakes was the most important of his 4 juvenile victories and on his reappearance in 1971 he decisively beat Mill Reef for the 2000 Guineas. The Sussex and Champion Stakes were among his other 5 races that year, and in 1972 he extended his brilliant unbeaten sequence to 15, culminating in the Eclipse and the King George VI and Queen

Elizabeth Stakes, before Roberto defeated him at York.

15 — Squanderer (1973)

Indian champion and triple crown hero Squanderer won 18 of his 19 races. After losing on his fourth start, he won the Bangalore Derby and Indian 2000 Guineas in 1976, while at 4 years his 8 victories included the Indian Derby and St Leger, and the President of India Gold Cup, a race which also figured among his 5 successes in 1978.

14 — Lucifer (1813)

Lucifer was a Scottish horse who won his last 9 races in 1817 and first 5 in 1818, notably the Gold Cup and King's Plate at Edinburgh. He had 2 walk-overs and 8 races in heats.

14 — Friponnier (1864)

Friponnier was the most prolific winner in Great Britain in 1867, when he lost on only the fifth of his 19 starts. Thereafter he walked over in 7 races, including the Goodwood Derby, and twice beat Derby winner Hermit, notably in the Grand Duke Michael Stakes.

14 — Prince Charlie (1869)

Prince Charlie, the 2000 Guineas hero of 1872, was one of the fastest and most popular horses ever to run in England. He won his last race at 3 years, all 10 at 4 years, including the Queen's Stand Plate at Ascot and a walk-over, and his first three in 1874. He won 25 of his 29 career starts, mostly over sprint distances, and was never beaten at Newmarket.

14 — Springfield (1873)

Springfield won 17 of his 19 races and was probably the best specialist sprinter-miler of the 19th century in England. He swept unbeaten through his last 2 seasons and numbered the Fern Hill Stakes, inaugural July Cup and 2 walk-overs among his tally of nine in 1876. He won 5 more races in 1877 including the Queen's Stand Plate, July Cup and inaugural Champion Stakes.

14 — Man o' War (1917)

Man o' War is widely regarded as the greatest of all American champions, having won 20 of his 21 races over 2 seasons. Trained by Louis Feustel for Samuel Riddle, he was unluckily beaten by Upset on his seventh juvenile start, the Sanford Memorial Stakes at Saratoga, and had 3 more races that year, notably the Hopeful Stakes and Belmont Futurity. He did not contest the Kentucky Derby but his 11 races in 1920 included the Preakness, Withers, Belmont, Dwyer, Travers, Lawrence Realization and Jockey Club Stakes; he set 5 American record times during that all-conquering campaign. 'Big Red' proved a successful stallion and died in 1947.

14 — Phar Lap (1926)

Phar Lap's claims to being regarded as the greatest of all Australasian Thoroughbreds are challenged only by Carbine. This New Zealand-bred gelding proved himself overwhelmingly the best 3-year-old in Australia in 1929–30 and recorded 14 consecutive wins in a brilliant campaign at 4 years, highlighted by an easy victory under 9 st 12 lb in the Melbourne Cup and also including the W.S. Cox Plate and Melbourne and Futurity Stakes. In early 1932 he was sent to North America and won in Mexico for his 37th win in 51 starts before falling victim to a sudden, mysterious and fatal illness.

14 — Nearco (1935)

Nearco, bred, owned and trained by Federico Tesio, was an outstanding Italian champion who went unbeaten through a career of 14 starts. His 7 races as a juvenile included the Gran Criterium, Premio Tevere and Premio Chiusura, and in 1938 he added seven more, notably the Premio Parioli, Derby Italiano, Gran Premio di Milano and Grand Prix de Paris. He stood at stud in Newmarket and became perhaps the most influential sire of the 20th century, dying in 1957.

After recording 13 wins in his native Italy, Nearco closed his career with a smooth victory in the Grand Prix de Paris. A few days later he was purchased for stud duty in England (where this photo was taken) and the extent of his influence as a stallion caused him to be regarded as the most significant import to England since the Godolphin Arabian more than two centuries earlier.

13 — Hippolitus (1767)

Hippolitus was an Irish gelding who won his last 12 races in 1773, nearly all of them run in heats at minor meetings, and then scored at The Curragh on his reappearance as a 7-year-old.

13 — Phoenomenon (1780)

Phoenomenon won his last 2 races in 1783, gaining a narrow success in the St Leger, all 10 in 1784, notably a victory over Dungannon in the Doncaster Cup, and his only start as a 5-year-old before being retired. He had 4 walk-overs and one race in heats.

13 — Dungannon (1780)

Dungannon came second in the Derby and developed into a champion in his last 2 campaigns, being unbeaten in 9 races in 1785 and four in 1786. Most of them, including a King's Plate, were at Newmarket, and he had 3 walk-overs and 2 contests in heats. He won 26 of his 29 career starts and was second in the other three.

13 — Rockingham (1781)

Rockingham was a top-class English horse who won his last 3 races in 1786 and 16 out of 17 in 1787, the first 10 of them consecutively. These included the Jockey Club Plate at Newmarket and 5 King's Plates, three of them run in heats.

13 — Timoleon (1813)

Timoleon, the best horse of his day in America, was based in Virginia and enjoyed his long run of success in 1816 and 1817, often walking over for Jockey Club purses after frightening away the opposition. He sired the great champion Boston.

13 — Effie Deans (1815)

Effie Deans graduated from selling plates to become the most prolific winner of the season in Great Britain in 1819, when she took her last 13 races including 10 in heats (notably the King's Plate at Salisbury) and 2 walk-overs.

13 — The Flying Dutchman (1846)

The Flying Dutchman was one of the greatest champions of the 19th century. He won 5 races as a juvenile, notably the July and Champagne Stakes, six in 1849, including the Derby, St Leger and 3 walk-overs, and added the Emperor of Russia's Plate (Ascot Gold Cup) and one other prize in 1850 before being upset by Voltigeur in the Doncaster Cup, the only defeat of his career.

13 — Planet (1855)

Planet was the best horse in America just before the Civil War, winning 27 of his 31 starts. He raced throughout the southern states and his long spell of success in 1859 and 1860 included victories in the Great Post and Planet Post Stakes, both in 4-mile heats at New Orleans.

13 — Mollie McCarthy (1873)

Champion American mare Mollie McCarthy won the first 13 races of her career in California but was then distanced in the first heat of a match with Ten Broeck at Churchill Downs in July 1878.

13 — Tremont (1884)

Tremont's career was a brief flash of brilliance, his 13 races all coming within 10 weeks in New York and New Jersey in the summer of 1886, and in that time he proved himself by far the best 2-year-old in America. Trained by Frank McCabe for the brothers Phil and Mike Dwyer, he was a phenomenally fast starter and was never headed for a single stride. His victories included the Juvenile, Great Post, Atlantic, Tyro and Junior Champion Stakes, but he could not stand further training.

13 — Kingston (1884)

Kingston won a career total of 89 races, which still stands as an American record; they included his last 13 as a 5-year-old in 1889, when he was just about the best older horse in the country. He was unplaced only 4 times in 138 starts and before his retirement at the age of 10 had become America's leading earner, his most valuable victory coming in the Select Stakes as a juvenile. He became champion sire twice.

13 — Polar Star (1904)

Polar Star was England's champion 2-year-old of 1906, winning all his 12 races including the Gimcrack and Criterion Stakes. On his reappearance at three years he took the Kempton Park Great Jubilee Handicap, but was never as good again.

13 — Limerick (1923)

New Zealand champion Limerick won 4 races in his native land, notably the Canterbury Cup, as a 4-year-old in 1927–28 and numbered the All Aged Stakes and King's Cup in Sydney among 5 further victories that season. At 5 years the gelding extended his sequence to 13, the last of them a dead-heat.

Bula, who was unraced on the Flat, won his first 13 races over hurdles. Here, on the left, he begins to draw clear of Persian War (right) in the 1971 Champion Hurdle.

13 — Sweet Wall (1925)

Sweet Wall, the best filly of her generation in Ireland, won her last 6 races as a 3-year-old, culminating in the Irish Cambridgeshire under top weight, and all seven in her farewell season of 1929, including 2 walk-overs.

13 — Grano de Oro (1937)

Grano de Oro was successful in Ireland in 1940 under his original name of Roe, and when exported to Venezuela the gelding won his first 13 races in Caracas.

13 — Bula (1965)

Bula never ran on the Flat and was unbeaten in his first 2 seasons over timber. In 1970 he won a division of the Gloucestershire Hurdle and the following year took the first of his 2 Champion Hurdles, dethroning Persian War, as well as the Welsh Champion Hurdle.

13 — Weimar (1968)

Italian champion Weimar won his first 13 races, comprising three as a juvenile, 8 in 1971 — notably the Gran Premio d'Italia, Gran Premio di Milano, St Leger Italiano and Gran Premio del Jockey Club — and his first two in 1972, but he never won again.

Longest Losing Sequences

It is a well-established fact that most horses are incapable of winning a race, and usually owners are quite swift to recognise the futility of persevering with animals of no evident merit. But there have been instances of remarkable reluctance to admit defeat.

The all-time record for consistent failure probably belongs to Ouroene, a mare bred and raced in Australia by George and Lorraine Chiotis. Foaled in 1974, this daughter of Farnworth became a figure of fun on Sydney tracks over a long period, racing 124 times without a single victory between December 1976 and November 1983. But the sequence was not all gloom, being punctuated with two second and seven third places, which contributed $14,605 towards the mare's upkeep. The saga seemed to have ended when Ouroene's owners took her home after the 124th failure, but in December 1984 came the announcement that she was to try again and she was put back into training at Canterbury.

Britain's nearest equivalent to Ouroene was Elsich, a gelding of uncertain breeding who worked between the shafts down on the farm as part of his preparation for steeplechasing. Foaled in 1936, Elsich had to make a late start to his jumping career because National Hunt racing was suspended for much of World War II. He made up for lost time by having his first two races on the same afternoon at Cheltenham in February 1945. He fell in both. For more than two years his intrepid and eccentric owner-trainer Charles Edwards ran him all over the country, including three times in the Cheltenham Gold Cup (ran out, fell, pulled up) and once in the Grand National (fell at the first fence). He completed the course in less than a third of his 50 races, sometimes even then only after being remounted. Edwards was keen to persevere and was highly indignant when, in June 1947, the authorities informed him that they would accept no further entries for Elsich.

The gelding had never been nearer than second—and that when beaten a distance in a two-horse race.

On the other hand, there are cases of horses coming good after promising little. Perhaps the most remarkable concerns Reckless, an Australian-bred son of Better Boy who had only a couple of seconds and a couple of thirds to show for 30 efforts in his first three seasons. He finally got his head in front in his 33rd start, when already five years old, and the following season improved out of all recognition. Before being retired at the age of seven he had won the Sydney, Adelaide and Brisbane Cups—all Group I events—and finished second, beaten a length, in the Melbourne Cup. He began duties as a stallion in Victoria in 1978.

Unbeaten Horses

The following 137 horses were never beaten during their racing careers. They are ranked according to how many races they had, and also given are their dates of birth and the countries in which they ran.

54—Kincsem (1874) filly: Austria-
   Hungary, Germany, England,
   France
18—Eclipse (1764) England
   Karayel (1970) Turkey
16—Ormonde (1883) England
   Prestige (1903) France
   Ribot (1952) Italy, France, England
15—Colin (1905) USA
   Macon (1922) Argentina
14—Nearco (1935) Italy, France
13—Tremont (1884) USA
12—Highflyer (1774) England
   Ardrossan (1809) Scotland
   Crucifix (1837) filly: England
   Asteroid (1861) USA
   Barcaldine (1878) Ireland, England
   Braque (1954) Italy
11—Goldfinder (1764) England
10—Nereïde (1933) filly: Germany
9—Regulus (1739) England
   Grand Flaneur (1877) Australia
   St Simon (1881) England
   Patience (1902) filly: Austria-
      Hungary, Germany
   Bahram (1932) England
   Combat (1944) England
8—Sweetbriar (1769) England
   American Eclipse (1814) USA
   Sensation (1877) USA
   Tiffin (1926) filly: England
   Caracalla (1942) France, England
7—Woodpecker (1828) USA
   Rodolph (1831) USA
   Bay Middleton (1833) England
   Monarch (1834) USA
   Salvator (1872) France
   El Rio Rey (1887) USA

The Tetrarch (1911) England
Mannamead (1929) England
Claude (1964) Italy
Viani (1967) Italy
6—Dismal (1733) England
   Quintessence (1900) filly: England
   Aldford (1911) England
   Hurry On (1913) England
   Tolgus (1923) England
   Payaso (1929) Argentina
   Albany Girl (1935) filly: England
   Windsor Slipper (1939) Ireland
   Manantial (1955) Argentina
5—Albert (1827) England
   Norfolk (1861) USA
   Frontin (1880) France
   Ajax (1901) France
   Landgraf (1914) Germany
   Pazman (1916) Austria
   Dice (1925) USA
   Cavaliere d'Arpino (1926) Italy
   Melody (1947) filly: Argentina
   Paddy's Sister (1957) filly: Ireland,
      England
   Emerson (1958) Brazil
   Star Shower (1976) Australia
   Landaluce (1980) filly: USA
   Precocious (1981) England
4—Snap (1750) England
   Ball's Florizel (1801) USA
   Tennessee Oscar (1814) USA
   Clairvaux (1880) England
   Saphir (1894) Germany, Austria-
      Hungary
   Morazzona (1939) filly: Italy
   Ocarina (1947) France
   Pharsalia (1954) filly: England
   Raise a Native (1961) USA

Drone (1966) USA
Blood Royal (1971) Ireland, England
Madelia (1974) filly: France
Golden Fleece (1979) Ireland,
   England
Saratoga Six (1982) USA
3—Lath (1732) England
   Slamerkin (1769) filly: New York,
      Pennsylvania
   Cobweb (1821) filly: England
   Achmet (1834) England
   Suspender (1889) England
   Meddler (1890) England
   Boniform (1904) Australia, New
      Zealand
   Inchcape (1918) USA
   Prince Meteor (1926) Ireland
   Early School (1934) England
   Rosewell (1935) Ireland
   Pharis (1936) France
   Blue Train (1944) England
   Berberis (1949) filly: West Germany
   Sagitaria (1951) filly: Argentina
   Pronto (1958) Argentina
   Whistling Wind (1960) Ireland,
      England
   Hardicanute (1962) England, Ireland
   Sir Wimborne (1973) Ireland, England
   Solar (1976) filly: Ireland
   Danzig (1977) USA
2—Flying Childers (1715) England
   Monkey (1725) England
   Shock (1729) England
   Selima (1745) filly: Maryland, Virginia
   Sailor (1817) England
   Battledore (1824) England
   Ghuznee (1838) filly: England
   Sir Amyas (1869) England

Thyestes (1928) England
Tai-Yang (1930) England
Quisquillosa (1941) filly: Argentina
Burg-el-Arab (1942) USA
Labrador (1953) Argentina
Abdos (1959) France
Royal Indiscretion (1960) filly: Ireland, England
Calchaqui (1960) France
Groton (1962) USA
Embroidery (1969) filly: Ireland, England

Morston (1970) England
Le Melody (1971) filly: Ireland
Lady Seymour (1972) filly: Ireland
Brahms (1974) Ireland
Fairy Bridge (1975) filly: Ireland
Tarona (1975) filly: France
1—Young Marske (1771) England
Sister to Tuckahoe (1814) filly: USA
Fillagree (1815) filly: England
Beeswing's dam (1817) filly: England

Middleton (1822) England
Amato (1835) England
Chattanooga (1862) England
Hero (1872) England
Plebeian (1872) England
Chouberski (1902) France
Cherimoya (1908) filly: England
Puits d'Amour (1932) France
Tourzima (1939) filly: France
Atan (1961) USA
Balkan Knight (1970) Ireland
Seneca (1973) filly: France

Oldest Horses

The greatest age at which any horse has won a race is 18, and of the 5 horses who share the record Wild Aster is the only one to win 3 times at that age.

Wild Aster, foaled in 1901, started his career in England and was then sent to France, where he dead-heated for a valuable steeplechase, the Grand Prix de la Ville de Nice, in 1909. The gelding returned to England and, at the age of 18, won 3 hurdle races within a week in March 1919. He dead-heated for the Selling Handicap Hurdle at Wolverhampton on 4 March; finished second in the Farm Selling Handicap Hurdle at Haydock Park on 8 March but was awarded the race because the jockey on the original winner had been warned off; and dead-heated for the Milverton Selling Handicap Hurdle at Warwick on 10 March, only to be awarded the race outright when the jockey on the other dead-heater dismounted in the wrong place.

Sonny Somers, foaled in 1962, was an English steeplechaser who gained his last 2 victories in 1980. He won the Star and Garter Handicap Chase at Southwell by 8 lengths on 14 February and the Westerham Handicap Chase at Lingfield Park by 5 lengths on 28 February.

On the Flat 2 stallions, 18-year-old Revenge and 14-year-old Tommy (the 1779 St Leger winner) took part in a bizarre match over 2 miles at Shrewsbury on 23 September 1790. Revenge beat his younger rival.

Marksman, foaled in 1808, was a high-class gelding who won the Wokingham Stakes at Ascot in 1814, the King's Plate at Lewes in 1817 and the Yeomen's Plate at Ashford, Kent on 4 September 1826. He lost the first heat of that race but won the next two, galloping a total of 7½ miles for his £50 prize.

Jorrocks, foaled in 1833, was the best horse to emerge in the early days of Australian racing. He gained the last of his 65 recorded wins in the Publican's Purse at Bathurst on 28 February 1851, though the only other runner threw his rider and galloped loose before the race.

The oldest horse to take part in a race is Creggmore Boy. Foaled in 1940, this veteran enjoyed his last victory in the Furness Selling Handicap Chase at Cartmel, Lancashire in 1957 and 5 years later, at the age of 22, ended his career by running fourth in the same race on 9 June 1962. He once finished second as a 21-year-old.

The remarkable Sonny Somers, with Ben de Haan in the saddle, takes the last fence on the way to victory in the Westerham Handicap 'Chase at Lingfield Park on 28 February 1980. It proved to be his last win, and his second at the age of 18.

Breeding Records

Champion Sires in Great Britain and Ireland

		Races won	£			Races won	£
1751	Blaze	13	973	1815	Rubens	30	7,998
1752	Cade	17	1,170	1816	Walton	28	9,366
1753	Cade	28	3,299	1817	Orville	41	6,403
1754	Regulus	25	2,052	1818	Walton	29	9,990
1755	Regulus	32	3,117	1819	Soothsayer	18	6,790
1756	Regulus	38	4,470	1820	Phantom	21	9,303
1757	Regulus	39	4,127	1821	Rubens	48	7,217
1758	Cade	45	6,130	1822	Rubens	56	10,572
1759	Cade	53	5,120	1823	Orville	22	9,978
1760	Cade	42	3,762	1824	Phantom	35	11,435
1761	Regulus	37	5,576	1825	Election	27	9,295
1762	Blank	41	7,180	1826	Whalebone	60	12,140
1763	Regulus	40	9,423	1827	Whalebone	66	8,133
1764	Blank	42	7,301	1828	Filho da Puta	78	8,394
1765	Regulus	24	7,535	1829	Blacklock	62	8,380
1766	Regulus	15	5,267	1830	Emilius	46	15,762
1767	Snap	28	5,149	1831	Emilius	57	18,378
1768	Snap	41	8,078	1832	Sultan	35	9,605
1769	Snap	35	9,389	1833	Sultan	47	10,348
1770	Blank	25	6,786	1834	Sultan	43	12,777
1771	Snap	46	11,457	1835	Sultan	46	10,993
1772	Matchem	82	22,046	1836	Sultan	53	20,580
1773	Matchem	81	17,177	1837	Sultan	50	13,297
1774	Matchem	79	19,512	1838	Camel	24	8,215
1775	Marske	59	16,054	1839	Priam	33	8,228
1776	Marske	66	21,243	1840	Priam	37	9,986
1777	Herod	56	15,828	1841	Taurus	37	9,413
1778	Herod	101	23,060	1842	Touchstone	18	9,630
1779	Herod	95	22,017	1843	Touchstone	37	19,544
1780	Herod	97	18,160	1844	Bay Middleton	48	13,648
1781	Herod	121	20,520	1845	Slane	35	11,445
1782	Herod	101	18,429	1846	Venison	58	12,369
1783	Herod	113	14,213	1847	Venison	73	19,963
1784	Herod	91	14,038	1848	Touchstone	39	21,475
1785	Highflyer	54	9,801	1849	Bay Middleton	28	14,804
1786	Highflyer	86	12,885	1850	Epirus	24	8,665
1787	Highflyer	91	12,906	1851	Orlando	21	12,181
1788	Highflyer	77	11,517	1852	Irish Birdcatcher	75	17,149
1789	Highflyer	91	15,722	1853	Melbourne	53	21,299
1790	Highflyer	109	15,778	1854	Orlando	72	16,974
1791	Highflyer	87	16,549	1855	Touchstone	55	20,147
1792	Highflyer	88	11,748	1856	Irish Birdcatcher	80	17,041
1793	Highflyer	70	11,561	1857	Melbourne	51	18,206
1794	Highflyer	48	7,020	1858	Orlando	63	15,283
1795	Highflyer	61	6,292	1859	Newminster	72	17,338
1796	Highflyer	77	12,729	1860	Stockwell	51	18,201
1797	King Fergus	29	4,352	1861	Stockwell	84	24,029
1798	Highflyer	34	4,916	1862	Stockwell	81	33,336
1799	Sir Peter Teazle	37	6,004	1863	Newminster	81	22,465
1800	Sir Peter Teazle	39	5,850	1864	Stockwell	88	28,708
1801	Sir Peter Teazle	44	5,351	1865	Stockwell	88	33,302
1802	Sir Peter Teazle	41	6,887	1866	Stockwell	132	61,391
1803	Trumpator	46	6,383	1867	Stockwell	113	42,521
1804	Sir Peter Teazle	72	8,097	1868	Buccaneer	68	33,713
1805	Sir Peter Teazle	85	10,688	1869	Thormanby	58	15,857
1806	Sir Peter Teazle	119	18,943	1870	King Tom	45	20,376
1807	Sir Peter Teazle	85	12,456	1871	King Tom	23	18,116
1808	Sir Peter Teazle	95	14,833	1872	Blair Athol	69	14,537
1809	Sir Peter Teazle	80	12,773	1873	Blair Athol	84	18,362
1810	Waxy	47	8,453	1874	Adventurer	35	21,667
1811	Sorceror	51	12,944	1875	Blair Athol	67	19,704
1812	Sorceror	42	10,948	1876	Lord Clifden	52	19,288
1813	Sorceror	42	13,599	1877	Blair Athol	62	28,830
1814	Selim	43	7,711	1878	Speculum	84	27,071

Year	Sire	Races won	£	Year	Sire	Races won	£
1879	Flageolet	10	18,657	1932	Gainsborough	33	34,789
1880	Hermit	66	30,907	1933	Gainsborough	32	38,138
1881	Hermit	49	27,223	1934	Blandford	57	75,707
1882	Hermit	81	47,311	1935	Blandford	22	57,538
1883	Hermit	62	30,406	1936	Fairway	38	57,931
1884	Hermit	75	29,418	1937	Solario	25	52,888
1885	Hermit	59	30,737	1938	Blandford	27	31,840
1886	Hermit	54	22,817	1939	Fairway	35	53,481
1887	Hampton	62	31,454	1940	Hyperion	25	13,407
1888	Galopin	51	30,211	1941	Hyperion	38	25,837
1889	Galopin	22	43,516	1942	Hyperion	30	13,801
1890	St Simon	27	32,799	1943	Fairway	31	12,133
1891	St Simon	25	26,890	1944	Fairway	32	15,704
1892	St Simon	47	53,504	1945	Hyperion	60	39,727
1893	St Simon	45	36,369	1946	Hyperion	64	54,021
1894	St Simon	44	42,092	1947	Nearco	42	45,087
1895	St Simon	35	30,469	1948	Nearco	40	41,541
1896	St Simon	38	59,734	1949	Nearco	49	52,545
1897	Kendal	31	28,845	1950	Fair Trial	39	37,887
1898	Galopin	18	21,699	1951	Nasrullah	36	44,664
1899	Orme	29	46,643	1952	Tehran	31	86,072
1900	St Simon	27	58,625	1953	Chanteur	30	57,296
1901	St Simon	33	28,964	1954	Hyperion	28	46,894
1902	Persimmon	16	36,868	1955	Alycidon	34	54,954
1903	St Frusquin	36	26,526	1956	Court Martial	61	49,237
1904	Gallinule	28	30,925	1957	Court Martial	47	58,307
1905	Gallinule	45	25,229	1958	Mossborough	42	66,471
1906	Persimmon	31	21,737	1959	Petition	44	75,955
1907	St Frusquin	45	25,355	1960	Aureole	28	90,088
1908	Persimmon	28	28,484	1961	Aureole	27	90,898
1909	Cyllene	29	35,550	1962	Never Say Die	31	65,902
1910	Cyllene	30	42,518	1963	Ribot	11	121,290
1911	Sundridge	31	33,284	1964	Chamossaire	13	141,819
1912	Persimmon	7	21,993	1965	Court Harwell	29	145,336
1913	Desmond	42	30,973	1966	Charlottesville	19	109,817
1914	Polymelus	34	29,607	1967	Ribot	9	128,530
1915	Polymelus	16	17,738	1968	Ribot	11	119,355
1916	Polymelus	15	16,031	1969	Crepello	42	88,538
1917	Bayardo	15	12,337	1970	Northern Dancer	14	247,450
1918	Bayardo	8	16,650	1971	Never Bend	9	133,160
1919	The Tetrarch	30	27,376	1972	Queen's Hussar	23	185,337
1920	Polymelus	42	40,447	1973	Vaguely Noble	5	127,908
1921	Polymelus	47	34,307	1974	Vaguely Noble	8	151,885
1922	Lemberg	45	32,888	1975	Great Nephew	29	313,284
1923	Swynford	30	37,897	1976	Wolver Hollow	37	210,765
1924	Son-in-Law	33	32,008	1977	Northern Dancer	13	380,982
1925	Phalaris	34	41,471	1978	Mill Reef	27	312,922
1926	Hurry On	26	59,109	1979	Petingo	21	471,574
1927	Buchan	37	45,918	1980	Pitcairn	16	463,693
1928	Phalaris	31	46,393	1981	Great Nephew	23	559,999
1929	Tetratema	35	53,025	1982	Be My Guest	28	469,421
1930	Son-in-Law	48	44,588	1983	Northern Dancer	21	442,206
1931	Pharos	27	43,922	1984	Northern Dancer	27	1,041,346

Champion Sires in North America

Year	Sire	Races won	$	Year	Sire	Races won	$
1829–30	Sir Charles	38	–*	1842	Priam	53	–
1831	Sir Charles	19	–	1843	Leviathan	26	–
1832	Sir Charles	43	–	1844	Priam	36	–
1833	Sir Charles	23	–	1845	Priam	23	–
1834	Monsieur Tonson	28	–	1846	Priam	16	–
1835	Bertrand	30	–	1847	Glencoe	34	–
1836	Sir Charles	28	–	1848	Leviathan/Trustee	19	–
1837	Leviathan	38	–	1849	Glencoe	21	–
1838	Leviathan	92	–	1850	Glencoe	22	–
1839	Leviathan	48	–	1851	Boston	31	–
1840	Medoc	61	–	1852	Boston	46	–
1841	Medoc	51	–	1853	Boston	56	–

		Races won	$				Races won	$
1854	Glencoe	56	–		1920	Fair Play	72	269,102
1855	Glencoe	42	–		1921	Celt	124	206,167
1856	Glencoe	45	–		1922	McGee	125	222,491
1857	Glencoe	62	–		1923	The Finn	31	285,759
1858	Glencoe	60	–		1924	Fair Play	84	296,204
1859	Albion	37	–		1925	Sweep	185	237,564
1860	Revenue	48	49,450		1926	Man o' War	49	408,137
1861	Lexington	27	22,425		1927	Fair Play	77	361,518
1862	Lexington	14	9,700		1928	High Time	109	307,631
1863	Lexington	25	14,235		1929	Chicle	88	289,123
1864	Lexington	38	28,440		1930	Sir Gallahad	49	422,200
1865	Lexington	87	58,750		1931	St Germans	47	315,585
1866	Lexington	112	92,725		1932	Chatterton	93	210,040
1867	Lexington	86	54,030		1933	Sir Gallahad	78	136,428
1868	Lexington	92	68,340		1934	Sir Gallahad	92	180,165
1869	Lexington	81	56,375		1935	Chance Play	88	191,465
1870	Lexington	82	129,360		1936	Sickle	128	209,800
1871	Lexington	102	109,095		1937	The Porter	104	292,262
1872	Lexington	82	71,915		1938	Sickle	107	327,822
1873	Lexington	71	71,565		1939	Challenger	99	316,281
1874	Lexington	70	51,889		1940	Sir Gallahad	102	305,610
1875	Leamington	32	64,518		1941	Blenheim	64	378,981
1876	Lexington	34	90,570		1942	Equipoise	82	437,141
1877	Leamington	49	41,170		1943	Bull Dog	172	372,706
1878	Lexington	36	50,198		1944	Chance Play	150	431,100
1879	Leamington	56	70,837		1945	War Admiral	59	591,352
1880	Bonnie Scotland	137	135,700		1946	Mahmoud	101	638,025
1881	Leamington	67	139,219		1947	Bull Lea	128	1,259,718
1882	Bonnie Scotland	169	103,475		1948	Bull Lea	147	1,334,027
1883	Billet	48	89,998		1949	Bull Lea	165	991,842
1884	Glenelg	108	69,862		1950	Heliopolis	167	852,292
1885	Virgil	56	73,235		1951	Count Fleet	124	1,160,847
1886	Glenelg	136	113,638		1952	Bull Lea	136	1,630,655
1887	Glenelg	120	120,031		1953	Bull Lea	107	1,155,846
1888	Glenelg	134	130,746		1954	Heliopolis	148	1,406,638
1889	Rayon d'Or	101	175,877		1955	Nasrullah	69	1,433,660
1890	St Blaise	105	185,005		1956	Nasrullah	106	1,462,413
1891	Longfellow	143	189,334		1957	Princequillo	147	1,698,427
1892	Iroquois	145	183,026		1958	Princequillo	110	1,394,540
1893	Himyar	138	249,502		1959	Nasrullah	141	1,434,543
1894	Sir Modred	137	134,318		1960	Nasrullah	122	1,419,683
1895	Hanover	133	106,908		1961	Ambiorix	148	936,976
1896	Hanover	157	86,853		1962	Nasrullah	107	1,474,831
1897	Hanover	159	122,374		1963	Bold Ruler	56	917,531
1898	Hanover	124	118,590		1964	Bold Ruler	88	1,457,156
1899	Albert	64	95,975		1965	Bold Ruler	90	1,091,924
1900	Kingston	110	116,368		1966	Bold Ruler	107	2,306,523
1901	Sir Dixon	94	165,682		1967	Bold Ruler	135	2,249,272
1902	Hastings	63	113,865		1968	Bold Ruler	99	1,988,427
1903	Ben Strome	91	106,965		1969	Bold Ruler	90	1,357,144
1904	Meddler	55	222,555		1970	Hail to Reason	82	1,400,839
1905	Hamburg	60	153,160		1971	Northern Dancer	93	1,288,580
1906	Meddler	54	151,243		1972	Round Table	98	1,199,933
1907	Commando	34	270,345		1973	Bold Ruler	74	1,488,622
1908	Hastings	93	154,061		1974	T.V. Lark	121	1,242,000
1909	Ben Brush	67	75,143		1975	What a Pleasure	101	2,011,878
1910	Kingston	41	85,220		1976	What a Pleasure	108	1,622,159
1911	Star Shoot	103	53,895		1977	Dr Fager	124	1,593,079
1912	Star Shoot	126	79,973		1978	Exclusive Native	106	1,969,867
1913	Broomstick	114	76,009		1979	Exclusive Native	104	2,872,605
1914	Broomstick	90	99,043		1980	Raja Baba	149	2,483,352
1915	Broomstick	108	94,387		1981	Nodouble	115	2,800,884
1916	Star Shoot	216	138,163		1982	His Majesty	86	2,675,823
1917	Star Shoot	167	131,674		1983	Halo	86	2,773,637
1918	Sweep	69	139,057		1984	Seattle Slew	49	5,361,259
1919	Star Shoot	108	197,233					

*From 1829–30 to 1859 the championship was determined on the basis of races won, and no account was made of prize money earned.

Champion Sires in Australia

		Races won	£			Races won	£
1883/4	St Albans	48	8,260	1934/5	Heroic	91	26,540
1884/5	St Albans	59	10,523	1935/6	Heroic	105	26,703
1885/6	Musket	75	16,503	1936/7	Heroic	108	32,825
1886/7	Robinson Crusoe	25	8,387	1937/8	Heroic	141	53,213
1887/8	Chester	27	12,605	1938/9	Heroic	101	35,496
1888/9	Musket	54	30,023	1939/40	Beau Père	71	31,295
1889/90	Chester	28	17,872	1940/1	Beau Père	89	41,710
1890/1	Musket	24	19,844	1941/2	Beau Père	42	23,410
1891/2	Chester	30	13,391	1942/3	Spearfelt	75	25,784
1892/3	Chester	38	13,505	1943/4	Manitoba	48	31,039
1893/4	Newminster	38	10,894	1944/5	Manitoba	57	40,217
1894/5	Grand Flaneur	25	9,162	1945/6	Emborough	94	37,248
1895/6	Trenton	53	13,126	1946/7	The Buzzard	74	39,676
1896/7	Newminster	30	9,181	1947/8	Midstream	62	52,407
1897/8	Lochiel	97	15,222	1948/9	Helios	74	71,297
1898/9	Gozo	54	12,683	1949/50	The Buzzard	60	56,794
1899/1900	Lochiel	110	16,137	1950/1	Midstream	58	64,528
1900/1	Lochiel	120	12,668	1951/2	Midstream	68	63,700
1901/2	Trenton	19	11,843	1952/3	Delville Wood	59	59,090
1902/3	Pilgrim's Progress	44	12,329	1953/4	Delville Wood	87	94,974
1903/4	Grafton	107	15,154	1954/5	Delville Wood	49	64,829
1904/5	Lochiel	97	15,227	1955/6	Delville Wood	58	59,364
1905/6	Lochiel	98	19,064	1956/7	Delville Wood	22	72,709
1906/7	Grafton	164	22,831	1957/8	Khorassan	26	54,437
1907/8	Grafton	195	20,443	1958/9	Star Kingdom	61	81,241
1908/9	Grafton	183	22,833	1959/60	Star Kingdom	79	77,515
1909/10	Maltster	145	36,972	1960/1	Star Kingdom	79	81,862
1910/11	Maltster	145	27,629	1961/2	Star Kingdom	85	74,521
1911/12	Maltster	163	32,957	1962/3	Wilkes	110	94,529
1912/13	Ayr Laddie	145	26,140	1963/4	Wilkes	97	110,244
1913/14	Maltster	167	31,592	1964/5	Star Kingdom	83	105,138
1914/15	Maltster	183	25,274				$
1915/16	Wallace	25	24,945	1965/6	Better Boy	85	176,220
1916/17	Linacre	115	21,396	1966/7	Alcimedes	40	216,977
1917/18	Linacre	102	26,883	1967/8	Agricola	49	212,776
1918/19	The Welkin	73	31,371	1968/9	Wilkes	124	312,148
1919/20	Comedy King	75	30,803	1969/70	Alcimedes	71	254,520
1920/1	The Welkin	61	32,112	1970/1	Better Boy	123	285,236
1921/2	The Welkin	88	40,374	1971/2	Better Boy	129	283,605
1922/3	Comedy King	92	43,114	1972/3	Oncidium	64	363,775
1923/4	Valais	29	28,379	1973/4	Matrice	107	365,011
1924/5	Valais	47	38,876	1974/5	Oncidium	75	756,981
1925/6	Valais	58	57,368	1975/6	Showdown	116	472,266
1926/7	Valais	62	43,455	1976/7	Better Boy	74	563,195
1927/8	Valais	69	36,166	1977/8	Showdown	106	584,269
1928/9	Magpie	96	44,231	1978/9	Century	58	621,093
1929/30	Night Raid	27	48,359	1979/80	Bletchingly	58	876,575
1930/1	Night Raid	21	27,449	1980/1	Bletchingly	92	623,200
1931/2	Limond	26	24,332	1981/2	Bletchingly	96	950,610
1932/3	Heroic	94	25,468	1982/3	Sir Tristram	83	1,982,315
1933/4	Heroic	103	32,851	1983/4	Vain	157	1,508,175

Champion Sires in New Zealand

		Races won	£			Races won	£
1892/3	St Leger	—*	—	1904/5	Stepniak	—	8,785
1893/4	St George	—	—	1905/6	Multiform	—	11,634
1894/5	St Leger	—	—	1906/7	Seaton Delaval	—	9,114
1895/6	St Leger	—	5,090	1907/8	Stepniak	—	10,411
1896/7	St Leger	—	6,981	1908/9	Soult	—	16,000
1897/8	St Leger	—	8,283	1909/10	Soult	—	16,044
1898/9	Castor	—	6,928	1910/11	Soult	—	18,483
1899/1900	St Leger	—	6,707	1911/12	Soult	—	16,678
1900/1	St Leger	—	9,999	1912/13	Soult	—	20,685
1901/2	St Leger	—	11,327	1913/14	Martian	—	15,173
1902/3	Stepniak	—	8,098	1914/15	Martian	—	22,848
1903/4	Seaton Delaval	—	8,783	1915/16	Martian	—	17,750

		Races won	£
1916/17	Martian	—	18,586
1917/18	Martian	—	13,980
1918/19	Martian	—	22,951
1919/20	Demosthenes	—	27,756
1920/1	Martian	—	30,735
1921/2	Absurd	—	36,498
1922/3	Absurd	—	26,313
1923/4	Absurd	—	29,690
1924/5	Solferino	—	28,281
1925/6	Absurd	—	27,606
1926/7	Absurd	—	23,309
1927/8	Lucullus	—	17,489
1928/9	Paper Money	79	22,067
1929/30	Chief Ruler	75	20,136
1930/1	Limond	49	16,033
1931/2	Chief Ruler	88	14,098
1932/3	Hunting Song	93	9,646
1933/4	Hunting Song	104	10,301
1934/5	Hunting Song	113	15,194
1935/6	Hunting Song	123	14,013
1936/7	Hunting Song	111	16,054
1937/8	Hunting Song	114	19,761
1938/9	Beau Père	51	17,950
1939/40	Beau Père	61	24,490
1940/1	Foxbridge	79	23,459
1941/2	Foxbridge	61	21,003
1942/3	Foxbridge	37	21,225
1943/4	Foxbridge	59	28,256
1944/5	Foxbridge	75	40,874
1945/6	Foxbridge	98	62,111
1946/7	Foxbridge	121	80,620
1947/8	Foxbridge	114	76,382
1948/9	Foxbridge	85	55,350
1949/50	Foxbridge	100	65,829
1950/1	Foxbridge	60	51,695

		Races won	£
1951/2	Balloch	67	47,798
1952/3	Balloch	65	44,945
1953/4	Ruthless	31	37,732
1954/5	Fair's Fair	58	48,030
1955/6	Count Rendered	58	43,837
1956/7	Ruthless	50	47,150
1957/8	Faux Tirage	53	34,908
1958/9	Fair's Fair	56	40,657
1959/60	Summertime	65	42,289
1960/1	Summertime	63	40,549
1961/2	Le Filou	45	40,086
1962/3	Count Rendered	62	57,157
1963/4	Le Filou	42	43,139
1964/5	Summertime	58	47,251
1965/6	Le Filou	67	68,207
1966/7	Le Filou	59	59,447

		Races won	$
1967/8	Copenhagen	93	101,537
1968/9	Pakistan	78	103,388
1969/70	Copenhagen	56	104,305
1970/1	Pakistan	90	138,360
1971/2	Better Honey	71	146,105
1972/3	Mellay	103	188,569
1973/4	Pakistan	76	222,767
1974/5	Copenhagen	88	180,787
1975/6	Copenhagen	77	187,970
1976/7	Mellay	133	266,198
1977/8	Bandmaster	32	214,225
1978/9	Gate Keeper	53	185,230
1979/80	Alvaro	48	232,392
1980/1	War Hawk	41	275,640
1981/2	Noble Bijou	87	434,452
1982/3	Noble Bijou	88	367,512
1983/4	Noble Bijou	80	362,740

*Figures unavailable.

Most national sires' championships

The record number of sires' championships won in any one country is 16, achieved by the great American horse Lexington. His stock dominated US racing to a remarkable degree virtually throughout the 1860s and 1870s, and he headed the list from 1861 to 1874 inclusive, and again in both 1876 and 1878.

The English-bred horse Buccaneer (foaled 1857) also compiled a formidable score. He topped the British table in 1868, by which time he had already been exported to Austria-Hungary. In due course he led the Hungarian list 15 times and was four times top in Germany, giving him a total of 20 championships.

Champion sires on both sides of the Atlantic

The first horse to head the sires' lists on both sides of the Atlantic was 1830 Derby winner Priam. Champion in Britain in 1839 and 1840, he topped the American lists for 1842, 1844, 1845 and 1846.

Nasrullah (foaled 1940) was another exported horse to achieve this feat. He was top in Great Britain and Ireland in 1951 and afterwards collected five championships in North America—in 1955, 1956, 1959, 1960 and 1962.

The only horse to have won both championships without having himself changed locations is Northern Dancer (foaled 1961). He was the 1971 leader in North America and has dominated four seasons in Great Britain and Ireland—in 1970, 1977, 1983 and 1984.

Champion sire in Britain and France in same season

Blandford (1919–35), who stood as a stallion in both Ireland and England, achieved the unique feat of heading the lists in both Britain and France in the year of his death.

Most winners sired in a season

Star Shoot, an English-bred son of Triple Crown winner Isinglass, is credited as the horse whose

Nasrullah, a gifted but unwilling athlete, is shown in unco-oper-ative mood as Gordon Richards tries to entice him to the start of the 1943 New 2000 Guineas, in which he eventually finished fourth. In due course he became an immensely influential sire, heading the list on both sides of the Atlantic.

stock won most races in a single season. Foaled in 1898, and exported to the USA as a 3-year-old, he became champion North American sire on five occasions, recording a score of 216 races won by 87 individual offspring in 1916.

Most mares covered in one stud season

Spread Eagle, the 1795 Derby winner, attracted huge demand for his services after his importation to Virginia in 1798. It is recorded that in 1801 he covered no fewer that 234 mares. He was subsequently transferred to Kentucky and died there in 1805. Other horses are known to have covered more than 200 mares in a season in America at around that time.

Oldest active stallions

Many stallions have continued to cover until a ripe old age, perhaps most notably the 1780 Derby winner Diomed. He was active at stud in Virginia at the age of 30 and was due to cover again when he died at 31 in March 1808.

The most notable instance of a big race winner sired by a horse at an advanced age concerns Tetotum, who won the Oaks of 1780. Her sire Matchem was 28 years old at the time of her conception.

Most consistently productive broodmare

Queen Esther (foaled 1864), a daughter of St Leger winner Warlock, ran four times without success as a two-year-old before being put to stud. She proceeded to produce a foal every year for 21 seasons (1868–88) before proving barren for the first time. She died in 1890 after giving birth to a dead filly, her 22nd foal in 23 years.

Oldest productive broodmare

Contract (foaled 1862), a mare by Stockwell who won 12 of her 63 races, had her first foal at the age of seven and was sold to France for 200 gns when nine. In 1893, at the age of 31, she was safely delivered of a filly by Begonia at the Haras de la Bourdonnière.

Contract's record may have been matched by Flora, a mare by Regulus who produced a colt by Chillaby in 1780, when she was either 30 or 31 years old.

In more recent times the Brumeux mare Wayward Miss produced a filly by Pendragon at the age of 30 in 1966. Her final mating was with Kolper, when she was 31 and the horse was 24, but she failed to get in foal.

North America's Record Auction Yearlings

The first yearling auctioned in North America for $25,000 was Sun Turret (b c Sunstar – Marian Hood, by Martagon), bought by John Ross in 1919.

Four years later Gifford Cochran gave the same sum for each of five colts submitted to the Saratoga Sales, but they formed part of a package deal and were not submitted to public auction. Subsequent record holders have been as follows, those from 1954 onwards ranking as the world's highest-priced yearlings:

		Buyer	$
1925	**War Feathers** (ch f Man o' War – Tuscan Red, by William Rufus)	Hamilton Farm	50,500
1927	**Hustle On** (b c Hurry On – Fatima, by Radium)	William Coe	70,000
1928	**New Broom** (ch c Whisk Broom – Payment, by All Gold)	Eastland Farms Syndicate	75,000
1954	**Nalur** (ch c Nasrullah – Lurline B., by Alibhai)	F. J. Adams Syndicate	86,000
1956	**Rise 'n Shine** (gr c Hyperion – Deodora, by Dante)	Mrs Liz Lunn	87,000
1961	**Swapson** (ch c Swaps – Obedient, by Mahmoud)	John Olin	130,000
1964	**One Bold Bid** (br c Bold Ruler – Forgetmenow, by Menow)	Mrs Velma Morrison	170,000
1966	**Bold Discovery** (br c Bold Ruler – La Dauphine, by Princequillo)	Frank McMahon	200,000
1967	**Majestic Prince** (ch c Raise a Native – Gay Hostess, by Royal Charger)	Frank McMahon	250,000
1968	**Exemplary** (b c Fleet Nasrullah – Sequence, by Count Fleet)	Mrs Ada Martin	280,000
1968	**Reine Enchanteur** (ch f Sea-Bird – Libra, by Hyperion)	Wendell Rosso	405,000
1970	**Crowned Prince** (ch c Raise a Native – Gay Hostess, by Royal Charger)	Frank McMahon	510,000
1973	**Wajima** (b c Bold Ruler – Iskra, by Le Haar)	East-West Stable	600,000
1974	**Kentucky Gold** (b c Raise a Native – Gold Digger, by Nashua)	Wallace Gilroy	625,000
1975	**Elegant Prince** (ch c Raise a Native – Gay Hostess, by Royal Charger)	Franklin Groves	715,000
1976	**Canadian Bound** (ch c Secretariat – Charming Alibi, by Honeys Alibi)	Theodore Burnett et al	1,500,000
1979	**Hoist the King** (br c Hoist the Flag – Royal Dowry, by Royal Charger)	Kazuo Nakamura	1,600,000
1980	**Lichine** (b c Lyphard – Stylish Genie, by Bagdad)	Stavros Niarchos	1,700,000
1981	**Ballydoyle** (br c Northern Dancer – South Ocean, by New Providence)	Robert Sangster et al	3,500,000
1982	**Empire Glory** (b c Nijinsky – Spearfish, by Fleet Nasrullah)	Robert Sangster et al	4,250,000
1983	**Foxboro** (b c Northern Dancer – Desert Vixen, by In Reality)	Robert Sangster et al	4,250,000
1983	**Snaafi Dancer** (b c Northern Dancer – My Bupers, by Bupers)	Sheikh Mohammed	10,200,000

Europe's Record Auction Yearlings

Auction sales of yearlings came into vogue in England in the late 1820s, and 1837 brought the first transaction of more than 1,000 guineas. The following have held, or have shared, the European record:

		Buyer	Guineas
1837	**Glenlivat** (ch c Rowton or Cetus – Camarine, by Juniper)	5th Duke of Richmond	1,010
1854	**Voivode** (ch c Surplice – Hybla, by The Provost)	James Merry	1,020
1855	**Lord of the Hills** (br c Touchstone – Fair Helen, by Pantaloon)	William Stirling Crawfurd	1,800
1866	**St Ronan** (ch c St Albans – Elspeth, by Irish Birdcatcher)	Henry Chaplin	2,000
1866	**Angus** (b c Newminster – Lady Elcho, by Sleight-of-Hand)	12th Duke of Hamilton	2,500
1876	**Maximilian** (b c Macaroni – Duchess, by St Albans)	1st Duke of Westminster	4,100
1890	**La Flèche** (br f St Simon – Quiver, by Toxophilite)	Baron Maurice de Hirsch	5,500
1891	**Childwick** (br c St Simon – Plaisanterie, by Wellingtonia)	John Blundell Maple	6,000
1900	**Cupbearer** (b c Orme – Kissing Cup, by Hampton)	2nd Duke of Westminster	9,100
1900	**Sceptre** (b f Persimmon – Ornament, by Bend Or)	Bob Sievier	10,000
1919	**Westward Ho** (br c Swynford – Blue Tit, by Wildfowler)	1st Baron Glanely	11,500
1920	**Blue Ensign** (ch c The Tetrarch – Blue Tit, by Wildfowler)	1st Baron Glanely	14,500
1936	**Colonel Payne** (b c Fairway – Golden Hair, by Golden Sun)	Miss Dorothy Paget	15,000
1945	**Sayajirao** (b c Nearco – Rosy Legend, by Dark Legend)	HH Maharaja of Baroda	28,000
1966	**Rodrigo** (b c Charlottesville – Rosmerta, by Nearula)	Tim Vigors and Co.	31,000
1967	**Exalt** (ch c Exbury – San Luis Rey, by Hard Sauce)	Charles Engelhard	31,000
1967	**Démocratie** (b f Immortality – Review, by Panorama)	Mme Pierre Wertheimer	36,000
1968	**Entrepreneur** (b c Ribot – Montea, by Seaulieu)	William Harder and Herbert Allen	37,000
1969	**La Hague** (b f Immortality – Review, by Panorama)	Souren Vanian	51,000
1970	**Cambrienne** (br f Sicambre – Torbella, by Tornado)	John Mulcahy	65,000
1971	**Bigivor** (b c Sir Ivor – Clorinda, by Set Fair)	Lady Beaverbrook	81,000
1971	**Princely Review** (b c Native Prince – Review, by Panorama)	Sir Douglas Clague	117,000
1975	**Be My Guest** (ch c Northern Dancer – What a Treat, by Tudor Minstrel)	Mrs Diana Manning et al	127,000
1975	**Million** (ch c Mill Reef – Lalibela, by Honeyway)	Lady Beaverbrook	202,000
1977	**Link** (b c Lyphard – Chain, by Herbager)	Mrs Diana Manning et al	250,000
1978	**Millième** (b f Mill Reef – Hardiemma, by Hardicanute)	Stavros Niarchos	250,000
1978	**Sand Hawk** (ch c Grundy – Parsimony, by Parthia)	Khalid Bin Abdullah	264,000
1979	**Centurius** (ch c Great Nephew – Word from Lundy, by Worden)	Jim McCaughey	270,000
1979	**Ghadeer** (b c Lyphard – Swanilda, by Habitat)	Hamdan Al Maktoum	625,000
1981	**South Atlantic** (b c Mill Reef – Arkadina, by Ribot)	Robert Sangster et al	640,000
1983	**Trojan Prince** (b c Troy – Princess Matilda, by Habitat)	Sheikh Mohammed	1,120,000
1983	**Convention** (b c General Assembly – Sarah Siddons, by Le Levanstell)	Khalid Bin Abdullah	1,400,000
1983	**Hero Worship** (ch c Hello Gorgeous – Centre Piece, by Tompion)	Robert Sangster et al	1,550,000
1984	**Authaal** (b c Shergar – Galletto, by Nijinsky)	Sheikh Mohammed	2,588,000*

*Figure converted from 3,100,000 Irish guineas, to nearest 1,000 guineas.

Record Times

World's Fastest Times

It is one of the ironies of horse racing that while, throughout the history of the Thoroughbred, man's constant quest has been for the horse who can run fastest between two given points, records in terms of time have tended to be meaningless. Hand-timing could never be thoroughly reliable, but even since electric timing became commonplace, other factors have been apt to make time alone a poor and misleading guide to racing class. Of course, in all but a tiny minority of races, horses are ridden with the intention of beating other horses, not of beating the clock. As a consequence, many recognised top horses do not break time records, whereas many manifestly ordinary horses do.

The condition and contours of the track and wind direction commonly have as much to do with the setting of time records as the intrinsic merit of the record-breaker, and comparisons between time records set in various parts of the world have little significance. Inevitably, most of the world's fastest times attributed to British horses were set at Epsom and Brighton, courses which feature sharp descents, and while the American record-holders might seem more legitimate on account of the almost uniformly level tracks, it is American practice to clock races from a flying start and to return times to the nearest fifth of a second, as opposed to the one-hundredth of a second common in other countries.

Distance	Time	Name	Age	Weight (lb)	Course	Date
5 furlongs	53.6*	**Indigenous**	4	131	Epsom, England	2 June 1960
	53.70	**Spark Chief**	4	110	Epsom, England	30 Aug 1983
	55.2	**Chinook Pass**	3	113	Longacres, USA	17 Sep 1982
6 furlongs	1:06.2*	**b g (unnamed) Blink – Broken Tendril**	2	123	Brighton, England	6 Aug 1929
	1:07.2	**Grey Papa**	6	112	Longacres, USA	4 Sep 1972
	1:07.2	**Petro D. Jay**	6	120	Turf Paradise, USA	9 May 1982
1 mile	1:31.8*	**Soueida**	4	126	Brighton, England	19 Sep 1963
	1:31.8*	**Loose Cover**	3	110	Brighton, England	9 June 1966
	1:31.8*	**Traditional Miss**	6	132	Chepstow, Wales	27 June 1981
	1:31.8*	**Traditional Miss**	6	132	Chepstow, Wales	31 Aug 1981
	1:32.0	**Royal Heroine**	4	123	Hollywood Park, USA	10 Nov 1984
1¼ miles	1:57.4	**Double Discount**	4	113	Santa Anita, USA	6 Oct 1977
1½ miles	2:23.0	**Fiddle Isle**	5	124	Santa Anita, USA	21 Mar 1970
	2:23.0	**John Henry**	5	126	Santa Anita, USA	16 Mar 1980
2 miles	3:16.75	**Il Tempo**	7	130	Trentham, NZ	17 Jan 1970
2½ miles	4:14.6	**Miss Grillo**	6	118	Pimlico, USA	12 Nov 1948

*Hand-timed.

Polls and Ratings

English Poll

In May 1886 the leading English racing newspaper *The Sporting Times* sent a circular to about 100 of the most prominent figures on the Turf, including owners, trainers, jockeys, journalists and officials, asking each of them to name the 10 best horses of the 19th century. The most popular nominations, with the number of voters who placed them in their top 10, were published on 17 July 1886.

1. Gladiateur (1862)	65
2. West Australian (1850)	63
3. Isonomy (1875)	62
4. St Simon (1881)	53
5. Blair Athol (1861)	52
6. The Flying Dutchman (1846)	49
7= Virago (1851)	36
St Gatien (1881)	36
9. Ormonde (1883)	34
10. Robert the Devil (1877)	31
11. Cremorne (1869)	30
12= Foxhall (1878)	27
Plaisanterie (1882)	27
14. Stockwell (1849)	24
15. Bay Middleton (1833)	22
16. Barcaldine (1878)	21
17. Thormanby (1857)	16
18. Plenipotentiary (1831)	15
19. Galopin (1872)	14
20= Crucifix (1837)	13
Teddington (1848)	13
22= Touchstone (1831)	12
Blink Bonny (1854)	12
Springfield (1873)	12
Bend Or (1877)	12

26.	Wheel of Fortune (1876)	11
27=	Priam (1827)	9
	Fisherman (1853)	9
	Achievement (1864)	9
30=	Velocipede (1825)	8
	Voltigeur (1847)	8
	Blue Gown (1865)	8

Of these, the French champion Plaisanterie was the only one who was not trained in England. Virago, Plaisanterie, Crucifix, Blink Bonny, Wheel of Fortune and Achievement were fillies.

The poll was taken before Ormonde won the Derby and there is little doubt that he would have come first had it been conducted later that year. Despite the bias towards recent champions St Simon, who had been retired less than 12 months before, was decisively outvoted by 3 earlier champions.

The experts were also asked to name absolutely the best horse they had ever seen. The most popular nominations, with the number of votes they received, were as follows:

1.	Gladiateur	11
2.	Isonomy	10
3.	West Australian	9
4.	St Simon	8
5=	Virago	6
	Blair Athol	6

American Polls

In 1973 the American magazine *The Thoroughbred Record* asked its readers to list, in order of merit, the 10 greatest horses of all time. The result, published on 17 November 1973, was determined by awarding 10 points for each first-place vote down to one point for each tenth-place vote. Most voters ignored foreign horses and Ribot was the only one to reach the final top 10. These top-rated champions, with the number of points they received, were as follows:

1.	Man o' War (1917)	1487
2.	Citation (1945)	1021
3.	Secretariat (1970)	923
4.	Kelso (1957)	780
5.	Native Dancer (1950)	520
6.	Count Fleet (1940)	455
7.	Buckpasser (1963)	357
8.	Ribot (1952)	320
9.	Dr Fager (1964)	259
10.	Tom Fool (1949)	241

In December 1983 the American magazine *The Blood-Horse* published a list of the 41 Horses of

Gladiateur, pictured with Harry Grimshaw up, was nicknamed "Avenger of Waterloo" when he became the first French-bred winner of the Derby in 1865. Many regarded him as the best horse of the 19th century.

the Year in the United States from 1936 to 1982 plus the best horses of 1933 (Equipoise), 1934 (Cavalcade) and 1935 (Discovery). From those 44 champions of the previous half-century, it asked its readers to name the best 10 in no particular order. The top 20 champions, with the percentage of voters who nominated them, were published on 23 June 1984.

1.	Secretariat (1970)	89
2.	Kelso (1957)	88
3.	Citation (1945)	74
4.	Native Dancer (1950)	70
5.	Forego (1970)	67
6.	Seattle Slew (1974)	58
7.	Affirmed (1975)	55
8.	Spectacular Bid (1976)	53
9.	Round Table (1954)	53
10.	John Henry (1975)	50
11.	Buckpasser (1963)	46
12.	Swaps (1952)	45
13.	Count Fleet (1940)	30
14.	Nashua (1952)	29
15.	Bold Ruler (1954)	26
16.	War Admiral (1934)	23
17.	Tom Fool (1949)	19
18=	Equipoise (1928)	16
	Seabiscuit (1933)	16
	Whirlaway (1938)	16

Among the racing journalists who took part in the poll, the most popular choices were Secretariat (100 per cent), Citation (97 per cent) and Kelso (83 per cent).

The American Racing Manual is America's most authoritative racing annual and among its features is a section on 'Great Horses of the 20th Century'. The 15 champions currently included are:

Sysonby (1902)	Native Dancer (1950)
Colin (1905)	Nashua (1952)
Exterminator (1915)	Swaps (1952)
Man o' War (1917)	Kelso (1957)
Equipoise (1928)	Secretariat (1970)
Count Fleet (1940)	Forego (1970)
Citation (1945)	Affirmed (1975)
Tom Fool (1949)	

Notable Thoroughbreds

In 1980 a huge, meticulously-researched book called *Notable New Zealand Thoroughbreds* was published by Alister Taylor in New Zealand. At the heart of it was a series of 54 chapters, each

Recognised as one of the greatest horses in United States racing history, Native Dancer lost only one of 22 starts, and that unluckily in the 1953 Kentucky Derby. Here he records an easy victory later that season in the Arlington Classic.

describing in detail the career of a great New Zealand champion selected by the authors on the basis of racecourse performance alone. Two companion volumes, *Notable Australian Thoroughbreds* and *Notable English and Irish Thoroughbreds*, were published in 1981 and 1984 respectively.

The 54 Notable New Zealand Thoroughbreds were:

Lurline (1869) filly	Royal Chief (1934)
Welcome Jack (1879)	Defaulter (1935)
Nelson (1880)	Beaulivre (1936)
Trenton (1881)	Beau Vite (1936)
Lochiel (1882)	Kindergarten (1937)
Carbine (1885)	Sleepy Fox (1939) gelding
Multiform (1894)	Soneri (1942) filly
Advance (1896)	Beaumaris (1946)
Cruciform (1898) filly	Mainbrace (1947)
Menschikoff (1898)	Dalray (1948)
Achilles (1899)	Rising Fast (1949) gelding
Gladsome (1900) filly	Redcraze (1950) gelding
Machine Gun (1900)	Somerset Fair (1951)
Bobrikoff (1904) gelding	Great Sensation (1952) gelding
Warstep (1910) filly	Syntax (1952)
Desert Gold (1912) filly	Yahabeebe (1953) filly
Sasanof (1913) gelding	Cadiz (1956) gelding
Gloaming (1915) gelding	Even Stevens (1957)
Amythas (1916) gelding	Il Tempo (1962) gelding
The Hawk (1918) gelding	Daryl's Joy (1966)
Rapine (1919) gelding	Battle Heights (1967) gelding
Ballymena (1920) gelding	Show Gate (1969) filly
Reremoana (1920) gelding	Grey Way (1970) gelding
Limerick (1923) gelding	Good Lord (1971) gelding
Nightmarch (1925)	Balmerino (1972)
Phar Lap (1926) gelding	La Mer (1973) filly
Cuddle (1929) filly	Uncle Remus (1974)

The 51 Notable Australian Thoroughbreds were:

Jorrocks (1833) gelding	Shannon (1941)
The Barb (1863)	Royal Gem (1942)
Chester (1874)	Comic Court (1945)
Grand Flaneur (1877)	Delta (1946)
Malua (1879)	Carioca (1947)
Abercorn (1884)	Hydrogen (1948)
Carbine (1885)	Rising Fast (1949) gelding
Wakeful (1896) filly	Sailor's Guide (1952)
Poseidon (1903)	Todman (1954)
Poitrel (1914)	Tulloch (1954)
Eurythmic (1916)	Sky High (1957)
Heroic (1921)	Wenona Girl (1957) filly
Windbag (1921)	Light Fingers (1961) filly
Amounis (1922) gelding	Galilee (1962) gelding
Manfred (1922)	Tobin Bronze (1962)
Phar Lap (1926) gelding	Rain Lover (1964)
Rogilla (1927) gelding	Vain (1966)
Chatham (1928)	Baguette (1967)
Peter Pan (1929)	Gunsynd (1967)
Hall Mark (1930)	Leilani (1970) filly
Ajax (1934)	Maybe Mahal (1972) filly
High Caste (1936)	Surround (1973) filly
Tranquil Star (1937) filly	Dulcify (1975) gelding
Bernborough (1939)	Manikato (1975) gelding
Flight (1940) filly	Kingston Town (1976) gelding
Russia (1940)	

Carbine, Phar Lap and Rising Fast appeared in both the New Zealand and the Australian volumes.

The 50 Notable English and Irish Thoroughbreds were:

Eclipse (1764)	Ormonde (1883)
Highflyer (1774)	Orme (1889)
Dungannon (1780)	Isinglass (1890)
Sir Peter Teazle (1784)	Persimmon (1893)
Hambletonian (1792)	Flying Fox (1896)
Eleanor (1798) filly	Sceptre (1899) filly
Velocipede (1825)	Pretty Polly (1901) filly
Priam (1827)	Bayardo (1906)
Plenipotentiary (1831)	The Tetrarch (1911)
Touchstone (1831)	Hurry On (1913)
Bay Middleton (1833)	Gay Crusader (1914)
Beeswing (1833) filly	Fairway (1925)
Crucifix (1837) filly	Hyperion (1930)
Alice Hawthorn (1838) filly	Windsor Lad (1931)
The Flying Dutchman (1846)	Bahram (1932)
Stockwell (1849)	Sun Chariot (1939) filly
West Australian (1850)	Tudor Minstrel (1944)
Virago (1851) filly	Abernant (1946)
Blink Bonny (1854) filly	Pinza (1950)
Blair Athol (1861)	Petite Etoile (1956) filly
Gladiateur (1862)	Nijinsky (1967)
Galopin (1872)	Brigadier Gerard (1968)
Isonomy (1875)	Mill Reef (1968)
Wheel of Fortune (1876) filly	Alleged (1974)
St Simon (1881)	Shergar (1978)

Timeform Ratings

The Timeform organisation in Halifax, Yorkshire was founded by Phil Bull in 1947 and is famous for the ratings contained in its annual publication *Racehorses of 19—*. A rating is given to each horse that has run on the Flat in Great Britain during the year, and also to the best horses in Ireland and France. The ratings are expressed in pounds on an unvarying scale, so that champions of different eras can be compared. The highest annual Timeform ratings have been:

COLTS: 3-YEAR-OLDS AND OLDER

145	Sea-Bird (1965)	137 Pinza (1953)
144	Tudor Minstrel (1947)	Never Say Die (1954)
	Brigadier Gerard (1972)	Princely Gift (1955)
142	Abernant (1950)	Right Boy (1959)
	Ribot (1956)	Molvedo (1961)
141	Mill Reef (1971, 1972)	Ragusa (1963)
140	Vaguely Noble (1968)	Reliance (1965)
	Shergar (1981)	Rheingold (1973)
139	Pappa Fourway (1955)	Grundy (1975)
138	Alycidon (1949)	Troy (1979)
	Exbury (1963)	Moorestyle (1980)
	Nijinsky (1970)	
	Alleged (1978)	

FILLIES: 3-YEAR-OLDS AND OLDER

136	Allez France (1974)	133 Hula Dancer (1963)
	Habibti (1983)	Noblesse (1963)
135	Coronation (1949)	Pistol Packer (1971)
	Dahlia (1974)	San San (1972)
134	Petite Etoile (1959, 1960)	Lianga (1975)
	All Along (1983)	Rose Bowl (1975)
		Dunfermline (1977)
		Three Troikas (1979)
		Marwell (1981)

Allez France, rated by Timeform and many other authorities as the best racemare in Europe at middle distances since World War II, shown at Chantilly with Angel Penna, who trained her as a four-and five-year-old.

2-YEAR-OLD COLTS

142 Windy City (1951)
137 Apalachee (1973)
136 My Babu (1947)
135 Floribunda (1960)
    Petingo (1967)
134p Abdos (1961)
134 Skindles Hotel (1956)
    Sing Sing (1959)
    Sir Ivor (1967)
    My Swallow (1970)
    Deep Diver (1971)
    Grundy (1974)
    Tromos (1978)
    Storm Bird (1980)

2-YEAR-OLD FILLIES

138 Star of India (1955)
136 Texana (1957)
135 La Tendresse (1961)
134 Zabara (1951)
133 Apollonia (1955)
    Hula Dancer (1962)
    Jacinth (1972)

GELDINGS

133 Admetus (1974)
131 Combined Operations (1948)
    Durante (1955)
130 Morecambe (1958)

LOWEST-RATED WINNERS OF BIG RACES

Oaks: 112 Long Look (1965)
1000 Guineas: 113 Night Off (1965, rated 124 in 1964)
2000 Guineas: 120 Rockavon (1961)
Derby: 123 Blakeney (1969, rated 126 in 1970)
    125 Morston (1973), Snow Knight (1974)
St Leger: 124 Ridge Wood (1949), Intermezzo (1969, rated
    125 in 1970), Boucher (1972)
King George: 125 Nasram (1964)
Arc: 128 La Sorellina (1953)
    129 Topyo (1967)

STEEPLECHASERS

182 Captain Christy (1975/76)
179 Badsworth Boy (1982/83)
177 Bregawn (1982/83)
176 Little Owl (1980/81)
175 Brown Lad (1975/76)
    Night Nurse (1980/81)
    Silver Buck (1981/82)
    Burrough Hill Lad (1983/84)
    Wayward Lad (1983/84)
174 Bula (1975/76)

HURDLERS

182 Night Nurse (1976/77)
180 Monksfield (1978/79)
176 Birds Nest (1975/76, 1976/77)
    Golden Cygnet (1977/78)
175 Sea Pigeon (1976/77 to 1980/81
    inclusive)
    Gaye Brief (1982/83)
174 Dramatist (1976/77)
    For Auction (1981/82)
173 Dawn Run (1983/84)

It is rare for any stallion to sire a horse of much greater merit than himself. According to Timeform ratings, the most startling examples have been:

45 Rolfe (rated 77 in 1976) sired Mighty Flutter (rated 122? in 1984)
23 Bewildered (102 in 1951) sired Operatic Society (125 in 1960)
21 Grit (95 in 1955) sired Chalkey (116 in 1962)
21 Maestoso (94 in 1964) sired Welsh City (115 in 1972).

From 1975/76 the Timeform organisation has given a rating to each jumper in Great Britain, and also to the best in Ireland, in its *Chasers & Hurdlers* annual. The highest annual Timeform ratings for jumpers have been:

Since the early 1960s Timeform has published similar ratings for jumpers in its weekly 'black book'. Arkle was rated 220 in early 1966 and later that year his stablemate Flyingbolt was assessed at 210.

IV
HUMAN
ACHIEVEMENT

Lester Piggott and Bill Shoemaker, riders of more than 12 000 winners between them, photographed at Ascot in 1982 on the occasion of a challenge match. The race was won by Shoemaker's mount, Princes Gate.

Owners

Most lifetime wins Marion H. Van Berg (1896–1971), from Nebraska, owned the winners of 4,775 races in North America over a period of 35 years.

Most wins in a year The record for number of wins in a year is held by Dan R. Lasater, whose horses won 494 races in North America in 1974.

The British record for races won in a year is 115, set by David Robinson in 1973.

Breeders

Most lifetime wins Kentucky-based John E. Madden (1856–1929) is generally credited as the breeder whose produce won most races. Reliable authorities credit him as breeder of winners of more than 10,000 races, but as official statistics were not kept during most of his career on the Turf the exact number cannot be determined.

Most wins in a year Eddie Taylor, owner of Windfields Farms in Ontario, Canada, and Maryland, USA, bred the winners of 442 races in North America in 1978.

The British record for wins in a year is 52, achieved by Lionel Holliday in 1954.

Trainers

Most lifetime wins The world's most successful trainer, in terms of number of races won, is the American Jack Van Berg, whose total to the end of 1984 was 4,412.

Most wins in a year The record for most wins in a year is 496, set in 1976, also by Jack Van Berg.

The British record for wins in a season is 146, set by John Day, jr in 1867. The best score in the 20th century is 128 by Henry Cecil in 1979.

The record for a trainer over jumps is held by Michael Dickinson, whose horses won 120 races in the 1982/83 season.

Most wins in a day The world record for most wins in a day is 12, established by Michael Dickinson on Boxing Day, 27 December 1982. He sent out a total of 21 runners, winning with Marnik and Thornacre at Huntingdon, W Six Times and Fearless Imp at Market Rasen, Londolozi and B Jaski at Sedgefield, Wayward Lad at Kempton, Delius and Happy Voyage at Wetherby, and Brunton Park, Prominent Artist and Slieve Bracken at Wolverhampton.

The world record for Flat race wins in a day is 10, achieved by Colin Hayes in Australia on 23 January 1982. He scored a treble at Caulfield with Mysterious Ways, McCabe and Glaisdale, and collected seven wins on the eight-race card at Victoria Park with Open Menu, High Drifter, War

Chest, Ronleigh Bisque, Frivolous Lass, Black Mandate and Supertrack.

Trained first 5 in championship race Michael Dickinson's 5 runners (Bregawn, Captain John, Wayward Lad, Silver Buck and Ashley House) filled the first 5 places in a field of 11 for the Cheltenham Gold Cup on 17 March 1983.

The most notable comparable performance on the Flat was that of James Croft, whose 4 runners (Theodore, Violet, Professor and Corinthian) filled the first 4 places in a field of 23 for the St Leger at Doncaster on 16 September 1822.

Jockeys

Most lifetime wins The world's most successful jockey, in terms of number of races won, is Bill Shoemaker, whose tally between 1949 and the end of 1984 exceeds 8,400. The Texas-born jockey has held the record since September 1970, when he passed the 6,032 wins (6,026 in North America) recorded by the English-born Johnny Longden.

The record for a jockey in British racing is 4,870, achieved by (Sir) Gordon Richards between 1921 and 1954. Richards rode only rarely in other countries, unlike his successor as Britain's leading jockey, Lester Piggott, whose global score almost certainly exceeds the Richards tally. To the end of 1984 Piggott had ridden 4,315 winners in Britain and several hundred more abroad, including 306 in France.

The world record for wins over jumps belongs to John Francome, whose total in Britain alone was 1,138 between December 1970 and April 1985. He took the record in May 1984 from Stan Mellor, who retired in 1972 with a career score of 1,035 wins.

Most wins in a year The highest number of wins recorded in a single year is 546 (from a record 2,199 mounts) by Massachusetts-born Chris McCarron in 1974.

The British record is 269 wins, by Gordon Richards in 1947. Richards also had most mounts in a season, exactly 1,000 in 1936.

The record for the number of wins in a jumping season is 149, set by Jonjo O'Neill in 1978/79.

Most wins in a day The highest number of wins recorded on a single programme is 8. The feat was first achieved by apprentice Hubert Jones (out of 13 mounts) at Caliente, California, on 11 June 1944, and later matched by Oscar Barattuci (8 consecutive mounts) at Independencia, Rosario City, Argentina, on 15 December 1957, and by Dave Gall (out of 10 mounts) at Cahokia Downs, Illinois, on 18 October 1978.

Jorge Tejeira rode at both Keystone (Pennsylvania) and Atlantic City (New Jersey) on 16 June 1976, winning with 8 out of a total of 12 mounts.

The scene is Alexandra Park in October 1927, as two of the most gifted jockeys of the century, Steve Donoghue (left) and Gordon Richards, return to the paddock. Donoghue was then the fading star, the last of his six Derby victories having been achieved two years earlier, whereas Richards was in only the second of 26 championship seasons.

The only recorded instances of jockeys riding 7 winners from 7 mounts on a single programme are those by Albert Whittaker (at Huntley, New Zealand, on 19 February 1910), W. Thomas (at Townsville, Australia, on 29 July 1929), and by Richard DePass (at Florida Downs, USA, on 15 March 1980).

In Britain there have been only two instances of a jockey 'going through the card' on a 6-race programme. The feat of Gordon Richards, at Chepstow on 4 October 1933, was emulated by Alec Russell, at Bogside, on 19 July 1957.

George Fordham won with 6 of his 7 mounts on an 8-race card at Stockbridge on 18 June 1867. He also dead-heated for first place on his other mount, but was beaten in the run-off.

Fred Archer twice won on all 6 of his mounts on 7-race cards, at Newmarket on 19 April 1877 and at Lewes on 5 August 1882.

Joe Mercer had 6 wins from 10 rides on 14 July 1965, scoring 4 times from 5 attempts at Yarmouth in the afternoon and twice more at the Doncaster evening fixture.

The world record over jumps (and for an amateur rider) is held by Charlie Cunningham, who won with 6 of his 7 mounts on an 8-race card at Rugby on 29 March 1881.

Most consecutive wins There have been two authenticated instances of jockeys riding 12 consecutive winners. The first was by Gordon Richards, who won on his last mount at Nottingham on 3 October 1933, all 6 at Chepstow on 4 October and the first 5 at Chepstow on 5 October. The feat was matched in Southern Rhodesia (now Zimbabwe) in June and July 1958 by Pieter Phillipus Stroebel.

Obituary notices of George Herring (killed in a race fall at Hull on 27 July 1796) credited him with having achieved 19 consecutive wins, but details were lacking and the feat cannot be verified.

Champion in two countries The only jockey to have won championships in both North America and Britain is Steve Cauthen. He headed the American list in 1977 and topped the British table in 1984.

Tommy Burns, North American champion in 1898 and 1899, was the leader in Germany in 1907.

Charlie Maidment was champion in Ireland in 1866 and 1867, and shared the championship in Britain in both 1870 and 1871. Steve Donoghue led the Irish list in 1908 and was champion in Britain from 1914 to 1923, jointly on the last occasion. Pat Eddery, champion in Britain from 1974 to 1977, topped the Irish table in 1982.

The world's oldest jockey was Harry Beasley (1852–1939), an Irishman who started his career in his teens. He rode Come Away to win the Grand National in 1891 and, at the age of 83, partnered his own filly Mollie to be unplaced in the Corinthian Plate, a Flat race for amateur riders at Baldoyle, Co Dublin on 10 June 1935.

The oldest jockey to record his first win was Victor Morley Lawson, who was 67 when partnering his own gelding Ocean King to victory in a division of the Corinthian Amateur Riders' Maiden Stakes at Warwick, England on 16 October 1973.

The identity of the world's youngest jockey is a matter for debate, though claims have been made on behalf of Frank Wootton. He was born in Australia in December 1893 and was not yet ten years old when riding winners in South Africa in 1903. His family then moved to England, where he became the youngest-ever champion jockey at the age of 15 in 1909.

The most notable victory by a disabled jockey was achieved by amateur Frank Wise, who wore an artificial leg when winning the 1929 Irish Grand National. Mr Wise had suffered war injuries, losing a leg and the tops of 3 fingers on his right hand, but he rode the favourite Alike (a mare whom he also owned and trained) to win Ireland's premier steeplechase at Fairyhouse on 1 April 1929. The partnership had finished fourth in the same race the previous year.

Gerald Foljambe rode 2 steeplechase winners at the Melton Hunt meeting, Leicestershire on 2 April 1925 despite having had a leg amputated just below the knee.

POSTSCRIPT

English Classic races, 2000 Guineas (page 19)

1985 Maktoum al Maktoum's b c **Shadeed** J: Lester Piggott 4/5 Fav £94,689 T: Michael Stoute, Newmarket B: Cherry Valley Farm Inc and The Gamely Corporation Sire: Nijinsky 2. Bairn 3. Supreme Leader head, 1½l 1:37.41 14 ran

Shadeed and Bairn were both bred in USA; Supreme Leader started at 50/1; richest first prize; 4th win for Lester Piggott.

1000 Guineas (page 31)

1985 Sheikh Mohammed's ch f **Oh So Sharp** J: Steve Cauthen 2/1 Fav £85,647 T: Henry Cecil, Newmarket B: Dalham Stud Farms Ltd Sire: Kris 2. Al Bahathri 3. Bella Colora short head, short head 1:36.85 17 ran

Smallest margins ever between winner and 3rd; Al Bahathri bred in USA; fastest time; 2nd richest first prize; 3rd win for Henry Cecil.

Derby (page 39)

1985 9th Baron Howard de Walden's b c **Slip Anchor** J: Steve Cauthen 9/4 Fav £204,160 T: Henry Cecil, Newmarket B: Owner Sire: Shirley Heights 2. Law Society 3. Damister 7l, 6l 2:36.23 14 ran

Greatest recorded margins between winner and 3rd; Law Society trained in Ireland; Law Society and Damister both bred in USA; 2nd richest first prize.

Oaks (page 51)

1985 Sheikh Mohammed's ch f **Oh So Sharp** J: Steve Cauthen 6/4 Fav £111,744 T: Henry Cecil, Newmarket B: Dalham Stud Farms Ltd Sire: Kris 2. Triptych 3. Dubian 6l, ¾l 2:41.37 12 ran

Equal 6th greatest winning margin; Triptych trained in Ireland; Triptych bred in USA; 2nd richest first prize.

Classic Summary (page 69)

Most successful trainers, (*add*)
  Henry Cecil 1975–1985 2 3 1 1 1 8
Most successful jockeys, (*amend*)
  Lester Piggott 1954–1985 4 2 9 6 8 29

Multiple Classic-Winning Horses (page 70)

1000 Guineas, Oaks, (*add*) Oh So Sharp (1985)

US Triple Crown Races, Kentucky Derby (page 103)

1985 Hunter Farm's b c **Spend A Buck** A Cordero

Preakness Stakes (page 107)

1985 E. V. & Mrs Klein's b c **Tank's Prospect** P Day

Belmont Stakes (page 108)

1985 Brushwood Stable's b g **Creme Fraiche** E Maple

World Record Earnings (page 112)

Spend A Buck has beaten Slew o' Gold's record for most money earned in one year. His victory in the Jersey Derby at Garden State Park, New Jersey, on 27 May 1985 was the most lucrative in racing history, for he won the $600,000 first prize plus a $2 million bonus for having already won the Cherry Hill Mile, the Garden State Stakes and the Kentucky Derby. This took Spend A Buck's 1985 earnings to a record $3,330,524 and his career earnings to $3,998,509, placing him 2nd to John Henry in that category.

Longest Winning Sequences (page 130)

Between August 1984 and March 1985 the Australian 5-year-old Picnic in the Park compiled a sequence of 21 wins in sprint races at Queensland 'bush' tracks. He was injured and beaten when attempting to record his 22nd consecutive win. After his 19th victory he returned a positive dope test, and he was disqualified, but connections appealed. At the time of going to press the matter had not been resolved, but it seemed likely that Picnic in the Park would be reinstated as winner and his sequence of 21 wins restored. As he never won on a metropolitan track, his true status was a matter of conjecture, but not even his connections claimed that he owned the class of Desert Gold and Gloaming, true champions who each recorded 19 wins in a row.

Oldest Active Stallions (page 148)

It was reported in May 1985 that the 31-year-old French-bred stallion Mystic would cover five mares at Windfields Farm, Maryland in the current breeding season.

Jockeys, most wins in a day (page 156)

Chris Loreth rode 8 winners from 10 mounts at Exhibition Park, Vancouver, Canada, on 9 April 1984.

Index

Page numbers in italics refer to illustrations